ADDRESS BOOK FOR
GERMANIC GENEALOGY

Sixth Edition

Address Book

FOR

Germanic GENEALOGY

◆

Sixth Edition

Ernest Thode

Published by Genealogical Publishing Co., Inc.
1001 N. Calvert St., Baltimore, MD 21202
Second printing, 2000
Library of Congress Catalogue Card Number 96-79326
International Standard Book Number 0-8063-1526-1
Made in the United States of America

INTRODUCTION

The previous editions of *Address Book for Germanic Genealogy* have been well received. This new sixth edition brings many addresses up to date and adds numerous others. This edition is especially strong in new municipal archive addresses and more local and regional European historical and genealogical society addresses.

Every postal code in Germany uses the 5-digit prefix. German codes are prefixed with D-, French with F-, Swiss with CH-, and Austrian with A-.

In cases where there are both a street address and a post office box, I opted for the box number as the mail address, but it may be helpful to know the street address, too, for instance when visiting an archive or museum.

There were numerous changes of archive addresses in the former German Democratic Republic (DDR), especially in Saxony. As always, society addresses change with different officers, and it is hard to keep up sometimes. If there are any outdated addresses, I would like to know so that they can be changed for the seventh edition.

Ernest Thode
RR 7, Box 306 AB, Kern Road
Marietta, OH 45750-9437
USA
19 October 1996

TITLE PAGE, INTRODUCTION, MAPS OF 1871-1918 GERMAN EMPIRE, MODERN POSTAL CODES

To find out the **exact origin** of your Germanic ancestors, which is essential, **do your homework first!** Check relatives, neighbors, friends, associations. Learn genealogical techniques; don't operate in a vacuum, but learn who else may be researching the same family or may have it already researched. **Join genealogical and historical groups** pertaining to your ancestor; put out queries.

Do your **genealogy at home** first! Search official sources such as censuses, passenger lists, and naturalization records for origins (usually generalized by German "state" or province, which is a clue).

Learn their religious affiliation, find what **religious records** are available for that group in that locality in that time period, and check them for places of origin (often generalized by German "state"), friends & relatives (baptismal sponsors, witnesses to marriage, survivors at death), genealogical clues (residence, cemetery, name of pastor of a group who came in a mass migration; ancestor's biography may give origin).

Study the **history, culture, and language** of your Germanic ancestors.

Inform yourself about the region of your Germanic ancestors and their sea journey **through maps and information on** the **ships**.

You must **first pin down** a **name** (spelling sometimes changed in English), a **place** (an exact village, or at least narrowed down to a German "state"), **and** a **year**) **of an event** (birth, confirmation, marriage, emigration). If the records are not available at home on microfilm or in publications, **then and only then** (except where comprehensive indexes for an area exist) should you **try to "cross the Atlantic"** without expert help. Send an ancestor chart and photocopies of the original source of place of origin (not just somebody's interpretation of a document in old German script). To send for vital records and church records see FORMLETTERS at end. It is usually possible **to obtain** emigration **records**, tax lists, land records, court records, and the like **from European government archives**.

GERMAN NATIONAL ARCHIVES AND ORGANIZATIONS

TABLE OF CONTENTS AND RESEARCH GUIDE

Obtain records of baptism, confirmation, marriage, death, sometimes communion, also pastor biographies and village chronologies **from religious archives**.

Regain family connections in formerly German areas now under Czech, Polish, Russian, Yugoslavian, or other administration.

Become a member of genealogical and historical groups for your ancestral homeland; enlist their help in searching their card-files; find references in their publications; place queries.

Obtain reference books and journals on Germanic genealogy, your ancestral region, etc., from publishers.

With specific citations of title and page, **obtain copies from** out-of-print **publications** and **learn from museums** pertaining to your ancestors or ancestral area.

If you run into difficulty "doing it yourself," **seek out a specialist** with experience.

When writing to Europe, until you gain more knowledge of the German language, **use good, simple English or customize your own letter from formletters** using additional phrases given.

THE GERMAN EMPIRE 1871-1918

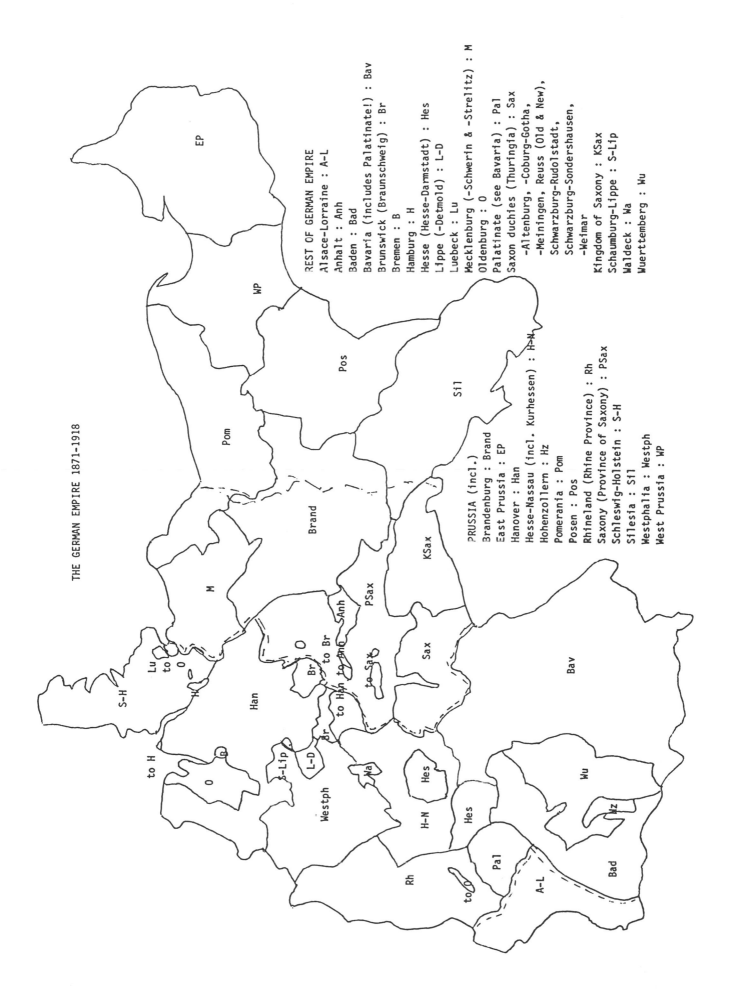

REST OF GERMAN EMPIRE
Alsace-Lorraine : A-L
Anhalt : Anh
Baden : Bad
Bavaria (includes Palatinate!) : Bav
Brunswick (Braunschweig) : Br
Bremen : B
Hamburg : H
Hesse (Hesse-Darmstadt) : Hes
Lippe (-Detmold) : L-D
Luebeck : Lu
Mecklenburg (-Schwerin & -Strelitz) : M
Oldenburg : O
Palatinate (see Bavaria) : Pal
Saxon duchies (Thuringia) : Sax
  -Altenburg, -Coburg-Gotha,
  -Meiningen, Reuss (Old & New),
  Schwarzburg-Rudolstadt,
  Schwarzburg-Sondershausen,
  -Weimar
Kingdom of Saxony : KSax
Schaumburg-Lippe : S-Lip
Waldeck : Wa
Wuerttemberg : Wu

PRUSSIA (incl.)
Brandenburg : Brand
East Prussia : EP
Hanover : Han
Hesse-Nassau (incl. Kurhessen) : H-N
Hohenzollern : Hz
Pomerania : Pom
Posen : Pos
Rhineland (Rhine Province) : Rh
Saxony (Province of Saxony) : PSax
Schleswig-Holstein : S-H
Silesia : Sil
Westphalia : Westph
West Prussia : WP

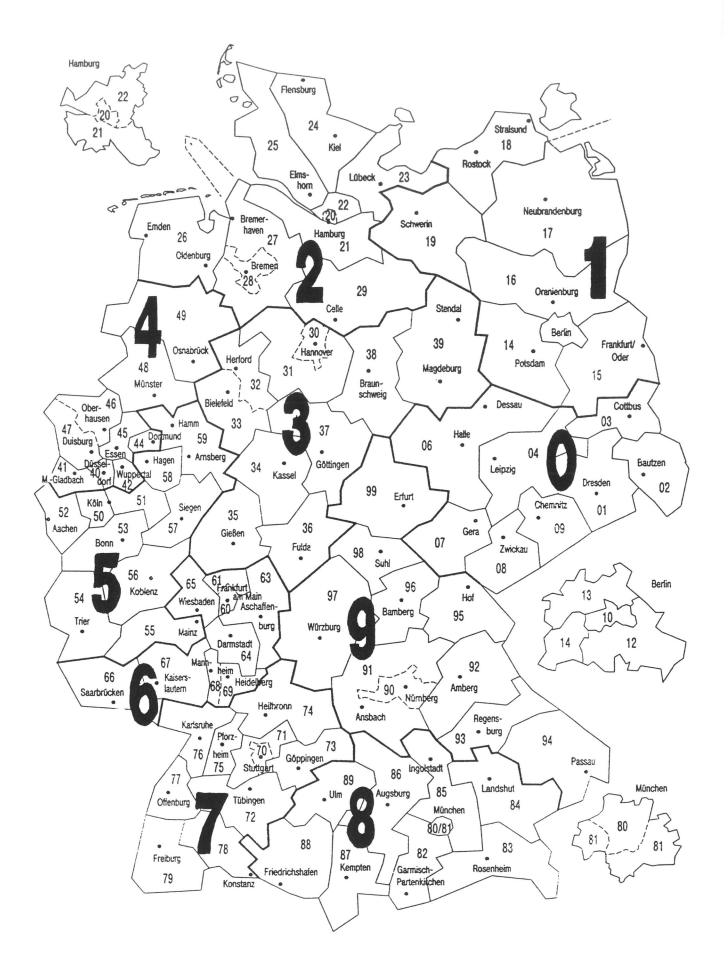

GERMAN ZIP CODE REGIONS

GENEALOGICAL, HISTORICAL, AND GERMAN-RELATED SOCIETIES OUTSIDE EUROPE

(Not all societies have secretarial help or time to reply to correspondence. Please keep correspondence scarce, brief, and to the point, and requests reasonable. Send one good letter to the correct place rather than dozens, mostly to the wrong place. Use a separate sheet for each family. Within your own country enclose a self-addressed, stamped envelope if a reply is desired; for foreign mail enclose two International Reply Coupons (available through post office) for air mail replies.) The value of an IRC is tied to the local postage rate, generally one for surface mail, two for air mail to a foreign country.

UNITED STATES.

Sécretariat Géneral
Conféderation Internationale de Généalogie et d'Héraldique
448 New Jersey Ave. SE
WASHINGTON DC 20003
(international "umbrella society" of major genealogical and heraldry societies; may be able to furnish current addresses of societies not found in this book, outdated, or otherwise not deliverable)

AASLH. See American Association for State and Local History.

ACCESS
401 E. 74th St., Suite 17D
NEW YORK NY 10021
(adoption newsletter for New York City area)

Adoption Circle
401 E. 74th St., Suite 17D
NEW YORK NY 10021
(nonprofit organization serving all those whose lives are touched by adoption)

Das Adoptionsdreieck. See Geborener Deutscher.

AFRA. See American Family Records Association.

American Association for State and Local History
530 Church St., Suite 600
NASHVILLE TN 37219
(national federation of state and local historical and genealogical societies and museums; may be able to provide current addresses of societies if address you have is not current)

American Antiquarian Society
185 Salisbury St. (at Park Ave.)
WORCESTER MA 01609
(national association for preservation of historical items; large newspaper collection, some of them German-language)

American Association of Teachers of German
523 Building, Suite 201
Route 38
CHERRY HILL NJ 08034
(professional society of German teachers at all levels in all types of institutions)

American Council on German Studies
P.O. Box J
PHILADELPHIA PA 19123
(national scholarly educational and cultural society for German studies)

American Council on Germany
680 Fifth Ave.
NEW YORK NY 10019
(council for international understanding)

American Council for Nationalities
20 W. 40th St.
NEW YORK NY 10018
(library and information center for nationality groups)

American Family Records Association
311 E. 12th St.
KANSAS CITY MO 64106
(national association of genealogical societies for family historians, one-name societies, etc.)

American Name Society
P.O. Box 340, Baruch College
NEW YORK NY 10010
(scholarly professional society dealing with surnames, given names, and place names; journal)

American Red Cross
Family Assistance Department
4700 Mount Hope Dr.
BALTIMORE MD 21215-3200
(will assist in search for records of prisoners in concentration camps through International Tracing Service in Arolsen, Germany)

American Translators Association
109 Croton Ave.
OSSINING NY 10562
(national professional society for translators)

American Turners
1550 Clinton Ave. N
ROCHESTER NY 14621
(national German-American gymnastics society headquarters)

Armorial Heritage Foundation
c/o Dr. Dieter Birk
Oakville, Ontario
CANADA
http://www.hookup.net/~dbirk/chf.html
(heraldry association, possibly commercial)

Association of the German Nobility in North America
(DAGNA - (Deutsche Adelsgesellschaft in Nordamerika)
3571 E. 8th St.
LOS ANGELES CA 90023
(exclusive society for individuals who are members of German nobility residing in North America)

Association for Gravestone Studies. See International Association for Gravestone Studies.

Association of Professional Genealogists
3421 M St. NW, Suite 126
WASHINGTON DC 20007
(national professional society for genealogists; publishes newsletter)

The Augustan Society, Inc.
P.O. Box P T
TORRANCE CA 90507-0210
(society for genealogy, heraldry, and history, including Germany ("Germania") and all of central Europe; publishes *The Omnibus Augustan* journal; library located at 1313 Sartori Ave., Torrance, CA)

The Balch Institute for Ethnic Studies
Temple University
18 S. 7th St.
PHILADELPHIA PA 19106
(scholarly immigration archive founded by Philadelphia Orphans Court in 1971 to fulfill Balch family wills; mission to document and interpret American immigration history and other ethnic life with photographs, foreign language newspapers (including German); originals of New York passenger arrival lists (being computerized for publications such as *Germans to America* series); papers of the Jewish Archives Center containing mostly Philadelphia Jewish families; records of Swiss-American societies; records of the National Carl Schurz Association)

Board for Certification of Genealogists
P.O. Box 14291
WASHINGTON DC 20044
(national certification board for various classes of genealogical researchers)

Center for Family and Community History
335 KMB
Brigham Young University
PROVO UT 84602
(publishes *The Community History Newsletter* and *The Family Historian*)

Center for Historical Population Studies
316 Carlson Hall
University of Utah
SALT LAKE CITY UT 84112
(scholarly center for studying migrations and demographic make-up of given populations)

Center for Migration Studies
209 Flagg Place
NEW YORK NY 10304
(scholarly nonprofit institute for studying sociological, demographic, and historic migration and ethnicity; publishes *International Migration Review*; primarily Italian and Catholic library holdings (11,000); has a working relationship with a Center for Migration Studies in Munich, among other places)

The Conference of Americans of Germanic Heritage
P.O. Box 20554
SAN JOSE CA 95160
(possibly a political organization)

Council for European Studies
1509 International Affairs Bldg.
Columbia University
NEW YORK NY 10027
(scholarly research center; publishes guides to libraries and archives in Europe)

DAGNA. See Association of German Nobility.

DANK. See German-American National Congress.

Deutsche Adelsgesellschaft. See Association of German Nobility.

Ellis Island. See Statue of Liberty.

Ellis Island Foundation
52 Vanderbilt Ave.
NEW YORK NY 10017-3898
(foundation for the restoration and preservation of Ellis Island immigrant screening center)

Family History Department of the Church of Jesus Christ of Latter-day Saints
Correspondence Section
35 N. West Temple St.
SALT LAKE CITY UT 84103
(largest genealogical organization in the world; enormous microfilm collection; International Genealogical Index on CD-ROM and microfiche; Ancestral File on CD-ROM)

Federation of American Citizens of German Descent
460 Chapman St.
IRVINGTON NJ 07111
(national political and social organization for German-Americans)

Federation of Genealogical Societies (FGS)
P.O. Box 830220
RICHARDSON TX 75083-0220
(umbrella organization of local, state, and national genealogical societies in USA; may be able to provide current addresses of societies if address you have isn't current)

Foreign Language Genealogical Researchers Association
2463 Ledgewood Dr.
W JORDAN UT 84084
(national association for genealogists researching foreign-language areas; publishes directory)

Geborener Deutscher
c/o Leonie D. Boehmer
805 Alvarado NE
ALBUQUERQUE NM 87108
(newsletter for German-born adoptees)

Genealogical Library for the Blind and
   Physically Handicapped, Inc.
P.O. Box 88100
ATLANTA GA 30356-8100
(genealogical lending library for the handicapped)

German Genealogical Society of America
P.O. Box 517
LA VERNE CA 91750-0517
(national society for German-American genealogy;
newsletter; library located at 2125 Wright Ave., LaVerne,
CA)

German Genealogy Group
c/o Donald E. Eckerle
24 Jonquill Lane
KINGS PARK NY 11754-3927
(German genealogical society; newsletter, surname
directory, computer matching; meetings at Plainview, NY,
Family History Center)

German Research Association, Inc.
P.O. Box 711600
SAN DIEGO CA 92171-1600
(national society for German-American genealogy;
newsletter)

German Research Index
Germanic Genealogy Society
P.O. Box 16312
ST PAUL MN 55116-0312
(nationwide index of German researchers, surnames, etc.)

German-American Heritage Center
P.O. Box 243
DAVENPORT IA 52805-0243
(German-American heritage center will be developed at
2nd and Gaines Streets in Davenport, IA, to exhibit the
heritage of Germans in the Midwest)

German-American Heritage Institute
Altenheim
7824 W. Madison St.
FOREST PARK IL 60130
(national centralized institute for advancement of
German-American studies, immigration studies for greater
Chicago and Illinois, historical studies, archival research,
exhibitions, and public educational programs)

German-American National Congress (D.A.N.K.)
4740 N. Western Ave.
CHICAGO IL 60625
(national civic and cultural organization for German-
Americans; political but non-partisan; has local chapters;
newsletter)

Germanic Genealogy Society
P.O. Box 16312
ST PAUL MN 55116-0312
(formerly German interest group of MN Genealogical
Society; publications; projects)
GGS. See Germanic Genealogy Society.

GGSA. See German Genealogical Society of America.

GRA. See German Research Association.

Heritage Resources, Inc.
P.O. Box 244
BOUNTIFUL UT 84010
(nationwide private membership genealogical microform
lending library)

Immigrant Genealogical Society (IGS)
P.O. Box 7369
BURBANK CA 91510-7369
(national society for genealogy of immigrant ancestors with
strong emphasis on German- American genealogy;
newsletter; library located at 1310 B W. Magnolia Blvd.,
Burbank, CA; German research committee will search
various resources)

Immigration Archives
826 Berry St.
ST PAUL MN 55114
(scholarly immigration archive with emphasis on minority
cultures)

International Association of Gravestone Studies
46 Plymouth St.
NEEDHAM MA 02194
(international association for study of gravestones; can
provide explanations for symbols found on tombstones)

International Soundex Registry
P.O. Box 2312
CARSON CITY NV 89702
(organization devoted to helping adopted children and birth
parents find one another through mutual computer
registration)

Johannes Schwalm Historical Association, Inc.
P.O. Box 99
PENNSAUKEN NJ 08110
(German-American historical and genealogy organization
for descendants of all "Hessian" soldiers of the
Revolutionary War, people from the Schwalm valley of
Hessen, and Johannes Schwalm; publishes annual volumes;
compiling list of all German soldiers who fought as
auxiliary troops (on the British side) in the American
Revolution; library at Lancaster County (PA) Historical
Society)

Latter-day Saints. See Family History Department.

LDS. See Family History Department.

Max Kade German-American Document and Research
  Center
2080 Wescoe Hall
University of Kansas
LAWRENCE KS 66045
(document center for historians, scholars, and genealogists
covering all German-speaking immigrants)

Max Kade German-American Center
IU-PU at Indianapolis
Athenaeum
401 E. Michigan St.
INDIANAPOLIS IN 46204
(center for historians, scholars, and genealogists covering
German-speaking immigrants)

Max Kade German-American Research Institute
The Pennsylvania State University
305 Burrowes Building
UNIVERSITY PARK PA 16802-6203
(center for historians, scholars, and genealogists covering
German-speaking immigrants)

Max Kade German-American Research Institute
100 Charles St., Room 1604
NEW YORK NY 10047
(center for historians, scholars, and genealogists covering
German-speaking immigrants)

Max Kade Institute for Austrian-German-Swiss Studies
2714 S. Hoover St.
LOS ANGELES CA 90000
(institute for study of German, Austrian, and Swiss
immigrants)

Max Kade Institute for German-American Studies
University of Wisconsin-Madison
901 University Bay Shore Drive
MADISON WI 53705
(center for historians, scholars, and genealogists covering
all German-speaking immigrants; ethnic book collection)

Military Information Enterprises
P.O. Box 340081
FT SAM HOUSTON TX 78234
(nationwide commercial locator database of over
110,000,000 names of 20th century military personnel)

Mormons. See Family History Department.

National Genealogical Society
Glebe House
4527 17th St., N
ARLINGTON VA 22207-2399
(national genealogical society for U.S. genealogy;
publishes journal, newsletter; International Liaison
Committee helps with guidance & addresses)

Overseas Brats
P.O. Box 29805
SAN ANTONIO TX 78229
(organization of former dependents of U.S. military,
government, and civilian personnel overseas; publishes a
magazine)

Palatines to America
Box 101, Capital University
COLUMBUS OH 43209-2394
(national society for German-American genealogy,
researching German ancestors; publishes quarterly journal,
The Palatine Immigrant, and quarterly newsletter, *Palatine
Patter*; has regional chapters, national annual meeting;
publishes *Surname Index*; library located in basement of
Saylor-Ackerman Hall, Capital University, Bexley
(Columbus), OH 43209)

Pastorius Home Association
P.O. Box 66
GERMANSVILLE PA 18053
(private association to provide a German "home away from
home" for Americans in the restored Pastorius home in Bad
Windsheim, Germany, now Pastorius-Kolleg with dorms,
library, classrooms, dining hall, individual bedrooms; daily
cultural programs and activities)

Red Cross. See American Red Cross.

Schwalm. See Johannes Schwalm.

SGAS. See Society for German-American Studies.

Sister Cities International
1625 Eye St. NW, Suite 434
WASHINGTON DC 20006
(international town affiliation program that links U.S. cities
and towns of all sizes with places in foreign countries for
cultural exchange)

Society for German-American Studies
c/o C. Richard Beam
406 Spring Dr.
MILLERSVILLE PA 17551
(national scholarly society for culture, history, and
genealogy pertaining to Germans, Austrians, and Swiss in
the United States; publishes journal, annual yearbook)

Soundex. See International Soundex Registry.

The Statue of Liberty - Ellis Island Foundation, Inc.
17 Battery Place
NEW YORK NY 10017-3808
(charitable foundation to restore and preserve Statue of
Liberty (first view of America for ca. 17 million
immigrants) and Ellis Island immigrant screening center
(1892-1954); establish computerized immigrant registration
file and lasting memorial to immigrants (American
Immigrant Wall of Honor); exhibits include The Peopling
of America, a William Randolph Hearst oral history studio,
a Library for Immigration Studies, and an Ellis Island
Theater showing "Island of Hope, Island of Tears")

Steuben Society of America
6705 Fresh Pond Rd.
RIDGEWOOD NY 11385
(national civic and cultural organization for
German-Americans)

United German-American Committee of the USA, Inc.
515 Huntingdon Pike
ROCKLEDGE PA 19046-4451
(umbrella federation of German-American societies in the
United States; may be able to provide current addresses of
societies if address you have is not current; hope to
establish a national German-American Heritage Museum
and Cultural Center)

United States Air Force
Air Force Military Personnel MPCD003
Records Division
Attention: Worldwide Locator
Randolph Air Force Base
SAN ANTONIO TX 78148
(address locator for U.S. air force personnel and veterans)

United States Army
Worldwide Locator Service, EERC
U.S. Army Personnel Support Center
FT BENJAMIN HARRISON IN 46249
(address locator for U.S. army personnel and veterans)

United States Coast Guard
Commandant
G-CP-3
WASHINGTON DC 20593-0001
(address locator for U.S. Coast Guard personnel and
veterans)

United States Marine Corps
Commandant of the Marine Corps
CMCMMRE-10
Bldg. 2008
QUANTICO VA 22134
(address locator for U.S. Marine Corps personnel and
veterans)

United States Navy
Navy Locator Service
NMPC-0216
Navy Department
WASHINGTON DC 20370
(address locator for U.S. naval personnel and veterans)

GENEALOGICAL, HISTORICAL, AND GERMAN-RELATED SOCIETIES OUTSIDE EUROPE

STATE.

Colorado Chapter, Palatines to America
C.R. "Dick" Spielman
7079 S. Marshall St.
LITTLETON CO 80123-4607
(state chapter of national organization; publishes
"CO-PAL-AM")

Illinois Chapter, Palatines to America
Mrs. Nadine Blocker
8045 S. Mulligan
BURBANK IL 60459-1864
(Illinois chapter of national organization; publishes
newsletter)

Indiana German Heritage Society
Das Deutsche Haus - Athenaeum
401 E. Michigan St.
INDIANAPOLIS IN 46204
(state historical, genealogical, and cultural society for
German-Americans in Indiana; publishes newsletter)

Indiana Chapter, Palatines to America
Miss Beth Ann Kroehler
1801 N. Duane Rd.
MUNCIE IN 47304-2648
(Indiana chapter of national organization; publishes
newsletter)

German Interest Group
Iowa Genealogical Society
P.O. Box 3815
DES MOINES IA 50322
(state interest group for German-Americans in Iowa)

German-Acadian Coast Historical and Genealogical
    Society
P.O. Box 517
DESTREHAN LA 70047
(history & genealogy of Louisiana Germans)

Broad Bay Family History Project
c/o Richard Castner
P.O. Box 10
WALDOBORO ME 04572
(project on family history of Broad Bay/Waldoboro
Germans)

Society for the History of Germans in Maryland
107 E. Chase St.
P.O. Box 22585
BALTIMORE MD 21203-4585
(state historical and cultural society for German-Americans
in Maryland)

Minnesota Historical Society
Archives and Manuscripts Collection
1500 Mississippi St.
ST PAUL MN 55101
(has state of Minnesota alien registrations for those residing
in state in 1918)

New York Chapter, Palatines to America
Ralph Weller
P.O. Box 14
ALCOVE NY 12007-0014
(New York chapter of national organization; publishes
"Yorker Palatine")

Palatine Settlement Society
10 W. Main St.
ST JOHNSVILLE NY 13452
(society for history of New York's early Palatine
settlements (ca. 1710))

Ohio Chapter, Palatines to America
Robert Strock
P.O. Box 399
DALTON OH 44618-0399
(Ohio chapter of national organization; publishes "Ohio
Palatine Heritage")

German American Heritage Association of Oklahoma
Modern Language Department
Oklahoma City University
2501 N. Blackwelder
OKLAHOMA CITY OK 73106
(society for German-American heritage in Oklahoma)

Pennsylvania German Society
P.O. Box 397
BIRDSBORO PA 19508
(society for history, genealogy, and folklife of the
Pennsylvania Germans; publishes journal, *Der Reggeboge*,
and books)

German Society of Pennsylvania
1305 Locust St.
PHILADELPHIA PA 19107
(literary reading club for German-Americans in
Pennsylvania; library and educational organization; not
primarily genealogical)

The Pennsylvania German Folklife Society, Inc.
P.O. Box 1053
LANCASTER PA 17601
(Pennsylvania German culture, customs)

Pennsylvania Chapter, Palatines to America
David P. Hively
375 Manor Rd.
RED LION PA 17356-9245
(Pennsylvania chapter of national society; publishes
"Penn Pal")

Pennsylvania German Research Society
c/o Carolyn B. Dryfoos
RD 1
SUGARLOAF PA 18249
(Pennsylvania German genealogical society)

GENEALOGICAL, HISTORICAL, AND GERMAN-RELATED SOCIETIES OUTSIDE EUROPE

Center for Pennsylvania German Studies
Millersville University
MILLERSVILLE PA 17551
(scholarly society devoted to study of Pennsylvania
German language and folklife)

Charleston County Library
King St.
CHARLESTON SC 29403
(library with holdings on Swiss in South Carolina)

German-Texas Heritage Society
P.O. Box 684171
AUSTIN TX 78768-4171
(state historical, genealogical, and cultural society for
Germans in Texas; physical location at German Free
School, 507 E. 10th St., Austin; publishes "The Journal")

Texas Wendish Heritage Society
c/o LaVerne Gersch
P.O. Box 311
GIDDINGS TX 78942
(state historical, genealogical, and cultural society for
Wends (Sorbs) in Texas)

Virginia Chapter, Palatines to America
Mrs. Monika E. Edick
3249 Cambrridge Ct.
FAIRFAX VA 22030-1942
(Virginia chapter of national society; publishes "That
Wagon Road")

West Virginia Chapter, Palatines to America
Mrs. Antielee Garletts
572 Plymouth Ave.
MORGANTOWN, WV 26505
(West Virginia chapter of national society; publishes
"Pal-Am Mountaineer")

GENEALOGICAL, HISTORICAL, AND GERMAN-RELATED SOCIETIES OUTSIDE EUROPE

LOCAL/AREA.
(listed alphabetically by state)

Sacramento German Genealogy Society
P.O. Box 660061
SACRAMENTO CA 95866-0061
(study group for German-American genealogy in
Sacramento area; newsletter)

German Research Group
c/o Ed Sarbach
P.O. Box 7683
BOISE ID 83707
(local study group for German-American genealogy in
Idaho)

Germanic Interest Group
Chicago Genealogy Society
P.O. Box 1160
CHICAGO IL 60690
(local subgroup of genealogical society for
German-Americans in Chicago area)

Kentuckiana Germanic Heritage Society
P.O. Box 37271
LOUISVILLE KY 40233-7271
(group formed April 1991 to promote, study, advertise, and
publicize the Germanic heritage of Kentucky and Indiana;
monthly newsletter *Louisville Anzeiger*)

German Interest Group
Louisville Genealogical Society
c/o Eugene Goodbub
913 Ormsby Lane
LOUISVILLE KY 40242
(local subgroup of genealogical society for German-
Americans in Louisville area)

The Mid-Atlantic Germanic Society (MAGS)
P.O. Box 2642
KENSINGTON MD 20891-2642
(local study group for German-American genealogy in
Maryland/Virginia/DC area; publishes "Der Kurier")

German Heritage Society of Greater Washington
c/o Robert E. Lee
2827 Vixen Lane
SILVER SPRING MD 20906
(local German heritage society for Washington, DC, area)

Frankenmuth Historical Museum
613 S. Main St.
FRANKENMUTH MI 48734
(local historical museum for area with strong German
heritage; 620 surnames in database)

New Ulm Historical Society
New Ulm Public Library
27 N. Broadway
NEW ULM MN 56073
(historical society for New Ulm area of German settlement
in MN)

The German Society of New York
6 E. 87th St.
NEW YORK NY 10011
(immigrant aid society founded in 1785)

The German Seaman's Mission of New York
Seaman and International House
123 E. 15th St.
NEW YORK NY 10011
(Lutheran church and mission for German seamen; a
continuation of several groups, the oldest founded in 1860
as "Das deutsche Emigrantenhaus," the Lutheran
Emigrants' Association)

German Genealogical Society of Chillicothe
c/o Glenda Zonner
40 Coventry Dr.
North Fork Village
CHILLICOTHE OH 45601
(local genealogical society for German-Americans in
Chillicothe area)

German Interest Group
Hamilton County Chapter
Ohio Genealogical Society
P.O. Box 15185
CINCINNATI OH 45215
(local subgroup of genealogical society for
German-Americans in Cincinnati area)

German Interest Group
Western Reserve Historical Society
10825 East Blvd.
CLEVELAND OH 44106
(local subgroup of genealogical society for
German-Americans in Cleveland area)

German-American Historical Society of Greater Cleveland
21210 Mastick Rd.
CLEVELAND OH 44126
(historical society for German-Americans of Cleveland
area)

Federation of German-American Societies of Greater
    Cleveland
21210 Mastick Rd.
CLEVELAND OH 44126
(umbrella organization of German-American societies of
Cleveland area)

Yamhill County Genealogical Society
German Interest Group
c/o Evelyn R. Wolfer
1300 E. 18th St.
McMINNVILLE OR 97128
(local subgroup of genealogical society for Yamhill
County, OR, area)

GENEALOGICAL, HISTORICAL, AND GERMAN-RELATED SOCIETIES OUTSIDE EUROPE

Berks Co. Genealogical Society
940 Centre Ave.
P.O. Box 14774
READING PA 19612
(local society in predominantly German area; newsletter)

Bucks Co. Genealogical Society
P.O. Box 1092
DOYLESTOWN PA 18901
(local society in predominantly German area; newsletter)

Germantown Historical Society
5208 Germantown Ave.
PHILADELPHIA PA 19144
(historical society for area of first German settlement in
U.S. 1683 and following)

Lancaster Mennonite Historical Society
2215 Millstream
LANCASTER PA 17602
(local historical society for Mennonites and all early
religious groups in the Lancaster and southeastern PA area;
journal; large card file)

Lehigh County Historical Society
Trout Hall
414 Walnut St.
ALLENTOWN PA 18102
(historical society for Lehigh County, an area of heavy
German settlement in 1700's)

German Interest Group
Western Pennsylvania Genealogical Society
c/o Ruth Hohnadel
4338 Bigelow Blvd.
PITTSBURGH PA 15213
(local subgroup of regional genealogical society for
German-Americans)

Pennsylvania Dutch Folk Culture Society
Baver Memorial Library
Folklife Museum
Main and Willow Streets
LENHARTSVILLE PA 19534
(society for Pennsylvania German Folk Culture)

Tulpehocken Settlement Historical Society
P.O. Box 53
WOMELSDORF PA 19567
(local society for history of German settlement)

Winedale Historical Center
P.O. Box 11
FM Rd. 2714
ROUND TOP TX 78954

German Interest Group
South King County Genealogical Society
c/o Emma H. Livermore
19455 132nd Ave. SE
RENTON WA 98058
(interest group for German genealogy in Seattle area)

Germany Area Interest Group
Milwaukee County Genealogical Society
P.O. Box 27326
MILWAUKEE WI 53227
(special interest group for Germanic genealogy in
Milwaukee area)

German Interest Group
Walworth County Genealogical Society
4327 Milton Ave.
JANESVILLE WI 55546
(special interest for Germanic genealogy in southern WI
area)

CANADA.

The German Canadian Association
207 Mary St. E
Thunder Bay, Ontario
CANADA P7E 4J7
(association for German-Canadians)

Canadian Association of University Teachers of German
c/o Prof. J. W. Dyck
Germanic Studies
University of Waterloo
Waterloo, Ontario
CANADA N2L 3G1
(scholarly association of Canadian university teachers of
German)

German-Canadian Historical Association
Horst Martin, President
Dept. of Germanic Studies
University of British Columbia
Vancouver, British Columbia
CANADA V6T 1W5
(scholarly association for the study of German-Canadian
history)

Historical Society of Mecklenburg Upper Canada, Inc.
c/o Dr. Hartmut Froeschle
Dept. of German
St. Michael's College
81 St. Mary St.
Toronto, Ontario
CANADA M5S 1J4
(historical society of the Mecklenburg Upper Canada
region with many ethnic Germans)

German Interest Group
Ottawa Branch
Ontario Genealogical Society
P.O. Box 8346, Station J
Ottawa, Ontario
CANADA K1G 3H8

German Historical Society
Main P.O. Box 64
Hamilton, Ontario
CANADA L8N 3A2
(German-Canadian historical society)

OTHER RELATED COUNTRY OR ETHNIC GROUPS.

Society of Australian Genealogists
Richmond Villa
The Rocks
AUS-2000 Sydney, NSW
AUSTRALIA
(Australian national genealogical society)

Queensland Family History Society
Central European Group
c/o Eric Kopittke
P.O. Box 171
Indooroopilly
AUS-4068 Brisbane, Queensland
AUSTRALIA

German Interest Group
Genealogical Society of Queensland
c/o Ms. Margaret Jenner
73 Plimsoll St.
Greenslopes
AUS-4120 Brisbane, Queensland
AUSTRALIA
(subgroup of provincial genealogical society in Australia
for Germans)

American Austrian Society
c/o Monroe Korasik
1156 15th St., NW
WASHINGTON DC 20005
(social and cultural organization for Austrian-Americans)

The Balkan and Eastern European-American Genealogical
    Society
4843 Mission St.
SAN FRANCISCO CA 94112
(genealogical society for Americans with Balkan or eastern
European ancestry)

The Belgian Researchers
Fruitdale Lane 62073
LA GRANDE OR 97850
(society of professional researchers for Belgian-Americans)

Bukovina Heritage Society of the Americas
c/o Joe Erbert
510 Madison
ELLIS KS 67637
(society for descendants of people from Bukovina)

Carpatho-Rusyn Research Center
P.O. Box 131-B
ORWELL VT 05760
(research center for Carpathians)

Carpatho-Rusyn Society
125 Westland Dr.
PITTSBURGH PA 15217
(society for Carpathians)

German Historical Society
Main P.O., Box 64
Hamilton, Ontario
CANADA L8N 3A2
(historical society for German-Canadians)

Society for Descendants of Charlemagne
Office of the Governor General
P.O. Box 76
SYLVESTER WV 25193
(society for descendants of Charlemagne, who was quite
prolific)

The Croatian Ethnic Institute, Inc.
4851 S. Drehel Blvd.
CHICAGO IL 60615
(institute with central national and international collection
on Croatians and their descendants in the U.S., Canada,
etc.)

The Croatian Genealogical and Heraldic Society
936 Industrial Ave.
PALO ALTO CA 94070
(American genealogical society for persons of Croatian,
Slovenian, or Serbian ancestry)

Czechoslovak Genealogy Society International
1650 Carroll Ave.
P.O. Box 16225
ST PAUL MN 55116-0225
(genealogical society for Slovak, Moravian, Ruthenian,
Bohemian, Silesian, German, Rusyn, Jewish, and
Hungarian research)

Augustine Hermann Czech American Historical Society
700 N. Collington Ave.
BALTIMORE MD 21205
(historical society for Czech-Americans)

Archives of the Czechs and Slovaks Abroad
Special Collections
Regensburg Library
1100 E. 57th St.
CHICAGO IL 60637

Danish Immigrant Archival Listing
Grandview College Archives
1351 Grandview Ave.
DES MOINES IA 50316
(listing of Danish immigrants to U.S. and Danish-American
archival materials)

Danish Immigrant Museum
2212 Washington St.
P.O. Box 178
ELK HORN IA 51531

Danish-American Center
4200 Cedar Ave. S
MINNEAPOLIS MN 55467
(center for Danish-Americans)

GENEALOGICAL, HISTORICAL, AND GERMAN-RELATED SOCIETIES OUTSIDE EUROPE

Danish-American Genealogy Group
Minnesota Genealogical Society
c/o Paula Warren
1869 Laurel Ave.
ST PAUL MN 55104-5938
(regional genealogical society for Danish-Americans)

Danish-American Heritage Society
Grandview College
1351 Grandview Ave.
DES MOINES IA 50316
(society for Danish-Americans)

Danish-American Heritage Society
2961 Dane Lane
JUNCTION CITY OR 97448
(society for Danish-Americans)

Danube Swabian Genealogical Society
127 Route 156
TRENTON NJ 08620
(genealogical society for Danube Swabians)

Association of Danube Swabians
214 Main St.
Toronto, Ontario
CANADA M4E 2W1
(national association for Danube Swabians in Canada)

Dutch Family Heritage Society
2463 Ledgewood Dr.
W JORDAN UT 84084
(society for Dutch genealogy)

East Europe Connection
1711 Corwin Drive
SILVER SPRING MD 20910-1533
(possibly commercial eastern European research group)

Federation of Eastern-European Family History Societies
P.O. Box 510898
SALT LAKE CITY UT 84151-0898
(umbrella organization of genealogical societies pertaining
to eastern Europe)

Emsland Heritage Society
Albert Olthaus
4325 St. Lawrence Ave.
CINCINNATI OH 45205
(Emsland genealogical society)

Genealogical Society of Flemish Americans
18740 Thirteen Mile Rd.
ROSEVILLE MI 48161
(national genealogical society for Flemish-Americans)

The American-French Genealogical Society
P.O. Box 2113
PAWTUCKET RI 02861-0113
(genealogy for French-Americans, including those from
Alsace, Lorraine, Montbéliard)

Frisian Information Bureau
c/o Geart B. Droege
3043 Ruhl Ave.
BEXLEY OH 43209
(information on Frisian culture, language, history, etc.;
publishes "Frisian News Items")

Frisian Information Bureau
Book Service
1229 Sylvan Ave., SE
GRAND RAPIDS MI 49506
(books on Frisian culture, language, history, etc.)

Galizien German Descendants
12637 SE 214th St.
KENT WA 98031-2215
(Galician German genealogical society)

The Memorial Foundation of the Germanna Colonies, Inc.
P.O. Box 693
CULPEPER VA 22701
(genealogy and history of the Germanna ironworker
colonists of Virginia in 1714, 1717, etc.)

Beyond Germanna
c/o John Blankenbaker
P.O. Box 120
CHADDS FORD PA 19317
(newsletter for descendants of Germanna colonists)

The American Historical Society of Germans from Russia
631 D St.
LINCOLN NE 68502-1199
(historical and genealogical society for Germans from
Russia; publishes journal, "Clues," books, including one
listing ca. 20,000 immigrant families from Germany to
Russia 1763-1862; ca. 57 chapters; archives; historical
library; chapters in Bakersfield, Belle Fourche, Billings,
Boise, Bremerton, Calgary, Cheyenne, Chicago, Denver,
Detroit, Eau Claire (MI), Edmonton, Endicott, Falls
Church, Flint, Fresno, Grand Junction, Greeley/Ft. Collins,
Hastings, Hays, Kansas City, Lakin, Lexington (NE),
Lincoln, Lodi, Los Angeles, McCook, Milwaukee,
Minneapolis/St. Paul, Odessa, Ogden, Oklahoma City,
Oshkosh, Pasco, Phoenix, Portage, Portland, Regina,
Russell, Sacramento, Saginaw, Salina, San Francisco,
Scottsbluff, Seattle, Shattuck, Sheboygan, Spokane,
Sterling, Topeka, Tucson, Walla Walla, Wenatchee,
Wichita, Winnipeg, Yakima, and Yankton;
ahsgr@aol.com)

The American Historical Society of Germans from Russia
9504 Austin O'Brien Rd.
Edmonton, Alberta T6B 2C3
CANADA
(Canadian branch of above society)

Germans from Russia Heritage Society
1008 E. Central Ave.
P.O. Box 1671
BISMARCK ND 58502
(society for the emigration of 1763 to 1850 from Germany
to Russia and subsequently from 1860 to 1930 to the
Americas, especially "Black Sea Germans")

Germans from Russia Heritage Collection
North Dakota Institute for Regional Studies
NDSU Library
FARGO ND 58105
(sponsors library collection on Germans from Russia)

Germans from Russia Heritage Society
First California Chapter
c/o Tom Hoffman
5070 Ducas Place
SAN DIEGO CA 92124
(state chapter of national society for Germans from Russia)

The Glueckstal Colonies Research Association
c/o Mrs. Margaret Freeman
611 Esplanade
REDONDO BEACH CA 90277-4130
(society researching Bergdorf, Glueckstal, Kassel, and
Neudorf in Russia)

The Gottschee Tree
Liz Information Service
P.O. Box 725
LOUISVILLE CO 80027-0725
(newsletter for descendants from the German-speaking
Gottschee cultural enclave in Slovenia; Elizabeth A. Nick)

Gottscheer Research and Genealogy Association
215634 American River Dam
SONORA CA 95370-9112
(Gottschee genealogical society)

Old Economy Village
14th and Church Streets
AMBRIDGE PA 15003
(archive of history of the Harmony Society (Rappites) from
1805 to 1905)

German Order of Harugari
c/o Max Math
7625 Hooker St.
WESTMINSTER CO 80030
(headquarters of German lodge organization with 4 state
groups)

Johannes Schwalm Historical Association, Inc.
Mark A. Schwalm
800-F Westbury Place
4807 Old Spartanburg Rd.
TAYLORS SC 29687
(society concentrating on Schwalm area and Hessian
soldiers)

The National Huguenot Society
c/o Arthur Finnell
9033 Lyndale Ave. S, Suite 108
BLOOMINGTON MN 55420-3535
(national society for Protestant descendants over 18 years
of age of Huguenots)

Huguenot Historical Society
14 Forest Glen Rd.
NEW PALTZ NY 10028
(historical society concerned with history of Huguenots)

Hungarian Genealogical Society of America
c/o Kathy Karocki
124 Esther St.
TOLEDO OH 43805-1435
(national genealogical society for Hungarian genealogy)

Jewish: See AMERICAN RELIGIOUS ARCHIVES.

Krefeld Immigrants and Their Descendants
7677 Abaline Way
SACRAMENTO CA 95823
(publication and group for descendants of immigrants from
Krefeld and vicinity ca. 1683-1700, mostly to Germantown,
PA)

Lithuanian-American Genealogy Society
c/o Balzakas Museum of Lithuanian Culture
6500 Pulaski Rd.
CHICAGO IL 60629-5136
(Lithuanian-American genealogical society)

Our Heritage
Louis Dylus
3176 Colchester Brook Lane
FAIRFAX VA 22031
(Lithuanian genealogy newsletter)

Luxembourgers of America, Inc.
806 S. Na-wa-ta Ave.
MT PROSPECT IL 60056
(society for descendants of immigrants from Luxembourg)

Wahlert Memorial Library
Loras College
11450 Alta Vista
DUBUQUE IA 52001
(has complete set of *Luxemburger Gazette* with obituaries
of Luxemburgers in America; several volumes of translated
extracts are in Carnegie-Stout Public Library in Dubuque)

Luxembourg Society of Wisconsin
c/o Old World Wisconsin
EAGLE WI 53119
(society for descendants of Luxembourg-Americans in
Wisconsin)

Mennonite Family History
P.O. Box 171
ELVERSON PA 17602
(journal for Americans of Mennonite heritage)

Moravian Heritage Society
31910 Road 160
VISALIA CA 93292-9044
(society for descendants of emigrants from Moravia)

New Zealand Society of Genealogists
Central European Interest Group
P.O. Box 8795
Auckland 3
NEW ZEALAND
(special interest group of New Zealand society for German and central European genealogy)

Vesterheim Genealogical Center
415 W. Main St.
MADISON WI 53702
(Norwegian local histories, family histories, passenger lists, church records, censuses)

Orangeburg German-Swiss Genealogical Society
James W. Green III
Rt. 5, Box 20
WINNSBORO SC 29180-9566
(genealogical society for descendants of Orangeburg Germans and Swiss in Carolina; newsletter)

Ostfriesen Ancestral Research Association
Rev. Kenneth De Wall
143 Virginia Ave.
BETHALTO IL 62010
(genealogical society for persons of East Frisian ancestry)

Ostfriesland Genealogical Society
P.O. Box 381
RUTHVEN IA 51358
(genealogical society for persons of East Frisian ancestry)

National Polish Genealogical Society
Polish Museum of America
984 N. Milwaukee Ave.
CHICAGO IL 60622-4101
(national genealogical society for Polish-Americans, including Germans, Jews, Lithuanians within present Polish borders)

The Polish Genealogical Society of Michigan
Burton Historical Collection
Detroit Public Library
5201 Woodward Ave.
DETROIT MI 48203
(genealogical society for Polish-Americans in Michigan, including Germans, Jews, and Lithuanians)

The Polish Nobility Association
419 Dunkirk Rd.
ANNAPOLIS MD 21212
(national association for Polish nobility)

The American Institute of Polish Culture, Inc.
1440 79th St. Causeway
MIAMI FL 33141
(national association for Polish-American culture)

Polish-American Archives
Central Connecticut State University
NEW BRITAIN CT 06050
(archives for Polish-American material)

Polish Genealogical Society of California
P.O. Box 713
MIDWAY CITY CA 92655
(genealogical society for Polish-Americans in California)

Polish Genealogical Society of Massachusetts
P.O. Box 381
NORTHAMPTON MA 01061
(genealogical society for Polish-Americans in Massachusetts)

Polish Genealogical Society of the Northeast
8 Lyle Rd.
NEW BRITAIN CT 06053
(genealogical society for Polish-Americans in northeastern states)

Polish Genealogical Society of Texas
3915 Glenheather
HOUSTON TX 77068
(genealogical society for Polish-Americans in Texas)

Polish Genealogical Society of Wisconsin
P.O. Box 37476
MILWAUKEE WI 53237
(genealogical society for Polish-Americans in Wisconsin)

Die Pommerschen Leute
c/o Myron and Norma Gruenwald
1260 Westhaven Dr.
OSHKOSH WI 54904
(newsletter/society for Pomeranian genealogy and culture)

Pommerscher Verein
c/o Leroy Boehlke
N112 W13102 Mequon Rd.
MEQUON WI 53022
(Pomeranian Society headquarters in U.S.)

Pommerscher Verein Freistadt
P.O. Box 204
GERMANTOWN WI 53022
(Pomeranian Society cultural information)

Russian Historical and Genealogical Society
971 First Ave.
NEW YORK NY 10022
(American historical and genealogical society for persons of Russian ancestry)

The Georgia Salzburger Society
9375 Whitfield Ave.
SAVANNAH GA 31406
(society for descendants of emigrants from Salzburg (now Austria) to Ebenezer (now Rincon), GA; first group landed 12 March 1734 in Charleston, SC)

GENEALOGICAL, HISTORICAL, AND GERMAN-RELATED SOCIETIES OUTSIDE EUROPE

The Scandinavian-American Genealogical Society
P.O. Box 16006
ST PAUL MN 55105
(society for Scandinavian-Americans, including Danes
(Schleswig-Holstein), etc.)

Schlaraffia Nordamerika
Dr. Karl Hormann
986 Memorial Dr.
CAMBRIDGE MA 02138
(headquarters of lodge for German-Americans with 30 local
chapters)

The American/Schleswig-Holstein Heritage Society
P.O. Box 313
DAVENPORT IA 52805-0313
(society to promote interest in the heritage of Schleswig-
Holstein, encourage cultural exchanges, sponsor study of
family history research, and encourage study of the
language and history of Schleswig-Holstein)

Schwaben International, Inc.
1 World Trade Center, Suite 1145
NEW YORK NY 10048
(international cultural, trade, tourism, and history group
relating to Swabians and Swabian Americans "for better
world understanding")

Silesian-American Genealogical Society
P.O. Box 346
SALT LAKE CITY UT 81346-0346
(genealogical society for Silesian-Americans)

1683 Immigrants Descendants
Mrs. Donald V. Rhoads
9508 Wheel Pump Lane
PHILADELPHIA PA 19118
(listing of descendants of Op den Graef, Lucken, Tones,
Simons, Strepers, Kunders, etc. (pioneer immigrants of
1683; many spelling variants))

Slovak Heritage and Folklore Society International
Helene Cincebeaux, Editor
151 Colebrook Dr.
ROCHESTER NY 14617-2215
(historical and folklore society for Slovaks)

Slovak Genealogy Research Center
6962 Palmer Ct.
CHINO CA 91710
(genealogical research center for Slovaks in America)

Slovenian Genealogical Society
52 Old Farm Rd.
CAMP HILL PA 17011
(genealogical society for Slovenian-Americans)

Swiss-American Historical Society
c/o Erdmann Schmocker
6440 N. Bosworth
CHICAGO IL 60626
(U.S. historical society for Swiss-Americans)

Swiss-American Historical Society
Genealogy Committee
2526 Jackson Ave.
EVANSTON IL 60201
(genealogy subgroup of historical society for
Swiss-Americans)

American Swiss Association
60 E. 42nd St.
NEW YORK NY 10017
(cultural exchange organization; film rentals on
Switzerland)

North American Swiss Alliance
33 Public Square, Suite 404
CLEVELAND OH 44113
(U.S./Canada association of Swiss-Americans)

Swiss Historical Society of Gruetli, Tennessee
c/o Dola S. Tyler
524 Lanny Dr.
WINCHESTER VA 22601
(historical society for the Swiss heritage of Gruetli,
Tennessee)

The Swiss Connection
2845 N. 72nd St.
MILWAUKEE WI 53210
(newsletter for Swiss genealogy)

Central Union of Transylvanian Saxons
1436 Brush St.
DETROIT MI 48226
(umbrella organization of societies for Transylvanian
Saxons)

Ukrainian Genealogical and Heraldic Society
573 NE 102nd Ave.
MIAMI SHORES FL 33138
(genealogical and heraldic society for Ukrainians)

Valais/Wallis Immigration Project
c/o Robert Klinko
915 N. Clark St.
APPLETON WI 54911
(researching Swiss immigrants from Canton Valais
(German: Wallis))

The Wandering Volhynians
Irmgard Hein Ellison
P.O. Box 97
OSSIAN IA 52161-0097
(U.S. contact for newsletter on Germans from Volhynia)

The Wandering Volhynians
Ewald Wuschke
3492 W. 39th Ave.
Vancouver, British Columbia
CANADA V6N 3A2
(Canadian contact for newsletter on Germans from
Volhynia)

GENEALOGICAL, HISTORICAL, AND GERMAN-RELATED SOCIETIES OUTSIDE EUROPE

Texas Wendish Heritage Society
Rt. 2, Box 155
GIDDINGS TX   78942-9802
(historical society for Wends (Sorbs) in Texas)

American Westphalian Historical Association
905 Vale Park Rd., 3-D
VALPARAISO IN   46383
(historical society for Westphalians in America)

Westphalian Heritage Society
P.O. Box 244
WESTPHALIA MO 65085
(society for persons of Westphalian heritage)

EUROPEAN/AMERICAN.

Federation of German-American Clubs
Olgastrasse 11
D-70182 Stuttgart
GERMANY
(can arrange for members to meet American tourists)

Columbus Gesellschaft e.V. Muenchen
Karolinenplatz 3
D-80333 Muenchen/Munich
GERMANY
(German-American pen pal association for adults)

Genealogical Association of English-Speaking Researchers
        in Europe, Sitz Heidelberg
86th CSG/RSSRR
P.O. Box 142
APO NY 09063
or
Greg Hagen
Gauangelloch
Achatweg 3
D-69181 Leimen
GERMANY
(publishes *Family Finder*; promotes family history research
among US forces in Europe; strengthens cooperation
between European and American/ Canadian researchers;
sponsors educational programs; assists US Army in
Europe's library in acquisition and usage of genealogical
material; encourages careful documentation)

Oesterreichische Landsmannschaft
Lindengasse 42
A-1070 Wien/Vienna
Oesterreich/AUSTRIA
EUROPE
(society for Austrians living in other countries)

UNITED STATES.

Genealogical Department of the Church of Jesus Christ of
    Latter-day Saints
35 N. West Temple St.
SALT LAKE CITY UT 84103
(has microfilmed many United States and Canadian public
records, as well as those of most European countries; most
are available on loan from Salt Lake City to branch Family
History Libraries of the LDS ("Mormon") church for use
on branch premises at a non-profit rental fee; the world's
largest genealogy collection)

Central Information Division
National Archives
WASHINGTON DC 20408
Telephone: (202) 523-3220
(national archives of the United States; has censuses,
passenger lists, military records, etc.)

Reference Services Branch (NNIR)
National Archives and Records Service
8th and Pennsylvania Avenue, NW
WASHINGTON DC 20408
(branch of national archives of the United States which
issues forms (NATF Form 81) to request passenger arrival
record searches and then performs the requested search)

Military Service Branch (NNMS)
National Archives and Records Service
8th and Pennsylvania Avenue, NW
WASHINGTON DC 20408
(branch of national archives of the United States which
issues forms (NATF Form 80) to request military service
records (including Confederate Armed Forces), pension
application records, and bounty-land warrant application
records prior to World War I, and then performs the
requested search)

Office of Personnel Management
1900 E St. NW
WASHINGTON DC 20415
(records of retired military and civil service personnel)

National Archives - Alaska Region
654 W. 3rd Ave., Room 012
ANCHORAGE AK 99501
(regional archive for AK)

National Archives - Pacific Southwest Region
24000 Avila Rd.
P.O. Box 6719
LAGUNA NIGUEL CA 92607-6719
(regional archive for AZ, southern CA, and Clark County,
NV)

National Archives - Pacific Northwest Region
Seattle Branch
6125 Sand Point Way NE
SEATTLE WA 98115
(regional archive for ID, OR, and WA)

Federal Archives and Records Center
3150 Bertwynn Dr.
DAYTON OH 45439
(regional records repository for certain federal agencies for
IN, MI, and OH)

National Archives - Pacific Sierra Region
1000 Commodore Dr.
SAN BRUNO CA 94066
(regional archive for most of CA, HI, most of NV, and the
Pacific)

National Archives - Rocky Mountain Region
Building 48, Denver Federal Center
P.O. Box 25307
DENVER CO 80225
(branch archive for CO, MT, ND, SD, UT, and WY)

National Archives - Southwest Region
501 W. Felix St.
P.O. Box 6216
FT WORTH TX 76115
(regional archive for AR, LA, NM, OK, and TX)

National Archives - Central Plains Region
Kansas City Branch
2312 E. Bannister Rd.
KANSAS CITY MO 64131
(regional archive for IA, KS, MO, and NE; has World War
I draft records for OR, RI, UT, VA, VT, WA, and WY)

National Archives - Great Lakes Region
7358 S. Pulaski Rd.
CHICAGO IL 60629
(regional archive for IN, MI, MN, OH, and WI; has World
War I draft records for IL)

National Archives - Southeast Region
1557 St. Joseph Ave.
EAST POINT GA 30344
(branch archive for AL, FL, GA, KY, MS, NC, SC, TN;
has 24,000,000 World War I draft records for most of
country except IL, OR, RI, UT, VA, VT, WA, WY; all men
b. 1873-1900; records include date & place of birth,
whether natural-born citizen, naturalized alien, or foreigner
who has declared intent)

National Archives - Mid-Atlantic Region
9th and Market Streets, Room 1350-3KRA
PHILADELPHIA PA 19107
(regional archive for DE, MD, PA, VA, WV)

Federal Records Center - Philadelphia
Market & 9th Streets, Room 1300
PHILADELPHIA PA 19107
(branch records repository for certain agencies for DE,
MD, PA, VA, WV)

National Archives - Northeast Region
201 Varick St.
NEW YORK NY 10014
(regional archive for NJ, NY, PR, VI; also entrance on
Houston St.)

National Archives - New England Region
380 Trapelo Rd.
WALTHAM MA 02154
(regional archive for CT, MA, ME, NH, RI, and VT)

Washington Federal Records Center
Eighth and Pennsylvania Avenue, NW
WASHINGTON DC 20409
(National Archives branch records center with case file
records of land-cntrics for government land transactions,
such as homesteading, some including declarations of
intent and naturalization papers for immigrants; use in
conjunction with Bureau of Land Management Office
records; records in process of relocation to National
Archives and should be completed in 1997)

United States Department of the Interior
Bureau of Land Management
7450 Boston Blvd.
SPRINGFIELD VA 22304
(United States land management office; has copies of more
than 5,000,000 land patents (original deeds from United
States government to original land grantees ("entrymen")
for eastern United States; most western states have own
land offices; automated Land Information System being
completed; name & state enough)

Census Microfilm Rental Program
P.O. Box 2940
HYATTSVILLE MD 20784
(means for rental of census microfilm (which in 1850 and
later censuses gives birthplaces, usually by country but
sometimes by province); operated by DDD Company of
Landover, MD, by contract with the National Archives)

Cashier
National Archives Trust Fund Board
WASHINGTON DC 20408
(National Archives microfilm sales; catalogs available)

Personal Census Service Branch
Bureau of the Census
P.O. Box 1545
JEFFERSONVILLE IN 47131
(after 1 August 1991 source for "proof of age" document in
lieu of birth certificate for censuses since 1920; use new
form BC-600)

Historic Resources, Inc.
P.O. Box 244
BOUNTIFUL UT 84010
(private lending library (AGLL) with National Archives
and other microfilms for rental and/or purchase)

Scholarly Resources, Inc.
104 Greenhill Ave.
WILMINGTON DE 19805-1897
(private company with National Archives microfilms for
purchase)

Library of Congress
Local History and Genealogy Reading Room
Genealogy Reading Rooms Division
Thomas Jefferson Annex
10 First St. SE
WASHINGTON DC 20540
(official library of the U.S. Congress with photoduplication
services of materials held; publications on *Library of
Congress Publications in Print*, guides to genealogical
research; out of print materials; repository for all
copyrighted works in the U.S.; emigration records copied
between 1928 and 1932 from state archives in Amberg,
Bamberg, Berlin, Breslau, Coburg, Dresden, Hamburg,
Hannover, Karlsruhe, Koblenz, Magdeburg,
Muenchen/Munich, Muenster, Neuburg, Osnabrueck,
Stettin, Weimar, Wiesbaden, and Wuerzburg)

National Union Catalog
Library of Congress
WASHINGTON DC 20408
(national listing of books including scarce and rare books)

Immigration and Naturalization Service (INS)
U.S. Department of Justice
425 I St. NW
WASHINGTON DC 20536
(archive for all naturalizations in the United States after 26
September 1906; also birth certifications for alien children
(still under 21) later adopted by U.S. citizens and lawfully
admitted to the U.S.; also lists of German aliens, who were
required to register yearly with the U.S. Department of
Justice during World War I; explain that your request is of
a genealogical nature; use form G-641 for verification of
age or date of birth, naturalization or citizenship, and
genealogical information; use form G-639 for U.S.
citizenship papers; branches located in Anchorage,
Phoenix, Los Angeles, San Diego, San Francisco, Denver,
Hartford, Miami, Orlando, Atlanta, Honolulu, Chicago,
Indianapolis, Louisville, New Orleans, Portland (ME),
Baltimore, Boston, Detroit, Minneapolis-St. Paul, Kansas
City (MO), St. Louis, Omaha, Las Vegas, Reno, Newark,
Albany, Buffalo, New York City, Charlotte, Cincinnati,
Cleveland, Portland (OR), Philadelphia, Providence,
Memphis, Dallas, El Paso, Harlingen (TX), Houston, San
Antonio, Salt Lake City, Burlington (VT), St. Albans (VT),
Washington DC in Alexandria (VA), Norfolk, Seattle,
Spokane, Milwaukee, Agana (Guam), San Juan, Rome,
Mexico City, and Bangkok)

Immigration and Naturalization Service
75 Lower Weldon St.
ST ALBANS VT 05479-0001
(source for documentation on immigrants from Canada; St. Alban's is the repository for virtually all points of entry)

Passport Services
Correspondence Branch
U.S. Department of State
1425 K Street NW
WASHINGTON DC 20520
(records from passports from 1906 and later; also, reports of deaths of U.S. citizens who die in foreign countries, such as naturalized citizens who die on a return trip to the old homeland)

Diplomatic Records Branch
National Archives
Room 5E
WASHINGTON DC 20408
(passport applications for travel abroad (perhaps for a trip back to the old homeland) from 1905 and previous years)

Office of Special Consular Services
U.S. Department of State
WASHINGTON DC 20520
(U.S. government assistance in obtaining a copy of a foreign birth or death record, especially birth records of living persons)

Daughters of the American Revolution Library
Memorial Continental Hall
1776 D St. NW
WASHINGTON DC 20006-5392
(major genealogical library with copies of many colonial and federal records)

Office of Personnel Management
1900 E St. NW
WASHINGTON DC 20415
(records of retired military and civil service personnel)

Federal Records Center - St. Louis
National Personnel Records Center
Military Personnel Records
9700 Page Blvd.
ST LOUIS MO 63132
(records on Army officers separated after 1916 and Army enlisted personnel separated after 1912; other and earlier records are in National Archives; fire damage in July 1973 to 80% of Army personnel discharges from 1 November 1912 to 1 January 1960; 75% of Air Force personnel (Hubbad to Z) discharges from 24 September 1947 to 1 January 1964)

U.S. Army Military History Institute
Upton Hall
CARLISLE BARRACKS PA 17013-5008
(has over 200,000 books, 11,000 bound periodicals, ca. 12,000 papers, 500,000 photos, 50,000 audio-visual materials, 500,000 documents and publications on military history of U.S. and other countries, military maps)

Cemetery Service
National Cemetery System
Veterans Administration
810 Vermont Ave. NW
WASHINGTON DC 20422
(holds alphabetical card record identifying most soldiers buried in national cemeteries and other cemeteries under federal jurisdiction from 1861 to the present)

Monument Service
Department of Veterans Affairs
810 Vermont Ave NW
WASHINGTON DC 20420
(records of monuments for deceased veterans)

The U.S. Air Force Historical Research Center
Maxwell Air Force Base
MONTGOMERY AL 36122
(has unit histories for the U.S. Air Force)

The U.S. Army Library
Room 1 A 518
The Pentagon
WASHINGTON DC 20310
(has unit histories for the U.S. Army)

The U.S. Marine Corps Library
Bldg. 58, Navy Yard
WASHINGTON DC 20374
(has unit histories for the U.S. Marine Corps)

Social Security Administration
Office of Central Records Operations
Attn.: Freedom of Information Officer
Metro West Bldg.
300 W. Greene
BALTIMORE MD 21235
(address for inquiries to obtain copy of application for a Social Security number SS-5 or claim for benefits of a person now deceased; send a copy of death certificate)

Social Security Administration
Letter Forwarding Unit
6401 Security Blvd.
BALTIMORE MD 21235
(address for attempts to forward letters to persons whose address is unknown, with explanation of your need for contact and relationship, the person's name, Social Security number, birthplace, birthdate, and names of parents if possible; the letter addressed to the individual must be left unsealed; 37,058,000 recipients were on rolls by 1985)

Social Security Administration
P.O. Box 57
HYATTSVILLE MD 21203
(address for inquiries relating to place of birth of a person now deceased who was covered under the Social Security Act of 1934; use form SSA-L997, send a copy of death certificate)

U.S. Information Agency
German-American Contacts Staff
WASHINGTON DC 20547
(coordination of official German-American governmental
cooperation)

New York Municipal Archives
Department of Records & Information Services
52 Chambers St.
NEW YORK NY 10007
(address of archive holding New York City directories,
1890 New York City police census, etc.; important for new
arrivals in U.S. before moving on to eventual place of
settlement)

Pennsylvania Historical and Museum Commission
Division of Archives and Manuscripts
P.O. Box 1026
HARRISBURG PA 17108
(has Philadelphia passenger arrival lists)

Historical Society of Pennsylvania
1300 Locust St.
PHILADELPHIA PA 19107
(has records of lying-in hospital for immigrants not
admitted after ca. 1719)

Baltimore City Archives
211 E. Pleasant St., Room 201
BALTIMORE MD 21202
(has city lists of passenger arrivals in Baltimore 1833-1866
required by a Maryland state law of 22 March 1833)

Texas Seaport Museum
Pier 21
2016 Strand
GALVESTON ISLAND TX 77550
(has database of ca. 150,000 immigrants through
Galveston, mostly from Bremen, 1846-71, 1896-1921)

CANADA.

Public Archives of Canada
395 Wellington St.
Ottawa, Ontario
CANADA K1A 0N3
(national archives of Canada; has microfilm passenger
manifests for Quebec 1865-1908; Halifax 1880-1908; St.
John 1900-1908; Victoria 1905-1908; via U.S. ports
1905-1908; indexes for only 1865-1869 Quebec and
1880-1881 Halifax)

Records of Entry Unit
Canada Employment and Immigration Commission
Place du Portage
Phase IV
Hull, Quebec
CANADA K1A 0J9
(immigrant arrivals in Canada after 1908)

Citizenship Registration Branch
15 Eddy St.
Hull, Quebec
CANADA K1A 0M5
(branch of Canadian national archives; has card file of
naturalizations 1867-1917 and originals from 1917 to the
present)

Canadian Department of Manpower and Immigration
Entry Section
Employment and Immigration Commission
305 Rideau St.
Ottawa, Ontario
CANADA K1A 0J9
(Canadian government branch; has information on
immigrants not held in the Public Archives of Canada)

The Public Archives of Nova Scotia
6016 University Ave.
Halifax, Nova Scotia
CANADA B3H 1W4
(passenger arrivals in Nova Scotia)

Citizen Registration Branch
P.O. Box 7000
Sydney, Nova Scotia
CANADA
(naturalizations in Nova Scotia)

Archive for Germans in Northern Ontario
Institute for Northern Ontario Research and Development
Laurentian University Library
Ramsey Lake Rd.
Sudbury, Ontario
CANADA P3E 2C6
(German-Canadian archive for northern Ontario area)

NEW ZEALAND.

Shipping Archivist
New Zealand Society of Genealogists
2 Bruce Rd.
Glenfield
NZ- Auckland 10
NEW ZEALAND
(New Zealand passenger arrival lists)

(Determine present church group affiliation through national church directories such as *Yearbook of American and Canadian Churches* or *The Encyclopedia of American Religions*, etc.)

AMANA SOCIETY.

Amana Society Heritage
P.O. Box 81
AMANA IA 52203-0081
(has church records of the Amana Society or Ebenezer Society, first of Buffalo, New York, area, then Iowa County, Iowa)

AMISH. See also MENNONITE.

Amish Historical Library
c/o David Luthy
Route 4
Alymer, Ontario
CANADA N5H 2R3
(has settlement histories; 610 genealogies)

Amish Genealogy Project
Johns Hopkins University
School of Medicine
725 N. Wolfe St.
BALTIMORE MD 21205
(genetic study of highly interrelated Amish families)

ANABAPTISTS.
See AMISH, APOSTOLIC CHRISTIAN CHURCH, BRETHREN IN CHRIST, CHURCH OF THE BRETHREN, EPHRATA COMMUNITY, GERMAN BAPTIST BRETHREN, HUTTERIAN BRETHREN, MENNONITES.

APOSTOLIC CHRISTIAN CHURCH.

Apostolic Christian Church
P.O. Box 151
TREMONT IL 61568
(national headquarters for Apostolic Christian Church, an Anabaptist church mostly of Swiss descent)

AUGSBURG CONFESSION. See LUTHERAN.

BRETHREN. See CHURCH OF THE BRETHREN.

BRETHREN IN CHRIST.

Brethren in Christ Historical Society
Messiah College
GRANTHAM PA 17027
(historical society for Brethren in Christ, an Anabaptist church sometimes also known as River Brethren)

BRETHREN CHURCH (PROGRESSIVE). See CHURCH OF THE BRETHREN.

CALVINISTS. See REFORMED, HUGUENOTS.

CATHOLIC. (Many records are maintained by diocesan archives or local parishes, often in Latin.)

Archives of the Roman Catholic Central-Verein
3855 Westminster Place
ST LOUIS MO 63103
(the most important and extensive collection of German Catholic materials on the American Catholic Church, including German bishops, priests, religious orders, nuns, parishes, colonies, etc.)

Archives of the Leo House
332 W. 23rd St.
NEW YORK NY 10011
(records of the American branch of the St. Raphael Society for immigrants)

Center for Migration Studies of New York, Inc.
209 Flagg Place
NEW YORK NY 10304
(records on immigration and the Catholic Church's effect on immigrants; publishes "International Migration Review")

American Catholic Historical Society of Philadelphia
St. Charles Borromeo Seminary
P.O. Box 84
PHILADELPHIA PA 19105
(historical society for Roman Catholics in America; publishes "American Catholic Historical Society Records")

American Catholic Historical Association
Catholic University of America
WASHINGTON DC 20017
(historical society for Roman Catholics in America)

Catholic Archives of America
Notre Dame University
SOUTH BEND IN 46624
(archive for Roman Catholics in America)

Department of Archives and Manuscripts
Catholic University of America
WASHINGTON DC 20019
(archive for Roman Catholics in America)

Jesuit-Krauss-McCormick Library
E. 55th St.
CHICAGO IL 60615
(library with Catholic historical material)

CHURCH OF JESUS CHRIST OF LATTER-DAY SAINTS. See MORMONS.

GERMAN-AMERICAN RELIGIOUS ORGANIZATIONS

CHURCH OF THE BRETHREN. Formerly GERMAN
BAPTIST BRETHREN. (Not UNITED BRETHREN!)

Fellowship of Brethren Genealogists
1451 Dundee Ave.
ELGIN IL 60120-1694
(genealogical society covering the Church of the Brethren;
located at Brethren Historical Library and Archives in
National Headquarters; publishes quarterly newsletter)

Brethren Historical Committee
Church of the Brethren General Board
1451 Dundee Ave.
ELGIN IL 60120-1694
(historical society covering the Church of the Brethren)

Brethren Archives
Bethany Theological Seminary
Library
Butterfield and Meyers Roads
OAK BROOK IL 60521
(archive of the Church of the Brethren; has collection of
church history, some family history)

Brethren Archives
Ashland Theological Seminary
524 College Ave.
ASHLAND OH 44805
(archive of the Brethren Church (Progressive) branch
known since 1939 as Ashland Brethren)

Fellowship of Grace Brethren Churches
WINONA LAKE IN 46590
(headquarters of the Brethren Church (Progressive) branch
known since 1939 as Grace Brethren)

Miller Library
McPherson College
McPHERSON KS 67460
(library with emphasis on Church of the Brethren in KS
region)

Brethren Bible Seminary
Beeghly Library
Juniata College
HUNTINGDON PA 16652
(archive of the Church of the Brethren)

Brethren Heritage Center
6987 Union Rd.
CLAYTON OH 45402
(library and archive of Church of the Brethren, District of
Southern Ohio)

Funderburg Library
Manchester College
N MANCHESTER IN 46962
(library with emphasis on Church of the Brethren in IN)

Brethren Historical Room
Zug Memorial Library
Elizabethtown College
ELIZABETHOWN PA 17022
(library with emphasis on former Eastern District, Atlantic
Northeast District, and Southern District of Pennsylvania of
Church of the Brethren)

Alexander Mack Library
Bridgewater College
BRIDGEWATER VA 22812
(library with emphasis on Church of the Brethren in VA)

Library
University of LaVerne
LaVERNE CA 91750
(library with emphasis on Church of the Brethren in CA)

CHURCH OF THE UNITED BRETHREN. See UNITED
BRETHREN.

CHURCH OF GOD, WINEBRENNER. See
WINEBRENNER CHURCH OF GOD.

DUNKARDS. See CHURCH OF THE BRETHREN.

DUNKERS. See CHURCH OF THE BRETHREN.

EBENEZER SOCIETY. See AMANA SOCIETY.

EPHRATA COMMUNITY.

Ephrata Community
9400 Anthony Highway
WAYNESBORO PA 17268
(headquarters of the small modern Ephrata Community,
spiritual descendants of the Ephrata Sabbatarians)

Ephrata Cloister
EPHRATA PA 17522
(museum of the Ephrata Sabbatarians, also known as
Seventh Day Baptists, Women of the Wissahickon, etc.)

Seventh Day Baptist Library
Seventh Day Baptist Building
PLAINFIELD NJ 07060
(library of the Ephrata Sabbatarians/Seventh Day Baptists)

Seventh Day Baptist Historical Society
3120 Kennedy Road
P.O. Box 1678
JANESVILLE WI 53547
(headquarters of Seventh Day Baptist group of U.S. and
Canada)

EPHRATA SABBATARIANS.
See EPHRATA COMMUNITY.

EVANGELICAL AND REFORMED. See REFORMED.

EVANGELICAL ASSOCIATION. See METHODIST.

EVANGELICAL CHURCH. See METHODIST.

EVANGELICAL CONGREGATIONAL CHURCH.

Evangelical School of Theology
121 S. College St.
MYERSTOWN PA 17067
(archives of the Evangelical Congregational Church as
offshoots of Albright and the Evangelical Association)

EVANGELICAL LUTHERAN. See LUTHERAN.

EVANGELICAL UNITED BRETHREN.
See METHODIST.

HARMONY SOCIETY.

Old Economy Village
14th and Church Streets
AMBLER PA 15003
(history and archives of Harmony Society of Economy, PA,
and New Harmony, IN, from 1805 to 1905)

HEBREW. See JEWISH.

HERRNHUTER. See MORAVIANS.

HUGUENOTS. See also REFORMED.
See also listings under RELIGIOUS ARCHIVES:
PROTESTANT: FRANCE.
(Huguenots were massacred in Paris on 24 August 1572,
St. Bartholomew's Day; Protestant religious refugees from
France exiled after King Louis XIV of France in 1685
revoked the 1598 Edict of Nantes which had allowed
religious and civil liberty to Huguenots; some fled first to
Holland, England, Germany, Switzerland, etc., some then
to America, most remained in Europe)

Huguenot Society of America
122 E. 58th St.
NEW YORK NY 10022
(a national society for descendants of Huguenots)

The National Huguenot Society
6033 Lyndale Ave. S, Suite 108
BLOOMINGTON MN 55420-3535
(national federation of state historical and genealogical
societies for descendants of Huguenots)

Huguenot Historical Association
983 North Ave.
NEW ROCHELLE NY 10804
(historical society for Huguenots; has records 1702-1874;
library)

Huguenot Historical Society
P.O. Box 339
NEW PALTZ NY 12561
(library covering Huguenot (exiled French Protestant)
records from 1675 to 1865; small staff, cannot perform
research)

Huguenot Society of South Carolina
94 Church St.
CHARLESTON SC 29401
(society for South Carolina Huguenots)

Huguenot Society of Oxford
2 Maple Rd.
OXFORD MA 01540
(society for Huguenots in Massachusetts)

Huguenot Society of Canada
136 Tollgate Rd., Apt. 202
Brantford, Ontario
CANADA N3R 4Z7
(historical society for Huguenots in Canada)

The Secretary
Huguenot and Walloon Research
Malmaison
Church St.
Great Bedwyn, Wiltshire
ENGLAND 5N8 3PE

The Huguenot Society
54 Knatchball Rd.
London
ENGLAND SE5QY

The Secretary
Huguenot Society of London
The Huguenot Library
University College
Gower St.
London
ENGLAND WC1E 6BT
(library for Huguenots)

HUTTERIAN BRETHREN. See MENNONITES.

ISRAELITES. See JEWISH.

JEWISH. See also listings under GERMANY.

Association of Jewish Genealogical Societies
155 N. Washington Ave.
BERGENFIELD NJ 07621
(umbrella organization for local and regional Jewish
genealogical societies, encouraging research, promoting
societies, lobbying, and sponsoring projects, publishes
microfiche gazetteer of Eastern Europe, Jewish surname
indexes, etc.)

GERMAN-AMERICAN RELIGIOUS ORGANIZATIONS

American Jewish Historical Society
15 W. 16th St.
NEW YORK NY 10011
(historical society for American Jewish people; synagogue and educational records; organizational and institutional records; early American family documents)

Jewish Genealogical Society, Inc.
P.O. Box 6398
NEW YORK NY 10128
(national genealogical society for Jewish people; prize-winning quarterly publication *Dorot*; maintains Jewish Genealogical Family Finder)

American Jewish Archives
Klau Library, Hebrew Union College
Jewish Institute of Religion
3101 Clifton Ave.
CINCINNATI OH 45220
(center for North American Jewish history and genealogy; many genealogies, vital records, newspaper indices; archives: documents, letters, memoirs, organizational records, family trees, many before 1900)

American Jewish Periodical Center
Klau Library, Hebrew Union College
3101 Clifton Ave.
CINCINNATI OH 45220
(center for 836 microfilmed Jewish periodicals, newspapers, and bulletins in various languages from the 19th and 20th centuries)

Jewish Theological Seminary Library
3080 Broadway
NEW YORK NY 10027
(records of European Jewish communities; Hebrew subscription lists for 8,767 communities in Europe and N. Africa with names of over 350,000 Jews who paid for book publication)

Leo Baeck Institute
15 W. 16th St.
NEW YORK NY 10011
(collection of records on German-speaking Jews (Austria, Czechoslovakia, Germany, Romania, etc.); congregational histories, vital records; strong points Berlin, northern Germany; Baden, the Palatinate)

YIVO Institute for Jewish Research
15 W. 16th St.
NEW YORK NY 10011
(major repository of primarily eastern European Jewish records (Hungary, Lithuania, Poland, Romania, etc., Hebrew Immigrant Aid Society records, etc.) mostly in Yiddish, including many communal histories and records)
(temporary address 555 W. 57th St., Suite 1102, NY 10019)

Yeshiva University
Mandel Gottesman Library
500 W. 185th St. (at 2520 Amsterdam Ave.)
NEW YORK NY 10033
(Jewish synagogue archive of New York City; books and manuscripts dealing with pre-World War II Europe; also records of 58 early American Orthodox Jewish communities; inventory of Staatsarchiv Jewish records for 53 communities in Europe)

Brooklyn Jewish Center Library
667 Eastern Parkway
BROOKLYN NY 11213
(private Jewish library)

Hebrew Immigrant Aid Society
333 Seventh Ave.
NEW YORK NY 10001
(has microfilm records of all immigrants met since 1910)

B'nai B'rith Museum
1640 Rhode Island Ave. NW
WASHINGTON DC 20036
(museum of history of Jewish fraternal organization)

Research Foundation for Jewish Immigration, Inc.
570 Seventh Ave.
NEW YORK NY 10018
(scholarly research center for Jewish immigration)

Research Foundation for Jewish Immigration
570 Seventh Ave., 16th Floor (at 41st)
NEW YORK NY 10028
(information on 25,000 emigrés 1933-1945)

Jewish Division, New York Public Library
Fifth Ave. at 42nd St., Room 84
NEW YORK NY 10028
(227,000 books, microfilms, manuscripts, newspapers, periodicals, from around the world)

Jewish Historical Society
c/o Carlton Brooks
720 W. Edgewood Ave.
MESA AZ 85210
(historical society for American Jewish life)

Western Jewish History Center
Judah L. Magnes Memorial Museum
2911 Russell St.
BERKELEY CA 94705
(family histories of western U.S. Jewish families; manuscript and archival research library; newspaper *The Hebrew* 1854-1876, *Emanu-El* 1895-- ; books; vertical files; cemetery commission; surname index to manuscript collection)

Hebrew Union College
3077 University Ave.
LOS ANGELES CA 90007

Brandeis-Bardin Institute
BRANDEIS CA 93064

Jewish Family Name File
David L. Gold
67-07 215 St.
OAKLAND GARDENS NY 11364-2523

Roots and Branches
136 Sandpiper Key
SECAUCUS NJ 07094
(syndicated Jewish genealogy column by Miriam Weiner in
numerous U.S. Jewish newspapers)

Stammbaum
c/o Harry Katzman
1601 Cougar Ct.
WINTER SPRINGS FL 32708-3855
(German Jewish genealogy newsletter)

Gesher Galicia
3128 Brooklawn Terrace
CHEVY CHASE MD 20815
(Jewish Galician newsletter "The Gallitzianer")

Landsman
3701 Connecticut Ave. NW #228
WASHINGTON DC 20008
("Landsman" newsletter)

HSIG
P.O. Box 34152
CLEVELAND OH 44134
(publishes "Magyar Zsido" newsletter on Hungarian Jews)

ROM-SIG
P.O. Box 520583
LONGWOOD FL
(publishes "ROM-SIG News" on Romanian Jews)

International Registry of Holocaust Victims
201 S. Third Ave.
HIGHLAND PARK NJ 08904
(a listing by name of Holocaust victims)

A Living Memorial to the Holocaust
Museum of Jewish Heritage
1605 Ave. J
NEW YORK NY 11230
(library with memoirs, yizkor books, taped interviews,
photographs, artifacts, documents, in Battery Park)

Holocaust Documentation and Education Center
Florida International University
NE 151 St. and Biscayne Blvd.
NORTH MIAMI FL 33181

Survivors of the Shoah Visual History Foundation
P.O. Box 3168
LOS ANGELES CA 90078-3168

Holocaust and War Victims Tracing and Information
   Center
4700 Mount Hope Dr.
BALTIMORE MD 21215-3231

U.S. Holocaust Memorial Museum
100 Raoul Wallenberg Place SW
WASHINGTON DC 20024-2150
research@ushmm.org

Baltimore Hebrew College
Meyerhoff Library
BALTIMORE MD 21215

Dropsie College Library
Broad and York
PHILADELPHIA PA 19119

Philadelphia Jewish Archives Center
Balch Institute
18 S. 7th St.
PHILADELPHIA PA 19106-2314

Arizona Jewish Historical Society
Committee on Genealogy
720 W. Edgewood Ave.
MESA AZ 85210

Southern Arizona Jewish Historical Society
Committee on Genealogy
4181 E. Pontatoc Canyon Dr.
TUCSON AZ 85718

Jewish Genealogical Society of Los Angeles
P.O. Box 55443
SHERMAN OAKS CA 91343-0443

Jewish Genealogical Society of Orange County
11571 Cherry St.
LOS ALAMITOS CA 90720

Jewish Genealogical Society of South Orange County
2370-D Via Mariposa W
LAGUNA HILLS CA 92075-1903

Jewish Genealogical Society of Sacramento
2351 Wyda Way
SACRAMENTO CA 95825

Jewish Genealogical Society of San Diego
255 S. Rios Ave.
SOLANA BEACH CA 95825

GERMAN-AMERICAN RELIGIOUS ORGANIZATIONS

San Francisco Bay Area Jewish Genealogical Society
3916 Louis Rd.
PALO ALTO CA 94303

Jewish Genealogical Society of Colorado
P.O. Box 224400
DENVER CO 80222

Jewish Genealogical Society of Connecticut
17 Salem Walk
MILFORD CT 06430

Jewish Genealogical Society of Greater Washington
P.O. Box 412
VIENNA VA 22183-0412

Jewish Genealogical Society of Broward County
P.O. Box 17251
FT LAUDERDALE FL 33318

Jewish Genealogical Society of Greater Miami
9370 SW 88th Terrace
MIAMI FL 33176

Jewish Genealogical Society of Central Florida
P.O. Box 520583
LONGWOOD FL 32752

Jewish Genealogical Society of Greater Orlando
P.O. Box 941332
MAITLAND FL 32794-1332

Jewish Genealogical Society of South Palm
2247 North West 62 Dr.
BOCA RATON FL 33434

Jewish Genealogical Society of Georgia
4430 Mt. Paran Parkway NW
ATLANTA GA 30327-3747

Jewish Genealogical Society of Illinois
P.O. Box 515
NORTHBROOK IL 60065-0515

Illiana Jewish Genealogical Society
404 Douglas
PARK FOREST IL 60466

Jewish Genealogical Society of Louisville
Israel T. Naamani Library
3600 Dutchman Lane
LOUISVILLE KY 40205

Jewish Genealogical Society of New Orleans
P.O. Box 7811
MATAIRIE LA 70010-7811

Genealogy Department
Jewish Genealogical Society of Maryland
2707 Moores Valley Dr.
BALTIMORE MD 21209

Jewish Genealogical Society of Greater Boston
P.O. Box 366
NEWTON HIGHLANDS MA 02161-0003

Jewish Genealogical Society of Michigan
4275 Strathdale Lane
W BLOOMFIELD MI 48323

Jewish Historical Society of Upper Midwest
Hamline University Library
1536 Hewitt Ave.
ST PAUL MN 53104

Jewish Historical Society of St. Louis
Jewish Community Library
12 Millstone Campus Dr.
ST LOUIS MO 63146

Jewish Genealogical Society of Las Vegas
P.O. Box 29342
LAS VEGAS NV 89126

Jewish Genealogical Society of Southern Nevada
2653 Topaz Square
LAS VEGAS NV 89126

Jewish Genealogical Society of North Jersey
1 Bedford Rd.
POMPTON LAKES NJ 07442

Genealogy and Family History Committee
New Mexico Jewish Historical Society
1428 Miracerros S
SANTA FE NM 87501

Albany Jewish Genealogical Society
P.O. Box 3850
ALBANY NY 12203

Jewish Genealogical Society of Greater Buffalo
174 Peppertree Dr. #7
AMHERST NY 14228

Jewish Genealogical Society of Long Island
37 Westcliff Dr.
DIX HILLS NJ 11746

Jewish Genealogical Society, Inc.
P.O. Box 6398
NEW YORK NY 10128

Jewish Genealogical Society of Rochester
205 Viennawood Dr.
ROCHESTER NY 14618

Jewish Genealogical Society of Cleveland
996 Eastlawn Dr.
HIGHLAND HEIGHTS OH 44143

Cleveland Jewish Genealogy Society
Menorah Park
27100 Cedar Rd.
BEACHWOOD OH 44122

Jewish Genealogical Society of Dayton
P.O. Box 338
DAYTON OH 45406

Jewish Genealogical Society of Oregon
Mittleman Jewish Community Center
6651 SW Capitol Highway
PORTLAND OR 97219

Jewish Genealogical Society of Philadelphia
332 Harrison Ave.
ELKINS PARK PA 19117-2662

Jewish Genealogical Society of Pittsburgh
213 Fifth Ave.
PITTSBURGH PA 15219

Dallas Jewish Historical Society
Jewish Genealogy Division
7900 Northaven Rd.
DALLAS TX 75230

Jewish Genealogical Society of Salt Lake City
3510 Fleetwood Dr.
SALT LAKE CITY UT 84109

Jewish Genealogical Society of Tidewater
Jewish Community Center
7300 Newport Ave.
NORFOLK VA 23505

Jewish Genealogical Society of Washington
14222 NE 1st Lane
BELLEVUE WA 98007

Wisconsin Jewish Genealogical Society
9280 N. Fairway Dr.
MILWAUKEE WI 53217

The Canadian Jewish Congress
1590 McGregor Ave.
Montréal, Quebec
CANADA H3G 1C5
(records on Jewish immigrants to Canada)

Jewish Genealogical Society of Southern Alberta
914 Royal Ave. SW
Calgary, Alberta
CANADA T2T 0L5

Jewish Historical Society of Western Canada
404-365 Hargrave St.
WINNEPEG, Manitoba
CANADA R3B 2K3

Jewish Genealogical Society of Canada
P.O. Box 446, Station "A"
Willowdale, Ontario
CANADA M2N 5T1
(publishes "Shem Tov")

Jewish Genealogical Society of Montréal
5787 McAloor Ave.
Côte St. Luc, Quebec
CANADA H4W 2H3

Genealogical Institute of the Jewish Historical Society of
Western Canada
365 Hargrave St., Suite 404
Winnipeg, Manitoba
CANADA R3B 2K3

LATTER-DAY SAINTS. See MORMONS.

LDS. See MORMONS.

LUTHERAN.

Concordia Historical Institute
801 DeMun Avenue
ST LOUIS MO 63105
(historical institute and archive for the Lutheran Church -
Missouri Synod (national) and Lutherans in general; many
parish vital registers beginning 1843; also has 38 district
archives in North America)

The Evangelical Lutheran Church in America
Ms. Elisabeth Wittman, Archivist
8765 W. Higgins Rd.
CHICAGO IL 60631-4198
(1 January 1988 merger of Lutheran Church in America,
American Lutheran Church, and Association of Evangelical
Lutheran Churches; has microfilmed records of ca. 5,000
congregations of both former American Lutheran Church
(**ALC**), a 11,160-congregation body composed largely of
Scandinavian and German settlers near and west of the
Mississippi River in the mid-to-late 1800's; and of former
Lutheran Church in America (**LCA**): Lutheran General
Synod, Lutheran General Council, Lutheran United Synod
in the South, all prior to 1918; United Lutheran 1918-1962;
Lutheran Church in America 1962-1987; microfilming still
not comprehensive; microfilms not available on loan but
may be used at archive; archive will respond to short,
specific genealogical questions; regional archives listed
below have paper copy of records of dissolved ALC &
LCA congregations; **AELC**, a modern creation, consisted
mostly of former Missouri Synod churches; archives
physically located at 5400 Milton Parkway, Rosemont, IL)

GERMAN-AMERICAN RELIGIOUS ORGANIZATIONS

Region 1 Archives
Evangelical Lutheran Church in America
Ms. Kerstin Ringdahl
Archives and Special Collections
Mortvedt Library
Pacific Lutheran University
TACOMA WA 98447
(regional ELCA archive for AK, ID, MT, OR, WA)

Region 2 Archives
Evangelical Lutheran Church in America
Rev. Ray Kibler III
4249 N. LaJunta Dr.
CLAREMONT CA 91711-3199
(temporary regional ELCA contact person for AZ, CA, CO,
III, NM, NV, UT, WY; an archival center will be located at
Pacific Lutheran Theological Seminary, Berkeley, CA.)

Region 3 Archives
Evangelical Lutheran Church in America
Mr. Paul Daniels
2481 Como Ave. W
ST PAUL, MN 55108-1445
(regional ELCA archive for MN, ND, SC)

Region 4 Archives
Evangelical Lutheran Church in America
(AR, KS, LA, MO, NE, OK, TX; write ELCA archives in
Chicago above)

Region 5 Archives
Evangelical Lutheran Church in America
333 Wartburg Place
DUBUQUE IA 52001
(regional ELCA archive for IL, IA, WI, and Upper
Michigan; has master list of formal
and informal names of all Lutheran congregations in US)

Region 6 Archives
Evangelical Lutheran Church in America
(IN, KY, Lower Michigan, OH; write ELCA
archives in Chicago above)

Region 7 Archives ELCA
The Lutheran Archives Center at Philadelphia
Mr. John E. Peterson
Krauth Memorial Library
Evangelical Lutheran Church in America
7301 Germantown Ave., Mt. Airy
PHILADELPHIA PA 19119
(regional archive for NY, NJ, eastern PA, all of New
England, and the non-geographic Slovak Zion Synod,
except Metropolitan New York Synod as noted below)

Dr. David Gaise
32 Neptune Rd.
TOMS RIVER NJ 08753
(archivist for Metropolitan New York Synod, Evangelical
Lutheran Church in America; located within Region 7)

New York Historical Society
170 Central Park W
NEW YORK NY 10024-5194
(now has records of St. Paul's Evangelical Lutheran
Church to 1880; New York was major immigration center)

Region 8 of Evangelical Lutheran Church in America
includes MD, central and western PA, WV, and
metropolitan Washington, DC.

Dr. Paul Mueller
Thiel College
GREENVILLE PA 16125
(archivist for western Region 8, including western PA,
WV, and western MD)

Mr. Donald Matthews
Lutheran Theological Seminary
GETTYSBURG PA 17325
(archivist for eastern Region 8, including central
PA, eastern MD, and metropolitan Washington, DC)

Region 9 of Evangelical Lutheran Church in America
includes AL, FL, GA, MS, NC, SC, TN, VA, and the
Caribbean Synod. A Cooperative Center for Archives in
Region 9 will be located at Lutheran Theological Southern
Seminary, 4201 N. Main St., Columbia, SC 29203; until it
is established, write ELCA archives in Chicago above.

Adams County (PA) Historical Society
Old Dorm
Seminary Campus
Drawer A
GETTYSBURG PA 17325
(now custodians of typed transcripts of Lutheran parish
vital registers of Pennsylvania formerly housed at Abdel
Wentz Library of Lutheran Theological Seminary,
Gettysburg, Pennsylvania)

Luther College Preus Library
DECORAH IA 52101

Grand View College
1351 Grandview Ave.
DES MOINES IA 50316

Concordia College
Ylvisaker Library
MOOREHEAD MN 56560

St. Olaf College
Rolvaag Library
NORTHFIELD MN 55057

Dana College
Dana Library
BLAIR NE 68008

Upsala College Library
Prospect St. E
ORANGE NJ 07019

Muhlenberg College
Haas Library
ALLENTOWN PA 18104

Thiel College
Langenheim Library
GREENVILLE PA 16125

Augustana College
Mikkelson Library
SIOUX FALLS SD 57197

Rev. Martin Westerhaus
Archives
Wisconsin Lutheran Seminary
1831 N. Seminary Dr., 65W
MEQUON WI 52092
(archives for Wisconsin Evangelical Lutheran Synod
(WELS))

Historical Institute of the Wisconsin Evangelical Lutheran
        Synod (WELS)
2929 N. Mayfair Rd.
MILWAUKEE WI 53222
(historical institute of the Wisconsin Evangelical Lutheran
Synod, founded 1850 (nationwide, despite name))

American Association of Lutheran Churches
Rev. Duane R. Lindberg, Presiding Pastor
P.O. Box 416
WATERLOO IA 50701
(head of small association, breakaway group from ELCA)

Apostolic Lutheran Church of America
Rev. Allen Tumberg
NEW YORK MILLS MN 56567
(head of 57-congregation church body)

Association of Free Lutheran Congregations
Rev. Richard Snipstead
3110 E. Medicine Lake Blvd.
MINNEAPOLIS MN 55441
(head of 193-congregation church group)

Church of the Lutheran Brethren of America
Rev. Robert M. Overgaard Sr.
P.O. Box 655
FERGUS FALLS MN 56537
(head of 128-congregation church body)

Church of the Lutheran Confession
Rev. Daniel Fleischer
460 75th Ave. NE
MINNEAPOLIS MN 55432
(head of 67-congregation church body)

Concordia Lutheran Archives
7100 Ada Blvd.
Edmonton AB
CANADA T5B 4E4
(archives for Lutheran churches in Canada)

Estonian Evangelical Lutheran Church
Rev. Karl Raudsepp
30 Sunrise Ave., Apt. 216
Toronto, Ontario M4A 2R3
CANADA
(Bishop in North America for Estonian Lutherans)

Texas Lutheran College
Blumberg Library
SEGUIN TX 78155
(records on Lutheran churches in TX)

MENNONITE.
(Note: Mennonites are mainly of Swiss descent, though
some are of German or Dutch descent)

Mennonite Church
528 E. Madison St.
LOMBARD IL 60148
(headquarters for the Mennonite Church)

Lancaster Mennonite Conference Historical Society
Landis Library
2215 Mill Stream Road
LANCASTER PA 17602-1499
(historical society for Mennonites of the Lancaster
Conference, Amish, and southeastern PA; library of ca.
55,000 volumes; publishes *Pennsylvania Mennonite
Heritage*)

Mennonite Historical Library
Musselman Library
280 W. College Ave.
Bluffton College
BLUFFTON OH 45817-1195
(library and archive of Mennonite Church, especially
Swiss, French, and south German Mennonites, especially
Central District Conference)

Mennonite Historical Library
Goshen College
1700 S. Main St.
GOSHEN IN 46526
(archive of the Mennonite Church; personal manuscripts,
photos, tape recordings)

Center for Mennonite Brethren Studies
Mennonite Brethren Biblical Seminary
4824 E. Butler
FRESNO CA 93727-5097
(official depository of Mennonite Brethren General
Conference; Anabaptist/Mennonite historical library)

Fresno Pacific Library (Mennonite)
1717 S. Chestnut
FRESNO CA 93702

Associated Mennonite Seminary
3003 Benham
ELKHART IN 46517

Mennonite Historical Library
Goshen College
1700 S. Main St.
GOSHEN IN 46526
(historical library for Mennonites; index to obituaries in
Herald of Truth and *Gospel Herald*; index to over 100
Amish families)

Mennonite Library and Archives
Information and Research Center
Bethel College
300 E. 27th St.
NORTH NEWTON KS 67117
(catalog cards on family history and church records;
Mennonite passenger lists)

Center for Mennonite Brethren Studies
Tabor College
400 S. Jefferson
HILLSBORO KS 67063
(historical library for Mennonite Brethren Church in U.S.)

Mennonite Historian of Eastern Pennsylvania
565 Yoder Rd. Box 82
HARLEYSVILLE PA 19438

Mennonite Heritage Center
24 S. Main St.
SOUDERTON PA 18964
(heritage center for Mennonites; art, artifacts, literature,
documents)

Menno Simons Historical Library and Archive
Eastern Mennonite College
1200 Park Rd.
HARRISONBURG VA 22801
(historical library of 15,700 volumes and archive for
Mennonites; also local Virginia books)

Juniata Mennonite Historical Center
RD 1
RICHFIELD PA 17086
(historical center for Mennonites; 1,500 volumes on history
and genealogy of central PA and Mennonites)

Central Mennonite Library
c/o Ella Nafziger
304 Vine St.
ARCHBOLD OH 43502
(historical library for Mennonites)

Illinois Mennonite Historical and Genealogical Society
P.O. Box 819
METAMORA IL 61548
(historical and genealogical society for Illinois Mennonites;
library; archive)

Mennonite Genealogy, Inc.
P.O. Box 393
Winnipeg, Manitoba
CANADA R3C 2H6
(genealogy library with 156,000 cards on Mennonites;
Prussia/Russia)

Freeman Jr. College Library
748 S. Main St.
FREEMAN SD 57209
(genealogies, papers on Northern District Conference of
General Conference; Hutterian Brethren)

Mennonite Archives of Ontario
Conrad Grabel College
Waterloo, Ontario
CANADA N2L 3G6
(historical archive for Ontario Mennonites)

Archives of the Evangelical Mennonite Conference
P.O. Box 1268
Steinbach, Manitoba
CANADA R0A 2A0
(historical research on Evangelical Mennonites; tape
recordings, etc.)

Mennonite Library and Archives of Eastern Pennsylvania
1000 Forty Foot Rd.
LONSDALE PA 19446
(family records; genealogy; cemetery records for
Mennonites of eastern PA)

Iowa Wesley College Library
MT PLEASANT IA 52614
(records on Mennonites of Iowa)

Mennonite Historical Society of Iowa
P.O. Box 576
KALONA IA 61761
(historical society for Mennonites in Iowa)

OMII (Ohio, Michigan, Illinois, Indiana) Genealogical
    Project
David Habegger
6929 Hillshire Ct.
FORT WAYNE IN 46835

Saskatchewan Mennonite Brethren Archives
Bethany Bible Institute
Hepburn, Saskatchewan
CANADA S0K 1Z0
(historical records of Bethany Bible Institute and
Mennonite Brethren of Saskatchewan)

Muddy Creek Farm Library
N. Muddy Creek Rd.
Route 3
DEMAR PA 17517
(Old Order Mennonite records)

Center for Mennonite Brethren Studies
c/o Rachel Hiebert
4824 E. Butler St.
FRESNO CA 93727
(study center for Mennonite Brethren)

Mennonite Heritage Centre
600 Shaftesbury Blvd.
Winnepeg, Manitoba
CANADA R3P 0M4
(heritage centre for Mennonites, mainly Prussian and
Russian Germans, in Canada)

Mennonite Historical Society of British Columbia Archives
2825 Clearbrook Rd.
Clearbrook, BC
CANADA V2T 2Y2
(family histories, genealogies, church histories, etc.)

Conference of Mennonites in British Columbia
c/o Peter Kehler
P.O. Box 2204
Clearbrook, BC
CANADA V2T 3XB
(historical documents on provincial conference and 26
congregations)

Center for Mennonite Brethren Studies in Canada
Mennonite Brethren Historical Library
1-169 Riverton Ave.
Winnepeg, Manitoba
CANADA R2L 2E5
(study center and historical library for Mennonite Brethren
in Canada)

Archives of the Pacific Coast Conference
Western Mennonite School
9045 Wallace Rd. NW
SALEM OR 97304
(unindexed records of Pacific Coast Conference of the
Mennonite Church)

Center for Mennonite Brethren Studies in Canada
169 Riverton Ave.
Winnepeg, Manitoba
CANADA R2L 2E5
(center sponsored by Historical Committee of Canadian
Conference of the Mennonite Brethren Church)

Hutterian Genetic Study Project
University of Chicago
Medical School
5640 S. Ellis Ave.
CHICAGO IL 60637
(genetic study project on highly intermarried Hutterian
Brethren)

METHODIST.
(includes German-language Methodist or Methodist
Episcopal churches, also the Evangelical Association,
Evangelical Church, United Evangelical Church,
Evangelical United Brethren, and United Brethren in
Christ, which were largely German)

Historical Society
United Theological Seminary
1810 Harvard Building
DAYTON OH 45406
(formerly held records of (largely German-language)
Evangelical Association/Evangelical United Brethren
churches)

Evangelical United Brethren Genealogical Newsletter
"The Bush Meeting Dutch"
c/o Dr. David H. Koss
Associate Professor of History
Illinois College
JACKSONVILLE IL 62650

General Commission on Archives and History of the
United Methodist Church
Drew University
P.O. Box 127
MADISON NJ 07940
(commission on archives and history for the Methodist
church in America; has general denominational archival
records; records of Methodist churches are usually kept
locally)

Methodist Historical Society
St. George Church
326 New St.
PHILADELPHIA PA 19106
(historical society for Methodists)

United Methodist Historical Society Archives
2200 St. Paul St.
BALTIMORE MD 21218
(historical society for Methodists)

MORAVIANS.
(a religious group, not necessarily ethnic Moravians, also
known as UNITAS FRATRUM or HERRNHUTER, with
centers of activity in Bethlehem and Nazareth,
Pennsylvania, and Salem, North Carolina, among other
places; founded in Europe; active in mission work)

Moravian Historical Society
214 E. Center St.
NAZARETH PA 18064
(historical society with museum and library on members of
the Moravian Church in the United States)

GERMAN-AMERICAN RELIGIOUS ORGANIZATIONS

Moravian Archives
Moravian Church Central Archives North
1228 Main St.
BETHLEHEM PA 18018
(archive with records of the Northern Province of the
Moravian Church in the United States, e.g. Bethlehem and
Nazareth, PA; many memoirs of church members; records
mention other Germans)

Moravian Archives Central Archives South
4 E. Bank St.
Drawer M, Salem Station
WINSTON-SALEM NC 27108
(archive with records of the Southern Province of the
Moravian Church in the United States, e.g. Salem, North
Carolina; many memoirs of church members; records
mention other Germans)

Salem College
Granly Library
Salem Square
WINSTON-SALEM NC 27108

"MORMONS."

Family History Department of the Church of Jesus Christ of
Latter-day Saints
35 N. West Temple St.
SALT LAKE CITY UT 84103
(the largest genealogical library in the world;
comprehensive; has microfilms of many parish vital
registers of many religions worldwide, as well as civil
records, including many in Germany, Austria, Switzerland,
etc.)

PRESBYTERIAN. For German-Americans who were
supposedly (or actually) Presbyterians, see also
REFORMED.

Presbyterian and Reformed Church Historical Foundation
Assembly Drive
MONTREAT NC 18757
(Presbyterian and Reformed church archives)

QUAKERS. For German-Americans who were supposedly
(or actually) Quakers, especially after 1700, see
MENNONITE.

RAPPITES. See HARMONY SOCIETY.

REFORMED. See also HUGUENOTS.

Historical Commission of the United Church of Christ
Lancaster Archives
555 W. James St.
LANCASTER PA 17603
(historical society and archive for the former Evangelical
and Reformed Church, now part of the United Church of
Christ (UCC))

Philip Schaff Memorial Library
Lancaster Theological Seminary
James St. & College Ave.
LANCASTER PA 17603
(has parish vital registers of Reformed churches in
Pennsylvania, etc.)

Eden Theological Seminary
475 E. Lockwood Ave.
WEBSTER GROVES MO 63119
(has records of Reformed churches especially in the
Midwest, some as far east as western Pennsylvania)

Commission on History
Reformed Church in America
New Brunswick Theological Seminary
NEW BRUNSWICK NJ 08901
(Reformed Church in America (Dutch Reformed) records)

Presbyterian and Reformed Church Historical Foundation
Assembly Drive
MONTREAT NC 18757
(Presbyterian and Reformed church archives)

Calvin College and Seminary Library
Colonial Origins Collection
Heritage Hall
3207 Barton St. SE
GRAND RAPIDS MI 49506
(Christian Reformed church records)

Committee in the East of Historical Documents of the
        Christian Reformed Church
PASSAIC NJ 07055
(Christian Reformed church records)

Holland Society of New York
122 E. 58th St.
NEW YORK NY 10022
(manuscript collection of Dutch Reformed Church records)

Syracuse University Library
SYRACUSE NY 13210
(manuscript collection of Dutch Reformed Church records)

Hope College
VanZoeren Library
HOLLAND MI 49423
(manuscript collection of Dutch Reformed Church records)

RIVER BRETHREN. See BRETHREN IN CHRIST.

ROMAN CATHOLIC. See CATHOLIC.

GERMAN-AMERICAN RELIGIOUS ORGANIZATIONS

SALVATION ARMY.
(traces missing living relatives worldwide; check with local branch of Salvation Army for details)

Archives and Research Center
Salvation Army
145 W. 15th St.
NEW YORK NY 10011
(national headquarters for official records; records on immigration, women, medicine, the family, Salvation Army officers/ministers)

Territorial Headquarters of the Salvation Army
860 N. Dearborn St.
CHICAGO IL 60610-3392
or
Territorial Headquarters of the Salvation Army
120 W. 14th St.
NEW YORK NY 10011
or
Territorial Headquarters of the Salvation Army
1424 Northwest Expressway
ATLANTA GA 30329-2088
or
Territorial Headquarters of the Salvation Army
30840 Hawthorne Blvd.
RANCHO PALOS VERDES CA 90274

SCHWENKFELDERS.

Schwenkfelder Historical Society Library
Carnegie Library Building
Perkiomen School
1 Seminary Avenue
PENNSBURG PA 18073
(archives of Schwenkfelder Church)

SEVENTH DAY BAPTISTS.
See EPHRATA COMMUNITY.

SOCIETY OF FRIENDS. See QUAKERS.

TUNKERS. See CHURCH OF THE BRETHREN.

UNITAS FRATRUM. See MORAVIANS.

UNITED BRETHREN.

United Brethren Archives
Huntington College
RichLyn Library
HUNTINGTON IN 46750
(archive of United Brethren church)

UNITED CHURCH OF CHRIST.
See also REFORMED.
(UCC founded 1957 by merger of Evangelical & Reformed Church and Congregational Christian Church; national headquarters now at 700 Prospect Ave., Cleveland, OH)

United Church of Christ
Eden Archives and Library
475 E. Lockwood Ave.
WEBSTER GROVES MO 63119
(archive and library of the United Church of Christ; has German-language records from former Evangelical Synod and "German Evangelical Protestant" Churches or German-speaking Reformed churches in US)

UNITED EVANGELICAL CHURCH.
See METHODIST.

WINEBRENNER CHURCH OF GOD.

Findlay College
100 N. Main St.
FINDLAY OH 45840
(historical depository of Winebrenner Church of God)

Winebrenner Theological Seminary
FINDLAY OH 45840
(historical depository of seminary of Winebrenner Church of God)

WOMEN OF THE WISSAHICKON. See EPHRATA COMMUNITY.

GERMAN-AMERICAN AND/OR AMERICAN GENEALOGICAL BOOKSELLERS AND IMPORTERS

(listed alphabetically by name of firm)

AKB Publications
691 Weavertown Rd.
MYERSTOWN PA 17067
(publisher of books on emigrants from the Palatinate/ Pfalz, etc., to Pennsylvania and surrounding areas in colonial times)
(Annette Kunselman Burgert)

Ancestry, Inc.
350 S 400 E
P.O. Box 476
SALT LAKE CITY UT 84110
(publishing house for genealogy source & "how-to" books)

Arno Press
330 Madison Ave.
NEW YORK NY 10017
(publishing house for the "American Immigration Collection")

Edna M. Bentz
13139 Old West Ave.
SAN DIEGO CA 92129
(publisher of *If I Can, You Can Decipher German Script*)

Beverly Boehl
3925 Amy
GARLAND TX 75043
(publisher of *Deciphering the Church Records of Germany*)

Books on Demand Order Department
University Microfilms International
P.O. Box 1467
ANN ARBOR MI 48106
(books, theses, dissertations, etc., by special request in book form, sometimes also on microfilm)

Carl Boyer, 3rd
P.O. Box 220333
SANTA CLARITA CA 91322-0333
(publisher of early ship passenger lists)

Gail E. Breitbard
Route 1, Box 1160
ESTERO FL 33928
(publisher of *The Lost Palatine*, monthly genealogy letter on Palatines, Huguenots; surname-specific booklets on Palatines)

Buch-Bruecke
Rt. 2, Sweet Rd.
BALLSTON LAKE N Y 12019
(book importer)

Der Buchwurm
P.O. Box 268
TEMPLETON CA 93465
(book importer)

Calmar Publications
202 Wildwood Lane
LOUISVILLE KY 40223
(seller of genealogies of German Turners during the Civil War)

Closson Press
1935 Sampson Dr.
APOLLO PA 15613-9209
(publishing house for genealogical records of western Pennsylvania)
(Bob & Mary Closson)

Stephen Conte
P.O. Box 962
W CALDWELL NJ 07007
(German and other specialized genealogy videos)

Continental Book Company
80-00 Cooper Ave.
Bldg. #29
GLENDALE NY 11385
(book importer; textbooks, readers, cultural material, dictionaries, reference material)

Cottonwood Books
1216 Lillie Circle
SALT LAKE CITY UT 84121
(publishing house for *How to Trace Your Ancestors to Europe*)
(Hugh T. Law)

Council for European Studies
1429 International Affairs Bldg.
Columbia University
NEW YORK NY 10027
(center for scholarly research; publishes guides to libraries and archives in Europe)

Deutsche Buchhandlung
Route 5, Box 443A
HAGERSTOWN MD 21740
(book importer)

Marcel Didier (Canada) Ltée
2050 Bleury Street, Suite 50
Montréal, Quebec
CANADA H3A 2J4
(book importer)

Russell D. Earnest Associates
P.O. Box 490
DAMASCUS MD 20872
(publications on Fraktur documents of baptisms, marriages, etc.)

European Book Company
925 Larkin St.
SAN FRANCISCO CA 94109
(book importer)

Everton Publishers, Inc.
P.O. Box 368
LOGAN UT 84323-0368
(large genealogical publishing house with many titles on
Germany, immigration, naturalization, "how-to" books,
etc.)

Fox Smith Books
915 King St., Suite B38
ALEXANDRIA VA 22314
(dealer of books on Germany and Poland)

Gale Research Company
835 Penobscot Bldg.
DETROIT MI 48226-4094
(publishing house for reference books, including passenger
list indexes and passenger list bibliographies)

Gemuetlichkeit
2892 Chronicle Ave.
HAYWARD CA 94542-9981
(travel letter for Germany, Austria, Switzerland, and the
new Europe)

Genealogical Publishing Company
1001 N. Calvert St.
BALTIMORE MD 21202-3897
(largest U.S. publisher of genealogy reference books,
textbooks, manuals, and how-to books)

Genealogical Research Directory
Mrs. Jan Jennings
3324 Crail Way
GLENDALE CA 91206-1107
(U.S. distributor of worldwide *Genealogical Reference
Directory* and related CD's)

Genealogical Research Directory
Mrs. Jeanette Tyson
94 Binswood Ave.
Toronto, Ontario
CANADA M4C 3N9
(Canadian distributor of worldwide *Genealogical
Reference Directory* and related CD's)

Genealogical Research Directory
K.A. Johnson
17 Mitchell St.
P.O. Box 795
AUS-2060 North Sydney, New South Wales
AUSTRALIA
(Australian distributor of worldwide *Genealogical
Reference Directory* and related CD's)

Genealogy Unlimited, Inc.
P.O. Box 537
OREM UT 84059-0537
(genealogy books and European maps; special interest in
central and eastern Europe; European town locating
service; telephone 1-800-663-4363)
(Carol and Don Schiffman)

German Book Boutiques Ltd.
37 Queen St.
Ottawa, Ontario
CANADA K1P 5C4
(book importer)

German Genealogical Digest
245 N. Vine St., No. 106
SALT LAKE CITY UT 84103-1948
(quarterly German genealogical publication)

German House Research
c/o Juergen Eichhoff
The Pennsylvania State University
305 Burrowes Bldg.
UNIVERSITY PARK PA 16802-6203
(publications and posters on immigration research)

German Language Publications International
153 S. Dean St.
ENGLEWOOD CLIFFS NJ 07632
(books, etc.)

German Language Video Center
Heidelberg Haus Imports
7625 Pendleton Pike
INDIANAPOLIS IN 46226
(video cassettes: popular German films, language-learning,
history, all formats; converter between formats:
NTSC/PAL/SECAM)
(Juergen Jungbauer)

German Life
Zeitgeist Publishing
P.O. Box 609
GRANTSVILLE MD 21536
(German cultural magazine for Americans)

German News Company
218 E. 86th St.
NEW YORK NY 10028
(subscriptions to German periodicals)

Gerold International Booksellers, Inc.
35-23 Utopia Parkway
NEW YORK NY 11358
(branch of Wien/Vienna (Austria) bookshop)

Gessler Publishing Co., Inc.
900 Broadway
NEW YORK NY 10003-1291
(German and other foreign language records, tapes, maps,
games, puppets, posters, reference books, and other
learning aids)

GERMAN-AMERICAN AND/OR AMERICAN GENEALOGICAL BOOKSELLERS AND IMPORTERS

Goodspeed's Book Shop, Inc.
18 Beacon St.
BOSTON MA 02108
(genealogical bookseller; carries out-of-print genealogy and
local history books)

Myron and Norma Gorges Gruenwald
1260 Westhaven Dr.
OSHKOSH WI 54904
(publishers of *Die Pommerschen Leute* English-language
newsletter on Pomeranian-Americans, books on
Pomeranian history)

Gary T. Hawbaker
P.O. Box 207
HERSHEY PA 17033-0207
(importer of German genealogical books; publisher of
Lancaster County Connections)

Hearthstone Bookshop
5735-A Telegraph Rd.
ALEXANDRIA VA 22303-1205
(large genealogical bookseller)
(Stuart and Tammy Nixon)

Hebert Publications
RR 2, Box 572
CHURCH POINT LA 70525
(publisher of genealogies of Louisiana Germans)

Heritage Books, Inc.
1540E Pointer Ridge Place
BOWIE MD 20716-1859
(genealogical publisher, many books on German-
Americana)
(Laird Towle)

Heritage International
P.O. Box 21346
SALT LAKE CITY UT 84121
(publisher of *Palatine Pamphlet*, a book listing origins of
German & Swiss passengers on 1727-1808 ships to
Pennsylvania)
(Charles M. Hall)

Heritage Quest
P.O. Box 40
ORTING WA 98360-0040
(genealogy magazine with German column, sells
discounted genealogy aids to members)
(Leland K. Meitzler, now AGLL)

Heritage Surveys
P.O. Box 344
MCLEAN VA 22101
(publisher's representative for 2-volume set *Luxembourgers
in the New World*)
(Robert E. Owen)

Hippocrene Books, Inc.
171 Madison Avenue
NEW YORK NY 10016
(publishers of German-English dictionaries)

Hoenstine Rental Library
414 Montgomery St.
P.O. Box 208
HOLLIDAYSBURG PA 16648
(extensive mail-order rental library of books on
Pennsylvania, mostly Pennsylvania Germans)

Brent H. Holcomb
P.O. Box 21766
COLUMBIA SC 29221
(publisher of books on the German-Americans
of South Carolina, etc.)

House of Tyrol
P.O. Box 909
Gateway Plaza
CLEVELAND GA 30528
(book importer)

Image Recovery Service
P.O. Box 31275
DAYTON OH 45431
(service that uses ultraviolet light and/or infrared energy to
"recover" faded ink, pencil, etc., that once was visible)

International Book Import Services (IBIS)
(book imports; telephone 1-800-277-4247)

International Bookfinders
P.O. Box 1
PACIFIC PALISADES CA 90272-0001
(locater of out-of-print and hard-to-find books)

Jensen Publications
P.O. Box 700
PLEASANT GROVE UT 84062
(publisher of guides for German genealogy, quarterly
Germanic Genealogy Digest)
(Larry O. Jensen)

Dr. Arta F. Johnson
153 Aldrich Rd.
COLUMBUS OH 43214
(she is publisher of many self-help and background German
genealogy books)

Hank Jones (= Henry Z Jones, Jr.)
P.O. Box 261388
SAN DIEGO CA 92196-1388
(publisher of books documenting New York "Palatines" of
1708-1710, ca. 600 of 847 also documented in Europe;
Pennsylvania)

Iris Carter Jones
7677 Abaline Way
SACRAMENTO CA 95823
(publisher of periodical *Krefeld Immigrants and Their Descendants*)

Kerekes Brothers, Inc.
177 E. 87th St., 5th Floor
NEW YORK NY 10128
(book importer)

Kinship, Inc.
60 Cedar Heights Rd.
RHINEBECK NY 12572
(publisher of records of German-American
"Palatines" in upstate New York from 1709)
(Arthur Kelly)

LDS Church Distribution Center
1999 W 1700 S
SALT LAKE CITY UT 84150
(series of Genealogical Society of Utah Research Papers,
including Austria, Denmark, France, Germany,
Netherlands, Poland, and Switzerland; World Conference
on Records papers 1969 and 1980, etc.)

LDS
The Family History Department
35 N. West Temple St.
SALT LAKE CITY UT 84150
(sells microfiche of International Genealogical Index,
Family History Library Catalog, etc.)

Langenscheidt Publishers, Inc.
46-35 54th Rd.
MASPETH NY 11378
(publisher of language learning materials, dictionaries)

Libra Publications
P.O. Box 29
LINTHICUM HEIGHTS MD 21090
(publishing house for directories of genealogical and
historical societies)
(Mary Keysor Meyer)

The Linden Tree
1204 W. Prospect
CLOQUET MN 55720
(publisher of German "how-to" books)
(Marilyn Lind)

Lineages, Inc.
P.O. Box 417
SALT LAKE CITY UT 84110
(publisher of *Before Germanna* on origins of Germanna
settlers in VA 1714-1717)

Lucent Technologies
2855 N. Franklin Rd.
P.O. Box 19901
INDIANAPOLIS IN 46219
(official U.S. importer of telephone directories from over
100 foreign countries, including Austria, Belgium,
Czechoslovakia, Denmark, France, Germany, Luxembourg,
Poland, Romania, and Switzerland; telephone
1-800-432-6600, fax 1-800-566-9568)

Alfred Mainzer
27-08 40th Avenue
LONG ISLAND CITY NY 11101
(publisher of German-language greeting cards, etc.)

Mansfield Book Market
2065 Mansfield St.
Montréal, Quebec
CANADA H3A 1Y2
(book importer)

Masthof Press
Route 1, Box 20
MORGANTOWN PA 19543
(journal *(Mennonite Family History)* and book publisher
and dealer; Mennonite, Amish, Brethren connections)
(LeMar and Lois Mast)

Midwest European Publications
915 Foster St.
EVANSTON IL 60201
(book importer; retail and mail order)

Multicultural Books and Videos, Inc.
28880 Southfield Rd. Suite 183
LATHRUP VILLAGE MI 48076

National Archives
WASHINGTON DC 20408
(publisher of book on genealogical research in the National
Archives, catalogs of National Archives microfilm
available, including passenger lists)

NCSA Literatur
430 S. Kelp Grove Rd.
NASHVILLE IN 47448
(self-teaching book for learning old German script, other
German-American literature)

Sylvia Lee Nimmo
6201 Kentucky Rd.
Route 21
PAPILLION NE 68133
(publisher of passenger immigration lists)

Noodle-Doosey Press
P.O. Box 716
MANCHESTER MD 21102
(publishing house for series of German church book
translations in Maryland)
(the Rev. Frederick S. Weiser)

GERMAN-AMERICAN AND/OR AMERICAN GENEALOGICAL BOOKSELLERS AND IMPORTERS

Oro Press
217 W. First Ave.
DENVER CO 80223
(sells tourist history of Germany and Austria)

Jerome S. Ozer, Publisher, Inc.
475 Fifth Ave.
NEW YORK NY 10017
(publishing house for the "American Immigration Library"
with many titles)

Pacific Crest Stamps
alanstal@ix.netcom.com
(source for unused foreign stamps in lieu of SASEs)

Palatines to America
Box 101, Capital University
COLUMBUS OH 43209-2394
(national society with German surname-index publications,
immigrant ancestor charts, etc.)

Pennsylvania German Society
P.O. Box 397
BIRDSBORO PA 19508
(society with annual publications of folklife, historical, or
genealogical interest on "Pennsylvania Germans" as well as
special publications)

Albert J. Phiebig, Inc.
P.O. Box 352
WHITE PLAINS NY 10602
(book importer; search service for both current and
out-of-print books)

Polonia Book Store
2886 N. Milwaukee Avenue
CHICAGO IL 60618
(importer of Polish books and maps)

Pommerscher Verein Freistadt
13102 W. Mequon Rd.
P.O. Box 204
GERMANTOWN WI 53022
(importer of books on German history, names, and culture,
especially on Pomerania)

The Preservation Emporium
Stemmons Freeway
P.O. Box 226309
DALLAS TX 75222
(materials for preserving old letters, documents, books,
photographs, etc.)
(DeWayne Lener)

R and E Research Associates, Inc.
4843 Mission St.
SAN FRANCISCO CA 94112
(publisher of short bibliographies for ethnic groups)

Robert Rabe
14466 Sunrise Dr. NE
BAINBRIDGE ISLAND WA 98110
(publisher of "Gateway to Germany" newsletter)

Robert D. Reed
18581 McFarland Ave.
SARATOGA CA 95070
(publisher of how-to books on researching ethnic groups,
including German, Jewish, and Polish)

Reed Publishing Co.
121 Chanlon Rd.
NEW PROVIDENCE NJ 07974
(formerly R.R. Bowker; publishing house for *Encyclopedia
of German-American Genealogical Research* and
American Genealogical Resources in German Archives)

Repeat Performance
2911 Crabapple Lane
HOBART IN 46342
(tapes of genealogical lectures)

Roots International
3239 N. 58th St.
MILWAUKEE WI 53216
(publisher of "how-to" books and finding aids for central
European genealogical research)
(Maralyn Wellauer)

Mary S. Rosenberg, Inc.
P.O. Box 99
1455 New Rd.
MOUNTAINDALE NY 12763-0099

Ruesch International Monetary Services, Inc.
825 14th St. NW
WASHINGTON DC 20005
toll-free phone (800) 424-2923
(source to use for paying in German and other foreign
currency; also offices in New York, Los Angeles, Chicago,
Atlanta, and Boston)

The Rev. Paul Miller Ruff
18 Fosterville Rd.
GREENSBURG PA 15601
(publisher of translations of western Pennsylvania
German-language church records)

Schoenhof's Foreign Books
76 Mt. Auburn St.
CAMBRIDGE MA 02138
(book importer)

Scholarly Resources, Inc.
104 Greenhill Avenue
WILMINGTON DE 19805-1897
(publishing house with genealogical publications on Dutch
emigration, Pennsylvania records, major *Germans to
America* series of passengers from 1850 on)

GERMAN-AMERICAN AND/OR AMERICAN GENEALOGICAL BOOKSELLERS AND IMPORTERS

Dr. George K. Schweitzer
407 Regent Ct.
KNOXVILLE TN 37923
(publisher of genealogy "how-to" and source books)

Shenandoah History
P.O. Box 98
EDINBURG VA 22824
(publishing house for German-American history of the
Shenandoah Valley of Virginia, West Virginia, Maryland)
(Klaus Wust)

Kenneth L. Smith
4936 Whisper Cove Ct.
COLUMBUS OH 43230
(publisher of books on German genealogical
correspondence, dating systems, calendars,
genealogical photography, etc.)

Southwest Pennsylvania Genealogical Services
P.O. Box 253
LAUGHLINTOWN PA 15655
(publishing house for (all) Pennsylvania research, including
Pennsylvania Germans)

Summit Publications
(publisher of *German Family Research Made Simple* and
similar works; see Ye Olde Genealogie Shoppe)
(J. Konrad, pseudonym of J.B. Koesterer)

Ernest Thode
RR 7, Box 306 AB, Kern Road
MARIETTA OH 45750-9437
(compiler of *Address Book for Germanic Genealogy*,
German-English Genealogical Dictionary, *Genealogical
Gazetteer of Alsace-Lorraine*, also seller of maps)
(Ernest Thode)

Bette Butcher Topp
1304 W. Cliffwood Ct.
SPOKANE WA 99218-2917
(publisher of periodical, *German Queries*)

Westland Publications
P.O. Box 117
MCNEAL AZ 85617
(publishing house for many monographs on "Hessian"
soldiers, emigration from specific areas of Germany, etc.)
(Clifford Neal Smith)

Ye Olde Genealogie Shoppe
P.O. Box 39128
INDIANAPOLIS IN 46239
(large genealogy bookseller and Heritage House publisher)
(Ray and Pat Gooldy)

FOREIGN OFFICES IN NORTH AMERICA

AUSTRIA.

Austrian Information Service
31 E. 69th St.
NEW YORK NY 10021
(general information about Austria)

Austrian National Tourist Office
500 Fifth Ave.
NEW YORK NY 10017
(tourist information about Austria; brochure "Tracing Your
Heritage in Austria"; also has branch offices in Chicago,
Los Angeles, and Portland, OR)

Austrian National Tourist Office
500 N. Michigan Ave.
CHICAGO IL 60611
(tourist information about Austria)

Austrian Embassy
2343 Massachusetts Ave., NW
WASHINGTON DC 20008
(chief Austrian diplomatic office in the United States)

Austrian National Tourist Office
2 Bloor St. E, Suite 3330
Toronto, Ontario
CANADA M4W 1A8
(tourist information on Austria; also has branch offices in
Montréal and Vancouver)

BELGIUM.

Belgian National Tourist Office
745 Fifth Ave.
NEW YORK NY 10022
(tourist information on Belgium)

DENMARK.

Danish Information Office
588 Fifth Ave.
NEW YORK NY 10036
(general information on Denmark)

The Danish Tourist Board
633 Third Ave.
NEW YORK NY 10027
(tourist information on Denmark; brochure "Tracing Your
Danish Ancestors and Relatives")

GERMANY.
(IN THE UNITED STATES)

German Information Center
950 Third Ave., 24th floor
NEW YORK NY 10022
(212) 888-9840
(general information on German public life, history, and
current events; publishes weekly free newsletters *The Week
in Germany* and *Deutschland Nachrichten*, also online)
(Internet: gicl@ix.netcom.com)

German National Tourist Office
122 E. 42nd St.
Chanin Bldg., 52nd Floor
NEW YORK NY 10168-0072
(212) 661-7200
(tourist information about Germany)

German National Tourist Office
444 S. Flower St., Suite 2230
LOS ANGELES CA 90017-2997
(213) 688-7332
(tourist information about Germany)

German Federal Railroad
630 Fifth Ave., Suite 1418
NEW YORK NY 10020
(information about German railroads, tourist information
about Germany)

German Federal Railroad
625 Statler Office Bldg.
BOSTON MA 02116
(information about German railroads, tourist information
about Germany)

German Federal Railroad
1121 Walker St.
HOUSTON TX 77002
(information about German railroads, tourist information
about Germany)

German Federal Railroad
10100 Santa Monica Blvd.
LOS ANGELES CA 90063
(information about German railroads, tourist information
about Germany)

Lufthansa German Airlines
680 Fifth Ave.
NEW YORK NY 10019
(information on German air travel)

Embassy of Germany
4645 Reservoir Rd., NW
WASHINGTON DC 20007-1998
(chief U.S. diplomatic office of Federal Republic of
Germany; also serves DC, DE, MD, VA, and WV)

Consulate General of Germany
1000 Peachtree Center
Cain Tower
299 Peachtree St., NE
ATLANTA GA 30043-3201
(serves AL, FL, GA, MS, NC, SC, and TN)

Consulate General of Germany
535 Boylston St.
BOSTON MA 02116
(serves CT except Fairfield Co., MA, ME, NH, RI, and
VT)

Consulate General of Germany
Monroe Bldg., 10th Floor
104 S. Michigan Ave.
CHICAGO IL 60603
(serves IA, IL, KS, MN, MO, ND, NE, SD, and WI)

Consulate General of Germany
Edison Plaza, Suite 2100
660 Plaza Dr.
DETROIT MI 48226
(serves IN, KY, MI, and OH)

Consulate General of Germany
1330 Post Oak Blvd, Suite 1850
HOUSTON TX 77056-3007
(serves AR, (LA), NM, OK, and TX)

Consulate General of Germany
6435 Wilshire Blvd.
LOS ANGELES CA 90048
(serves AZ and southern CA)

Consulate General of Germany
Branch Office
100 N. Biscayne Blvd.
MIAMI FL 33132
(branch of Atlanta; serves Miami and south FL)

Consulate General of Germany
Branch Office
2834 International Trade Mart
2 Canal St.
NEW ORLEANS LA 70130
(branch of Houston; serves Louisiana)

Consulate General of Germany
460 Park Ave.
NEW YORK NY 10022
(serves NJ, NY, PA, and Fairfield Co., CT)

Consulate General of Germany
6th Floor, International Bldg.
601 California St.
SAN FRANCISCO CA 94108-2870
(serves most of CA; CO, HI, NV, UT, WY, and American
Midway)

Consulate General of Germany
1617 IBM Bldg.
1200 Fifth Ave.
SEATTLE WA 98101
(serves AK, ID, MT, OR, and WA)

(also Honorary Consulates-General or Honorary Consulates
of Federal Republic of Germany in Albuquerque,
Anchorage, Buffalo, Charlotte, Cincinnati, Cleveland,
Corpus Christi, Dallas, Denver, Honolulu, Indianapolis,
Jacksonville, Kansas City, Louisville, Memphis,
Minneapolis, Mobile, Norfolk, Oklahoma City,
Philadelphia, Phoenix, Pittsburgh, Portland, Salt Lake City,
San Diego, St. Petersburg, Savannah, Spokane, and San
Juan, Puerto Rico)

Embassy of Germany
P.O. Box 444
10 Waterloo Rd.
Kingston 10
JAMAICA
(serves Puerto Rico and Virgin Islands)

Goethe-Institut Ann Arbor Branch
City Center Building
220 E. Huron, Suite 210
ANN ARBOR MI 48104
(German cultural center)

Goethe-Institut Atlanta
Colony Square, Plaza Level
1197 Peachtree St. NE
ATLANTA GA 30361
(German cultural center)

Goethe-Institut Boston
170 Beacon St.
BOSTON MA 02116
(German cultural center)

Goethe-Institut Chicago
401 N. Michigan Ave., Room 1334
CHICAGO IL 60611
(German cultural center)

Goethe-Institut Cincinnati
559 Liberty Hill, Pendleton House
CINCINNATI OH 45201
(German cultural center)

Goethe-Institut Houston
3120 Southwest Freeway, Suite 100
HOUSTON TX 77098
(German cultural center)

Goethe-Institut Los Angeles
5700 Wilshire Blvd., Suite 110
LOS ANGELES CA 90036
(German cultural center)

Goethe House New York
1014 Fifth Ave.
NEW YORK NY 10028
(German cultural center)

Goethe-Institut St. Louis
326 N. Euclid Ave., 2nd Floor South
ST. LOUIS MO 63108
(German cultural center)

Goethe-Institut San Francisco
530 Bush St.
SAN FRANCISCO CA 94108
(German cultural center)

FOREIGN OFFICES IN NORTH AMERICA

Goethe-Institut Seattle
Mutual Life Building
605 First Ave., Suite 401
SEATTLE WA 98104
(German cultural center)

Goethe-Institut Washington
820 Seventh St. NW
WASHINGTON DC 20001-3718
(German cultural center)

(IN CANADA)

German Embassy Ottawa
1 Waverley St.
Ottawa, Ontario
CANADA K2P 0T8

Consulate General of Germany
77 Admiral Road
Toronto, Ontario
CANADA M5S 2T1
(serves most of Canada)

Consulate General of Germany
3455 Mountain St.
Montréal, Quebec
CANADA H3A 1R3
(serves eastern and French-speaking Canada)

German National Tourist Office
47 Fundy
P.O. Box 417
Place Bonaventura
Montréal, Quebec
CANADA H3A 1R3
(tourist information on Germany)

German National Tourist Office
175 Bloor St. East
North Tower, #604
Toronto, Ontario
CANADA M4W 3R8
(tourist information on Germany)

Lufthansa German Airlines
55 Yonge St.
Toronto, Ontario
CANADA M5E 1J4
(information on German air travel)

Lufthansa German Airlines
666 Sherbrooke St., W
Montréal, Quebec
CANADA H3A 1E7
(information on German air travel)

Goethe-Institut Montréal
418 rue Sherbrooke est
Montréal, Quebec
CANADA H2L 1J6
(German cultural center)

Goethe-Institut Ottawa
25, University
University of Ottawa
Ottawa, Ontario
CANADA K1N 6N5
(German cultural center)

Goethe Institute Toronto
1067 Yonge St.
Toronto, Ontario
CANADA M4W 2L2
(German cultural center)

Goethe-Institut Vancouver
944 W. 8th Avenue
Vancouver, BC
CANADA V5Z 1E5
(German cultural center)

Canadian German Chamber of Industry and
    Commerce
Yale Building, Suite 1110
Montréal, Quebec
CANADA H3A 1T8
(office for international trade between Germany and
Canada)

German Federal Railroad
45 Richmond St. W
Toronto, Ontario
CANADA M5H 1Z2
(information about German railroads, tourist information
about Germany)

DENMARK.

The Danish Tourist Board
655 Third Ave.
NEW YORK NY 10017
(tourist information on Denmark)

FRANCE.

French Government Tourist Office
610 Fifth Ave.
NEW YORK NY 10020-2452
(tourist information on France, including Alsace-Lorraine)

French Government Tourist Office
372 Bay St., Suite 610
Toronto, Ontario
CANADA M5H 2W9
(tourist information on France)

HOLLAND. See NETHERLANDS.

LUXEMBOURG.

Luxembourg National Tourist Office
1 Dag Hammarskjold Plaza
NEW YORK NY 10017
(tourist information on Luxembourg)

FOREIGN OFFICES IN NORTH AMERICA

NETHERLANDS.

Netherlands National Tourist Office
576 Fifth Ave.
NEW YORK NY 10036
(tourist information on Netherlands)

Netherlands National Tourist Office
1 Dundas St. W
Toronto, Ontario
CANADA M5G 1Z3
(tourist information on Netherlands)

POLAND.

ORBIS
Polish Travel Office
500 Fifth Ave.
NEW YORK NY 10036
(official Polish travel bureau)

SWITZERLAND.
(IN THE UNITED STATES)

Swiss National Tourist Office
104 S. Michigan Ave.
CHICAGO IL 60603
(tourist information on Switzerland)

Swiss National Tourist Office
The Swiss Center
608 Fifth Ave.
NEW YORK NY 10020
(tourist information on Switzerland)

Swiss National Tourist Office
222 N. Sepulveda Blvd. Suite 1570
EL SEGUNDO CA 90245
(tourist information on Switzerland)

Swiss National Tourist Office
260 Stockton St.
SAN FRANCISCO CA 94108
(tourist information on Switzerland)

Embassy of Switzerland
2900 Cathedral Ave., NW
WASHINGTON DC 20008-3499
(chief diplomatic office of Switzerland in the United States)

Consulate General of Switzerland
1275 Peachtree St. NE, Suite 425
ATLANTA GA 30309
(serves southeastern United States)

Consulate General of Switzerland
737 N. Michigan Ave.
CHICAGO IL 60611
(serves midwestern United States)

Consulate General of Switzerland
First Interstate Bank Plaza, Suite 5670
1000 Louisiana
HOUSTON TX 77002
(serves mid-southern United States)

Consulate General of Switzerland
3440 Willshire Blvd., Suite 817
LOS ANGELES CA 90010
(serves southwestern United States)

Consulate General of Switzerland
665 Fifth Ave.
NEW YORK NY 10022
(serves northeastern United States)

Consulate General of Switzerland
456 Montgomery St.
SAN FRANCISCO CA 94104
(serves northwestern United States and northern California)

(IN CANADA)

Swiss National Tourist Office
154 University Avenue, Suite 610
Toronto, Ontario
CANADA M5H 3Y9
(tourist information on Switzerland)

Swiss National Tourist Office
1572 Av. Dr. Penfield
Montréal, Quebec
CANADA H3G 1C4
(tourist information on Switzerland)

Embassy of Switzerland
5 Av. Marlborough
Ottawa, Ontario
CANADA K1N 8E6
(chief diplomatic office of Switzerland in Canada)

Consulate General of Switzerland
1572 Av. Dr. Penfield
Montréal, Quebec
CANADA H3G 1C4
(serves eastern and French-speaking region of Canada)

Consulate General of Switzerland
154 University Avenue
Toronto, Ontario
CANADA M5H 3Y9
(serves central region of Canada)

Consulate General of Switzerland
790-999 Canada Place
Vancouver, British Columbia
CANADA V6C 3E1
(serves western region of Canada)

GERMAN-LANGUAGE NEWSPAPERS IN NORTH AMERICA

(Major German newspapers listed alphabetically by state; consult *The German Language Press of the Americas* by Karl J.R. Arndt and May E. Olson for names of newspapers published, dates, editors, circulations, and political affiliations, plus which libraries hold which copies; *Newspapers in Microform, Foreign Countries* (1948-1983); *United States Newspaper Program: National Union List* (1985-) of microform titles)

Neue Zeitung
9471 Hidden Valley Place
BEVERLY HILLS CA 90210
(German-language weekly newspaper for <u>Los Angeles</u>)

California Staats-Zeitung
1201 N. Alvarado St.
LOS ANGELES CA 90026
(German-language weekly newspaper)

Los Angeles Kurier
5858 Hollywood Blvd.
LOS ANGELES CA 90028
(German-language weekly newspaper)

San Francisco Neue Presse
23987 Craftsman Rd.
CALABASAS CA 91302
(German-language weekly newspaper)

Washington Journal
1113 National Press Bldg.
WASHINGTON DC 20045
(German-language newspaper in nation's capital)

Abendpost-Sonntagspost
223 W. Washington St.
CHICAGO IL 60606
(German-language daily newspaper; published continuously since 2 September 1889)

Amerika-Woche
Courier Press
955 Alexander Ave.
Winnipeg, Manitoba
CANADA R3C 2X8
(German-language weekly newspaper; edited in <u>Chicago</u>, printed in Winnipeg)

Wochenzeitung "Eintracht"
9456 N. Lawler St.
SKOKIE IL 60077
(German-language weekly newspaper)

Baltimore Correspondent und Wochenend-Magazin
1211 Havenwood Rd.
BALTIMORE MD 21201
(weekly general newspaper in German)

Detroiter Abend-Post
1436 Brush St.
DETROIT MI 48226
(German-language semi-weekly newspaper, daily until 1944; published continuously since 5 September 1868)

Deutsche Wochenschrift
P.O. Box 28218
ST. LOUIS MO 63132
(German-language weekly newspaper; recent)

New Jersey Freie Zeitung
500 S. 31st St.
KENWILWORTH NJ 07033
(German-language weekly newspaper)

New Yorker Staats-Zeitung und Herold
160 W. 71st St.
NEW YORK NY 11101
(influential German-language daily newspaper, formerly weekly and tri-weekly before 1843; published continuously since 24 December 1834)

Aufbau
2121 Broadway
NEW YORK NY 10023
(German-language Jewish-oriented weekly newspaper published since 1 December 1934 covering life in Germany and Israel)

Amerkanische Schweizer Zeitung
608 Fifth Ave.
NEW YORK NY 10020
(weekly newspaper in German for Swiss)

Der Staats-Anzeiger
622 12th St.
BISMARCK ND 58501
(German-language weekly newspaper)

Volkszeitung Tribune
4614 Dodge St.
OMAHA NE 68132
(German-language weekly newspaper)

Die Weltpost
4614 Dodge St.
OMAHA NE 68132
(German-language weekly newspaper)

Cincinnati Kurier
5117 Lee St.
SKOKIE IL 60076
(German-language weekly newspaper)

Plattdeutsche Post
4164 Lorain Ave.
CLEVELAND OH 44113
(Low German dialect weekly newspaper)

Waechter und Anzeiger
4162 Lorain Ave.
CLEVELAND OH 44113
(weekly German-language newspaper; published since
1852)

Milwaukee Deutsche Zeitung
5463 S. Lake Dr.
P.O. Box 711
CUDAHY WI 53110
(German-language daily newspaper)

Milwaukee Herold
2321 W. Kenboern Dr.
GLENDALE WI 53209
(German-language weekly newspaper)

CANADA.

Deutsche Presse
455 Spadina Ave., Suite 303
Toronto, Ontario
CANADA M5S 2G8
(German-language weekly newspaper)

MAP SOURCES

Please note that names of places are often (maybe usually!) misspelled in documents; often there are several places with the same name; often various geographical entities are confused, so that "County" or "Township" or "Forest" (of course, in Europe: "Duchy" or "Principality," etc.) are erroneously thought to be villages -- and most of our ancestors did come from villages, not the nearest large city or capital. Cities and capitals are mistakenly often believed to be the place of origin, because larger places are more recognizable for the sake of identification.

Thode Translations
RR 7, Box 306 AB, Kern Road
MARIETTA OH 45750-9437
(has detailed maps and atlases of areas of Germany and central & eastern Europe for sale, as well as ATLAS FOR GERMANIC GENEALOGY, etc.; assistance in finding difficult places for a fee)

American Geographical Society Collection
Golda Meir Library
The University of Wisconsin - Milwaukee Library
P.O. Box 399
MILWAUKEE WI 53201
(large collection of maps and gazetteers (place-name dictionaries); if really stuck on locating places, send photocopy of your source of information, what is nearby, in what district or near what river or lake or mountain range or ocean, etc.)

American Map Company
46-35 54th Rd.
MASPETH NY 11378
(member of Langenscheidt Publishing Group, distributes Euro-Atlas series of maps)

Bundesamt fuer Eich- und Vermessungswesen
Krotenthaller Gasse 3
A-1080 Wien/Vienna
Oesterreich/AUSTRIA
EUROPE
(official cartographic office for **Austria**; maps of Austria)

Landesvermessungsamt **Baden-Wuerttemberg**
Buechsenstrasse 54
Postfach 102962
D-70025 Stuttgart
GERMANY *(Street address D-70174)*
(state map office of Baden-Wuerttemberg)

Bayerisches Landesvermessungsamt
Alexandrastrasse 4
D-80538 Muenchen
GERMANY
(state map office of **Bavaria**/Bayern)

Institut Géographique National
Service Documentation et Vente
Abbaye de la Cambre 13
B-1050 Bruxelles/Brussels 5
Belgique/BELGIUM
(national map office for **Belgium**)

Stadt **Berlin**
Senatsverwaltung fuer Bau-und Wohnungswesen,
Abteilung V - Vermessungswesen
Mansfelder Strasse 16
D-10713 Berlin
GERMANY
(map office for city of Berlin)

Landesvermessungsamt **Brandenburg**
Aussenstelle Potsdam
Heinrich-Mann-Allee 103
D-14473 Potsdam
GERMANY
(state map office for Brandenburg)

Hansestadt **Bremen**
Kataster-und Vermessungsverwaltung
Wilhelm-Kaisen-Bruecke 4
D-28195 Bremen
GERMANY
(state map office for city-state of Bremen)

Kartographischer Verlag **Busche** GmbH
Kaiserstrasse 129
Postfach 101141
D-44011 Dortmund *(Street address D-44143)*
GERMANY
(publisher of maps and atlases of Germany, etc., in the ARAL series; available from Thode Translations; see first listing)

National Map Library
Public Archives of Canada
395 Wellington St.
Ottawa, Ontario
CANADA K1A 0N3
(large map holdings; many available through interlibrary loan)

Artia
Ve Smeckách 3 C
11127 Praha 1 (Prague)
CZECH REPUBLIC
(national map office of **Czech Republic**)

Geodaetisk Institut
Rigsdagsgården 7
DK-1218 København K
Danmark/DENMARK
(official cartographic office of **Denmark**; topographic maps of Denmark)

C.H. Bielefeldt, Boghandel
Kronprinsensgade 10
DK- København/Copenhagen K
Danmark/DENMARK
(bookseller that sells maps of **Denmark**)

MAP SOURCES

Defense Mapping Agency
Topographic Center
6500 Brook Lane
GLEN ECHO MD 20812
(official center for maps related to U.S. national defense,
including central and eastern Europe; maps and U.S. Board
of Geographic Names Gazetteers; some security restrictions
may apply)

Deutsche Bundesbahn
Zentrale Transportleitung
Kartenstelle
Kaiserstrasse 3
Postfach 1569
D-55005 Mainz
GERMANY
(maps of railroad lines in Germany)

Deutsches Hydrographisches Institut
Bernhard-Nocht-Strasse 78
D-20359 Hamburg
GERMANY
(German hydrographic institute; maps of oceans, etc.)

East View Publications
3020 Harbor Lane North
MINNEAPOLIS MN 55447
(distributor of maps of Russia and newly independent states
in **eastern Europe**)

Falk-Verlag
Burchardstrasse 8
D-20095 Hamburg
GERMANY
(publisher of various maps, city maps, atlases, etc.)

Institut Géographique National (IGN)
107 Rue La Boétie
F-75008 Paris
FRANCE
(official cartographic office for France; maps of France)

French and European Publications
610 Fifth Ave.
NEW YORK NY 10022
(importer of various maps of France, Germany, etc.)

Freytag-Berndt und Artaria KG
Kartographische Anstalt
Schottenfeldgasse 62
A-1071 Wien/Vienna
Oesterreich/AUSTRIA
EUROPE
(publisher of maps of Austria, Poland, Czechoslovakia,
Yugoslavia, Romania, and Bulgaria)

Genealogy Unlimited, Inc.
P.O. Box 537
OREM UT 84059-0537
(genealogical bookseller that carries several series of maps
of Europe; also finding aids for localities in central and
eastern Europe)

GEO Center
Internationales Landkartenhaus
Schockriedstrasse 44
Postfach 800830
D-70508 Stuttgart *(Street address D-70565)*
GERMANY
(distributor of maps of Germany, Austria, etc.)

Vermessungsamt der Freien und Hansestadt Hamburg
Wexstrasse 7
Postfach 300531
D-20302 Hamburg
GERMANY *(Street address D-20355)*
(state map office for city-state of **Hamburg**)

Geographia Map & Travel Bookstore
4000 Riverside Dr.
Toluca Lake
BURBANK CA 91505
(map store in Los Angeles area)

Bundeszentrale fuer politische Bildung
Berliner Freiheit 7
D-53111 Bonn
GERMANY
(new political map of **Germany** issued by government)

Haupka
Auf der Krautweide
D-65812 Bad Soden
GERMANY
(publisher of 1:100,000 series of maps for Germany,
Deutsche Ausflugskarte)

Hessisches Landvermessungsamt
Schaperstrasse 16
Postfach 3249
D-65022 Wiesbaden
GERMANY *(Street address D-65195)*
(surveying office of **Hessen**; catalog in German available at
a nominal cost describing 1:100,000 and more detailed
maps for sale by states of Germany; each state has its own
catalog); map office for state of Hessen)

Hippocrene Books, Inc.
171 Madison Ave.
NEW YORK NY 10016
(importer of maps and tour guides of Germany and other
European countries)

Topografischer Dienst
Westvest 9
NL-2611 Ax Delft
Nederland/NETHERLANDS
(official cartographic office of **Holland**; maps of the
Netherlands)

Cartographia
Pf. 132
H-1443 Budapest
HUNGARY
(cartographic office of **Hungary**; maps of Hungary)

MAP SOURCES

Institut fuer angewandete Geodaesie
Aussenstelle Berlin
Stauffenbergstrasse 11-13
D-10785 Berlin
GERMANY
(official cartographic distribution center for Germany; has
detailed official topographic maps of Germany)
(telephone +30-2611157, fax +30-2629499)

Institut fuer angewandte Geodaesie
Richard-Strauss-Allee 11
D-60598 Frankfurt am Main
GERMANY
(administrative offices of the above-listed map distribution
center)

Jensen Publications
P.O. Box 700
PLEASANT GROVE UT 84062
(has set of maps of 1871 German Empire)

Jewish Genealogical Society of Illinois
Map Department
Mrs. Freda Maslow
5819 W. Kenney St.
MORTON GROVE IL 60053
(village location service for central and eastern Europe)

Buchhandlung Justus **Koch**
Rotebuehlplatz 30
D-70193 Stuttgart
GERMANY
(sells atlas of Poland, map of Romania)

Kuemmerly & Frey
Kartographischer Verlag
Hallerstrasse 6-10
CH-3001 Bern
Schweiz/SWITZERLAND
(publisher of maps of Switzerland, etc.)

European Reference Section
The Family History Department
The Church of Jesus Christ of **Latter-day Saints**
35 N. West Temple St.
SALT LAKE CITY UT 84103
(maps, including the Mitteleuropa series, with the German
Empire, much of the Austro-Hungarian Empire, and
Poland; microfilm #1,181,580)

Library of Congress
Geography and Map Division
WASHINGTON DC 20540
(library of United States Congress with over 2,000,000
maps)

Niedersaechsisches Landesverwaltungsamt
Landesvermessung
Warmbuechenkamp 2
Postfach 107
D-30001 Hannover
GERMANY
(street address D-30159)
(state map office for **Lower Saxony**/ Niedersachsen)

Cadastre de **Luxembourg**
Avenue Gaston Diederich 54
L- Luxembourg Ville
LUXEMBOURG
(official cartographic office for Luxembourg; maps of
Luxembourg)

Mairs Geographischer Verlag
Postfach 3151
D-73751 Ostfildern
GERMANY
(publisher of Shell series of 1:200,000 maps covering
Germany, Austria, and Switzerland; Shell Atlas; etc.)

The Map Store
5821 Karric Square Dr.
DUBLIN OH 43017
(imports many series of maps from Europe)

Landesvermessungsamt **Mecklenburg-Vorpommern**
Luebecker Strasse 289
D-19059 Schwerin
GERMANY
(map office for state of Mecklenburg-Nearer Pomerania)

Michelin Guides and Maps
P.O. Box 19008
GREENVILLE SC 29602-9008
(United States branch of French publisher of maps of
France, Switzerland, and Germany; travel guides in
English, French, and German; available from Thode
Translations; see first listing)

Cartographic and Architectural Branch (NNSC)
National Archives and Records Administration (NARA)
WASHINGTON DC 20408
(will make 4" x 8" negative and 8" x 10" glossy of German
villages if you can provide coordinates or otherwise
pinpoint the location)

National Cartographic Information Center
United States Geological Survey
507 National Center
Room 1-C-107
12201 Sunrise Valley Drive
RESTON VA 22092
(United States government cartographic center for special
maps (such as aerial and satellite maps) and inquiries about
out-of-print topographic maps)

Landesvermessungsamt Nordrhein-Westfalen
Bad Godesberg
Muffendorfer Strasse 19-21
D-53177 Bonn
GERMANY
(state map office for Nordrhein-Westfalen/**North Rhine-Westphalia**)

Omega Translation Services
P.O. Box 745
IOWA CITY IA 52244-0745
(offers service of place finding in Europe; Timothy Parrott)

Polonia Book Store
2886 N. Milwaukee Ave.
CHICAGO IL 60618
(bookseller that sells maps of **Poland**)

Dudley Blank
7037 Cedar Creek Rd.
CEDARBURG WI 53012
(seller of maps & souvenirs of **Pomerania**)

Pomerania. See also Mecklenburg.

Ravenstein-Verlag
Wielandstrasse 31-35
D-60318 Frankfurt am Main
GERMANY
(publisher of maps of Germany, etc.)

Landesvermessungsamt Rheinland-Pfalz
Ferdinand-Sauerbruch-Strasse 15
Postfach 1428
D-56014 Koblenz
GERMANY *(Street address D-56073)*
(state map office of Rheinland-Pfalz/ **Rhineland-Palatinate**)

RV- Reise- und Verkehrsverlag GmbH
Luetzowstrasse 105
D-10785 Berlin
GERMANY
(German map publisher)

Landesvermessungsamt des Saarlandes
Von der Heydt 22
D-66115 Saarbruecken
GERMANY
(state map office of the **Saarland**)

Landesvermessungsamt Sachsen
Olbrichtplatz 3
Postfach 306
D-01073 Dresden
GERMANY *(Street address D-01099)*
(state map office of **Saxony**)

Landesamt fuer Landesvermessung und Datenverarbeitung
    Sachsen-Anhalt
Barbarastrasse 2
D-06110 Halle (Saale)
GERMANY
(state map office of **Saxony-Anhalt**)

Landesvermessungsamt **Schleswig-Holstein**
Mercatorstrasse 1
Postfach 5070
D-24062 Kiel-Wik
GERMANY
(street address D-24106)
(state map office of Schleswig-Holstein)

Schmorl und von Seefeld
Postfach 5526
D-30055 Hannover
GERMANY
(map dealer)

Schropp Fachbuchhandlung
Potsdamer Strasse 100
D-10785 Berlin
GERMANY
(topographic maps)

Jonathan **Sheppard** Books
Empire State Plaza Station
Box 2020
ALBANY NY 12220
(bookseller and publisher; has historical map reproductions of Germany and central Europe, also originals of historical maps)
(Mel Wolfgang)

Edward **Stanford** Ltd.
12-14 Long Acre
London
ENGLAND WC2E 9LP
(map seller with maps including eastern Europe)

Stevenson Supply
230 W 1230 N
PROVO UT 84601
(genealogical bookseller with maps of Denmark, etc.)

Eidgenoessische Landestopographie
Seftigenstrasse 264
CH-3084 Wabern-Bern
Schweiz/**SWITZERLAND**
(official Swiss cartographic office; has official detailed maps of Switzerland)

Thode Translations. See first listing, this section.

Thomsen's Genealogical Supplies
P.O. Box 568
BOUNTIFUL UT 84011
(atlas of 1871-1918 German empire, Austrian Empire)

MAP SOURCES

Thueringer Landesverwaltungsamt
Landesvermessungsamt
Schmidtstedter Ufer 7
D-99084 Erfurt
GERMANY
(state map office for **Thuringia**)

Travel Essentials
253 E. Main St.
ASHLAND OR 97520
(German maps, including ADAC 1:150,000
from German automobile club)

United States Department of the Interior
Bureau of Land Management
Eastern States Office
350 S. Pickett St.
ALEXANDRIA VA 22304-4704
(United States land management office; has copies of more
than 5,000,000 land patents (original deeds from United
States government to original land grantees) for eastern
United States; most western states have own land offices)

United States Geologic Survey
Map Distribution
P.O. Box 25286
Federal Center Building 41
DENVER CO 80225
(United States Geologic Survey topographical map
distribution center for maps of entire United States)

Washington National Records Center
(Suitland, Maryland)
Eighth and Pennsylvania Avenue, NW
WASHINGTON DC 20408
(**United States** National Archives branch records center
with case file records of land-entries, some including
declarations of intent and naturalization papers,
incidentally; use in conjunction with Bureau of Land
Management Office records above)

SHIP AND RIVERBOAT RECORDS

The Mariner's Museum
100 Museum Dr.
NEWPORT NEWS VA 23606-3759
(seafaring museum; ships' logs; information on ships;
35,000 artifacts, over 500,000 photos)
(telephone 804-596-2222)

Mystic Seaport Museum
G. W. Blunt White Library
Greenmanville Ave.
P.O. Box 6000
MYSTIC CT 06355
(telephone 202-572-0711)

The Steamship Historical Society of America, Inc.
H. C. Hall Building
345 Blackstone Blvd.
PROVIDENCE RI 02906
(national steamship historical society)

The Steamship Historical Society of America
Langsdale Library
Laura Brown, Librarian
University of Baltimore
1420 Maryland Ave.
BALTIMORE MD 21201
(library with over 100,000 photographs of steamships)

Peabody Essex Museum of Salem
East India Square
161 Essex St.
SALEM MA 01970
(seafaring museum)

San Francisco Maritime National Historical Park
Hyde Street Pier
SAN FRANCISCO CA 94109
(national maritime park)

National Maritime Museum
J. Porter Shaw Library
Foot of Polk St.
SAN FRANCISCO CA 94109
(national seafaring museum; ships' logs)

South Street Seaport Museum
207 Front St.
NEW YORK NY 10038
(museum of immigration 1820-1880 to port of New York)

Library of Congress
Maritime Division
10 First St.
WASHINGTON DC 20540
(may have drawings of ships)

Genealogical Publishing Co., Inc.
1001 N. Calvert St.
BALTIMORE MD 21202-3897
(sells *Ships of Our Ancestors*, a book with photographs of
many ships; also many other books on German emigration
and ships' passenger lists)

Inland Rivers Library
Public Library of Cincinnati and Hamilton Co.
800 Vine St.
CINCINNATI OH 45202-2071
(records of steamboats on inland waterways)

Great Lakes Historical Society
480 Main St.
VERMILION OH 44089
(ships' logs from the Great Lakes)

Transatlantic Research and Advisory Board
P.O. Box 8797
UNIVERSAL CITY CA 91608
(researcher on ships and immigration)

Newport Historical Society
82 Touro St.
NEWPORT RI 02840
(ships' logs)

Bernice P. Bishop Museum
1355 Kalihi St.
HONOLULU HI 96819
(ships' logs)

Priston's
Main Street Wharf
GREENPORT NY 11944
(dealer in marine prints)

City of London
Guildhall Library
Aldermanbury
London EC2P 2EJ
ENGLAND
(has Lloyd's Marine Collection, deposited there in 1979)

Sons and Daughters of Pioneer Rivermen
c/o Mrs. J. W. Rutter
126 Seneca Dr.
MARIETTA OH 45750
(society for descendants of pioneer rivermen and others
interested in steamboating and river lore)

Maritime Archaeological and Historical Institute (MAHRI)
P.O. Box 159
BRISTOL ME 04539
(study group searching for significant maritime sites, e.g.
shipwrecks)

Judicial, Fiscal, Social Branch
National Archives
WASHINGTON DC 20408
(records of shipwrecks)

Deutsches Schiffahrtsmuseum
Van-Ronzelen-Strasse
W-27568 Bremerhaven
GERMANY
(German national seafaring museum)

SHIP AND RIVERBOAT RECORDS

Bremer Landesmuseum (Focke-Museum)
Schwachhauser Heerstrasse
D-28203 Bremen
GERMANY
(museum of Bremen with seafaring museum)

Ueberseemuseum
Bahnhofsplatz 13
D-28195 Bremen
GERMANY
(emigration and ethnographic museum of Bremen)

Schloss Schoenebeck
Im Dorfe 3-5
D- 28757 Bremen
GERMANY
(castle museum: information on ships, pictures of ships)

Schiffahrts-Museum
Mitteldeichstrasse 49
D-26919 Brake
GERMANY
(seafaring museum)

Museum fuer Hamburgische Geschichte
Holstenwall 24
D-20355 Hamburg
GERMANY
(Hamburg history museum with exhibits on shipping, the
harbor, displays of emigrants who left for America through
Hamburg; emigrant passenger list research)

HAPAG-Lloyd
Ballindamm 25
Postfach 102626
D-20018 Hamburg
GERMANY *(Street address D-20095)*
(merger of the major German passenger ship lines, the
Hamburg-American Line and Norddeutscher Lloyd of
Bremen)

Seemannskartei
Reimerstwiete 2
D-20457 Hamburg
GERMANY
(card file of Hamburg ships' crews)

NAUSA
Universitaet Oldenburg
Abteilung Politik II
Ammerlaender Heerstrasse 114-118
Postfach 2503
D-26015 Oldenburg
GERMANY *(Street address D-26111)*
(has complete emigration microfilms for Germany and
North America)

GERMAN NATIONAL ARCHIVES AND ORGANIZATIONS

Bundesarchiv
Potsdamer Strasse 1
Postfach 320
D-56003 Koblenz
GERMANY
(Street address D-56075)
(national archives of Federal Republic; recent records, after 23 May 1945; most files barred to the public; has Third Reich records of Germans in foreign lands; German-Americans; emigration lists for 20th century)

Bundesarchiv-Aussenstelle Frankfurt
Seckbaecher Gasse 4
D-60311 Frankfurt (Main)
GERMANY
(archival records of the Reich and the German confederation to 1866, including the 1848-49 government)

Zentrales Staatsarchiv
Historische Abteilung I (Potsdam)
Berliner Strasse 98-101
D-14467 Potsdam
GERMANY
(national archives created 1949 for German Democratic Republic, founded 1946; records of the former Reich 1867-1945, including some genealogical files)

Geheimes Staatsarchiv Preussischer Kulturbesitz
Archivstrasse 12-14
D-14195 Berlin
GERMANY
(archival records from East Prussia, Brandenburg, West Prussia, etc., some church books, genealogical and seal collections; military church records)

Saechsisches Staatsarchiv Leipzig
Abteilung Deutsche Zentralstelle fuer Genealogie
Schongauer Strasse 1
Postfach 274
D-04007 Leipzig
GERMANY
(Street address D-04109)
(genealogical center, has specialized "Rolandsverein" genealogy library, *Deutsche Ahnengemeinschaft* ancestor card-file of 1,400,000 people, burial sermons, 16,000 church books - originals, copies, and microfilms)

Berlin Document Center
Wasserkaefersteig 1
D-14163 Berlin
GERMANY
(20th century official records, including 2.5 million file cards on foreign Germans, 10.7 million NSDAP membership cards, 600,000 SS and 500,000 SA membership files, 100,000 People's Court files; files presently barred to public; formerly controlled by U.S. mission to Berlin; will be available on microfilm in U.S. National Archives)

Deutsche Zentrale fuer Tourismus
Beethovenstrasse 69
D-60325 Frankfurt am Main
GERMANY
(German national tourist board; tourist information on Germany)

Deutscher Fremdenverkehrsverband e.V.
Niebuhrstrasse 16b
D-53113 Bonn
GERMANY
(German association of local and regional tourist offices; should be able to direct you to tourist information on any region of Germany)

Deutsches Bundesarchiv, Abteilung IV
Militaerarchiv
Wiesenthalstrasse 10
D-79115 Freiburg im Breisgau
GERMANY
(military records covering 1867 to 1945, some incomplete; includes Prussian records; many records were destroyed on 14 April 1945)

Militaergeschichtliches Forschungsamt
Zeppelinstrasse 127-128
D-14471 Potsdam
GERMANY
(military history records)

Krankenbuchlager Berlin
Wattstrasse 11
D-13355 Berlin (Wedding)
GERMANY
(military wounded prior to 1919 including Prussia, Baden, and Alsace-Lorraine; also World War II, including POW's in England, France, and Belgium)

Deutsches Bundesarchiv
Zentralnachweisstelle des Militaerarchivs
Kornelimuenster, Abteigarten 6
D-52076 Aachen-Kornelimuenster
GERMANY
(recent personal military service records)

Deutsche Dienststelle fuer die Benachrichtigung der
      naechsten Angehoerigen von Gefallenen der
      ehemaligen deutschen Wehrmacht
(Wehrmacht Angehoerigen Stelle - **WASt**)
Eichborndamm 179
Postfach 510657
D-13366 Berlin
GERMANY
(Street address D-13403)
(military archives of the *Wehrmacht*, marines and sailors; central card-file, information on POW's; for family members only)

International Red Cross
Agence Central de Recherches
Avenue de la Paix 7
CH-1211 Genève/Geneva
Suisse/Switzerland
(documentation of persons missing in wartime, displaced persons, etc.)

Deutsches Rotes Kreuz
Friedrich-Ebert-Allee
D-53113 Bonn
GERMANY
(German headquarters of the Red Cross)

GERMAN NATIONAL ARCHIVES AND ORGANIZATIONS

Zentralverwaltungsarchiv des Deutschen Roten Kreuzes
Kaitzerstrasse
D-01069 Dresden
GERMANY
(German Red Cross central administrative archive for
former DDR "East Germany"; may have records of refugees
from former eastern territories)

Deutsches Rotes Kreuz
Suchdienst Hamburg
Blomkamp 31
D-22549 Hamburg
GERMANY
(Red Cross service for Germans in eastern and southeastern
Europe, reuniting families)

Deutsches Rotes Kreuz
Suchdienst Muenchen
Infantriestrasse 7a
D-80797 Muenchen
GERMANY
(Red Cross searching for deported persons, German
soldiers missing in action, support for prisoners of war in
non-German custody, search service for children; 320,000
deceased prisoners of war)

Verband der Lebensversicherungsunternehmen e.V.
Eduard-Pflueger-Strasse 55
D-53113 Bonn
GERMANY
(umbrella organization of German life insurance
companies; way to trace current addresses of individuals in
Germany)

Sonderstandesamt Arolsen
Grosse Allee 5-9
D-34454 Arolsen
GERMANY
(International Tracing Service; documentation of persons in
concentration camps and used for forced labor in various
German firms; ca. 46,000,000 documents pertaining to ca.
13,000,000 individuals; master index has ca. 39,700,000
cards referring to ca. 3,735,000 documents; Buchenwald &
Dachau records almost complete; Flossenburg,
Mauthausen, Mittelbau, Natzweiler, Niederhagen-
Wewelsburg and Stutthof fairly complete; Auschwitz,
Krakow-Plaszow, Gross Rosen, Lublin, Neuengamme, and
Sachsenhausen incomplete; also records of 400,000
prisoners liberated by Soviet soldiers at end of World War
II)

Foerderverein Deutsches Auswanderermuseum
The German Emigration Museum
Inselstrasse 6
D-27568 Bremerhaven
GERMANY
(regional center with archives and library on emigration;
holds an exhibition)

Fuerst Thurn und Taxis Zentralarchiv
Hofbibliothek
Emmeramsplatz
Postfach 110246
D-93015 Regensburg
GERMANY
(Street address D-94037
(German postal archive))

Institut fuer Zeitgeschichte
Leonrodstrasse 46 b
D-80636 Muenchen/Munich
GERMANY
(archive on German exiles during the National Socialist
(Nazi) period)

United Restitution Organization
Wiesenau 53
D-60323 Frankfurt am Main
GERMANY
(central file of material claims filed by victims of National
Socialist (Nazi) persecution, crimes, and displacement
during World War II, and by their heirs)

Heimatauskunftstelle Uebersee
Contrescarpe 73
D-28195 Bremen
GERMANY
(center for information for Germans in foreign countries
seeking information about homelands, home towns, etc., in
former German areas)

Statistisches Bundesamt
Gustav-Stresemann-Ring 11
Postfach 5528
D-65045 Wiesbaden
GERMANY
(federal statistical office; documenting existence of old
place names)

Westdeutsche Rektorenkonferenz
Ahrstrasse 39
D-53175 Bonn
GERMANY
(association of rectors of advanced educational institutions)

Institut fuer Auslandsbeziehungen
Charlottenplatz 17
D-70173 Stuttgart
GERMANY
(information on foreigners on cultural aspects of German
life, including publications on famous people of German
origin, foreign newspapers in German, cultural exchange
promotion)

Bundesbeauftragter fuer die Unterlagen des
Staatssicherheitsdienstes der ehemaligen
Deutschen Demokratischen Republik
Glinkastrasse 35
D-10117 Berlin
GERMANY
(files of the former STASI internal intelligence agency in the former
German Democratic Republic; over 540,000,000 feet(!) of material
on residents 1949-1990; waiting list to see files)

Inter Nationes e.V.
Kennedyallee 91-103
D-53175 Bonn-Bad Godesberg
GERMANY
(educational foundation with information on all aspects of life in
Germany; promotes international goodwill)

Steuben-Schurz-Gesellschaft e.V. Berlin
Kurfuerstendamm 188
D-10707 Berlin
GERMANY
(society promoting cultural exchanges)

GERMAN REGIONAL ARCHIVES.

Standesamt I in Berlin (West)
Rheinstrasse 54
D-12161 Berlin
GERMANY
(various civil registers of over 1,500 places from 1874 to 1945,
including 12 of the 21 districts of Berlin; consular records; records
of formerly occupied eastern areas: eastern Poland, Belarus,
Ukraine, the Baltic states, Poland, etc.)

Standesamt I in Berlin (Ost)
Rueckertstrasse 9
D-12163 Berlin
GERMANY
(special civil registration archive, including 9 of the 21 districts of
Berlin)

Hauptstandesamt Hamburg
Johanniswall 4
D-200095 Hamburg
GERMANY
(special civil registration archive; coverage not limited to Hamburg)

GERMAN SPECIALIZED ARCHIVES.

Frau Dr. Ingrid Schoeberl
Fachbereich 8
Historisches Seminar
Universitaet Hamburg
Von-Melle-Park 6
D-20146 Hamburg
GERMANY
(university research project on German emigration movement
America in 19th and 20th centuries; bibliography, textual and
pictorial documentation)

Standortkatalog der deutschen Presse
Staats- und Universitaetsbibliothek Bremen
Bibliothekstrasse 1
Postfach 330440
D-28334 Bremen   *(Street address D-28353)*
GERMANY
(central catalog of German newspapers found in libraries)

Institut fuer Zeitungsforschung der Stadt Dortmund
Wiss-Strasse 4
D-44137 Dortmund
GERMANY
(institute for the history of newspapers)

EUROPEAN STATE OR PROVINCIAL ARCHIVES

ALSACE.

Archives départementales du Bas-Rhin
5-9, rue Fischart
F-67000 Strasbourg
France
(lower (northern) Rhine and northern Alsace area,
including city of Strasbourg; microfilm church and civil
records prior to 1880)

Archives de la ville Strasbourg
8, place de l'Hospital
Boîte postale No 1049-1050 F
F-67070 Strasbourg
France
(municipal archive of Strassburg/Strasbourg; church and
civil records of Strasbourg city; no photocopies allowed)

Archives départementales du Haut-Rhin
Cité administrative
3, Rue Fleischauer
F-68000 Colmar
France
(upper (southern) Rhine and southern Alsace area, except
city of Mulhouse; church and civil records prior to 1880)

Centre Départemental d'Histoire des Familles
Ancien Couvent des Dominicains
F-68500 Guebwiller
FRANCE
(genealogical division of the district archives of Haut-Rhin,
upper (southern) Rhine and southern Alsace)

Archives de la ville de Mulhouse
Boîte postale 3089
F-68062 Mulhouse
FRANCE
(municipal archive of Mülhausen/Mulhouse; church and
civil records of Mulhouse city)

AUSTRIA.
NATIONAL ARCHIVES.
(Note: Civil registration began in Austria in 1938 except
Wiener Neustadt in 1872 and the province of Burgenland
in 1895. Persons of all religions were recorded in the
Catholic registers until 1849. For dates prior to 1918 make
sure the place is in present-day Austria; see also POLAND,
CZECH REPUBLIC, HUNGARY, former
YUGOSLAVIA, etc.)

Oesterreichisches Staatsarchiv
Abteilung I: Haus-, Hof- und Staatsarchiv
Bibliothek
Minoritenplatz 1
A-1010 Wien/Vienna
Oesterreich/AUSTRIA
EUROPE
(Austrian "national archives")

Oesterreichisches Staatsarchiv
Abteilung II: Allgemeines Verwaltungsarchiv
Wallnerstrasse 6a
A-1010 Wien/Vienna
Oesterreich/AUSTRIA
EUROPE
(Austrian royal administrative archive)

Oesterreichisches Staatsarchiv
Abteilung III: Hofkammer-Archiv
Himmelpfortgasse 4-8
A-1010 Wien/Vienna I
Oesterreich/AUSTRIA
EUROPE
(Austrian royal chancellery archive, including records of
German colonization of the Banat and Transylvania in the
17th and 18th centuries, filed by settlements)

Oesterreichisches Staatsarchiv
Abteilung IV: Kriegsarchiv
Nottendorfergasse 2
A-1030 Wien/Vienna
Oesterreich/AUSTRIA
EUROPE
(Austrian military archive; muster rolls 1740-1820, pension
documents 1749-1920; until 1802 soldiers served for life;
1802-1869 for 10 years; from 1869 universal conscription
in the Austro-Hungarian Empire with 3 years of required
service, 2 years since 1912; muster rolls 1760-1900)

Oesterreichisches Staatsarchiv
Archiv der Republik
Nottendorfergasse 2
A-1030 Wien/Vienna
Oesterreich/AUSTRIA
EUROPE
(archive of the Austrian Republic)

Standesamt
Waehringerstrasse 39
A-1100 Wien-Alsergrund (=Vienna-Als...)
Oesterreich/AUSTRIA
EUROPE
(Austrian special civil registry with duplicate records since
1870 of free-thinkers, Arminian-Orientals, Lipponauers,
Mennonites, Moravian Brethren, Muslims, and members of
no recognized denomination, also marriage records for all
marriages that required dispensations)

Oesterreichisches Staatsarchiv fuer Verkehrswesen
Aspangstrasse 33
A-1030 Wien/Vienna
Oesterreich/AUSTRIA
EUROPE
(Austrian state archive for traffic and transportation (road
and rail workers?))

Bundesministerium fuer Inneres Wien VII
Abteilung 9/M
Karl-Schweighofer-Gasse 3
A-1070 Wien/Vienna
Oesterreich/AUSTRIA
EUROPE
(Austrian Ministry of the Interior; vital statistics for
military personnel to 1919 if military post or discharge date
is known)

Statistisches Zentralamt
Heldenplatz
Neue Burg
A-1010 Wien/Vienna
Oesterreich/AUSTRIA
EUROPE
(Austrian central statistics office with records of censuses
for the Austro-Hungarian Empire 1869, 1890, 1900, 1910,
and Austria 1923, 1934, 1951, 1961, 1971, and 1981)

AUSTRIA: PROVINCIAL OR REGIONAL ARCHIVES.

Burgenlaendisches Landesarchiv
Freiheitsplatz 1
A-7001 Eisenstadt
Oesterreich/AUSTRIA
EUROPE
(Burgenland state archive; archives of 11 Jewish
communities; books of mines since 1767; land records
since 1850)

Kaerntner Landesarchiv
Praesenzbibliothek
Landhaus
Herrengasse 14
A-9020 Klagenfurt
Oesterreich/AUSTRIA
EUROPE
(state archive of Carinthia)

Niederoesterreichisches Landesarchiv
Abteilung I - Regierungsarchiv fuer Oesterreich
Herrengasse 11-13
A-1014 Wien/Vienna
Oesterreich/AUSTRIA
EUROPE
(Lower Austria state archive, administrative archive for
Austria)

Niederoesterreichisches Landesarchiv
Abteilung II - Staendsches Archiv
Teinfalterstrasse 8
A-1014 Wien/Vienna
Oesterreich/AUSTRIA
EUROPE
(Lower Austria state archive for nobility, contains feudal
tenure books of 16th to 18th centuries including names of
serfs and masters)

Landesarchiv Salzburg
Michael-Pacherstrasse 20
A-5020 Salzburg
Oesterreich/AUSTRIA
EUROPE
(Salzburg state archive; has documents on the emigration
of Protestants 1731-1744)

Steiermaerkisches Landesarchiv
Buergergasse 2
A-8010 Graz
Oesterreich/AUSTRIA
EUROPE
(Styria state archive; has provincial censuses from as early
as 1707)

Amt des Tiroler Landesarchivs
Herrengasse 1
A-6010 Innsbruck
Oesterreich/AUSTRIA
EUROPE
(Tirol/Tyrol state archive)

Oberoesterreichisches Landesarchiv
Anzengruberstrasse 19
A-4020 Linz
Oesterreich/AUSTRIA
EUROPE
(Upper Austria state archive)

Vorarlberger Landesarchiv
Kirchstrasse 28
A-6901 Bregenz
Oesterreich/AUSTRIA
EUROPE
(Vorarlberg state archive; 14th century to 1938)

Magistrat der Stadt Wien
Magistratsabteilung 8
Wiener Stadt- und Landesarchiv
Neues Rathaus
Felderstrasse 1
A-1082 Wien/Vienna
Oesterreich/AUSTRIA
EUROPE
(provincial archive for the city-state of Vienna; combined
with city archive)

Zentralmeldeamt Wien
Berggasse 43
A-1090 Wien/Vienna
Oesterreich/AUSTRIA
EUROPE
(central (address) registry for inhabitants of Vienna)

AUSTRIA: SPECIAL ARCHIVES

Deutschordens-Zentralarchiv
Singerstrasse 7
A-1010 Wien/Vienna 1
Oesterreich/AUSTRIA
EUROPE
(archive of the Teutonic Knights)

Niederoesterreichisches Burgenarchiv
Teinfaltstrasse 8
A-1010 Wien/Vienna
Oesterreich/AUSTRIA
EUROPE
(castles in Lower Austria)

BADEN.

Badisches Generallandesarchiv
Noerdliche Hilda-Promenade 2
D-76133 Karlsruhe
GERMANY
(state archive for Baden; has civil registers (church book
duplicates) for communities in Baden for 1810-1869;
military records for Baden army before 1871)

Badisches Generallandesarchiv
Aussenstelle Freiburg
Colombistrasse 4
Postfach 323
D-79003 Freiburg im Breisgau
GERMANY
(Freiburg branch of state archive)

Staatsarchiv Wertheim
Muehlenstrasse 26
D-97877 Wertheim
GERMANY
(state archive for Wertheim area)

Hauptstaatsarchiv Stuttgart
Konrad-Adenauer-Strasse 4
D-70173 Stuttgart
GERMANY
(has military records for Baden army after 1871)

BADEN-WUERTTEMBERG.
See BADEN and WUERTTEMBERG. (The present state
of Baden-Wuerttemberg is an artificial combination after
World War II.)

BAVARIA.
See also PALATINATE, which was Bavarian until 1948.

Bayerisches Hauptstaatsarchiv I
Schoenfeldstrasse 5
Postfach 200507
D-80005 Muenchen *(Munich) (Street address D-80539)*
GERMANY
(Bavarian state archive headquarters; different branches
have military records, legal emigration records, mortgage
records, land records, etc.)

Bayerisches Geheimes Staatsarchiv
Abteilung IV
Ludwigstrasse 14
D-80539 Muenchen *(Munich)*
GERMANY
(files of Bavarian State Chancellery, important for foreign
diplomatic relations and domestic policy)

Bayerisches Hauptstaatsarchiv
Kriegsarchiv, Abteilung V
Leonrodstrasse 57
Postfach 221152
D-80501 Muenchen *(Munich)   (Street address D-80636)*
GERMANY
(Bavarian military archive; military records 1648-1914;
Bavarian War Ministry and Army records to 1921; rolls of
1,460,000 Bavarians mobilized 1914-1918, police records
1919-1935; no military personnel files for Bavarian army
are available 1870-1914; no rosters from wars of 1866,
1870-1871)

Staatsarchiv Coburg
Schloss Ehrenburg
D-96450 Coburg
GERMANY
(Coburg (former Saxe-Coburg-Gotha) state archive)

Staatsarchiv fuer Niederbayern
Burg Trausnitz
D-84036 Landshut
GERMANY
(Lower Bavaria state archive, mostly pre-1900 records)

Staatsarchiv fuer Unterfranken
Residenzplatz 2
Residenz-Nordfluegel
D-97070 Wuerzburg
GERMANY
(Lower Franconia state archive, mostly pre-1900 records)

Staatsarchiv Nuernberg
Archivstrasse 17
Postfach 120346
D-90010 Nuernberg *(Nuremberg)(Street address D-90408)*
GERMANY
(state archive for Middle Franconia, mostly pre-1900
records)

Staatsarchiv Augsburg
Salomon-Idler-Strasse 2
D-86159 Augsburg
GERMANY
(state archve for Swabian part of Bavaria; former archive in
Neuburg/Donau closed)

Staatsarchiv fuer Oberbayern
Schoenfeldstrasse 3
D-80539 Muenchen *(Munich)*
GERMANY
(Upper Bavaria state archive; not for city of Munich nor for
Bavaria as a whole)

Staatsarchiv fuer Oberfranken
Hainstrasse 39
Postfach 2668
D-96017 Bamberg *(Street address D-96047)*
GERMANY
(Upper Franconia (northern Bavarian) state archive)

Staatsarchiv fuer Oberpfalz
Archivstrasse 3
D-92224 Amberg/Oberpfalz
GERMANY
(Uper Palatinate (northeastern Bavaria) state archive)

BELARUS.

The Belarus State Historical Archives in Minsk
ulica Kozlowa 26
Minsk 22038
BELARUS

The Belarus State Historical Archives in Grodno
pl. Lenina 2
Grodno 230023
BELARUS

BELFORT.

Direction des Services d'Archives
2, Rue de l'Ancien Théatre
F-90020 Belfort
FRANCE
(French state archive for Belfort and Montbéliard area;
birth, marriage, and death records prior to 1880)

BELGIUM.

Algemeen Rijksarchief
Ruisbroekstraat 2-6
  or (in French)
  Archives Générales du Royaume
  rue de Ruysbroeck 2-6
B-1000 Bruxelles/Brussels
Belgique/BELGIUM
(national royal archives of Belgium, including the province
of Brabant)

Rijksarchief te Antwerpen
Door Verstraeteplaats 5
B-2000 Antwerpen/Anvers/Antwerp
Belgique/BELGIUM
(state archive at port city, Antwerp; emigration records for
1855; civil records for province of Antwerp ca. 1800-1870)

Archives de l'État a Liège
rue Pouplin 8
B-4000 Liège/Luik
Belgique/BELGIUM
(state archive at Liège/Luettich; church and civil records of
formerly German Eupen and Malmedy)

Archives de l'État
Parc des Expositions
B-6700 Arlon
Belgique/BELGIUM
(state archive at Arlon; church and civil records of former
Luxembourgian areas)

Stadsarchief Antwerpen
Venusstraat 11
B-2000 Antwerpen/Anvers/Antwerp
Belgique/BELGIUM
(municipal archive for port city of Antwerp; hotel registers
1834-50; 1857-78; 1881-98; passports 1593-1690; 1702-
1735; 1793-1798)

Ministère des Affaires Étrangères
rue Quatre Bras 2
B-1000 Bruxelles/Brussels
Belgique/BELGIUM
(Belgian foreign ministry; emigrations of Belgians filed by
settlement areas)

BERLIN. See also BRANDENBURG and NATIONAL
ARCHIVES: GERMANY: SPECIAL.

Staatsarchiv
Archivstrasse 12-14
D-14195 Berlin
GERMANY
(state archive for the city-state of Berlin; also East Prussia,
etc.)

Landesarchiv Berlin
Kalckreuthstrasse 1-2
D-10777 Berlin
GERMANY
(mostly post-1948 records of the city of West Berlin)

Landesarchiv Berlin
Aussenstelle
Chausseestrasse 2
D-10115 Berlin
GERMANY
(branch of Berlin archives above)

Magistrat von Berlin
Breite Strasse 30/31
D-10178 Berlin
GERMANY
(state archive for East Berlin, central archive for eastern
sections of the city)

Landeseinwohnermeldeamt Berlin
Referat Meldeangelegenheiten
Rollbergstrasse 7
D-12035 Berlin
GERMANY
(residents registration office; referral to proper civil
registration office if street address in Berlin in known)

BESSARABIA.

Heimatmuseum der Deutschen aus Bessabien
Lindachstrasse 37
D-75417 Muehlacker
GERMANY
(homeland museum for Germans from Bessarabia; has
card-file of origins of resettlers from Bessarabia, also
genealogical indexes)

BOHEMIA. See CZECH REPUBLIC.

BRANDENBURG.

Brandenburgisches Landeshauptsarchiv Potsdam
An der Orangerie 3
Postfach 600449
D-14404 Potsdam *(Street address D-14469)*
GERMANY
(state archive for state, church, land, and court records of
the Kurmark, the Neumark, and Niederlausitz to ca. 1808-
1816, and Brandenburg and Berlin to 1945, including
police records of Berlin)

BRAUNSCHWEIG. See LOWER SAXONY.

BREMEN.

Staatsarchiv
Am Staatsarchiv 1
D-28203 Bremen
GERMANY
(state archive for the city-state of Bremen, including the
port of Bremerhaven, but Bremen passenger lists of
emigrants have been destroyed up to 20th century; has civil
birth records since 1811; 16,127 indexed *Stammtafeln*
(ancestral lines) for 1824-1933)

Prof. Dr. Tony Holtmann
Carl-von-Ossietzky-Univeritaet Oldenbburg
Abteilung Politik II
Ammerlaender Heerstrasse 114-118
Postfach 2503
D-26111 Oldenburg *(Street address D-26129)*
GERMANY
(project on German emigration from Hamburg, Bremen,
etc.)

BRUNSWICK See LOWER SAXONY.

CENTRAL GERMANY. See BRANDENBURG,
MECKLENBURG, SAXONY, THURINGIA.

CZECH REPUBLIC.

Johann-Gottfried-Herder Institut
Gisonenweg 7-9
D-35039 Marburg/Lahn
GERMANY
(repository on eastern German history and genealogy,
including Czech Republic)

Archívní Spravá MV
Trída Obráncy Miru 133
16621 Praha/Prague 6
CZECH REPUBLIC
(state archives administration for Czech Republic; for all
records to 1900 in Bohemia or Moravia (see also SLOVAK
REPUBLIC); specify money limit)

Mr. Ing. M. Stovicek
ARCHIVEX s.s.r.o.
P.O. Box 38
Premyslenska 81
CZ-18200 Praha 8 *(Prague)*
CZECH REPUBLIC
("privatized" national archives)

Statni Oblastni Archiv v Cheb
Frantiskanse nam. 14
CZ-35011 Cheb
CZECH REPUBLIC
(regional archive for Cheb/Eger for Egerland)

Vojensky historicky ustav
U Památniku 2
CZ-13000 Praha 3 *(Prague)*
CZECH REPUBLIC
(military historical institute with military records and
military files of all former Czechoslovakian soldiers,
including those in the Austro-Hungarian army in 1918)

Statní ústrední archiv
Mala Strana
Karmelitska 2
CZ-11801 Praha *(Prague)*
CZECH REPUBLIC
(state archive for Moravian area (see also SLOVAK
REPUBLIC); has no church registers)

Archívní Sprava
Trídi Obráncu Míru 133
CZ-16000 Praha 6 *(Prague)*
CZECH REPUBLIC
(state archive for Bohemian part of Czech Republic)

Statní Oblastní Archiv v Treboni
CZ-27911 Trebon-zámek
CZECH REPUBLIC
(regional archive for the Wittingau, southern Bohemia)

Statní Oblastní Archiv v Zámrsku
CZ-56543 Zámrsk-zámek
CZECH REPUBLIC
(regional archive for eastern Bohemia, the
Leitomischl/Hohenmauth area)

Statní Oblastní Archiv v Litomericích
Dominikansky Klaster
Krajiska 1
CZ-41274 Litomerice
CZECH REPUBLIC
(regional archive at Leitmeritz for northern Bohemia or the
Sudetenland)

Statní Oblastní Archiv v Plzní
Svedláckova ulica 44
CZ-30612 Plzen
CZECH REPUBLIC
(regional archive at Pilsen for western Bohemia)

Statní Oblastní Archiv v Praze
Na Karlove
Horská 7
CZ-12000 Praha 2 *(Prague)*
CZECH REPUBLIC
(regional archive at Prag/Prague for central Bohemia,
not including the city of Prag/Prague)

DANUBE GERMANS.

Landesarchiv
Scheidter Strasse 114
Postfach 102431
D-66024 Saarbruecken *(Street address D-66130)*
GERMANY
(records on German ethnics in the eastern Danube area)

DARMSTADT. See HESSE.

DENMARK. See also SCHLESWIG-HOLSTEIN.

Udvandrerarkivet
Arkivstrade 1
Postfack 1731
DK-9100 Aalborg
Danmark/DENMARK
hbender@inet.uni-c-dk
("Danes Worldwide Archive" for research on emigrants;
indexes based on U.S. and Canadian Lutheran churches
and newspapers; Copenhagen police lists of emigrants
1869-1900)

Rigsarkivet
9 Rigsdagsgården
DK-1218 København/Copenhagen K
Danmark/DENMARK
(Danish national archives in Copenhagen; censuses of
1787, 1801, 1834, 1840, 1845, and each 5 years thereafter
to 1860, then 1870, 1880, 1890, 1906, 1911; from 1845 on
birthplaces given; draft forms from 1788, originally only
peasant sons, who were registered at birth; from 1849 all
males, registered at 15; naval records from 1802)

Rigsarkivet 3. Afdeling
Forsvarets Arkiver
Rigsdagsgården 5
DK-1218 København/Copenhagen K
Danmark/DENMARK
(Danish military archive)

Landsarkivet for Sjaelland
Jagtvei 10
DK-2200 København/Copenhagen N
Danmark/DENMARK
(Danish state archive for the Copenhagen area; has
emigration records for 1868 to 1959)

Landsarkivet for de sønderjske Landsdele
Haderslevvej 45
DK-6200 Aabenraa
Danmark/DENMARK
(Danish state archive for south Jutland, including North
Schleswig; has civil registration from 1 October 1874 for
districts of Aabenraa-Sønderborg/Apenrade-Sonderburg,
Haderslev/Hadersleben, and Tønder/Tondern)

EAST FRISIA. See LOWER SAXONY.

"EAST GERMANY." See CENTRAL GERMANY!

EASTERN GERMANY. See also GERMANY, POLAND,
POMERANIA, POZNAN, PRUSSIA (EAST AND
WEST), SILESIA, CZECH REPUBLIC, SLOVAK
REPUBLIC, etc.

Johann-Gottfried-Herder-Institut
Gisonenweg 5-7
D-35037 Marburg/Lahn
GERMANY
(central repository in Germany for eastern German history
and genealogy, including eastern Germany, Poland, and
Czech Republic; publishes a continous catalog of all new
publications related to eastern Germany)

Buecherei des deutschen Ostens
Berliner Platz 11
D-44623 Herne
GERMANY
(library in Germany which collects literature from and
about the eastern areas of Germany; publishes a catalog of
its holdings; world-wide interlibrary loans)

Haus des deutschen Ostens
Koenigsworther Strasse 2
D-30167 Hannover
GERMANY
(center in Germany for eastern German culture)

Bundesarchiv
Abteilung Ostarchiv
Am Woellershof 12
D-56068 Koblenz
GERMANY
(eastern Germany section of national archive of Federal
Republic of Germany)

Bibliothek der Stiftung Haus des deutschen Ostens
Bismarckstrasse 90
D-40210 Duesseldorf
GERMANY
(library of the foundation that supports the center for
eastern German culture; publishes catalogs of its holdings)

Stiftung Ostdeutscher Kulturrat
Kaiserstrasse 113
D-53113 Bonn
GERMANY
(fund for eastern German culture; possibly being phased
out following unification)

EUROPEAN STATE OR PROVINCIAL ARCHIVES

Historisches Staatsarchiv
Ortenburg
D-02625 Bautzen
GERMANY
(regional state archive for the Bautzen area, homeland of
Sorbs or Wends)

Sorbisches Kulturarchiv (Macica-Archiv)
Institut fuer sorbische Volksforschung
Ernst-Thaelmann-Strasse
D-02625 Bautzen
GERMANY
(cultural archive of the Sorbs or Wends)

ENGLAND.

Public Record Office
Kew
UK- Richmond, Surrey
ENGLAND TW9 4DU
(a British state archive; has records of Colonial Office
concerning "Palatines" of 1708 and 1709 in Holland,
London, etc.; German-language newspapers; naturalization
and alien registration records)

Merseyside Maritime Museum
Albert Dock
Pier Head
UK- Liverpool
ENGLAND L34 AA
(records of passengers from Liverpool, if ship's name
known; library with published passenger lists (no
originals), emigration literature; emigrant letters and
drawers with database)

Army Record Centre
Bourne Ave.
GB- Hayes, Middlesex
ENGLAND UB3 1RF
(records of German Jewish British soldiers whose names
were changed)

ESTONIA.

Historical Archives
Eesti Ajaloo Arhiiv
J. Liivi 4
202400 Tartu
ESTONIA
(state historical archives to 1918 in Dorpat/Tartu)

RAGAS (Russian-American Genealogical Archival Source)
1929 18th St. NW, Suite 1112
WASHINGTON DC 20009
(source for genealogical contact with archives in former
Soviet Union)

FINLAND.

Institute of Migration
Piispanskatu 3
20500 Turku
FINLAND
(information on Finnish emigrants ca. 1890-1950)

FRANCE.
See also ALSACE, BELFORT, LORRAINE, MEUSE, and
VOSGES.

Archives nationale de France
60, rue des Francs-Bourgeois
F-75141 Paris 03
FRANCE
(national archives of France; section TT has material on
Huguenots with individual alphabetically indexed files on
cases of confiscation; section BB has nationality options of
Alsatians and Lorrainers in 1871; section F has passport
records from 19th century)

Service Historique de l'Armee de terre
Pavillon du Roi
Château de Vincennes
Poste 25-42
F-94304 Vincennes
FRANCE
(French military records; officers filed by name; soldiers
filed by regiment; has name-list book of French soldiers in
the American Revolution)

Archives départementales de la Seine-Maritime
Cours Clemenceau
F-76000 Rouen
FRANCE
(regional archive that holds ship passenger lists of the port
of Le Havre, 1752-1880; 500 pages per volume, ca. 10
volumes per year, only French-registered ships that
returned to port filed if and when they returned to port)

Service Historique de la Marine
Pavillon de la Reine
Château de Vincennes
F-94000 Vincennes
FRANCE
(French naval records; officers filed by name; soldiers filed
by regiment)

Ministère de la Marine
3, avenue Octave Grenard
F-75007 Paris
FRANCE
(French naval records)

Ministère des affaires ètrangeres
Service de l'État civil
F-44941 Nantes Cedex 9
FRANCE
(civil registrations of French born outside France)

Ministère des Anciens Combattants
139, rue de Bercy
F-75012 Paris
FRANCE
(indexed list giving birthplaces of 1,295,249 French
casualties in World War I)

FRANCONIA. See under BAVARIA.

FRANKEN. See under BAVARIA.

FRIESLAND. See DENMARK, HOLLAND, LOWER
SAXONY, SCHLESWIG-HOLSTEIN, etc.

FRISIA. See DENMARK, HOLLAND, LOWER
SAXONY, SCHLESWIG-HOLSTEIN, etc.

GALICIA. See also POLAND, RUSSIA, etc.

RAGAS (Russian-American Genealogical Archival Source)
1929 18th St. NW, Suite 1112
WASHINGTON DC 20009
(source for genealogical contact with archives in former
Soviet Union)

Urzad Stanu Cywilnego Warszawa Strodmiescie
Archiwum Akt Zabuzanskich
ulica Jeznicka 1-3
PL-00281 Warszawa/Warsaw
POLAND
(Polish state archive for eastern Galicia)

Bundesarchiv
Am Woellershof 1
D-5400 Koblenz 1
GERMANY
(national archive of Federal Republic of Germany; holds
incomplete file of genealogical questionnaires on Galicians
resettled in 1939/1940)

GERMANY.
See beginning of this section, before ALSACE.

HAMBURG.

Prof. Dr. Tony Holtmann
Carl-von-Ossietzky-Univeritaet Oldenbburg
Abteilung Politik II
Ammerlaender Heerstrasse 114-118
Postfach 2503
D-26111 Oldenburg *(Street address D-26129)*
GERMANY
(project on German emigration from Hamburg, Bremen,
etc.)

Staatsarchiv der Freien und Hansestadt Hamburg

ABC-Strasse 19E (Seiteneingang)
D-20354 Hamburg
GERMANY
(state archive for Hamburg; has direct Hamburg passenger
lists 1850-1934; index to direct lists 1856-1871; indirect
passenger lists 1854-1910; passport records for Hamburg
citizens and non-residents 1852-1929, indexed yearly
1851-1897, cumulatively 1897-1929; register of non-
citizen workers 1834-1890; birth records for Hamburg
proper; shipping and trade records; collection of local
coats-of-arms and shields, material also on LDS (Mormon)
microfilm)

Tourismus-Zentrale Hamburg
Elisabeth Sroka
Burchardstrasse 14
Historic Emigration Office
Postfach 102749
D-20015 Hamburg   *(Street address D-20095)*
GERMANY
(research center with Hamburg passenger lists for 1850-
1914; 274 microfilm rolls of nearly 5,000,000 emigrants
who left through Hamburg; lists also on LDS (Mormon)
microfilm)

HANNOVER (Kingdom or Province).
See LOWER SAXONY, also WESTPHALIA.

HANOVER (Kingdom or Province).
See LOWER SAXONY, also WESTPHALIA.

HESSE.

Staatsarchiv Darmstadt
Karolinenplatz 3
D-64289 Darmstadt
GERMANY
(state archive for Hessen-Darmstadt; has emigration file for
1800's and some from 1700's, also church book duplicates
ca. 1808-1876; records of Hessen-Darmstadt army before
1867)

Staatsarchiv Marburg
Friedrichsplatz 15
Postfach 540
D-35017 Marburg (Lahn) *(Street address D-35037)*
GERMANY
(state archive for Hessen-Kassel or Kurhessen (Electoral
Hesse) area; has records on "Hessian" soldiers in U.S.
Revolutionary War; has some church book duplicates ca.
1808-1876; records of Hessen-Kassel army before 1867)

Hessisches Hauptstaatsarchiv Wiesbaden
Mosbacher Strasse 55
D-65187 Wiesbaden
GERMANY
(state archive for Hesse-Nassau; headquarters for the
society of archivists in Germany; some church book
duplicates of the former Duchy of Hesse-Nassau; records of
Nassau army before 1867; emigrant card-file)

Staatsarchiv Muenster
Bohlweg 2
Postfach 7629
D-48041 Muenster
GERMANY
(state archive, together with the Wiesbaden state archive,
for the Nassau-Siegen area)

Bundesarchiv Abteilung Frankfurt
Berliner Strasse 22
D-60311 Frankfurt/Main
GERMANY
(branch of national archives of Federal Republic of
Germany; post-1949 records)

Beratungsstelle fuer Gemeindepflege beim Hessischen
    Landkreistag
Messeler Strasse 81
D-64291 Darmstadt
GERMANY
(central repository or clearing-house for municipal archives
of numerous Hessian villages)

Schwalm Emigrant Project
Dr. Robert von Friedeberg
Universitaet Bielefeld
Postfach 8640
D-33615 Bielefeld
GERMANY
(project on settlement in U.S. of emigrants from the
Schwalm region 1830-1866)

Prof. Dr. Peter Assion
Institut fuer Europaeische Ethnologie und Kulturforschung
Arbeitsgruppe Auswanderung
Bahnhofstrasse 5a
D-35037 Marburg
GERMANY
(research project on emigration from Hesse-Darmstadt,
Hesse-Kassel, and Nassau desiring letters, documents,
photographs, etc., of emigrants)

HESSEN. See HESSE.

HOHENZOLLERN. See WUERTTEMBERG.

HOLLAND.

Algemeen Rijksarchief (ARA)
Prins Willem Alexander Hof 20
NL-2595 BE s'Gravenhage/The Hague
Nederland/NETHERLANDS
(national archives of Holland; census records 1829 and
every 10 years thereafter; some emigration lists 1847-1878;
Dutch emigrant records *(Landverhuizerslijsten)*; books and
papers of Dutch East and West India Companies; archives
of Dutch Emigration Service *(Nederlandse Emigratie
Dienst)*

Rijksinspectie van de Bevolkingsregisters
NL- s'Gravenhage/The Hague
Nederland/NETHERLANDS
(population registers 1810 to present at 10-year intervals;
emigration records)

Central Bureau voor Genealogie
Postbus 11755
NL-2502 AT s'Gravenhage/The Hague
Nederland/NETHERLANDS
(quasi-official genealogy research bureau)

Gemeentelijke Archiefdienst
Amsteldijk 67
NL-1074 HZ Amsterdam
Nederland/NETHERLANDS
(municipal archives of Amsterdam; notarial records,
including indexed marriage banns, including some
emigrating couples)

Gemeentearchief Rotterdam
Robert Fruinstraat 52
NL-3021 XE Rotterdam
Nederland/NETHERLANDS
(archives of Waterschout, including passenger lists, were
destroyed in World War II; has archives of Holland-
America Line)

HUNGARY. See also DANUBE GERMANS.

Hungarian Embassy
2437 15th St. NW
WASHINGTON DC 20009
USA
(avenue for obtaining Hungarian archival records)

Magyar Országos Levéltár
Bécsi kapu-tér 4
Postafiók 3
H-1250 Budapest 1
HUNGARY
(Hungarian archives prior to 1944; has microfilms of all
parish vital registers to 1895, but only books to 1865 are
open, with church permission)

Levéltárok Országos Központia
Uri Utca 54-56
Postafiók 2
H- Budapest 1
HUNGARY
(national archives administration of Hungary)

IRELAND. See ENGLAND.

ITALY.

Staatsarchiv Bozen
Armando-Diaz-Strasse 8
I-39100 Bozen
Italia/ITALY
(state archive for the Bozen area and South Tirol/Tyrol)

Archivio di Stato di Trento
Via Roma 51
I-38100 Trento
Italia/ITALY
(state archive of the Trento area)

LATVIA.

RAGAS (Russian-American Genealogical Archival Source)
1929 18th St. NW, Suite 1112
WASHINGTON DC 20009
(source for genealogical contact with archives in former
Soviet Union)

Latvijas Valsts vestures arhivs
Slokaskielà 16
22607 Riga
LATVIA
(national historical archive for pre-Soviet era)

Centràlais Valsts arhivs
Bezdeligu ielà 1
26047 Riga
LATVIA
(national historical archive for Soviet era)

Dzimtsaraktu Arhives
24 Kalku St.
Riga
LATVIA
(vital statics 1906-1940)

LIECHTENSTEIN.

Liechtensteinisches Regierungsarchiv
Kanzlei
Regierungsgebaeude des Fuerstentums Liechtenstein
FL-9490 Vaduz
LIECHTENSTEIN
(civil registration bureau of Liechtenstein)

Liechtensteinisches Landesarchiv
Regierungsgebaeude des Fuerstentums Liechtenstein
FL-9490 Vaduz
LIECHTENSTEIN
(national archives of Liechtenstein)

LIPPE. See also WESTPHALIA.

Personenstandsarchiv fuer Westfalen-Lippe
Willi-Hofmann-Strasse 2
D-32756 Detmold
GERMANY
(state archive and vital records office for Lippe and
adjoining part of Westphalia; has church book duplicates
for roughly 1815-1874; records of Lippe-Detmold troops
before 1867)

Landschaftsverband Westfalen-Lippe
Westfaelisches Landesamt fuer Archivpflege
Warendorfer Strasse 24
D-48145 Muenster
GERMANY
(custodian or clearing-house for various local and private
archives in the Westphalia and Lippe area)

Staatsarchiv Detmold
Aussenstelle Schloss Alverdissen
Schlossstrasse 4
D-32683 Barntrup
GERMANY
(Barntrup branch of Detmold State Archive)

LITHUANIA.

RAGAS (Russian-American Genealogical Archival Source)
1929 18th St. NW, Suite 1112
WASHINGTON DC 20009
(source for genealogical contact with archives in former
Soviet Union)

Lietuvos valstybinis istorijos archyvas
Gerosios Vilites 10
2015 Vilna
LITHUANIA
(national historical state archive)

Lietuvos valstybinis metriku archyvas
21 Kalinausko
Vilna
LITHUANIA
(national archive for church book records)

Lietuvos valstybinis archyvas
21 Kareiviu 21
Vilna
LITHUANIA
(national vital record archive for civil births, marriages, and
deaths)

LORRAINE. See also MEUSE and VOSGES.

Archives départementales de la Moselle
Préfecture de la Moselle
Hôtel du Département
9 place de la Prêfecture
F-57036 Metz
FRANCE
(regional archive for Moselle region of northern Lorraine;
birth, marriage, and death registers prior to 1880)

Archives départementales de Meurthe-et-Moselle
1 rue de la Monnaie
F-54052 Nancy Cedex
FRANCE
(regional archive for southern Lorraine; birth, marriage,
and death registers prior to 1880)

Archives municipales de la ville Metz
6, rue Chèvremont
F-57000 Metz
FRANCE
(archive of the city of Metz)

LOWER BAVARIA. See BAVARIA.

LOWER FRANCONIA. See BAVARIA.

LOWER SAXONY.

Niedersaechsisches Hauptstaatsarchiv
Am Archiv 1
D-30169 Hannover
GERMANY
(state archive for former Electorate and Kingdom of
Hannover and the Hannover area; has records of Hannover
army before 1867)

Niedersaechsisches Staatsarchiv Aurich
Oldersumer Strasse 50
D-26603 Aurich
GERMANY
(state archive for East Frisian area)

Niedersaechsisches Staatsarchiv Bueckeburg
Schloss, Westfluegel
Postfach 1350
D-31665 Bueckeburg *(Street address D-31675)*
GERMANY
(state archive for Schaumburg-Lippe area; has records of
Schaumburg-Lippe army before 1867)

Niedersaechsisches Staatsarchiv Oldenburg
Damm 43
D-26135 Oldenburg
GERMANY
(state archive for former Duchy of Oldenburg; has records
of Oldenburg army until 1867)

Niedersaechsisches Staatsarchiv Osnabrueck
Schloss-strasse 29
D-49074 Osnabrueck
GERMANY
(state archive for Westphalian section of Lower Saxony
(see also under WESTPHALIA); has computerized
emigrant list)

Niedersaechsisches Staatsarchiv Stade
Am Sande 4C
D-21682 Stade
GERMANY
(state archive for Stade area; has church book duplicates of
parishes of the former duchies of Bremen and Verden
except Land Hadeln, generally for 1715-1726 and 1751-
1852, with some gaps)

Niedersaechsisches Staatsarchiv Wolfenbuettel
Forstweg 2
D-38302 Wolfenbuettel
GERMANY
(state archive for former Duchy of
Brunswick/Braunschweig; has copies of 95% of the
Protestant church books of Brunswick/Braunschweig until
1814; 80% of 1815-1875 Protestant church books; records
of Braunschweig army before 1867)

LÜBECK. See SCHLESWIG-HOLSTEIN.

LUEBECK. See SCHLESWIG-HOLSTEIN.

LUXEMBOURG. See also BELGIUM.

Archives de l'État
Plateau-du-St.-Esprit
Boîte postale 6
L-2010 Luxembourg Ville 2
LUXEMBOURG
(national archives of Luxembourg)

Greffe du Tribunal d'Arrondissement
Division État-civil
rue du Palais du Justice 9
L-1841 Luxembourg Ville
LUXEMBOURG
(one of two tribunals in Luxembourg where mandatory
copies of civil registrations since 1795 with decennial
indexes are kept)

Greffe du Tribunal d'Arrondissement
Division État-civil
Palais du Justice
Place des Recollets
L-9275 Diekirch
LUXEMBOURG
(one of two tribunals in Luxembourg where mandatory
copies of civil registrations since 1795 with decennial
indexes are kept)

Archives de la Ville de Luxembourg
Hôtel de ville
Place Guillaume
L- Luxembourg Ville
LUXEMBOURG
(municipal archive of Luxembourg city; passport records
1840-1849; 1851-1880)

MECKLENBURG.

Mecklenburgisches Landeshauptarchiv
Graf-Schack-Allee 2
D-19053 Schwerin
GERMANY
(state archive for Mecklenburg, including former
Mecklenburg-Guestrow, Mecklenburg-Schwerin, and
Mecklenburg-Strelitz, as well as Vorpommern (Nearer
Pomerania); has emigration records 1862-1914, as well as
indexes 1826-1861 for Mecklenburg-Schwerin only;
records of Mecklenburg army before 1867)

Staatsarchiv Ludwigslust
Schlossfreiheit 10
D-19288 Ludwigslust
GERMANY
(regional branch of Schwerin state archive)

MECKLENBURG-VORPOMMERN.
See MECKLENBURG.

MEUSE.

Archives départementales de la Meuse
20 rue Monseigneur Aimond
Boîte Postale 514
F-55012 Bar-le-Duc Cédex
FRANCE
(state archive of the Meuse region)

MIDDLE FRANCONIA. See under BAVARIA.

MITTELFRANKEN. See under BAVARIA.

MOEMPELGARD. See BELFORT.

MONTBÉLIARD. See BELFORT.

MORAVIA. See under SLOVAK REPUBLIC.

MOSELLE.

Archives départementales de la Moselle
1, allee du Château *(F-57050 Saint-Julien-les-Metz)*
Boîte Postale 1096
F-57036 Metz
FRANCE

NASSAU. See under HESSE.

NETHERLANDS. See HOLLAND.

NIEDERBAYERN. See under BAVARIA.

NIEDERSACHSEN. See LOWER SAXONY.

NORDRHEIN-WESTFALEN. See RHINELAND.

NORWAY.

The Norwegian Emigrant Museum
P.O. Box 1104
N-2301 Hamar
NORGE/Norway
(library and archives)

OBERBAYERN. See under BAVARIA.

OBERFRANKEN. See under BAVARIA.

OBERPFALZ. See under BAVARIA.

OLDENBURG. See under LOWER SAXONY.

PALATINATE.

Institut fuer pfaelzische Geschichte und Volkskunde
Benzinoring 6
Postfach 2860
D-67616 Kaiserslautern
GERMANY
(institute for Palatine history and folk culture with card-file
of ca. 1,000,000 by name, foreign destination or source,
Palatine home location on ca. 300,000 emigrants
from/to the Palatinate; formerly called the *Heimatstelle
Pfalz*; library; publications)

Landesarchiv Speyer
Otto-Mayer-Strasse 9
Postfach 1608
D-67326 Speyer/Rhein
GERMANY
(state archive for the southern Palatinate, including
Rheinhessen and the (formerly Bavarian) Rheinpfalz)

Staatsarchiv
Karmeliterstrasse 1-3
D-56068 Koblenz
GERMANY
(state archive for the northern Palatinate, Trier, and the
Rhine area)

PFALZ. See PALATINATE.

POLAND.

Naczelna Dyrekcja Archiwów Panstwowych
Miodowa 10
skrytka pocztowa 1005
PL-00950 Warszawa 10 *(Warsaw)*
Polska/POLAND
(national archives of Poland)

Urzad stanu cywilnego
Praezydium Dzielnacowej Rady Warodowej
Novy swiat 18/20
PL- Warszawa 1 *(Warsaw)*
Polska/POLAND
(Polish national center for civil registration records from
ca. 1 October 1874)

Urzad stanu cywilnego
Warszawa Stóamiescie
Archiwum Akt Zabuzanskich
ulica Jeznicka 1-3
L-00281 Warszawa *(Warsaw)*
Polska/POLAND
(many German church records and civil records)

Archiwum Glowne Akt Dawnych w Warszawie
ulica Dluga 7
PL-00950 Warszawa *(Warsaw)*
Polska/POLAND
(Polish national center for pre-1890 historical records)

Archiwum Akt Nowych
ulica Niepodleglosci 182
PL-02554 Warszawa *(Warsaw)*
Polska/POLAND
(Polish national center for newer historical records)

Centralne Archiwum Wojskowe
PL-00910 Warszawa 72 *(Warsaw)*
Polska/POLAND
(Polish military archive)

Archiwum Glównego Urzedu Statystcznego
ulica Niepodleglosci 208
PL-00925 Warszawa *(Warsaw)*
Polska/POLAND
(Polish central statistical office)

Johann-Gottfried-Herder-Institut
Gisonenweg 5-7
D-35037 Marburg (Lahn)
GERMANY
(central repository in Federal Republic of Germany for
eastern German history and genealogy, including "East"
Germany and Poland; publishes a continuous catalog of all
new publications on eastern Germany)

Osrodek Badan Genealogicznych "Piast"
ulica Zaulek 22
PL-06100 Pultusk woj. Ciechanowskie
Polska/POLAND
(Polish genealogical research center; covers families living
in the historical territories of Poland regardless of
nationality, religion, or social status)

Standesamt I in Berlin (West)
Rheinstrasse 54
D-12161 Berlin
GERMANY
(repository in Berlin for various civil registers of over
1,500 places from 1874 to 1945, including formerly
occupied portions of Poland)

Standesamt I in Berlin (Ost)
Rueckertstrasse 9
D-12163 Berlin
GERMANY
(repository in Berlin for various civil registers ca. 1874-
1945, including some portions of Poland)

The General Sikorski Historical Institute
20 Princes' Gate
BG- London S.W. 7
ENGLAND
(repository in England for some Polish military records)

Wojewódzkie Archiwum Panstwowe w Olsztynie Zamek
Zamkowa 2
PL-10074 Olsztyn
Polska/POLAND
(Polish state archive for Allenstein/Olsztyn district)

Archiwum Panstwowe Miasto Wroclawia i Wojewodztwa
Wroclawskiego
ulica Pomorska 2
PL-50215 Wroclaw
Polska/POLAND
(Polish state archive for Breslau/Wroclaw district; has
several church records)

Urzad Stanu Cywilnego Archiwum
ulica Wlodkowica 21-22
PL- Wroclaw
Polska/POLAND
(civil registration office for Breslau/Wroclaw city; has
preserved civil records)

Wojewódzkie Archiwum Panstwowe w Bydgoszczy
ulica Dworcowa 65
PL-83009 Bydgoszcz
Polska/POLAND
(Polish state archive for Bromberg/Bydgoszcz district)

Wojewódzkie Archiwum Panstwowe w Gdansku
ulica Waly Piastowskie 5
PL-80855 Gdansk
Polska/POLAND
(Polish state archive for Danzig/Gdansk district)

Wojewódzkie Archiwum Panstwowe w Zielonej Górze
Stary Kiselin 31
PL-66002 Zielona Góra
Polska/POLAND
(Polish state archive for Gruenberg/Grünberg/
Zielona Góra district)

Wojewódzkie Archiwum Panstwowe w Rzeszówie
Oddzial w Jasle
ulica Lenartowicza 9
PL-38200 Jaslo
Polska/POLAND
(Polish branch state archive for Jaslo near
Reichshof/Rzeszów)

Wojewódzkie Archiwum Panstwowe w Katowicach
ulica Jagiellonska 25
PL-40032 Katowice
Polska/POLAND
(Polish state archive for Kattowitz/Katowice district)

Wojewódzkie Archiwum Panstwowe w Koszalinie
ulica Zwyciestwa 117
skrytka pocztowa 149
PL-75950 Koszalin *(Street address PL-75601)*
Polska/POLAND
(Polish state archive for Koeslin/Köslin district)

Wojewódzkie Archiwum Panstwowe w Krakówie
ulica Kanoniczna 1
PL-32700 Kraków
Polska/POLAND
(Polish state archive for Krakau/Kraków district)

Wojewódzkie Archiwum Panstwowe
PL- Gorzow Wielkopolski
Polska/POLAND
(Polish state archive for Landsberg an der Warthe/Gorzow
Wielkopolski district)

Panstwowega Muzeum
Droga Meczennikow Majdanka 67
PL-20325 Lublin
POLAND
(museum with Majdanek concentration camp records)

Wojewódzkie Archiwum Panstwowe w Noiwym Saczu
ulica Królowej Jadwigi 10
PL-94400 Nowy Targ
Polska/POLAND
(Polish state archive for Neu-Sandez/Nowy Sacz district in
Galicia)

Wojewódzkie Archiwum Panstwowe w Opolu
ulica Zamkowa 2
PL-45016 Opole
Polska/POLAND
(Polish state archive for Oppeln/Opole district)

Panstwowe Muzeum
PL-32603 Osciwcim
POLAND
(museum for Auschwitz concentration camp)

Archiwum Panstwowe Miasto Poznanina iWojewodztwa
Poznanskiego
ulica 23 Lutego 41/43
PL-60967 Poznan 9
Polska/POLAND
(Polish state archive for Posen/Poznan district)

Wojewódzkie Archiwum Panstwowe w Przemyslu
ulica Polskiego Czerwonego Krzyza 4
PL-37700 Przemysl
Polska/POLAND
(Polish state archive for Przemysl district in Galicia)

Wojewódzkie Archiwum Panstwowe w Rzeszówie
ulica Boznicza 4
skrytka pocztowa 168
PL-35959 Rzeszów
Polska/POLAND
(Polish state archive for Reichshof/Rzeszów district in
 Galicia)

Archiwum Panstwowe
31A ulica Partyzentów
PL-72600 Słupsk
Polska/POLAND
(Polish district archie for Stolp/Slupsk area of Poland)

Wojewódzkie Archiwum Panstwowe w Szczecinie
ulica sw. Wojciecha 13
PL-70410 Szczecin
Polska/POLAND
(Polish state archive for Stettin/Szczecin district)

Wojewódzkie Archiwum Panstwowe w Tarnobrzegu
ulica Batosza 4
PL-27600 Sandomierz
Polska/POLAND
(Polish state archive for Tarnobrzeg district in Galicia)

Wojewódzkie Archiwum Panstwowe w Toruniu
plac Rapackiego 4
PL-87100 Torun
Polska/POLAND
(Polish state archive for Thorn/Torun district)

POMERANIA. See also POLAND, MECKLENBURG.

Geheimes Staatsarchiv Preussischer Kulturbesitz
Archivstrasse 12-14
D-14195 Berlin
GERMANY
(repository in West Berlin of Pomeranian pedigree files in
Lassahn-Spruth collection)

Vorpommersches Landesarchiv Greifswald
Alte Kaserne
Kreishaus
Martin-Andersen-Nexoe-Platz 11
Postschliessfach 323
D-17463 Greifswald *(Street address D-17489)*
GERMANY
(state archive of Pomerania from 12th to 20th centuries;
Wolgast archives; records of Swedish government at
Stralsund; some material from former Prussian archive at
Stettin/Szczecin)

Riksarkivet
Fack
S-10026 Stockholm 34
Sverige/SWEDEN
(Swedish state archive; contains important "Pomeranica"
and Gadebusch collections)

Krigsarkivet
Fack
S-10450 Stockholm 60
Sverige/SWEDEN
(Swedish military archive; contains muster rolls of
Swedish-Pomeranian regiments, biographies, etc.)

POMMERN. See POMERANIA.

PRUSSIA. See also EASTERN GERMANY, POLAND,
RUSSIA, etc. (Note: "Prussia" once included most of the
northern half of Germany plus Hohenzollern in
southwestern Germany; try to define a more specific
location)

Geheimes Staatsarchiv Merseburg
Koenig-Heinrich-Strasse 37
D-06217 Merseburg
GERMANY
(former Prussian Privy State Archives of East and West
Prussia)

Geheimes Staatsarchiv Preussischer Kulturbesitz
Archivstrasse 12-14
D-14195 Berlin
GERMANY
(repository in West Berlin of records from historical
Prussia; includes largely East Prussian and Danzig
microfilms of records from former state archive at
Koenigsberg)

Deutsches Zentralarchiv
Historische Abteilung II
An der weissen Mauer 48
D-06217 Merseburg
GERMANY
(former governmental archives of East and West Prussia
only)

RHEINBAYERN. See PALATINATE.

RHEINLAND. See RHINELAND.

RHEINPFALZ. See PALATINATE.

RHENANIA. See RHINELAND.

RHINE BAVARIA. See PALATINATE.

RHINELAND.
See also LIPPE, PALATINATE, and WESTPHALIA.

Landeshauptarchiv Koblenz
Karmeliterstrasse 1-3
Postfach 1340
D-56013 Koblenz *(Street address D-56068)*
GERMANY
(state archive for the southern Rhineland, the northern
Palatinate, and the Nassau area in the vicinity of Koblenz;
emigrant card-file)

NRW Hauptstaatsarchiv
Mauerstrasse 55
D-40476 Duesseldorf 30
GERMANY
(chief state archive for the Duesseldorf area; has records of
Duchy of Berg troops until 1815)

Landeshauptarchiv Koblenz
Aussenstelle Rommersdorf
D-56566 Neuwied
GERMANY
(branch of chief state archive of Koblenz in Rommersdorf;
notarial documents from 19th century files of the statistical
office; Neuwied municipal records)

NRW Staatsarchiv Muenster
Bohlweg 2
Postfach 7629
D-48041 Muenster
GERMANY
(state archive for Muenster area of northern Rhineland and
Westphalia)

NRW Personenstandsarchiv Rheinland
Schloss Augustusburg
Schlossstrasse 12
D-50321 Bruehl
GERMANY
(vital records archive for the Rhineland; church and civil
registration books and duplicates for most of the Rhineland
from ca. 1798 to 1874; also records of the Duesseldorf area
excluding Berg and Essen until June 1938; see also
Cologne listing)

Historisches Archiv
Stadt Koeln
Severinstrasse 222-228
D-50676 Koeln/Cologne
GERMANY
(historical archive of city of Koeln/Köln/Cologne; birth
records for city only)

Der Standesbeamte in Koeln
Stadt Koeln
Friedrichstrasse 42-44
D-50676 Koeln/Cologne
GERMANY
(civil registration office of city of Cologne for births and
deaths)

Der Standesbeamte in Koeln
Stadt Koeln
Rathaus, Eingang Portalsgasse
D-50667 Koeln/Cologne
GERMANY
(civil registration office of city of Cologne for banns and
marriages)

Archivberatungsstelle Rheinland in Koeln
Constantinstrasse 5
D-50679 Koeln/Cologne
GERMANY
(archive coordinating center for Koeln/Köln/ Cologne area;
may help sort out proper jurisdiction)

NRW Staatsarchiv, Aussenstelle Porz
Friedrich-Ebert-Strasse 64
D-50996 Koeln *(Cologne)*
GERMANY
(Porz branch of Westphalian state archive)

ROMANIA. See also DANUBE SWABIANS.

Directia Generala A
Archivelor Statului din RS România
B-dul Gheorghe Ghorgiu-Dej, Nr. 29
R-70602 Bucuresti/Bucharest, Sector VI
ROMANIA
(state archives of Romania; civil registers for Wallachia
since 1 May 1831; civil registers for Moldavia since
January 1832 kept by the Orthodox Church; passport
records 1885, 1890-1918 for Alba, Brasov, and Fagaras
districts in Transylvania)

RUMANIA. See ROMANIA.

RUSSIA. See also PRUSSIA.

RAGAS (Russian-American Genealogical Archival Source)
1929 18th St. NW, Suite 112
WASHINGTON DC 20009-1710
(source for genealogical contact with archives in former
Soviet Union)

Central State Archives
Boris Ivanovich Kaptelov
Bolshaja Pirogovskaja 17
119817 Moskva *(Moscow)*
RUSSIA
(national archives of the former USSR)

RAGAS (Russian-American Genealogical Archive Source)
P.O. Box 459
127349 Moskva *(Moscow)*
RUSSIA

Archive of the Russian Republic
Berezkovskaja Nat 3
Moskva/Moscow
RUSSIA
(state archive for the Republic of Russia)

Central State Historical Archives
Nabareznaya Krasnaya Flota 4
St. Petersburg
RUSSIA
(national historical archive for Russia; has parts of the
archives of the Consistorium General of the Lutheran
church in Russia and copies of records of all churches in
Russia, probably since 1722)

SAARLAND.

Landesarchiv
Scheidter Strasse 114
Postfach 102431
D-66024 Saarbruecken *(Street address D-66130)*
GERMANY
(state archive for the Saarland; has central file of civil
register decennial tables (indexes) for 1802-1862 for many
communities in the Saarland)

SACHSEN. See SAXONY.

SACHSEN-ANHALT. See SAXONY.

SALZBURGERS. See also under AUSTRIA.

Staatsarchiv
Schoenfeldstrasse 3
D-80539 Muenchen *(Munich)*
GERMANY
(records of Salzburgers in the Pflegegericht Rauschenberg
1731-1805)

SAXONY.

Saechsisches Hauptstaatsarchiv
Archivstrasse 14
D-01097 Dresden
GERMANY
(major state archive for the former Kingdom of Saxony
(capital at Dresden); has records of Electoral and Royal
Saxon army until 1919)

Aussenstelle Altenburg des Thueringischen
Hauptstaatsarchivs
Schloss 2a
D-04600 Altenburg
GERMANY
(state archive for former Duchy of Altenburg and Saxony-
Anhalt until 1920; has emigrant card file; military records
to 1867)

Staatsarchiv Dresden, Aussenstelle Bautzen
Schloss Ortenburg
Seidauer Strasse 2
D-02625 Bautzen
GERMANY
(state archive for the former province of Upper
Lusatia/Oberlausitz and the Sorbs or Wends while under
Prussian or Saxon government)

Staatsarchiv Coburg
Schloss Ehrenburg
D-96450 Coburg
GERMANY
(state archive for former Duchy of Saxe-Coburg-Gotha)

Staatsarchiv Dresden, Bergarchiv Freiberg
Kirchgasse 11
D-09559 Freiberg
GERMANY
(archive on mining in Saxony until 1952)

Aussenstelle Glauchau des Saechsischen
Hauptstaatsarchivs
Schloss Vordergleichau
D-08371 Glauchau
GERMANY
(branch of the Dresden state archive in Glauchau for the
former Schoenburg territories and several castles in the
region)

Thueringisches Hauptstaatsarchiv, Staatsarchiv Gotha
Schloss Friedenstein
D-99867 Gotha
GERMANY
(state archive for city of Gotha and district of Erfurt until
1920; Eisenach, Gotha, and Sonderhausen 1920-1945;
military records prior to 1867)

Thueringisches Staatsarchiv, Aussenstelle Greiz
Oberes Schloss 7
D-07973 Greiz
GERMANY
(branch of Weimar state archive for the former Principality
of Reuss, old line (Greiz), until 1920; Reuss, young line
(districts of Gera and Greiz), 1920-1952; military records
prior to 1867)

Saechsisches Staatsarchiv Leipzig
Paunsdorf
Schongauer Strasse 1
Postfach 100947
D-04009 Leipzig   *(Street address D-04329 Leipzig)*
GERMANY
(state archive for Leipzig area; collection on feudalism and
the rise of cities; large newspaper collection dating back to
1722)

Landeshauptarchiv Sachsen-Anhalt
Hegelstrasse 25
D-39104 Magdeburg
GERMANY
(state archive for Saxony-Anhalt, the Magdeburg church
lands, the Halberstadt church lands, and several estate
archives)

Staatsarchiv Meiningen
Schloss Bibrabau
D-98617 Meiningen
GERMANY
(state archive for former Duchy of Meiningen and County
of Henneberg; military records prior to 1867)

Staatsarchiv Magdeburg, Aussenstelle Oranienbaum
Schloss
D-06785 Oranienbaum bei Dessau
GERMANY
(state archive for former Principality of Anhalt and for
Blankenburg)

Aussenstelle Mockern des Staatsarchivs Weimar
D-39391 Moeckern
GERMANY
(branch of the chief state archive of Thuringia)

Thueringisches Staatsarchiv Rudolstadt
Schloss Heidecksburg
D-07407 Rudolstadt
GERMANY
(state archive for former Duchies of Schwarzburg-
Rudolstadt and Schwarzburg-Sondershausen, also parts of
Thuringia since 1920; military records prior to 1867)

Thueringisches Hauptstaatsarchiv Weimar
Marstallstrasse 2
Postfach 726
D-99408 Weimar (Street address D-99423)
GERMANY
(state archive for Thuringia 1920-1952)

Thueringisches Hauptstaatsarchiv Weimar
Beethovenplatz 3
Postfach 726
D-99408 Weimar (Street address D-99423)
GERMANY
(state archive for former Duchy of Saxony-Weimar-
Eisenach to 1920; military records prior to 1867)

Landeshauptarchiv Sachsen-Anhalt, Aussenstelle
    Wernigerode
Orangerie
Lustgarten 21
D-38855 Wernigerode (Harz)
GERMANY
(branch of chief Saxony-Anhalt state archive responsible
for a small portion of the state)

SCHAUMBURG-LIPPE. See HESSE, LIPPE, LOWER
SAXONY, WESTPHALIA.

SCHLESIEN. See SILESIA.

SCHLESWIG-HOLSTEIN. See also DENMARK.

Landesarchiv
Prinzenpalais
Gottorfstrasse 6
D-24837 Schleswig
GERMANY
(state archive for Schleswig-Holstein, especially while
under German rule; many early records now removed to
Copenhagen, Denmark; some military records prior to
1867)

Rigsarkivet
Rigsdagsgården 9
DK-1218 København/Copenhagen K
Danmark/DENMARK
(Danish national archives in Copenhagen; censuses of
1787, 1801, 1834, 1840, 1845, and each 5 years thereafter
to 1860, then 1870, 1880, 1890, 1906, 1911; from 1845 on
birthplaces given; draft forms from 1788, originally only
peasant sons, who were registered at birth; from 1849 all
males, registered at 15; naval records from 1802)

Rigsarkivet 3. Afdeling
Forsvarets Arkiver
Rigsdagsgården 5
DK-1218 København/Copenhagen K
Danmark/DENMARK
(military archive of Denmark)

Staatsarchiv Luebeck
St.-Annen-Strasse 12
D-23552 Luebeck
GERMANY
(state archive for Luebeck area)

Landsarkivet for de sønderjske Landesdele
Haderslevvej 45
DK-6200 Aabenraa
Danmark/DENMARK
(Danish state archive for parts of Schleswig-Slesvig now under Danish rule since 1920)

SCHWABEN. See SWABIA.

SCHWEIZ. See SWITZERLAND.

SILESIA. See under CZECH REPUBLIC, POLAND, AUSTRIA, etc.

SLESVIG. See SCHLESWIG-HOLSTEIN.

SLOVAK REPUBLIC.

Archívní Sprava
Odbur Archivnictus
Kriszkova 7
81104 Bratislavá
SLOVAK REPUBLIC
(archive at Bratislavá/Pressburg for Slovakia; has records to 1900; specify money limit; ask for extract of birth; marriage; death, etc.)

Statní Oblastní Archiv v Brno
Zerotínovo námestf 3-5
60000 Brno
SLOVAK REPUBLIC
(regional archive at Bruenn/Brünn for central and southern Moravia)

Statní Oblastní Archiv v Opave
Snemovní ul. 1
74600 Opava
SLOVAK REPUBLIC
(regional archive at Troppau for northern Moravia and former Austrian Silesia)

SOUTH AFRICA.

Secretary of the Interior
Private Bag X 114
Corner of Schoeman and van der Walt Street
Pretoria
UNION OF SOUTH AFRICA
(civil registration records of South Africa; earliest records deaths in Natal since 1868)

Records of the South African Constrabulary
Union Building
Pretoria
UNION OF SOUTH AFRICA
(South African archive of immigration and emigration records?)

Former SOVIET UNION. See RUSSIA, etc.

SUDETENLAND. See also under CZECH REPUBLIC.

Sudetendeutsches Archiv
Guellstrasse 7
D-80366 Muenchen *(Munich)*
GERMANY
(local history archive, photograph archive, and central repository for archives of Sudetenland homeland associations)

SWABIA. See BAVARIA, WUERTTEMBERG, also DANUBE GERMANS.

SWEDEN. See also POMERANIA.

The House of Emigrants
P.O. Box 201
S-35104 Växjö 1
Sverige/SWEDEN
(archives and library; database on 1,300,000 Swedish emigrants 1840-1930)

SWITZERLAND. (Note: The LDS church has microfilmed parish registers in Basel-Stadt, Basel-Land, Zuerich, Lucerne, St. Gallen, Appenzell, Ausser-Rhoden and Inner-Rhoden, Vaud/Watt, Geneva, and Solothurn cantons)

Schweizerisches Bundesarchiv
Archivstrasse 4
CH-3003 Bern
Schweiz/SWITZERLAND
(federal archives of Switzerland; because of the local character of Swiss citizenship and goverment, not as useful as individual cantonal archives)

Zentralstelle fuer genealogische Auskuenfte
Werner Hug
Unterwartweg 23/8
CH-4132 Muttenz
Schweiz/SWITZERLAND
(central genealogical inquiry center for all of Switzerland)

Eidgenoessisches Militaer-Department
Bibliothek
Bundeshaus Ost
CH-3000 Bern
Schweiz/SWITZERLAND
(military records of the Swiss citizen army, which has universal obligation for all able-bodied men between 20 and 45; post-1800 records)

Archives Héraldique Suisses
Chemin du Parc de Valency 11
CH-1005 Lausanne
Suisse/SWITZERLAND
(Swiss heraldry archives)

Schweizerisches Burgenarchiv
Stapfelberg 4
CH-4000 Basel
Schweiz/SWITZERLAND
(archive for Swiss castles)

EUROPEAN STATE OR PROVINCIAL ARCHIVES

Staatsarchiv des Kantons Aargau
Aargauerplatz
CH-5001 Aarau
Schweiz/SWITZERLAND
(Swiss cantonal archive for Canton Aargau; passport
records for districts of Aarau and Lenzburg; census 1837,
1850; citizens' registers in town clerk's offices since 1817)

Landesarchiv von Appenzell (Inner-Rhoden)
Landeskanzlei
CH-9050 Appenzell
Schweiz/SWITZERLAND
(Swiss cantonal archive for Canton Appenzell, Inner-
Rhoden)

Staatsarchivs des Kantons Appenzell (Ausser-Rhoden)
Kasernenstrasse 17B
CH-9100 Herisau
Schweiz/SWITZERLAND
(Swiss cantonal archive for Canton Appenzell, Ausser-
Rhoden; indexed passport records for 1806-1927, gaps
1811-1815)

Staatsarchiv Basel-Land
Wiedenhubstrasse 35
CH-4410 Liestal
Schweiz/SWITZERLAND
(Swiss cantonal archive for Canton Basel-Land; has
centralized vital records)

Staatsarchiv Basel-Stadt
Martinsgasse 2
CH-4001 Basel
Schweiz/SWITZERLAND
(Swiss cantonal archive for Canton Basel-Stadt; indexed
passport records 1738-1922; special register for America
1854-1861)

Staatsarchivs des Kantons Bern
Falkenplatz 4
CH-3012 Bern
Schweiz/SWITZERLAND
(Swiss cantonal archive for Canton Bern; indexed passport
records 1838-1887, gaps 1855-1859)

Landesarchiv des Kantons Glarus
Gerichtsgebaeude
Gerichtshof
Spielhof 6
CH-8750 Glarus
Schweiz/SWITZERLAND
(Swiss cantonal archive for Canton Glarus)

Staatsarchiv des Kantons Graubuenden
Reichsgasse
CH-7000 Chur
Schweiz/SWITZERLAND
(Swiss cantonal archive for Canton Graubuenden/ Grisons;
passport records since 1873)

Staatsarchiv des Kantons Luzern
Schuetzenstrasse 9
CH-6003 Luzern
Schweiz/SWITZERLAND
(Swiss cantonal archive for Canton Luzern/
Lucerne; indexed passport records 1790-1915, some gaps
since 1829)

Staatsarchiv des Kantons Nidwalden
Muergstrasse 12
CH-6370 Stans
Schweiz/SWITZERLAND
(Swiss cantonal archive for Canton Nidwalden)

Staatsarchiv Obwalden
Rathausplatz
CH-6060 Sarnen
Schweiz/SWITZERLAND
(Swiss cantonal archive for Canton Obwalden)

Staatsarchiv des Kantons St. Gallen
Regierungsgebaeude
CH-9000 St. Gallen
Schweiz/SWITZERLAND
(Swiss cantonal archive for Canton St. Gallen; indexed
passport records for District of Werdenberg 1846-1894)

Staatsarchiv Schaffhausen
Rathausbogen 4
CH-8200 Schaffhausen
Schweiz/SWITZERLAND
(Swiss cantonal archive for Canton Schaffhausen;
unindexed passport records 1807-1915)

Staatsarchiv des Kantons Schwyz
Bahnhofstrasse 20
CH-6430 Schwyz
Schweiz/SWITZERLAND
(Swiss cantonal archive for Canton Solothurn; has
centralized vital records; passport records 1822-1929,
indexed to 1915)

Staatsarchiv des Kantons Thurgau
Regierungsgebaeude
Promenadenstrasse 12
CH-8500 Frauenfeld
Schweiz/SWITZERLAND
(Swiss cantonal archive for Canton Thurgau)

** Unterwalden.
See under Nidwalden and Obwalden.

Staatsarchiv des Kantons Uri
Ankenwaage
CH-6460 Altdorf
Schweiz/SWITZERLAND
(Swiss cantonal archive for Canton Uri; indexed passport
records 1808-1894)

EUROPEAN STATE OR PROVINCIAL ARCHIVES

Archives cantonales du Vaud
Rue de la Mouline 32
CH-1022 Chavannes-Renens VD
Suisse/SWITZERLAND
(Swiss cantonal archive for Canton Vaud/Waadt)

Staatsarchiv des Kantons Zuerich
Predigerplatz 33
CH-8001 Zuerich
Schweiz/SWITZERLAND
(Swiss cantonal archive for Canton Zuerich; has centralized
vital records; unindexed passport records 1814-1926)

Staatsarchiv des Kantons Zug
Regierungsgebaeude
CH-6300 Zug
Schweiz/SWITZERLAND
(Swiss cantonal archive for Canton Zug; unindexed
passport records 1811-1935)

THURINGIA. See under SAXONY; Gotha, Greiz,
Meiningen, Rudolstadt, Weimar.

UKRAINE.

Ukraine
290006 L'viv 4
Tsentralnyi derzhavnyi arkhiv Ukrainy
pl. Vozziednannia 3A
UKRAINE
(state archive for Ukraine at Lvov)

Ukraine
252601 Kiev-1000
Tsentralnyi derzhavnyi arkhiv Ukrainy u.m. Kyievai
vul. Solomianska 24
UKRAINE
(state archive for Ukraine at Kiev)

UNION OF SOUTH AFRICA. See SOUTH
   AFRICA.

UNTERFRANKEN. See under BAVARIA.

UPPER BAVARIA. See under BAVARIA.

USSR. See RUSSIA, etc.

VOLHYNIA.

Urzad Stanu Cywilnego
Warszawa Strodmiescie
Archiwum Akt Zabuzanskich
ulica Jeznicka 1-3
PL-00281 Warszawa/Warsaw
POLAND
(state archive for western Volhynia)

VOSGES.

Archives départelemtales des Vosges
Allee des Hetres
La Voivre
Boîte postale 1002
F-80050 Epinal Cedex
FRANCE
(archive of the Département of Vosges)

WALDECK. See HESSE-KASSEL.

WESTPHALIA. See also LIPPE, LOWER SAXONY, and
RHINELAND.

NRW Hauptstaatsarchiv Duesseldorf
Mauerstrasse 55
D-40476 Duesseldorf
GERMANY
(chief state archive for the Rhineland and part of
Westphalia)

Staatsarchiv Muenster
Bohlweg 2
Postfach 7629
D-48041 Muenster
GERMANY
(state archive for Westphalia)

Geheimes Staatsarchiv Merseburg
Historische Abteilung II
Koenig-Heinrich-Strasse 37
D-06217 Merseburg
GERMANY
(state archive with holdings of the central organs of the
former Kingdom of Westphalia 1807-1813; since
unification, these may be transferred to Westphalia)

Westfaelisches Archivamt Muenster
Warendorfer Strasse 24
D-48145 Muenster
GERMANY
(caretaker archive for various local and private archives; for
area of Muenster, Arnsberg, and former Westphalia)

WUERTTEMBERG.

Hauptstaatsarchiv Stuttgart
Konrad-Adenauer-Strasse 4
D-70173 Stuttgart
GERMANY
(chief state archive for Stuttgart and the former Duchy of
Wuerttemberg; military records for the Wuerttemberg army
to 1871; card-index to Ludwigsburg emigration files)

Heeresarchiv
Gutenbergstrasse 109
D-70197 Stuttgart
GERMANY
(military archive for Wuerttemberg 1871-1919)

EUROPEAN STATE OR PROVINCIAL ARCHIVES

Staatsarchiv Ludwigsburg
Mathildenstrasse 1
D-71638 Ludwigsburg
GERMANY
(state archive for Ludwigsburg and northern Wuerttemberg;
has emigration records for all of Wuerttemberg, but you
must know the name of the village or the *Oberamt*
(governing district) the emigrant came from)

Staatsarchiv Sigmaringen
Steindorfer Strasse 11
D-72488 Sigmaringen
GERMANY
(state archive for Hohenzollern and southern
Wuerttemberg)

Staatsarchiv Sigmaringen
Abteilung Landesbeschreibung
Kurze Strasse 6
D-72072 Tuebingen
GERMANY
(geography division of Sigmaringen state archive for
Hohenzollern and southern Wuerttemberg)

(former) YUGOSLAVIA.

National Archives of Yugoslavia
Vase Pelagica 33
Beograd/Belgrade
SERBIA
(national archives of former Yugoslavia; state archives
below deal with civil registration and church records)

Archiv Vojvodina
Dunavska 35
21000 Novy Sad
VOIVODINA
(state archive for Neusatz area)

Archiv Croatija
Marulicevtrg 21
41000 Zagreb
CROATIA
(state archive for Croatia)

Archiv Bosnija-Hercegovina
Save Kovacevica 6
71001 Sarajevo
BOSNIZ-HERCEGOVINA
(state archive for Bosnia-Hercegovina)

Archiv Slovenija
Zvezdarska 1
61000 Ljubljana
SLOLVENIA
(state archive for the Ljubljana/Laibach and
Kocevje/Gottschee area and Carniola/Krain/ Slovenia)

"Deutsche Minderheit"
Historisches Seminar der Universitaet Hamburg
Von-Melle-Park 6, XI
D-20146 Hamburg
GERMANY
(research project of University of Hamburg on German
national minority in Yugoslavia from 1918 to 1945)

MUNICIPAL AND COUNTY ARCHIVES IN GERMANY

*(Listed alphabetically by city, town, or village name; omit **Bad** in names.)*
If your ancestor's village is not listed, try the nearest town or city, the *Kreisstadt* or "county seat" if known.
Stadtarchiv is municipal archive, for the city. *Kreisarchiv* or *Landkreisarchiv* is county archive, for the county/district.
If more than one postal code is shown, the preferred one is the post office box or code for a major postal customer rather than the street address.

Stadtarchiv, Fischmarkt 3, D-56062 Aachen, GERMANY

Stadtarchiv, Marktplatz 30, Postfach 1740,
   D-73430 Aalen, GERMANY

Stadtarchiv, D-93326 Abensberg, GERMANY

Stadtarchiv, Van-Delden-Strasse 6, D-48683 Ahaus,
   GERMANY

Stadtarchiv Ahrweiler, D-53474 Bad Neuenahr-Ahrweiler,
   GERMANY

Archiv des Landkreises Waldshut, Dr. Rudolf-Eberle-
   Strasse 32, D-79774 Albbruck, GERMANY

Stadtarchiv, Marktplatz 4-5, D-31061 Alfeld, GERMANY

Stadtarchiv, Am Marktplatz, D-36304 Alsfeld, GERMANY

Stadtarchiv, Oberer Markt 2, D-90518 Altdorf bei
   Nuernberg, GERMANY *(near Nuremberg)*

Stadtarchiv, D-04600 Altenburg, GERMANY

Stadtarchiv, D-55232 Alzey, GERMANY

Stadtarchiv, Zeughausstrasse 1, Postfach 2155,
   D-92224 Amberg, GERMANY

Stadtarchiv, D-35287 Amoeneburg, GERMANY

Amöneburg. See Amoeneburg.

Stadtarchiv, D-56626 Andernach, GERMANY

Stadtarchiv, D-17389 Anklam, GERMANY

Stadtarchiv, D-09456 Annaberg-Buchholz, GERMANY

Stadtarchiv, Rathaus, D-76855 Annweiler, GERMANY

Stadtarchiv, D-91522 Ansbach, GERMANY

Stadtarchiv, D-99510 Apolda, GERMANY

Stadtarchiv, Trauring 1, Postfach 2340, D-59759 Arnsberg,
   GERMANY

Stadtarchiv, D-99310 Arnstadt, GERMANY

Stadtarchiv, D-06556 Artern, GERMANY

Stadtarchiv, Postfach 1145, D-95653 Arzberg, GERMANY

Stadt- und Stiftsarchiv, Schoenborner Hof,
   Wermbachstrasse 15, Postfach 63, D-63701
   Aschaffenburg, GERMANY *(Street address D-63739)*

Stadtarchiv, D-06449 Aschersleben, GERMANY

Stadtarchiv, Markgroeninger Strasse 2, D-71679 Asperg,
   GERMANY

Stadtarchiv, Rathaus, Postfach 420, D-57428 Attendorn,
   GERMANY

Stadtarchiv, D-08280 Aue, GERMANY

Stadtarchiv, Fugger Strasse 12, Postfach 111960,
   D-86150 Augsburg, GERMANY

Baar. See Villingen.

Stadtarchiv, Marktstrasse 24, D-71520 Backnang,
   GERMANY *(Street address D-71522)*

(Bad Xxx. See under Xxx.)

Stadtarchiv, Steinstrasse 9, Postfach 920, D-76485
   Baden-Baden, GERMANY *(Street address D-76530)*

Stadtarchiv, D-72336 Balingen, GERMANY

Stadtarchiv, Domplatz 2, D-96049 Bamberg, GERMANY

Stadtarchiv, D-18356 Barth, GERMANY

Stadtarchiv, D-34225 Baunatal, GERMANY

Stadtarchiv, D-02625 Bautzen, GERMANY

Stadtarchiv, Luitpoldplatz 13, D-95440 Bayreuth,
   GERMANY *(Street address D-95444)*

Stadtarchiv, D-15848 Beeskow, GERMANY

Stadtarchiv, D-64625 Bensheim, GERMANY

Stadtarchiv, D-45455 Bad Bentheim, GERMANY

Stadtarchiv, Stadtverwaltung, Konrad-Adenauer-Platz 1,
   D-51462 Bergisch Gladbach, GERMANY
   (Street address D-51465)

Stadtarchiv, Rathaus, D-59192 Bergkamen, GERMANY

Stadtarchiv, Schloss, D-76887 Bad Bergzabern,
   GERMANY

Stadtarchiv, D-57319 Bad Berleburg, GERMANY

Stadtarchiv, Breitestrasse 30-31, Postfach 660,
   D-10128 Berlin, GERMANY

Stadtarchiv, D-16321 Bernau, GERMANY

Stadtarchiv, D-06406 Bernburg, GERMANY

Bersenbrück. See Bersenbrueck.

Archiv der Samtgemeinde, Rathaus, Lindenstrasse 2,
   D-49593 Bersenbrueck, GERMANY

Stadtarchiv, Marktplatz 12, D-74354 Besigheim,
   GERMANY

Stadtarchiv, Rathaus, Lindenstrasse 1, D-29549 Bad
   Bevensen, GERMANY

Stadtarchiv, Museumstrasse 6, D-88400 Biberach an
   der Riss, GERMANY *(City government D-88396; street
   address D-88400)*

Kreiskultur- und Archivamt, Rollinstrasse 9, Postfach
   1662, D-88386 Biberach an der Riss, GERMANY

Stadtarchiv, Rohrteichstrasse 19, D-33615 Bielefeld,
   GERMANY

Stadtarchiv, Marktplatz 11, D-74231 Bietigheim-
   Besigheim, GERMANY *(City government D-74319)*

Stadtarchiv, D-55411 Bingen am Rhein, GERMANY

Kreisarchiv, Schlossallee 11, Postfach 301240,
   D-55760 Birkenfeld, GERMANY

Stadtarchiv, D-01877 Bischofswerda, GERMANY

Stadtarchiv, D-06749 Bitterfeld, GERMANY

Stadtarchiv, Rathaus, Karlstrasse 2, D-89143 Blaubeuren,
   GERMANY

Stadtarchiv, D-32825 Blomberg, GERMANY

Böblingen. See Boeblingen.

Stadtarchiv, Muenster Strasse 76, D-46397 Bocholt,
   GERMANY *(City government D-46393)*

Stadtarchiv, Kronenstrasse 47, Postfach 102269,
   D-44787 Bochum, GERMANY
   (Street address D-44789; city government D-44777)

Stadtarchiv, Rathaus, D-31167 Bockenem, GERMANY

Stadtarchiv, Muenchhausenplatz 1, D-37619 Bodenwerder,
   GERMANY

Stadtarchiv, Pfarrgasse 2, D-71032 Boeblingen,
   GERMANY *(City government D-71029)*

Kreisarchiv, Parkstrasse 16, Postfach 1640,
   D-71006 Boeblingen, GERMANY
   (Street address D-71034)

Stadtarchiv, Stadthaus, Berliner Platz 2, D-53111
   Bonn, GERMANY *(City government D-53103)*

Stadtarchiv, Im Piepershagen 17, D-46322 Borken,
   GERMANY *(Street address D-46325)*

Kreisarchiv, Burloer Strasse 93, Postfach 1420,
D-46304 Borken, GERMANY *(Street address D-46325)*
Stadtarchiv, D-04552 Borna, GERMANY
Stadtarchiv, Bogenstrasse 40, D-46236 Bottrop,
GERMANY
Stadtarchiv, D-74336 Brackenheim, GERMANY
Stadtarchiv, Rathaus, Schrabberdeich 1, Postfach 1361,
D-26913 Brake, GERMANY *(Street address D-26919)*
Stadtarchiv, Am Markt, D-33034 Brakel, GERMANY
Stadtarchiv, Altstaedtischer Markt 6, D-14770
Brandenburg, GERMANY *(City government D-14767)*
Stadtarchiv, Herzog-Johann-Albrecht-Strasse 2,
D-38700 Braunlage, GERMANY
Stadtarchiv, Loewenwall 18 B, Postfach 3309, D-38023
Braunschweig, GERMANY
(Street address D-38100) *(Brunswick)*
Stadtarchiv, Frankfurter Strasse 38, Postfach 780,
D-58339 Breckerfeld, GERMANY
Stadtarchiv, Muensterplatz, D-79206 Breisach,
GERMANY
Stadtarchiv im Staatsarchiv, Am Staatsarchiv 1/
Fedelhoeren, D-28203 Bremen, GERMANY
(City government D-28189)
Stadtarchiv, Stadthaus Block 1, Postfach 3224, D-27501
Bremerhaven, GERMANY *(Street address D-27568)*
Stadtarchiv, Rathaus, D-27432 Bremervoerde, GERMANY
Bremervoerde. See Bremervörde.
Stadtarchiv, Rathaus, D-59929 Brilon, GERMANY
Stadtarchiv, Steinweg 1, D-50321 Bruehl, GERMANY
(City government D-50319)
Brühl. See Bruehl.
Brunswick: See Braunschweig.
Stadtarchiv, D-88422 Bad Buchau, GERMANY
Stadtarchiv, Wimpinaplatz 3, D-74722 Buchen,
GERMANY
Büdingen. See Buedingen.
Bückeburg. See Bueckeburg.
Stadtarchiv, D-31675 Bueckeburg, GERMANY
Stadtarchiv, Zum Stadtgraben 7, Postfach 1360,
D-63643 Buedingen, GERMANY
(Street address D-63654)
Stadtarchiv, Hauptstrasse 47, Postfach 1420,
D-77815 Buehl, GERMANY
Stadtarchiv, Bahnhofstrasse 13-15, D-32257 Buende,
GERMANY
Stadtarchiv, Rathaus, Burgstrasse 30, Postfach 1480,
D-33142 Bueren, GERMANY
Kreisarchiv, Kreis Paderborn, Lindenstrasse 12,
D-33142 Bueren, GERMANY
Bühl. See Buehl.
Bünde. See Buende.
Büren. See Bueren.
Stadtarchiv, Rathaus, Am Markt 1, Postfach 1140,
D-23763 Burg auf Fehmarn, GERMANY
Stadtarchiv, D-39288 Burg bei Magdeburg, GERMANY
Stadtarchiv, D-91593 Burgbernheim, GERMANY
Stadtarchiv, Marktstrasse 55, D-31300 Burgdorf,
GERMANY *(Street address D-31303)*
Stadtarchiv, Postfach 1240, D-84489 Burghausen,
GERMANY
Stadtarchiv, Vogtei 5, D-96224 Burgkunstadt, GERMANY

Stadtarchiv Burgsteinfurt, Wasserstrasse, D-48565
Steinfurt, GERMANY
Stadtarchiv, D-79325 Burkheim am Kaiserstuhl,
GERMANY
Stadtarchiv, Buergerhaus, Am Bollwerk 16, Postfach 109,
D-35501 Butzbach, GERMANY
(Street address D-35510)
Stadtarchiv, Stadthaus, Bahnhofstrasse 7,
D-21614 Buxtehude, GERMANY
Stadtarchiv, D-39240 Calbe, GERMANY
Stadtarchiv, Bischofstrasse 48, D-75365 Calw,
GERMANY *(City government D-75363)*
Stadtarchiv, D-65520 Bad Camberg, GERMANY
Camenz. See Kamenz.
Stadtarchiv, Europaplatz 1, D-44575 Castrop-Rauxel,
GERMANY
Stadtarchiv, Prinzengarten 2, D-29223 Celle, GERMANY
Landkreisarchiv, Speicher Strasse 14, D-29221 Celle,
GERMANY
Stadtarchiv, Spitalplatz 22, D-93411 Cham, GERMANY
(Street address D-93413)
Stadtarchiv, Aue 16, D-09112 Chemnitz, GERMANY
(City government D-93411)
Gemeindearchiv Oberharz (Samtgemeinde),
Bahnhofstrasse 2, D-38678 Clausthal-Zellerfeld,
GERMANY
Stadtarchiv, Rosengasse 1, D-96450 Coburg, GERMANY
Stadtarchiv, Markt 1, D-56812 Cochem, GERMANY
Stadtarchiv, Walkenbrueckenstrasse, Postfach 1729,
D-48637 Coesfeld, GERMANY
(Street address D-48653; city government D-48651)
Coethen. See Koethen.
Cologne: See Koeln below.
Cösfeld. See Coesfeld.
Stadtarchiv, D-06869 Coswig, GERMANY
Stadtarchiv, Altmarkt 21, D-03046 Cottbus, GERMANY
Stadtarchiv, Rathaus, D-97993 Creglingen, GERMANY
Stadtarchiv, D-08451 Crimmitschau, GERMANY
Cuxhaven. See also Otterndorf.
Stadtarchiv, Gorch-Fock-Strasse 8, D-27472 Cuxhaven,
GERMANY
Gemeindearchiv (Samtgemeinde), Postfach 1260,
D-29446 Dannenberg, GERMANY
Stadtarchiv im Hessischen Staatsarchiv, Karolinenplatz 3,
D-64289 Darmstadt, GERMANY
Stadtarchiv, D-37586 Dassel, GERMANY
Stadtarchiv, Stadthalle, Kolpingstrasse 1, D-45711 Datteln,
GERMANY
Stadtarchiv, Oestlicher Stadtgraben 28, D-94469
Deggendorf, GERMANY
Stadtarchiv, D-67146 Deidesheim, GERMANY
Stadtarchiv, D-04509 Delitzsch, GERMANY
Stadtarchiv, Rathausplatz 1, D-27747 Delmenhorst,
GERMANY *(Street address D-27749)*
Stadtarchiv, Joliot-Curie-Strasse 10, D-06844 Dessau,
GERMANY
Stadtarchiv, Postfach 1207, D-64802 Dieburg, GERMANY
Diemelstadt. See also Rhoden.
Stadtarchiv, D-34474 Diemelstadt, GERMANY
Stadtarchiv, Rathaus, Postfach 1620 D-49346 Diepholz,
GERMANY

Landkreisarchiv, Postfach 2840, D-49346 Diepholz, GERMANY

Stadtarchiv, Koenigstrasse 63, D-89165 Dietenheim, GERMANY

Stadtarchiv, Offenbacher Strasse 11, Postfach 1120, D-63111 Dietzenbach, GERMANY *(Street address D-63128; city government D-63126)*

Stadtarchiv, Pfaffengasse 27, D-65582 Diez, GERMANY

Stadtarchiv, Rathausstrasse 7, D-35683 Dillenburg, GERMANY

Stadtarchiv, Rathaus, Postfach 1210, D-89402 Dillingen, GERMANY

Stadtarchiv, D-84130 Dingolfing, GERMANY

Stadtarchiv, Rathaus, Segringer Strasse 30, D-91550 Dinkelsbuehl, GERMANY

Dinkelsbühl. See Dinkelsbuehl.

Stadtarchiv, Platz d'Agen 1, Postfach 100540, D-46535 Dinslaken, GERMANY

Stadtarchiv, Leonberger Strasse 7, D-71254 Ditzingen, GERMANY

Döbeln. See Doebeln.

Stadtarchiv, D-03253 Doberlug-Kirchhain, GERMANY

Stadtarchiv, D-04720 Doebeln, GERMANY

Stadtarchiv, Rathausgasse 1, Postfach 1453, D-86604 Donauwoerth, GERMANY *(Street address D-86609; city government D-86607)*

Donauwörth. See Donauwoerth.

Stadtarchiv, D-73072 Donzdorf, GERMANY

Stadtarchiv, D-39264 Dornburg (Elbe), GERMANY

Stadtarchiv, Bildungszentrum Maria-Lindenhof, Im Werth 6, D-46282 Dorsten, GERMANY

Stadtarchiv, Stadthaus, Olpe 1, D-44135 Dortmund, GERMANY

Stadtarchiv, Kirchplatz 1, Postfach 40, D-37125 Dransfeld, GERMANY *(Street address D-37127)*

Stadtarchiv, Buchschlager Allee 8, Postfach 102020, D-63266 Dreieich, GERMANY *(Street address D-63303; city government D-63299)*

Stadtarchiv, Marienallee 3, D-01099 Dresden, GERMANY

Stadtarchiv, Rathausstrasse 5, D-33014 Bad Driburg, GERMANY

Stadtarchiv, Hagener Strasse 2, D-57489 Drolshagen, GERMANY

Stadtarchiv, Christian-Blank-Strasse 1, Postfach 1160, D-37115 Duderstadt, GERMANY

Stadtarchiv, Markt 1-3, Postfach 1440, D-48235 Duelmen, GERMANY

Stadt- und Kreistarchiv, Rathaus, Kaiserplatz 2-4, D-54348 Dueren, GERMANY *(Street address D-54349)*

Stadtarchiv, D-67098 Bad Duerkheim, GERMANY

Stadtarchiv, Heinrich-Ehrhardt-Strasse 61, Stadtverwaltungsamt 10/8, D-40200 Duesseldorf, GERMANY *(Street address D-40468)*

Stadtarchiv, Alter Markt 21, Amt 41-03, Postfach 101351, D-47013 Duisburg, GERMANY *(Street address D-47051; city government D-47059)*

Dülmen. See Duelmen.

Düren. See Dueren.

Dürkheim. See under (Bad) Duerkheim.

Düsseldorf. See Duesseldorf.

Stadtarchiv, D-69412 Eberbach, GERMANY

Stadtarchiv, Rathaus, D-91320 Ebermannstadt, GERMANY

Stadtarchiv, Hauptstrasse 5, D-73061 Ebersbach an der Fils, GERMANY

Stadtarchiv, D-16225 Eberswalde-Finow, GERMANY

Stadtarchiv Ebingen, D-72458 Albstadt, GERMANY

Stadtarchiv, D-24340 Eckernfoerde, GERMANY

Eckernförde. See Eckernfoerde.

Stadtarchiv, D-67480 Edenkoben, GERMANY

Stadtarchiv, Stadtplatz 1, Postfach 1220, D-84302 Eggenfelden, GERMANY *(Street address D-84307)*

Stadtarchiv, Marktplatz 1, D-89584 Ehingen, GERMANY

Stadtarchiv, Marktplatz 1, Postfach 1344, D-85072 Eichstaett, GERMANY

Eichstätt. See Eichstaett.

Eickel. See Wanne.

Stadtarchiv, Marktplatz 1, D-04838 Eilenburg, GERMANY

Stadtarchiv, Steinweg 11, D-37574 Einbeck, GERMANY

Kreisarchiv, Markt 22-24, D-99817 Eisenach, GERMANY

Stadtarchiv, D-07607 Eisenberg Thueringen, GERMANY

Stadtarchiv, D-67304 Eisenberg (Pfalz), GERMANY

Stadtarchiv, D-98673 Eisfeld, GERMANY

Stadtarchiv, Markt 1, D-06295 Lutherstadt Eisleben, GERMANY

Stadtarchiv, Spitalstrasse 8, D-73479 Ellwangen (Jagst), GERMANY

Stadtarchiv, Matheus-Mueller-Strasse 3, Postfach 89, D-65337 Eltville, GERMANY

Stadtarchiv, Rathaus, Hauptstrasse 61, D-31008 Elze, GERMANY

Stadtarchiv, Rathaus am Delft, Postfach 2254, D-26721 Emden, GERMANY

Stadtarchiv, Rathaus, Marktplatz 1, D-79312 Emmendingen, GERMANY

Stadtarchiv, Martinikirchgang 2, D-46446 Emmerich, GERMANY

Stadtarchiv, Roemer Strasse 97, D-56130 Bad Ems, GERMANY

Stadtarchiv, Am Markt 1, Postfach 1254, D-48270 Emsdetten, GERMANY *(Street address D-48282)*

Stadtarchiv, Rathaus, D-79346 Endingen, GERMANY

Stadtarchiv, Rathaus, D-78234 Engen, GERMANY

Stadtarchiv, Kirchplatz 10 (Widukind-Museum), D-32130 Enger, GERMANY

Stadtarchiv, vom-Hofe-Strasse 2-6, D-58256 Ennepetal, GERMANY

Enzkreis. See Pforzheim.

Stadt- und Kreisarchiv, Rathaus, D-65817 Eppstein, GERMANY

Stadtarchiv, Neckarstrasse 3, D-64711 Erbach (Odenwald), GERMANY

Stadtarchiv, D-85435 Erding, GERMANY

Erftkreis. See Huerth.

Stadtarchiv, Bahnhofstrasse 1, D-50374 Erftstadt, GERMANY

Stadtarchiv, Fischmarkt 1, D-99084 Erfurt, GERMANY

Stadtarchiv, Johannismarkt 17, D-41812 Erkelenz, GERMANY

Stadtarchiv, Cedernstrasse 1, D-91054 Erlangen, GERMANY

Stadtarchiv, Eschenplatz 1, Postfach 5980, D-65734
Eschborn, GERMANY

Stadtarchiv, Postfach 1269, D-37629 Eschershausen,
GERMANY

Stadtarchiv, D-37269 Eschwege, GERMANY

Stadtarchiv, Rathaus, Wilhelm-Kern-Platz 1,
D-32337 Espelkamp, GERMANY
(Street address D-32339)

Stadtarchiv, Steeler Strasse 29, D-45121 Essen (Ruhr),
GERMANY *(Street address D-45127)*

Stadtarchiv, Marktplatz 20, D-73728 Esslingen am Neckar,
GERMANY

Landkreisarchiv, Pulverwiesen 42, Postfach 145, D-73702
Esslingen am Neckar, GERMANY
(Street address D-73728)

Stadtarchiv, Schloss, D-76275 Ettlingen, GERMANY

Stadtarchiv, Koelner Strasse 75, D-53879 Euskirchen,
GERMANY

Kreisverwaltungsarchiv, Juelicher Ring 32, D-53879
Euskirchen, GERMANY

Stadtarchiv, Kreissparkasse Ostholstein, Am Rosengarten,
D-23701 Eutin, GERMANY

Stadtarchiv, Vogteistrasse 1, D-29683 Fallingbostel,
GERMANY

Stadtarchiv, Rathaus, Hindenburgstrasse 5/7,
Postfach 1257, D-91552 Feuchtwangen, GERMANY
(Street address D-91555)

Stadtarchiv, Lang Strasse 83, Postfach 1180,
D-70772 Filderstadt, GERMANY
(Street address D-70794)

Stadtarchiv, Rathaus, D-24937 Flensburg, GERMANY

Stadtarchiv, St.-Martin-Strasse 8, D-91301 Forchheim,
GERMANY

Stadtarchiv, D-03149 Forst (Lausitz), GERMANY

Stadtarchiv, D-06567 Bad Frankenhausen, GERMANY

Stadtarchiv, Rathaus, D-67227 Frankenthal (Pfalz),
GERMANY

Stadtarchiv, Stadtverwaltung (Amt 41 A), Postfach 3882,
Karmeliterkloster, Karmelitergasse 5, D-60311
Frankfurt am Main, GERMANY
(municipal archive; has births and deaths prior to 1850,
marriages prior to 1848; see next entry)

Standesamt, Bethmannstrasse 3, D-60311 Frankfurt
am Main, GERMANY
(civil registration office; has births and deaths after
1850, marriages after 1848; see previous entry)

Kreisarchiv Main-Taunus Kreis, Bolongarostrasse 101,
Postfach 800460, D-65904 Frankfurt am Main,
GERMANY

Stadtarchiv, Collegienstrasse 8/9, D-15230 Frankfurt
(Oder), GERMANY

Stadtarchiv, Rathaus, Postfach 1960, D-50226 Frechen,
GERMANY

Stadtarchiv, Obermarkt 24, D-09599 Freiberg (Sachsen),
GERMANY

Stadtarchiv, Gruenwaelderstrasse 15,
D-79078 Freiburg im Breisgau, GERMANY

Landkreisarchiv Breisgau-Hochschwarzwald,
Stadtstrasse 2, D-79104 Freiburg im Breisgau,
GERMANY

Stadtarchiv, Rathaus, Obere Hauptstrasse 2, D-85354
Freising, GERMANY

Stadtarchiv, Markt 1, D-49832 Freren, GERMANY

Stadtarchiv, Bahnhofstrasse 18, D-57258 Freudenberg
(Westfalen), GERMANY

Stadtarchiv, Turnhallestrasse 45, D-72250
Freudenstadt, GERMANY

Landkreisarchiv, Herrenfelder Strasse 14, Postfach
620, D-72236 Freudenstadt, GERMANY
(Street address D-72250)

Stadtarchiv, Pfarrstrasse 6, Postfach 1453, D-86304
Friedberg (Bayern), GERMANY
(Street address D-86316)

Stadtarchiv, Haagstrasse 16, D-61169 Friedberg (Hessen),
GERMANY

Stadtarchiv, Katharinenstrasse 55, D-88045
Friedrichshafen, GERMANY

Kreisarchiv Bodenseekreis, Glaernischstrasse 1,
Postfach 1940, D-88009 Friedrichshafen, GERMANY
(Street address D-88045)

Stadtarchiv, Westerlilienstrasse 7, D-25840 Friedrichstadt
(Eider), GERMANY

Stadtarchiv, Rathaus, D-34560 Fritzlar, GERMANY

Stadtarchiv, Rathaus, D-58730 Froendenberg, GERMANY

Stadtarchiv, Postfach 1140, D-49578 Fuerstenau,
GERMANY

Stadtarchiv, Rathaus, Hauptstrasse 31, D-82256
Fuerstenfeldbruck, GERMANY

Stadtarchiv, D-15517 Fuerstenwalde, GERMANY

Stadtarchiv, Schlosshof 12, D-90768 Fuerth (Bayern),
GERMANY

Kloster- und Stadtarchiv, Lechhalde 3, D-87629 Fuessen,
GERMANY

Stadtarchiv, Palais Buttlar, Bonifatiusplatz 1-3, D-36037
Fulda, GERMANY

Fürstenau. See Fuerstenau.

Fürstenwalde. See Fuerstenwalde.

Fürth. See Fuerth.

Füssen. See Fuessen.

Staddtarchiv, Hauptstrasse 1, Postfach 1520,
D-76555 Gaggenau, GERMANY
(Street address D-76571)

Stadtarchiv, Schlossstrasse 20, Postfach 50, D-74401
Gaildorf, GERMANY
(Street address D-74405)

Marktarchiv, Rathausplatz 1, D-82467 Garmisch-
Partenkirchen, GERMANY

Stadtarchiv, Heimatmuseum, Dammstrasse,
D-30989 Gehrden (Hannover), GERMANY

Stadtarchiv, Altes Rathaus, Hauptstrasse 19, D-73312
Geislingen, GERMANY

Stadtarchiv, Issumer Tor 36, D-47608 Geldern,
GERMANY

Kreisarchiv Kreis Kleve, Kapuzinerstrasse 34,
D-47608 Geldern, GERMANY

Stadtarchiv, Rathaus, D-63571 Gelnhausen, GERMANY

Stadtarchiv, Bildungszentrum, Ebertstrasse 19, D-45879
Gelsenkirchen, GERMANY

Stadtarchiv, D-77723 Gengenbach, GERMANY

Stadtarchiv, D-49124 Georgsmarienhuette, GERMANY

Stadtarchiv, Enzianstrasse 23, D-07545 Gera, GERMANY

Stadtarchiv, Hauptstrasse 42, D-70839 Gerlingen,
GERMANY

Stadtarchiv, D-37339 Gernrode, GERMANY

Stadtarchiv, D-76953 Gernsbach, GERMANY

Stadtarchiv, Rathaus, Brunnengasse 5, D-97447 Gerolzhofen, GERMANY

Stadtarchiv, Lindenstrasse 2, Postfach 1361, D-48706 Gescher, GERMANY *(Street address D-48712)*

Stadtarchiv, D-59590 Geseke, GERMANY

Stadtarchiv, Rathausplatz 1, D-58285 Gevelsberg, GERMANY

Stadtarchiv, Postfach 1140, D-89537 Giengen, GERMANY

Stadtarchiv, Behoerdenzentrum, Berliner Platz 1, D-35930 Giessen, GERMANY

Stadtarchiv, Schlossstrasse, D-38505 Gifhorn, GERMANY

Kreisarchiv Landkreis Gifhorn, Postfach 1360, D-38503 Gifhorn, GERMANY

Stadtarchiv, Hochstrasse 2, D-45964 Gladbeck, GERMANY

Kreisarchiv, Muehlberg 7, D-08371 Glauchau, GERMANY

Glückstadt. See Glueckstadt.

Stadtarchiv, Dethlefsenmuseum, Brockdorff-Palais, Am Fleth 43, D-25348 Glueckstadt, GERMANY

Stadtarchiv, Rathaus, Markt 2, D-47574 Goch, GERMANY

Stadtarchiv Goddelau, D-64560 Riedstadt, GERMANY

Stadtarchiv, Schoenhengster Heimatbund e.V., Alter Kasten, Schlossstrasse 14, D-73033 Goeppingen, GERMANY

Landkreisarchiv, Lorcher Strasse 6, Postfach 809, D-73008 Goeppingen, GERMANY *(Street address D-73033)*

Stadtarchiv, Untermarkt 8, D-02826 Goerlitz, GERMANY

Stadtarchiv, Hiroshimaplatz 4, D-37083 Goettingen, GERMANY

Landkreisarchiv, Buergerstrasse 62, Postfach 2632-34, D-37016 Goettingen, GERMANY *(Street address D-37073)*

Göppingen. See Goeppingen.

Görlitz. See Goerlitz.

Stadtarchiv, Zehntstrasse 24, Postfach 2569, D-38615 Goslar, GERMANY *(Street address D-38640)*

Stadtarchiv, D-99867 Gotha, GERMANY

Göttingen. See Goettingen.

Graefrath. See Solingen.

Gräfrath. See Solingen.

Stadtarchiv, D-17489 Greifswald, GERMANY

Stadtarchiv, D-07973 Greiz, GERMANY

Kreisarchiv Kreis Neuss, Harnischstrasse 6, D-41515 Grevenbroich, GERMANY

Stadtarchiv, D-99718 Greussen, GERMANY

Stadtarchiv, Stadtbibliothek, Markt 16, D-04668 Grimma, GERMANY

Grodk Dolna Luzyca. See Spremberg.

Stadtarchiv, D-04838 Groitzsch, GERMANY

Stadtarchiv, Blankestrasse 16, D-31028 Gronau, GERMANY

Stadtarchiv, D-71723 Grossbottwar, GERMANY

Stadtarchiv, Marktstrasse 28, D-64398 Gross-Bieberau, GERMANY

Stadtarchiv, Postfach 1561, D-64526 Gross-Gerau, GERMANY

Stadtarchiv, Rathaus, Markt 1, D-64823 Gross-Umstadt, GERMANY

Stadtarchiv, D-35305 Gruenberg (Hessen), GERMANY

Stadtarchiv, D-67269 Gruenstadt (Pfalz), GERMANY

Grünberg. See Gruenberg.

Grünstadt. See Gruenstadt.

Stadtarchiv, D-03172 Guben, GERMANY

Stadtarchiv, D-18273 Guestrow, GERMANY

Stadtarchiv, Hohenzollernstrasse 30A, D-33330 Guetersloh, GERMANY

Stadtarchiv, Rathausplatz 1, D-51643 Gummersbach, GERMANY

Stadtarchiv, D-91710 Gunzenhausen, GERMANY

Güstrow. See Guestrow.

Gütersloh. See Guetersloh.

Stadtarchiv, Alexanderring 8, Postfach 1308, D-57622 Hachenburg, GERMANY *(Street address D-57627)*

Stadtarchiv, Rathausstrasse 12, Postfach 4249, D-58095 Hagen (Westfalen), GERMANY *(Street address D-58042)*

Stadt- und Kreisarchiv, Domplatz 49, D-38820 Halberstadt, GERMANY

Stadtarchiv, D-39340 Haldensleben, GERMANY

Stadtarchiv, Bredenstrassse 1, D-33790 Halle (Westfalen), GERMANY

Stadtarchiv, Rathausstrasse 1, D-06108 Halle (Saale), GERMANY

Stadtarchiv, D-59969 Hallenberg, GERMANY

Stadtarchiv, Rathaus 84, D-45712 Haltern, GERMANY

Archiv der Freien und Hansestadt Hamburg, ABC-Strasse 19a (Seiteneingang), D-20354 Hamburg, GERMANY

Stadtarchiv, Hochzeitshaus, Osterstrasse 2, D-31785 Hameln, GERMANY

Stadtarchiv, Altes Amtshaus, Kamener Strasse 177, D-59065 Hamm (Westfalen), GERMANY *(Street address D-59077)*

Stadtarchiv, Schlossplatz 2, D-63450 Hanau, GERMANY

Stadtarchiv, Am Bokemahle 14-16, D-30171 Hannover, GERMANY

Kreisarchiv Landkreis Hannover, Hildesheimer Strasse 20, D-30169 Hannover, GERMANY

Stadtarchiv, Schlossplatz 3, Postfach 1528, D-34335 Hannoversch Muenden, GERMANY *(Street address D-34346)*

Harburg. See Winsen.

Stadtarchiv, Neuer Markt 1, D-49733 Haren (Ems), GERMANY

Gemeindearchiv, Samtgemeinde, Amtshof, D-27243 Harpstedt, GERMANY

Stadtarchiv, D-77716 Haslach im Kinzigtal, GERMANY

Stadtarchiv, D-67454 Hassloch (Pfalz), GERMANY

Stadtarchiv, Postfach 440, D-45525 Hattingen, GERMANY

Stadtarchiv, Buergermeisteramt, Marktplatz 1, Postfach 222, D-72375 Hechingen, GERMANY *(Street address D-72379)*

Archiv der Stadt Heide, Heider Heimatmuseum, Brahmsstrasse 8, D-25746 Heide (Holstein), GERMANY

Stadtarchiv, Heiliggeist-Strasse 12, D-69117 Heidelberg, GERMANY

Stadtarchiv, Rathaus, Grabenstrasse 15, D-89522
Heidenheim, GERMANY

Heilbad Heiligenstadt. See Heiligenstadt.

Stadtarchiv, Eichgasse 1, Deutschhof, D-74072 Heilbronn
(Neckar), GERMANY

Kreisarchiv Landkreis Heilbronn, Lerchenstrasse 40,
D-74072 Heilbronn, GERMANY

Stadtarchiv, D-42579 Heiligenhaus, GERMANY

Kreisarchiv, Ratsgasse 9, D-37308 Heilbad Heiligenstadt,
GERMANY

Stadtarchiv, Rathaus, Markt 1, D-38350 Helmstedt,
GERMANY

Stadtarchiv, Hauptstrasse 116, D-58675 Hemer,
GERMANY

Stadtarchiv, D-64646 Heppenheim, GERMANY

Stadtarchiv, Rathaus, D-35145 Herborn, GERMANY

Stadtarchiv, Deichtorwall 2, D-32052 Herford,
GERMANY

Stadtarchiv, Eickeler Strassse 7, D-44651 Herne,
GERMANY

Stadtarchiv, Rathaus, D-71083 Herrenberg, GERMANY

Stadtarchiv, D-91217 Hersbruck, GERMANY

Stadtarchiv, Am Treppchen 1, D-36251 Bad Hersfeld,
GERMANY

Stadtarchiv, Kurt-Schumacher-Strasse 16-22, D-45699
Herten (Westfalen), GERMANY

Stadtarchiv, Radelandweg 6, D-04916 Herzberg (Elster),
GERMANY

Stadtarchiv, Marktplatz 13, Postfach 128, D-31833
Hessisch Oldendorf, GERMANY
(Street address D-31840)

Stadtarchiv, Rathaus, Im Herrngarten 1, D-63150
Heusenstamm, GERMANY

Stadtarchiv, Rathaus, Markt 13, Postfach 1360,
D-57261 Hilchenbach, GERMANY
(Street address D-57271)

Stadtarchiv, D-98646 Hildburghausen, GERMANY

Kreisarchiv, Eisfelder Strasse 12, D-98646
Hildburghausen, GERMANY

Landkreisarchiv, Kaiserstrasse 15, D-31134 Hildesheim,
GERMANY

Stadtarchiv, Am Holterhoefchen 34, D-40724 Hilden,
GERMANY

Stadtarchiv, Am Steine 7, Postfach 101255,
D-31112 Hildesheim, GERMANY
(Street address D-31134.)

Stadtarchiv, Burgeffstrasse 30, Postfach 1140,
D-65233 Hochheim am Main, GERMANY
(Street address D-65239)

Höchstädt. See Hoechstaedt.

Stadtarchiv, Obere Hauptstrasse 11, D-68766 Hockenheim,
GERMANY

Stadtarchiv, Bahnhofstrasse 10, D-89420
Hoechstaedt an der Donau, GERMANY

Stadtarchiv, Schulzentrum, D-37671 Hoexter, GERMANY

Stadtarchiv, Unteres Tor 9, D-95028 Hof (Saale),
GERMANY

Stadtarchiv, Markt 1, D-34369 Hofgeismar, GERMANY

Stadtarchiv, Kulturamt, Chinonplatz 2, Postfach 1340,
D-65703 Hofheim am Taunus, GERMANY
(Street address D-65719)

Hohenlohe. See Kuenzelsau.

Stadtarchiv, Rathaus, Postfach 1462, D-37594
Holzminden, GERMANY

Stadtarchiv, Rathaus, D-35315 Homberg (Ohm),
GERMANY

Stadtarchiv, Am Rondell, D-66424 Homburg (Saar),
GERMANY

Stadtarchiv, Gotisches Haus, Tannenwaldweg 102,
D-61350 Bad Homburg vor der Hoehe, GERMANY

Stadtarchiv, Postfach 1740, D-53587 Bad Honnef,
GERMANY

Stadtarchiv, Rathausplatz 4, D-32805 Horn-Bad Meinberg,
GERMANY

Stadtarchiv, Rathaus, D-72160 Horb am Neckar,
GERMANY

Stadtarchiv, D-38315 Hornburg, GERMANY

Höxter. See Hoexter.

Hückelhoven. See Hueckelhoven.

Hückeswagen. See Hueckeswagen.

Stadtarchiv, Altes Rathaus, D-41836 Hueckelhoven,
GERMANY

Stadtarchiv, D-42499 Hueckeswagen, GERMANY

Stadtarchiv, D-78183 Huefingen, GERMANY

Stadtarchiv, Rathaus, Friedrich-Ebert-Strasse 40,
D-50354 Huerth, GERMANY

Kreisarchiv Erftkreis, Friedrich-Ebert-Strasse 1,
D-50334 Huerth, GERMANY

Hüfingen. See Huefingen.

Hürth. See Huerth.

Stadtarchiv, Kaiser Strasse 7, D-35410 Hungen,
GERMANY

Stadtarchiv, Schlossstrasse, D-25813 Husum (Nordsee),
GERMANY

Stadtarchiv, Muensterstrasse 16, Postfach 1565,
D-49465 Ibbenbueren, GERMANY
(Street address D-49477)

Stadtarchiv, Am Markt 2, D-55743 Idar-Oberstein,
GERMANY

Stadtarchiv, Postfach 1140, D-65501 Idstein, GERMANY

Stadtarchiv, D-98693 Ilmenau, GERMANY

Staedtisches Archiv, D-87509 Immenstadt, GERMANY

Stadtarchiv, D-55128 Ingelheim, GERMANY

Stadtarchiv, Auf der Schanz 45, D-85049 Ingolstadt
(Donau), GERMANY

Stadtarchiv, Rathaus, D-97346 Iphofen, GERMANY

Stadtarchiv, An der Schlacht 14, D-58638 Iserlohn,
GERMANY

Stadtarchiv, Markt 15, D-46419 Isselburg, GERMANY

Stadtarchiv, Rathaus, Postfach 1140, D-88316 Isny,
GERMANY

Kreis- und Stadtarchiv, Markt 1, D-25524 Itzehoe,
GERMANY

Stadtarchiv, Ernst-Thaelmann-Strasse 19, D-07747
Jena, GERMANY

Stadtarchiv, D-26441 Jever, GERMANY

Kulturamt, Stadtarchiv, Rathaus, Markt 1, D-52428
Juelich, GERMANY

Stadtarchiv, D-14913 Jueterbog, GERMANY

Jülich. See Juelich.

Jüterbog. See Jueterbog.

Stadtarchiv, Rathaussstrasse 1, D-41564 Kaarst,
GERMANY

Stadtarchiv, Rathaus, Steinstrasse 9, Postfach 1320,
    D-67604 Kaiserslautern, GERMANY
    (Street address D-67657)
Kalbe. See Calbe.
Stadtarchiv, Hanselaer Strasse 5, D-47546 Kalkar,
    GERMANY
Stadtarchiv, Rathaus, D-59174 Kamen, GERMANY
Stadtarchiv, D-76870 Kandel, GERMANY
Stadtarchiv, Rathaus Klein-Karben, Rathausstrasse 35,
    Postfach 1107, D-61174 Karben, GERMANY
    (Streeet address D-61184)
Stadtarchiv, Buergerhaus Petterweil,
    Sauerbornsstrasse 12-14, D-61184 Karben, GERMANY
Karl-Marx-Stadt. See Chemnitz.
Amt fuer Archiv, Zaehringer Strasse 96/98,
    D-76133 Karlsruhe (Baden), GERMANY
Stadtarchiv, Helfensteinstrasse 2, D-97753
    Karlstadt, GERMANY
Stadtarchiv, Marstallgebaeude, Wildemannsgasse 1,
    D-34117 Kassel, GERMANY
Stadtarchiv, Hauberrisserstrasse 8, Postfach 1752,
    D-87577 Kaufbeuren, GERMANY
    (Street address D-87600)
Stadtarchiv, Alleestrasse 21, D-93309 Kelheim,
    GERMANY
Stadtarchiv, Gagernring 6, Postfach 1560, D-65765
    Kelkheim (Taunus), GERMANY
    (Street address D-65779)
Kreisarchiv und Stadtarchiv Viersen, Thomasstrasse 20,
    D-47906 Kempen, GERMANY
Stadtarchiv, Rathausplatz 3-5, D-87435 Kempten
    (Allgaeu), GERMANY
Stadtarchiv, Rathaus, Hauptstrasse 15, D-79341
    Kenzingen, GERMANY
Stadtarchiv, Koelner Strasse 17, Postfach 2109,
    D-50151 Kerpen, GERMANY
    (Street address D-50171)
Stadtarchiv, Postfach 176, D-47613 Kevelaer, GERMANY
Stadtarchiv, Rathaus, Fleethoern 9-17, D-24103 Kiel,
    GERMANY
Stadtarchiv, Friedrich-Ebert-Strasse 360, D-58566 Kierspe,
    GERMANY
Stadtarchiv, Wollmarktstrasse 30, D-73230 Kirchheim
    unter Teck, GERMANY
Gemeindearchiv, Hundemstrasse 40, D-57399
    Kirchhundem, GERMANY
Stadtarchiv, Kirchstrasse 3, Postfach 93, D-55602
    Kirn (Nahe), GERMANY *(Street address D-55606)*
Stadtarchiv, D-97318 Kitzingen, GERMANY
Stadtarchiv, Tiergartenstrasse 41, D-47533 Kleve
    (Niederrhein), GERMANY
Stadtarchiv, Burgstrasse 1, D-56068 Koblenz am Rhein,
    GERMANY
Stadtarchiv, Gereonskloster 12, D-50670 Koeln am Rhein,
    GERMANY *(Cologne)*
Stadtarchiv, Rathaus, D-97631 Bad Koenigshofen im
    Grabfeld, GERMANY
Stadtarchiv, Rathaus, D-38154 Koenigslutter, GERMANY
Stadtarchiv, D-61462 Koenigstein im Taunus, GERMANY
Stadtarchiv, Weiler 4, D-53639 Koenigswinter,
    GERMANY
Stadtarchiv, D-06366 Koethen (Anhalt), GERMANY

Köln. See Koeln.
Königshofen. See Koenigshofen.
Königslutter. See Koenigslutter.
Königstein. See Koenigstein.
Königswinter. See Koenigswinter.
Stadtarchiv, Benediktinerplatz 5, D-78467 Konstanz,
    GERMANY
Stadtarchiv, D-34497 Korbach-Edersee, GERMANY
Stadtarchiv, Jakob-Sigle-Platz 1, Postfach 1840,
    D-70799 Kornwestheim, GERMANY
    (Street address D-70806)
Köthen. See Koethen.
Koswig. See Coswig.
Kottbus. See Cottbus.
Stadtarchiv, D-47559 Kranenburg, GERMANY
Stadtarchiv, Girmesgath 120, Postfach 2740, D-47727
    Krefeld, GERMANY *(Street address D-47798)*
Stadtarchiv, Karl-Geib-Museum, Kreuzstrasse 69,
    D-55543 Bad Kreuznach, GERMANY
Stadtarchiv, Siegener Strasse 5, D-57223 Kreuztal,
    GERMANY
Krimmitschau. See Crimmitschau.
Stadtarchiv, Rathaus, Marktplatz 5, D-96317 Kronach,
    GERMANY
Stadtarchiv, Katharinenstrasse 7, Postfach 1280, D-61467
    Kronberg (Taunus), GERMANY
    (Street address D-61476)
Stadtarchiv, Hauptstrasse 41, D-74653 Kuenzelsau,
    GERMANY
Kreisarchiv Hohenlohekreis, Allee 17, Postfach 1362,
    D-74643 Kuenzelsau, GERMANY
    (Street address D-74653)
Stadtarchiv, Pestalozzistrasse 8, D-95326 Kulmbach,
    GERMANY
Künzelsau. See Kuenzelsau.
Stadtarchiv, D-66869 Kusel, GERMANY
Stadtarchiv, D-32791 Lage (Lippe), GERMANY
Stadtarchiv, D-56112 Lahnstein, GERMANY
Stadtarchiv, D-77933 Lahr (Schwarzwald), GERMANY
Stadtarchiv, D-76829 Landau (Pfalz), GERMANY
Stadtarchiv, D-86899 Landsberg (Lech), GERMANY
Stadtarchiv, Rathaus, D-84028 Landshut, GERMANY
Stadtarchiv, D-99947 Bad Langensalza, GERMANY
Stadtarchiv, D-35321 Laubach, GERMANY
Stadtarchiv, D-21481 Lauenburg (Elbe), GERMANY
Stadtarchiv, D-91207 Lauf (Pegnitz), GERMANY
Stadtarchiv, D-83410 Laufen (Salzach), GERMANY
Stadtarchiv, D-89415 Lauingen (Donau), GERMANY
Stadtarchiv, D-36341 Lauterbach, GERMANY
Stadtarchiv, D-67742 Lauterecken, GERMANY
Stadtarchiv, Burgplatz 1, D-04109 Leipzig, GERMANY
Stadtarchiv, D-32657 Lemgo, GERMANY
Stadtarchiv, Haus-Vorster-Strasse 11, D-51379
    Leverkusen, GERMANY
Stadtarchiv, D-35423 Lich, GERMANY
Stadtarchiv, D-96215 Lichtenfels, GERMANY
Stadtarchiv, D-65553 Limburg (Lahn), GERMANY
Stadtarchiv, D-88131 Lindau (Bodensee), GERMANY
Stadtarchiv, D-53545 Linz (Rhein), GERMANY
Stadtarchiv, Rathausstrasse, D-59555 Lippstadt,
    GERMANY
Löbau. See Loebau.

MUNICIPAL AND COUNTY ARCHIVES IN GERMANY

Stadtarchiv, D-02708 Loebau, GERMANY
Stadtarchiv, Rathausgasse, D-79540 Loerrach, GERMANY
Lörrach. See Loerrach.
Lübben. See Luebben.
Lübeck. See Luebeck.
Stadtarchiv, D-14943 Luckenwalde, GERMANY
Lüdenscheid. See Luedenscheid.
Stadtarchiv, D-71634 Ludwigsburg, GERMANY
Stadtarchiv, Rottstrasse 17, D-67061 Ludwigshafen
     am Rhein, GERMANY
Stadtarchiv, D-19288 Ludwigslust, GERMANY
Stadtarchiv, D-15907 Luebben, GERMANY
Archiv der Hansestadt Luebeck, Muehlendamm 1/3,
     D-23552 Luebeck, GERMANY
Stadtarchiv, Rathausplatz 2, D-58507 Luedenscheid,
     GERMANY
Stadtarchiv, D-32676 Luegde, GERMANY
Stadtarchiv, Rathaus, D-21339 Lueneburg, GERMANY
Stadtarchiv, D-44536 Luenen, GERMANY
Lügde. See Luegde.
Lüneburg. See Lueneburg.
Lünen. See Luenen.
Lutherstadt Eisleben. See Eisleben.
Lutherstadt Wittenberg. See Wittenberg.
Stadtarchiv, Bei der Hauptwache 4-6, D-39104
     Magdeburg, GERMANY
Main-Tauber-Kreis. See Tauberbischofsheim.
Stadtarchiv, Stadtbibliothek, Rheinallee 3 B,
     D-55116 Mainz, GERMANY
Stadtarchiv, Rathaus E 5, Postfach 102203, D-68022
     Mannheim, GERMANY
Stadtarchiv, D-09496 Marienberg, GERMANY
Stadtarchiv, Rathausplatz 1, D-88677 Markdorf,
     GERMANY
Stadtarchiv, D-95615 Marktredwitz, GERMANY
Stadtarchiv, D-45772 Marl (Westfalen), GERMANY
Stadtarchiv, D-75433 Maulbrunn, GERMANY
Stadtarchiv, Rosengasse 2, D-56727 Mayen, GERMANY
Stadtarchiv, D-67149 Meckenheim (Pfalz), GERMANY
Stadtarchiv, D-88709 Meersburg, GERMANY
Stadtarchiv, D-98617 Meiningen, GERMANY
Stadtarchiv, D-55590 Meisenheim, GERMANY
Stadtarchiv, D-01662 Meissen, GERMANY
Stadtarchiv, D-25704 Meldorf, GERMANY
Stadtarchiv, D-49324 Melle, GERMANY
Stadtarchiv, D-97638 Mellrichstadt, GERMANY
Stadtarchiv, D-87700 Memmingen, GERMANY
Stadtarchiv, D-58706 Menden, GERMANY
Stadtarchiv, D-88512 Mengen, GERMANY
Stadtarchiv, D-49716 Meppen, GERMANY
Stadtarchiv, D-97980 Bad Mergentheim, GERMANY
Stadtarchiv, D-06217 Merseburg, GERMANY
Stadtarchiv, D-88605 Messkirch, GERMANY
Stadtarchiv, D-48629 Metelen, GERMANY
Stadtarchiv, D-40822 Mettmann, GERMANY
Meurs. See Moers.
Stadtarchiv, D-04610 Meuselwitz, GERMANY
Stadtarchiv, D-64720 Michelstadt, GERMANY
Stadtarchiv, D-87719 Mindelheim, GERMANY
Stadtarchiv, Koenigstrasse 60, D-32427 Minden
     (Westfalen), GERMANY

Kommunalarchiv Minden, Tonhallenstrasse 7, D-32423
     Minden, GERMANY
Stadtarchiv, D-09648 Mittweida, GERMANY
Stadtarchiv, D-78532 Moehringen, GERMANY
Moenchengladbach. See also Rheydt.
Stadtarchiv, Bluecherstrasse 6, D-41061
     Moenchengladbach, GERMANY
Stadtarchiv, Rathaus, Neumarkt 6, D-47441 Moers,
     GERMANY
Möhringen. See Moehringen.
Mönchengladbach. See Moenchengladbach and Rheydt.
Stadtarchiv, D-52156 Monschau, GERMANY
Stadtarchiv, D-56140 Montabaur, GERMANY
Mörs. See Moers.
Stadtarchiv, D-84453 Muehldorf am Inn,
     GERMANY
Stadtarchiv, D-99974 Muehlhausen (Thueringen),
     GERMANY
Mühlhausen. See Muehlhausen.
Stadtarchiv, Stadtverwaltung, D-45468 Muelheim an
     der Ruhr, GERMANY
Stadtarchiv, D-95213 Muenchberg, GERMANY
Stadtarchiv, Winzererstrasse 68, D-80797 Muenchen,
     GERMANY *(Munich)*
Muenchen-Gladbach. See Moenchengladbach.
Muenden. See Hannoversch Muenden.
Stadtarchiv, D-97702 Muennerstadt, GERMANY
Stadtarchiv, Hoerster Strasse 28, D-48143 Muenster,
     GERMANY
Stadtarchiv, D-53902 Bad Muenstereifel, GERMANY
Mühldorf. See Muehldorf.
Mülheim. See Muelheim.
Münchberg. See Muenchberg.
München. See Muenchen.
München-Gladbach. See Moenchengladbach.
Munich: See Muenchen above.
Münster. See Muenster.
Münstereifel. See (Bad) Muenstereifel.
Stadtarchiv, D-56377 Nassau, GERMANY
Stadtarchiv, D-64569 Nauheim Kreis Gross-Gerau,
     GERMANY
Stadtarchiv, D-06618 Naumburg (Saale), GERMANY
Stadtarchiv, D-59755 Neheim-Huesten, GERMANY
Stadtarchiv, D-79395 Neuenburg am Rhein, GERMANY
Stadtarchiv, D-24534 Neumuenster, GERMANY
Neumünster. See Neumuenster.
Stadtarchiv, D-84524 Neuoetting, GERMANY
Neuötting. See Neuoetting.
Neuss. See also Grevenbroich.
Stadtarchiv, Oberstrasse 15, D-41460 Neuss, GERMANY
Stadtarchiv, D-91413 Neustadt an der Aisch, GERMANY
Stadtarchiv, D-93333 Neustadt an der Donau, GERMANY
Neustadt an der Haardt. See Neustadt (Weinstrasse).
Stadtarchiv, D-23730 Neustadt in Holstein, GERMANY
Stadtarchiv, Rathausgasse 2, D-97615 Bad Neustadt
     (Saale), GERMANY *(Street address D-97616)*
Stadtarchiv, Rathausstrasse, D-67433 Neustadt
     (Weinstrasse), GERMANY
Stadtarchiv, D-17235 Neustrelitz, GERMANY
Stadtarchiv, D-56566 Neuwied, GERMANY
Stadtarchiv, Rathaus, Marktplatz 1, D-86720 Noerdlingen,
     GERMANY

Stadtarchiv, D-99734 Nordhausen, GERMANY

Stadtarchiv, D-48531 Nordhorn, GERMANY

Nördlingen. See Noerdlingen.

Stadtarchiv, Zwinger 5, D-37154 Northeim, GERMANY

Stadtarchiv, Egidienplatz 23, D-90403 Nuernberg,
GERMANY *(Nuremberg)*

Stadtarchiv, D-72622 Nuertingen, GERMANY

Nuremberg. See Nuernberg above.

Nürtingen. See Nuertingen.

Oberharz. See Clausthal.

Stadtarchiv, Schloss, Sterkrader Strasse, Postfach
101505, D-46015 Oberhausen (Rheinland), GERMANY
(Street address D-46117)

Stadtarchiv, D-63785 Obernburg (Main), GERMANY

Stadtarchiv, Klosterstrasse 14, Postfach 1105, D-78720
Oberndorf (Neckar), GERMANY
(Street address D-78727)

Stadtarchiv, Rathaus, Postfach 1130, D-31676
Obernkirchen, GERMANY *(Street address D-31683)*

Stadtarchiv, Schulstrasse 32, D-61440 Oberursel,
GERMANY

Stadtarchiv, D-92526 Oberviechtach, GERMANY

Stadtarchiv, Rathaus, Postfach 1153, D-97195
Ochsenfurt, GERMANY

Stadtarchiv, D-88416 Ochsenhausen, GERMANY

Stadtarchiv, D-74613 Oehringen, GERMANY

Stadtarchiv, D-08606 Oelsnitz (Vogtland), GERMANY

Stadtarchiv, Hauptstrasse 31, Postfach 1106,
D-65367 Oestrich-Winkel, GERMANY
(Street address D-65375)

Stadtarchiv, Rathaus 1, Ostkorso 8, Postfach 101245,
D-32515 Bad Oeynhausen, GERMANY
*(Street address D-32545; city government address
D-32543)*

Stadtarchiv, Sandgasse 26, D-63065 Offenbach (Main),
GERMANY

Stadtarchiv, Ritterstrasse 10, D-77652 Offenburg,
GERMANY

Kreisarchiv Ortenaukreis, Badstrasse 20, Postfach
1960, D-77609 Offenburg, GERMANY
(Street address D-77652)

Stadtarchiv, D-99885 Ohrdruf, GERMANY

Öhringen. See Oehringen.

Stadtarchiv Oldenburg, Damm 43, D-26135 Oldenburg,
GERMANY

Stadtarchiv, Markt 1, D-23758 Oldenburg in Holstein,
GERMANY

Oldendorf, Hessisch. See Hessisch Oldendorf.

Stadtarchiv, Stadthaus, Hagenstrasse 42, Postfach 1220,
D-23832 Bad Oldesloe, GERMANY
(Street address D-23843)

Stadtarchiv, Kirchstrasse 5, Postfach 134, D-59396
Olfen, GERMANY *(Street address D-59399)*

Stadtarchiv, D-59939 Olsberg, GERMANY

Ölsnitz. See Oelsnitz.

Stadtarchiv, Franziskanerstrasse 776, D-57462 Olpe
(Biggesee), GERMANY

Kreisarchiv, Kirchhaus-Heinrich-Strasse 34,
Postfach 1560, D-57445 Olpe (Biggesee), GERMANY
(Street address D-57462)

Stadtarchiv, D-55276 Oppenheim, GERMANY

Ortenaukreis. See Offenburg.

Stadtarchiv, Stadtverwaltung, Lauterbacher Strasse 2,
D-68683 Ortenberg (Hessen), GERMANY

Stadtarchiv, D-04758 Oschatz, GERMANY

Stadtarchiv, D-39387 Oschersleben, GERMANY

Kreisarchiv, Strasse der Freundschaft 5, D-39387
Oschersleben

Osnabrück. See Osnabrueck.

Landkreisarchiv, D-39606 Osterburg, GERMANY

Landkreisarchiv, Osterholzer Strasse 23, D-27711
Osterholz-Scharmbeck, GERMANY

Stadtarchiv, Doergestrasse 40, Postfach 1720, D-37507
Osterode am Harz, GERMANY
(Street address D-37520)

Stadtarchiv, Rathaus Nellingen, Klosterhof 10,
Postfach 112, D-73747 Ostfildern, GERMANY
(Street address D-73760)

Östrich-Winkel. See Oestrich-Winkel.

Stadtarchiv, D-67697 Otterberg, GERMANY

Stadtarchiv, D-21762 Otterndorf, GERMANY

Kreisarchiv Landkreis Cuxhaven, Reichenstrasse 3,
D-21762 Otterndorf, GERMANY

Stadtarchiv, Buergermeisteramt, D-73277 Owen,
GERMANY

Stadtarchiv, Am Abdinghof 11, D-33098 Paderborn,
GERMANY

Kreisarchiv Kreis Paderborn. See under Bueren.

Stadtarchiv, Schuhmarkt 1, D-19370 Parchim, GERMANY

Stadtarchiv, Schrottgasse 1, Postfach 2447, D-94032
Passau, GERMANY *(Street address D-94034)*

Stadtarchiv, Markt 1, D-04523 Pegau, GERMANY

Stadtarchiv, Kantstrasse 5, Postfach 1760, D-31207
Peine, GERMANY

Landkreisarchiv, Postfach 1360, D-31203 Peine,
GERMANY *(Street address D-31224)*

Stadtarchiv, Rathaus, Grosser Markt, D-19348 Perleberg,
GERMANY

Stadtarchiv, Rathaus, Bahnhofstrasse 63, Postfach
1120, D-32458 Petershagen (Weser), GERMANY
(Street address D-32469)

Stadtarchiv, Brettener Strasse 19, D-75173 Pforzheim,
GERMANY

Kreisarchiv Enzkreis, Blumenhof 4, D-75175 Pforzheim,
GERMANY

Stadt- und Spitalarchiv, Buergermeisteramt,
D-88630 Pfullendorf (Baden), GERMANY

Stadtarchiv, Buergermeisteramt, D-72793
Pfullingen, GERMANY

Stadtarchiv, Kirchstrasse 12-14, D-64319 Pfungstadt

Kreisarchiv, Moltkestrasse 10, Postfach 1720,
D-25407 Pinneberg, GERMANY
(Street address D-25421)

Stadtarchiv, Klosterhof 3, D-01796 Pirna, GERMANY

Stadtarchiv, Unterer Graben 1, D-08523 Plauen
(Vogtland), GERMANY

Stadtarchiv, Postfach 1580, D-58815 Plettenberg,
GERMANY

Stadtarchiv, Schulstrasse 5, D-73207 Plochingen,
GERMANY

Archiv der Stadt Ploen, Schlossberg 4, D-24306 Ploen,
GERMANY

Kreisarchiv, Hamburger Strasse 17/18, D-24306 Ploen,
GERMANY

Plön. See Ploen.

Stadtarchiv, Rathaus, Markt 11, D-07381 Poessneck, GERMANY

Stadtarchiv, Postfach 1154, D-35411 Pohlheim, GERMANY

Stadtarchiv, Kempstrasse 1, D-32457 Porta Westfalica, GERMANY

Stadtarchiv Porz (Rhein), Friedrich-Ebert-Ufer 64, D-51143 Koeln, GERMANY

Pössneck. See Poessneck.

Stadtarchiv, Friedrich-Ebert-Strasse 79-81, D-14469 Potsdam, GERMANY

Stadtarchiv, Rathausstrasse 3, Postfach 1260, D-32353 Preussisch Oldendorf, GERMANY
(Street address D-32361)

Stadtarchiv, D-16928 Pritzwalk, GERMANY

Stadtarchiv, Rathaus, Postfach 1060, D-54591 Pruem, GERMANY

Prüm. See Pruem.

Stadtarchiv, Rathaus, D-66346 Puettlingen, GERMANY

Püttlingen. See Puettlingen.

Stadtarchiv, Brunnenstrasse 4, Postfach 1630, D-31798 Bad Pyrmont, GERMANY
(Street address D-31812; city government D-31810)

Quakenbrück. See Quakenbrueck.

Stadtarchiv, D-49610 Quakenbrueck, GERMANY

Stadtarchiv, Markt, D-06484 Quedlinburg, GERMANY

Stadtarchiv, Hohenfuhrstrasse 13, D-42477 Radevormwald, GERMANY

Stadtarchiv, Rathaus, D-78315 Radolfzell, GERMANY

Stadtarchiv, Lange Strasse 9, D-32369 Rahden (Westfalen), GERMANY

Stadtarchiv, Hauptstrasse 60, D-86641 Rain (Lech), GERMANY

Stadtarchiv, Herrenstrasse 11, D-76437 Rastatt, GERMANY

Stadtarchiv, D-14712 Rathenow, GERMANY

Stadtarchiv, Muelheimer Strasse 47, D-40878 Ratingen, GERMANY

Stadtarchiv, D-23909 Ratzeburg, GERMANY

Kreisarchiv, Domhof 13, D-23901 Ratzeburg, GERMANY

Rauxel. See Castrop.

Ravensberg, Landkreis. See Wangen.

Stadtarchiv, Marktstrasse 28, Postfach 2180, D-88212 Ravensburg, GERMANY

Stadt- und Vestisches Archiv, Hohenzollernstrasse 12, D-45659 Recklinghausen, GERMANY

Kreisarchiv, Postfach 100864/865, D-45608 Recklinghausen, GERMANY

Stadtarchiv, Postfach 1362, D-46459 Rees, GERMANY

Stadtarchiv, Rathaus, D-94209 Regen, GERMANY

Stadtarchiv, Baumhackergasse 6, D-93047 Regensburg, GERMANY

Stadtarchiv, D.-Martin-Luther-Strasse 1, Postfach 1560, D-95105 Rehau, GERMANY
(Street address D-95111)

Stadtarchiv, Bahnhofstrasse 105, D-08468 Reichenbach (Vogtland), GERMANY

Stadtarchiv, Rathaus, Hamburger Strasse 7, D-21465 Reinbek, GERMANY

Stadtarchiv, Stadtverwaltung, Cestasplatz 1, D-64354 Reinheim (Odenwald), GERMANY
(Located Kirchstrasse, Hofgut)

Stadtarchiv, D-53424 Remagen, GERMANY

Stadtarchiv, Scharffstrasse 4-6, Postfach 100860, D-42808 Remscheid, GERMANY
(Street address D-42853)

Gemeindearchiv, Foersterweg 7, D-71686 Remseck, GERMANY

Archiv der Stadt Rendsburg, Am Gymnasium 4, D-24768 Rendsburg, GERMANY

Stadtarchiv, Langestrasse 4, Postfach 1240, D-27335 Rethem (Aller), GERMANY
(Street address D-27336)

Stadtarchiv, Rathaus, Marktplatz 22, D-72764 Reutlingen, GERMANY

Landkreisarchiv, Bismarckstrase 16, D-72764 Reutlingen, GERMANY

Stadtarchiv, Rathausplatz 13, Postfach 2309, D-33351 Rheda-Wiedenbrueck, GERMANY
(Street address D-33378)

Rhein-Sieg-Kreis. See Siegburg.

Stadtarchiv, Vor dem Voigtstor 33, D-53359 Rheinbach, GERMANY

Stadtarchiv, Rathaus, D-47495 Rheinberg, GERMANY

Stadtarchiv, Marktstrasse 12, D-48431 Rheine, GERMANY

Stadtarchiv, Kirchplatz 2, Postfach 1560, D-79605 Rheinfelden (Baden), GERMANY
(Street address D-79618)

Stadtarchiv, D-47239 Duisburg-Rheinhausen, GERMANY

Stadtarchiv, Rathaus, D-41065 Moenchengladbach-Rheydt, GERMANY

Stadtarchiv Rhoden, D-34474 Diemelstadt-Rhoden, GERMANY

Stadtarchiv, Stadtverwaltung, D-88499 Riedlingen, GERMANY

Riedstadt. See Goddelau.

Stadtarchiv, Buergerzentrum, Schulgasse 4, D-97794 Rieneck, GERMANY

Stadtarchiv, D-01587 Riesa, GERMANY

Stadtarchiv, Ruegenstrasse 1, D-33397 Rietberg, GERMANY

Stadtarchiv, Am Markt 7, Postfach 1460, D-31724 Rinteln, GERMANY *(Street address D-31727)*

Stadtarchiv, Markt 1, D-09306 Rochlitz, GERMANY

Stadtarchiv, Hauptstrasse 30, Postfach 1109, D-48713 Rosendahl, GERMANY
(Street address D-48720)

Staedtisches Archiv, Max-Bram-Platz 2a, D-83022 Rosenheim, GERMANY

Stadtarchiv, Hinter dem Rathaus 5, D-18057 Rostock, GERMANY

Rotenburg an der Wuemme. See Rotenburg (Hannover).

Rotenburg an der Wümme. See Rotenburg (Hannover).

Stadtarchiv, Rathaus, Grosse Strasse 1, D-27356 Rotenburg (Hannover), GERMANY

Stadtarchiv, Kirchplatz 2, Postfach 40, D-91146 Roth bei Nuernberg (Mittelfranken), GERMANY
(Street address D-91154)

Stadtarchiv, Buettelhaus, Milchmarkt 2, D-91541
  Rothenburg ob der Tauber, GERMANY
Stadtarchiv, Obere Gasse 12, Postfach 29, D-72101
  Rottenburg am Neckar, GERMANY
  (Street address D-72108)
Stadtarchiv, D-78628 Rottweil, GERMANY
Kreisarchiv, Landratsamt Rottweil, Koenigstrasse 36,
  D-78628 Rottweil, GERMANY
Rüdesheim. See Ruedesheim.
Stadtarchiv, Rathaus, Markt 2, D-07407 Rudolstadt,
  GERMANY
Stadtarchiv, Stadtverwaltung, D-65385 Ruedesheim
  am Rhein, GERMANY
Stadtarchiv, In der Festung, Hauptmann-Scheuermann-
  Weg 4, D-65428 Ruesselsheim, GERMANY
Stadtarchiv, Hochstrasse 14, D-59602 Ruethen,
  GERMANY
Stadtarchiv, D-99842 Ruhla, GERMANY
Rüsselsheim. See Ruesselsheim.
Rüthen. See Ruethen.
Stadtarchiv, D-99996 Saalfeld bei Muehlhausen
  (Thueringen), GERMANY
Saarbrücken. See Saarbruecken.
Stadtarchiv, Rathaus, Nauwieser Strasse 3,
  D-66123 Saarbruecken, GERMANY
Stadtarchiv, Alte Brauereistrasse, Kaserne VI,
  D-66740 Saarlouis, GERMANY
Stadtarchiv, Bismarckstrasse 1, Postfach 1260,
  D-37438 Bad Sachsa, GERMANY
  (Street address D-37441)
Stadtarchiv, Aeusserer Schlosshof, Postfach 1260,
  D-74338 Sachsenheim (Wuerttemberg),
  GERMANY *(Street address D-74343)*
Säckingen. See Saeckingen.
Stadtarchiv, Rathausplatz 1, Postfach 1143,
  D-79702 Bad Saeckingen, GERMANY
  (Street address D-79713)
Saint or St. See under Sankt (=St.).
Stadtarchiv, Rathaus, St. Georgsplatz 1,
  D-31162 Bad Salzdetfurth, GERMANY
Salzgitter. See also Lebenstedt.
Stadtarchiv, Nord-Sued-Strasse 155, Postfach 100800,
  D-38206 Salzgitter, GERMANY
  (Street address D-38229)
Stadtarchiv, Hermannstrasse 32 (VHS-Haus), D-32105
  Bad Salzuflen, GERMANY *(City government D-32102)*
Stadtarchiv, Ratsstrasse 2, D-36433 Bad Salzungen,
  GERMANY
Stadtarchiv, D-29410 Salzwedel, GERMANY
Stadtarchiv, D-06526 Sangerhausen, GERMANY
Stadtarchiv, Markt 1, Postfach 1169, D-53729 Sankt (=St.)
  Augustin, GERMANY *(Street address D-53757)*
Stadtarchiv, Grundschule, Heerstrasse 22, D-56329
  Sankt (=St.) Goar, GERMANY
Stadtarchiv, Am Markt, D-66386 Sankt (=St.) Ingbert,
  GERMANY
Stadtarchiv, Rathaus, Schlossstrasse 7,
  D-66606 Sankt (=St.) Wendel, GERMANY
Stadtarchiv, Steinstrasse 13, D-31157 Sarstedt,
  GERMANY
Stadtarchiv, Buergermeisteramt, D-88348 Saulgau,
  GERMANY

Stadtarchiv, D-96528 Schalkau, GERMANY
Scharmbeck. See Osterholz.
Stadtarchiv, D-89601 Schelklingen, GERMANY
Stadtarchiv, Rathaus, Wallstrasse 1, Postfach 1265,
  D-32807 Schieder-Schwalenberg, GERMANY
  (Street address D-32816)
Stadtarchiv, Pfortengasse 3, D-07907 Schleiz, GERMANY
Stadtarchiv, Plessenstrasse 7, D-24837 Schleswig,
  GERMANY
Stadtarchiv, D-98553 Schleusingen, GERMANY
Stadtarchiv, An der Kirche 4, D-36110 Schlitz,
  GERMANY
Stadtarchiv, D-98574 Schmalkalden, GERMANY
Kreisarchiv, Schloss, Kuechenweg 15,
  D-98574 Schmalkalden, GERMANY
Stadtarchiv, Postfach 1140, D-57376 Schmallenberg,
  GERMANY
Stadtarchiv, D-04626 Schmoelln, GERMANY
Schmölln. See Schmoelln.
Stadtarchiv, Kirchgasse 2, D-08289 Schneeberg,
  GERMANY
Stadtarchiv, D-39218 Schoenebeck (Elbe), GERMANY
Stadtarchiv, Rathaus, D-38364 Schoeningen, GERMANY
Schönebeck (Elbe). See Schoenebeck (Elbe).
Schöningen. See Schoeningen.
Stadtarchiv, Muenzstrasse 1-3, D-86956 Schongau,
  GERMANY
Stadtarchiv, Archivstrasse 4, D-73614 Schorndorf
  (Wuerttemberg), GERMANY
Stadtarchiv, Rathaus, D-63679 Schotten, GERMANY
Stadtarchiv, Rathaus, D-78713 Schramberg, GERMANY
Stadtarchiv, Lenbachplatz 18, Postfach 1380,
  D-86523 Schrobenhausen, GERMANY
  (Street address D-86529)
Stadtarchiv, Rathaus, Postfach 1420, D-48459 Schuettorf,
  GERMANY
Schüttorf. See Schuettorf.
Stadtarchiv, Stadthalle, Schulstrasse 22, D-88427
  Bad Schussenried, GERMANY
Stadtarchiv, Postfach 1680, D-91106 Schwabach,
  GERMANY
Schwäbisch Gmünd. See Schwaebisch Gmuend.
Schwäbisch Hall. See Schwaebisch Hall.
Stadtarchiv, Augustiner Strasse 3, D-73525
  Schwaebisch Gmuend, GERMANY
Stadtarchiv, Am Markt 5, Postfach 100180, D-74501
  Schwaebisch Hall, GERMANY
  (Street address D-74523)
Schwabmünchen. See Schwabmuenchen.
Stadtarchiv, Fugger Strasse 50, D-86830
  Schwabmuenchen, GERMANY
Stadtarchiv, Marktplatz 1-2, Postfach 2710,
  D-65820 Schwalbach am Taunus, GERMANY
  (Street address D-65824)
Stadtarchiv, D-65307 Bad Schwalbach, GERMANY
Schwalenberg. See Schieder-Schwalenberg.
Stadtarchiv, Kirchengasse 1, Postfach 1880,
  D-92409 Schwandorf, GERMANY
  (Street address D-92421)
Stadtarchiv, Rathaus, Ritter-Wulf-Platz 1, D-21493
  Schwarzenbek, GERMANY
Schwarzwald. See Villingen.

Stadtarchiv, Bahnhofstrasse 21, D-16303 Schwedt, GERMANY

Stadtarchiv, Rathaus, Friedrich-Rueckert-Bau, Martin-Luther-Platz, D-97421 Schweinfurt, GERMANY

Stadtarchiv, Haus Martfeld, Hauptstrasse 150, D-58332 Schwelm, GERMANY

Schwenningen. See Villingen.

Stadtarchiv, Platz der Jugend 12-14, D-19053 Schwerin (Mecklenburg), GERMANY

Stadtarchiv, Postfach 1920, D-68723 Schwetzingen, GERMANY

Stadtarchiv, D-39615 Seehausen (Altmark), GERMANY

Stadtarchiv, Oldesloer Strasse 20, D-23795 Bad Segeberg, GERMANY

Stadtarchiv, Rathaus, Postfach 1150, D-95146 Selbitz (Oberfranken), GERMANY

Stadtarchiv, Giselastrasse 37, D-63500 Seligenstadt, GERMANY

Stadtarchiv, Rathaus, D-59379 Selm, GERMANY

Stadtarchiv, Rathaus, D-48324 Sendenhorst, GERMANY

Stadtarchiv, Postfach 1061, D-53708 Siegburg, GERMANY

Kreisarchiv Rhein-Sieg-Kreis, Kaiser-Wilhelm-Platz 1, D-53721 Siegburg, GERMANY

Stadtarchiv, Oranienstrasse 15, D-57072 Siegen, GERMANY

Landkreisarchiv, Karlstrasse 15, Postfach 440, D-72482 Sigmaringen, GERMANY *(Street address D-72488)*

Stadtarchiv, Rathausplatz, D-71063 Sindelfingen, GERMANY

Stadtarchiv, August-Ruf-Strasse 7, D-78224 Singen (Hohentwiel), GERMANY

Stadtarchiv, D-74889 Sinsheim, GERMANY

Stadtarchiv, Haus "Zum Spiegel," Jakobistrasse 13, Postfach 2252, D-59482 Soest (Westfalen), GERMANY *(Street address D-59494)*

Kreisarchiv, Osthofenstrasse 60-62, D-59494 Soest (Westfalen), GERMANY

Stadtarchiv, Klosterhof 4, D-42653 Solingen-Graefrath, GERMANY

Stadtarchiv, D-99706 Sondershausen, GERMANY

Stadtarchiv, Platz der Republik, D-96515 Sonneberg, GERMANY

Kreisarchiv, Karl-Marx-Strasse, D-96515 Sonneberg, GERMANY

Stadtarchiv, Rathaus, D-37242 Bad Sooden-Allendorf, GERMANY

Söst. See Soest.

Stadtarchiv, D-78549 Spaichingen, GERMANY

Stadtarchiv, Rathaus, Lange Strasse 52-56, D-32139 Spenge, GERMANY

Stadtarchiv, Maximilianstrasse 12, D-67346 Speyer, GERMANY

Stadtarchiv, D-03130 Spremberg, GERMANY

Stadtarchiv, Heimatmuseum, Auf dem Burghof 1, D-31832 Springe, GERMANY

Stadtarchiv, Johannisstrasse 1, D-21682 Stade, GERMANY

Stadtarchiv, D-31655 Stadthagen, GERMANY

Stadtarchiv, Hauptstrasse 10, Postfach 1680, D-82306 Starnberg, GERMANY *(Street address D-82319)*

Stadtarchiv, D-39418 Stassfurt, GERMANY

Kreisarchiv, Bernburger Strasse 12, D-39418 Stassfurt, GERMANY

Stadtarchiv, Emsdettener Strasse 40, Postfach 2480, D-48553 Steinfurt, GERMANY *(Street address D-48565)*

Stadtarchiv, Markt 1, D-39576 Stendal, GERMANY

Stadtarchiv, D-78333 Stockach, GERMANY

Stadtarchiv, Rathaus, Rathausstrasse 11-13, Postfach 1820, D-52205 Stolberg (Rheinland), GERMANY *(Street address D-52222)*

Stadtarchiv, Rathausstrasse 1, D-47638 Straelen, GERMANY

Strälen. See Straelen.

Stadtarchiv, Badenstrasse 13, D-18439 Stralsund, GERMANY

Stadtarchiv, Rathaus, Theresienplatz 20, Postfach 352, D-94303 Straubing, GERMANY *(Street address D-94315)*

Stadtarchiv, Silberburgstrasse 191, Postfach 106034, D-70049 Stuttgart, GERMANY *(Street address D-70178)*

Stadt- und Kreisarchiv, Strasse der Opfer des Faschismus 5, D-98527 Suhl, GERMANY

Stadtarchiv, Linden Strasse 26, Postfach 1240, D-27233 Suhlingen, GERMANY

Stadtarchiv, D-72172 Sulz am Neckar, GERMANY

Stadtarchiv, Buehlgasse 5, Postfach 1125, D-92229 Sulzbach-Rosenberg, GERMANY

Stadtarchiv, Postfach 1109, D-59831 Sundern, GERMANY

Stadtarchiv, Herrlichkeit 6, Postfach 1365, D-28847 Syke, GERMANY

Stadtarchiv, D-39590 Tangermuende, GERMANY

Tangermünde. See Tangermuende.

Kreisarchiv Main-Tauber-Kreis, Gartenstrasse 1, Postfach 1380, D-97933 Tauberbischofsheim, GERMANY *(Street address D-97941)*

Stadtarchiv, D-65232 Taunusstein, GERMANY

Stadtarchiv, Rathaus Binsfeld 4-6, Postfach 220, D-48284 Telgte, GERMANY *(Street address D-48291)*

Stadtarchiv, D-88069 Tettnang, GERMANY

Tiengen. See Waldshut.

Stadtarchiv, Rathaus, D-79822 Titisee-Neustadt

Stadtarchiv, D-84529 Tittmoning, GERMANY

Stadtarchiv, D-83646 Bad Toelz, GERMANY

Archiv der Stadt Toenning, Rathaus, D-23832 Toenning, GERMANY

Tölz. See (Bad) Toelz.

Tönning. See Toenning.

Stadtarchiv, D-04860 Torgau, GERMANY

Stadtarchiv, Stadtplatz 39, Postfach 1829, D-83278 Traunstein, GERMANY

Stadtarchiv, D-99830 Treffurt, GERMANY

Stadtarchiv, Weberbach 25, D-54290 Trier, GERMANY

Tübingen. See Tuebingen.

Stadtarchiv, Rathaus, Postfach 2540, D-72015 Tuebingen, GERMANY

Stadtarchiv, Alleenstrasse 10, D-78532 Tuttlingen, GERMANY

Landkreisarchiv, Koenigstrasse 55, Postfach 4453, D-78509 Tuttlingen, GERMANY *(Street address D-78532)*

Stadtarchiv, Am Markt 1, Postfach 1260, D-27234 Twistringen, GERMANY *(Street address D-27230)*

Überlingen. See Ueberlingen.

Stadtarchiv, Rathaus, D-88662 Ueberlingen (Bodensee), GERMANY

Stadtarchiv, D-29525 Uelzen, GERMANY

Landkreisarchiv, Veersser Strasse 53, D-29525 Uelzen, GERMANY

Stadtarchiv, Weinhof 12 (Schwoerhaus), D-89073 Ulm (Donau), GERMANY

Kreisarchiv Alb-Donau-Kreis, Olgastrasse 137, Postfach 2820, D-89018 Ulm (Donau), GERMANY *(Street address D-89073)*

Stadtarchiv, Hauptstrasse 9, D-35327 Ulrichstein, GERMANY

Ülzen. See Uelzen.

Stadtarchiv, Graf-Blumenthal-Strasse 15, D-53572 Unkel, GERMANY

Stadtarchiv, Rathausplatz, D-59423 Unna, GERMANY

Kreisarchiv, Friedrich-Ebert-Strasse 17, Postfach 1625, D-59406 Unna, GERMANY *(Street address D-59425)*

Stadtarchiv, D-61250 Usingen, GERMANY

Stadtarchiv, Muehlentor 6, D-37170 Uslar, GERMANY

Stadtarchiv, Spitalgasse 8, D-71665 Vaihingen (Enz), GERMANY

Stadtarchiv, Rathaus, D-26316 Varel, GERMANY

Stadtarchiv, Thomasstrasse 1, Zum Hardenberger Schloss 4, D-42551 Velbert, GERMANY

Stadtarchiv, D-27283 Verden (Aller), GERMANY

Landkreisarchiv, Bremer Strasse 4, Postfach 1509, D-27265 Verden (Aller), GERMANY *(Street address D-27283)*

Stadtarchiv, D-38690 Vienenburg, GERMANY

Stadtarchiv, Postfach 1380, D-68503 Viernheim, GERMANY

Viersen. See also Kempen.

Stadtarchiv, Rathaus, D-41747 Viersen, GERMANY

Stadtarchiv Villingen, Kanzleigasse 6, Postfach 1260, D-78002 Villingen-Schwenningen, GERMANY *(Street address D-78050)*

Stadtarchiv Schwenningen, Kronenstrasse 16, D-78054 Villingen-Schwenningen, GERMANY

Landkreisarchiv Schwarzwald-Baar, Kaiserring 2, D-78050 Villingen-Schwenningen, GERMANY

Stadtarchiv, Elsachstrasse 7, D-78147 Voehrenbach

Stadtarchiv, D-66333 Voelklingen, GERMANY

Stadtarchiv, Rathaus, Ulrich-Steinberger-Platz 12, D-85088 Vohburg an der Donau, GERMANY

Vöhrenbach. See Voehrenbach.

Stadtarchiv, Rathaus, D-97332 Volkach, GERMANY

Völklingen. See Voelklingen.

Stadtarchiv, Burgstrasse 14, D-48691 Vreden, GERMANY

Stadtarchiv, D-67157 Wachenheim (Weinstrasse), GERMANY

Stadtarchiv, Rathaus, Postfach 1740, D-71307 Waiblingen, GERMANY

Stadtarchiv, D-04736 Waldheim bei Doebeln (Sachsen), GERMANY

Stadtarchiv, Marktplatz 5, D-79183 Waldkirch (Breisgau), GERMANY

Stadtarchiv, Postfach 1420, D-88331 Bad Waldsee, GERMANY

Waldshut. See also Albbruck.

Stadtarchiv, Kaiser Strasse 28-32, D-79761 Waldshut-Tiengen, GERMANY

Stadtarchiv, Rathaus, Langestrasse 22, Postfach 1440, D-29654 Walsrode, GERMANY *(Street address D-29664)*

Stadtarchiv, Stadthalle, Jahnstrasse 21, D-88239 Wangen im Allgaeu, GERMANY

Landkreisarchiv Ravensburg, Marktplatz 5, D-88239 Wangen im Allgaeu, GERMANY

Stadtarchiv, Rathausstrasse, D-44649 Wanne-Eickel, GERMANY

Stadtarchiv, Sternstrasse 35, D-34414 Warburg, GERMANY

Stadtarchiv, Kesselstrasse 4, D-48231 Warendorf, GERMANY

Kreiszentralarchiv, Waldenburger Strasse 2, D-48231 Warendorf, GERMANY

Stadtarchiv, Dieplohstrasse 1, D-59581 Warstein, GERMANY

Stadtarchiv, Postfach 1680, D-83506 Wasserburg am Inn, GERMANY

Stadtarchiv, Rathausstrasse, D-44866 Bochum-Wattenscheid, GERMANY

Stadtarchiv, Kulturzentrum Hans Bauer, Pfarrplatz 4, D-92637 Weiden (Oberpfalz), GERMANY

Stadtarchiv, Postfach 9, D-97984 Weikersheim, GERMANY

Stadtarchiv, Schillerstrasse 1, D-79576 Weil am Rhein, GERMANY

Stadtarchiv, Rathaus, Postfach 1120, D-71255 Weil der Stadt, GERMANY

Stadtarchiv, Schlossplatz 1, Postfach 1420, D-35774 Weilburg, GERMANY

Stadtarchiv, Postfach 1154, D-73231 Weilheim an der Teck, GERMANY

Stadtarchiv, Admiral-Hipper-Strasse 20, D-82362 Weilheim (Oberbayern), GERMANY

Stadtarchiv, Rathaus, D-99423 Weimar, GERMANY

Stadtarchiv, Schuetzenstrasse 3/1, D-88250 Weingarten (Wuerttemberg), GERMANY

Stadtarchiv, Rathaus, D-69469 Weinheim an der Bergstrasse, GERMANY

Stadtarchiv, Am Markt 19, Postfach 27, D-96258 Weismain, GERMANY

Stadtarchiv, Jahnstrasse 2, Postfach 569, D-91774 Weissenburg in Bayern, GERMANY

Stadtarchiv, Grosse Burgstrasse 22, D-06667 Weissenfels, GERMANY

Stadtarchiv, D-86650 Wemding, GERMANY

Stadtarchiv, Goethestrasse 51, D-58791 Werdohl, GERMANY

Stadtarchiv, Rathaus, Hedwig-Dransfeld-Strasse 23, D-59457 Werl, GERMANY

Stadtarchiv, Postfach 1110, D-42904 Wermelskirchen, GERMANY

Historisches Stadtarchiv, Altes Amtshaus, Kirchhof
13, D-59368 Werne an der Lippe, GERMANY

Stadtarchiv, D-38855 Wernigerode, GERMANY

Stadtarchiv, D-97877 Wertheim, GERMANY

Stadtarchiv, D-46483 Wesel, GERMANY

Kreisarchiv, Reeser Landstrasse 31,
D-46483 Wesel, GERMANY

Stadtverwaltung, Rathaus, Am Markt 2,
D-26655 Westerstede, GERMANY

Stadtarchiv, Burgstrasse, Postfach 146,
D-58287 Wetter (Ruhr), GERMANY

Stadtarchiv, Rathaus, Herrengasse 17, Postfach 2120,
D-35531 Wetzlar, GERMANY
(Street address D-35578)

Wiedenbrück. See Rheda.

Wiedenbrueck. See Rheda.

Stadtarchiv, Im Rad 20, D-65187 Wiesbaden, GERMANY

Stadtarchiv, Hauptstrasse 25, D-73349 Wiesensteig,
GERMANY

Stadtarchiv, Postfach 1520, D-69156 Wiesloch,
GERMANY

Stadtarchiv, Am Markt 1, Postfach 1563,
D-34525 Bad Wildungen, GERMANY
(Street address D-34537; city government D-34535)

Wilhelm-Pieck-Stadt. See Guben.

Stadtarchiv, Rathausplatz 10, D-26382 Wilhelmshaven,
GERMANY

Stadtarchiv, Klosterhof 28, D-25554 Wilster, GERMANY

Stadtarchiv, Rathaus, Marktplatz 1,
D-74206 Bad Wimpfen, GERMANY

Stadtarchiv, Marktplatz 1, Postfach 260, D-91438
Bad Windsheim, GERMANY

Stadtarchiv, Postfach 1240, D-21412 Winsen (Luhe),
GERMANY

Landkreisarchiv Harburg, Rote-Kreuz-Strasse 6,
D-21423 Winsen (Luhe), GERMANY

Stadtarchiv, D-59955 Winterberg, GERMANY

Stadtarchiv, Hinter dem Rathaus, Vor dem Amtsgericht,
D-23966 Wismar, GERMANY

Stadtarchiv, Rathaus, Postfach 2280, D-58453 Witten,
GERMANY

Stadtarchiv, Schloss, D-06886 Lutherstadt Wittenberg,
GERMANY

Stadtarchiv, Rathaus, D-38304 Witzenhausen, GERMANY

Stadtarchiv, Rathaus, Zweigstrasse 1, Postfach 1663,
D-86819 Bad Woerishofen, GERMANY
(Street address D-86825)

Stadtarchiv, Rathaus, Hauptstrasse 41, D-77709 Wolfach,
GERMANY

Stadtarchiv, Marienplatz 1, Postfach 1460, D-82504
Wolfratshausen, GERMANY *(Street address D-82515)*

Stadtarchiv, Porsche Strasse 43c, Postfach 100944,
D-38440 Wolfsburg, GERMANY

Stadtarchiv, D-17438 Wolgast, GERMANY

Stadtarchiv, D-39326 Wolmirstedt, GERMANY

Wörishofen. See (Bad) Woerishofen.

Stadtarchiv, Raschi-Haus, Hintere Judengasse 6,
D-67547 Worms, GERMANY

Stadtarchiv, Wilhelmstrasse 189, D-42489 Wuelfrath,
GERMANY

Wülfrath. See Wuelfrath.

Stadtarchiv, Kaiserstrasse 26, Postfach 1160,

D-52135 Wuerselen, GERMANY

Stadtarchiv, Stadtentwaesserungsamt, Neubaustrasse 12,
D-97070 Wuerzburg, GERMANY

Stadtarchiv, D-95632 Wunsiedel, GERMANY

Stadtarchiv, Suedstrasse 1, D-31515 Wunstorf,
GERMANY

Stadtarchiv, Friedrich-Engels-Allee 89-91,
D-42285 Wuppertal-Barmen, GERMANY

Würselen. See Wuerselen.

Würzburg. See Wuerzburg.

Stadtarchiv, D-25938 Wyk auf Foehr, GERMANY

Stadtarchiv, Rathaus, Karthaus 2, Postfach 1164,
D-46509 Xanten, GERMANY

Stadtarchiv, D-06712 Zeitz (Elster), GERMANY

Zentrales Kreisarchiv, Museum Schloss Moritzburg,
Schlossstrasse 6, D-06712 Zeitz (Elster), GERMANY

Stadtarchiv, D-98544 Zella-Mehlis, GERMANY

Zellerfeld. See Clausthal.

Stadtarchiv, D-39261 Zerbst, GERMANY

Stadtarchiv, D-07937 Zeulenroda, GERMANY

Stadtarchiv, Rathaus, Fuerther Strasse 8, Postfach 1160,
D-90505 Zirndorf, GERMANY

Stadtarchiv, D-02763 Zittau, GERMANY

Stadtarchiv, Markt 21, D-53909 Zuelpich, GERMANY

Zülpich. See Zuelpich.

Zweibrücken. See Zweibruecken.

Stadtarchiv, Herzogstrasse 13, D-66482 Zweibruecken
(Pfalz), GERMANY

Stadtarchiv, Archivleiter, Lessingstrasse 1,
D-08058 Zwickau, GERMANY

Stadtarchiv, A-3300 Amstetten, Oesterreich, AUSTRIA, EUROPE

Stadtarchiv, A-8184 Anger, Oesterreich, AUSTRIA, EUROPE

Stadtarchiv, A-4082 Aschach, Oesterreich, AUSTRIA, EUROPE

Stadtarchiv, A-3361 Aschbach, Oesterreich, AUSTRIA, EUROPE

Stadtarchiv, A-2870 Aspang, Oesterreich, AUSTRIA, EUROPE

Stadtarchiv, A-2151 Asparn, Oesterreich, AUSTRIA, EUROPE

Bad Xxx. See under Xxx.

Stadtarchiv, A-2500 Baden bei Wien, Oesterreich, AUSTRIA, EUROPE

Stadtarchiv, Rathaus, Postfach 120, A-6700 Bludenz, Oesterreich, AUSTRIA, EUROPE

Stadtarchiv, A-5280 Braunau (Inn), Oesterreich, AUSTRIA, EUROPE

Stadtarchiv, Rathausstrasse 4, A-6900 Bregenz, Oesterreich, AUSTRIA, EUROPE

Stadtarchiv, A-2460 Bruck (Leitha), Oesterreich, AUSTRIA, EUROPE

Stadtarchiv, A-8600 Bruck (Mur), Oesterreich, AUSTRIA, EUROPE

Stadtarchiv, A-2345 Brunn am Gebirge, Oesterreich, AUSTRIA, EUROPE

Stadtarchiv, A-6850 Dornbirn, Oesterreich, AUSTRIA, EUROPE

Stadtarchiv, A-2265 Droessing, Oesterreich, AUSTRIA, EUROPE

Stadtarchiv, A-2095 Drosendorf, Oesterreich, AUSTRIA, EUROPE

Drössing. See Droessing.

Stadtarchiv, A-3601 Duernstein (Donau), Oesterreich, AUSTRIA, EUROPE

Dürnstein. See Duernstein.

Stadtarchiv, A-2490 Ebenfurth, Oesterreich, AUSTRIA, EUROPE

Stadtarchiv, A-4070 Eferding, Oesterreich, AUSTRIA, EUROPE

Stadtarchiv, A-3730 Eggenburg, Oesterreich, AUSTRIA, EUROPE

Stadtarchiv, A-7001 Eisenstadt, Oesterreich, AUSTRIA, EUROPE

Stadtarchiv, A-3644 Emmersdorf, Oesterreich, AUSTRIA, EUROPE

Stadtarchiv, A-4470 Enns, Oesterreich, AUSTRIA, EUROPE

Stadtarchiv, A-2162 Falkenstein, Oesterreich, AUSTRIA, EUROPE

Stadtarchiv, Palais Liechtenstein, A-6800 Feldkirch, Oesterreich, AUSTRIA, EUROPE

Stadtarchiv, A-4240 Freistadt, Oesterreich, AUSTRIA, EUROPE

Stadtarchiv, A-9360 Friesach, Oesterreich, AUSTRIA, EUROPE

Stadtarchiv, A-8280 Fuerstenfeld, Oesterreich, AUSTRIA, EUROPE

Fürstenfeld. See Fuerstenfeld.

Stadtarchiv, A-3511 Furth bei Krems, Oesterreich, AUSTRIA, EUROPE

Stadtarchiv, A-3334 Gaflenz, Oesterreich, AUSTRIA, EUROPE

Stadtarchiv, A-4210 Gallneukirchen, Oesterreich, AUSTRIA, EUROPE

Stadtarchiv, A-4713 Gallspach, Oesterreich, AUSTRIA, EUROPE

Stadtarchiv, A-3571 Gars am Kamp, Oesterreich, AUSTRIA, EUROPE

Stadtarchiv, A-3542 Gfoehl, Oesterreich, AUSTRIA, EUROPE

Gföhl. See Gfoehl.

Stadtarchiv, A-8200 Gleisdorf, Oesterreich, AUSTRIA, EUROPE

Stadtarchiv, A-3950 Gmuend (Niederoesterreich), Oesterreich, AUSTRIA, EUROPE

Gmünd. See Gmuend.

Stadtarchiv, A-4810 Gmuenden, Oesterreich, AUSTRIA, EUROPE

Stadtarchiv, A-5440 Golling, Oesterreich, AUSTRIA, EUROPE

Stadtarchiv, Hans-Sachs-Gasse 1, A-8010 Graz, Oesterreich, AUSTRIA, EUROPE

Stadtarchiv, A-4360 Grein (Donau), Oesterreich, AUSTRIA, EUROPE

Stadtarchiv, A-3264 Gresten, Oesterreich, AUSTRIA, EUROPE

Gröbming. See Groebming.

Stadtarchiv, A-8962 Groebming, Oesterreich, AUSTRIA, EUROPE

Stadtarchiv, A-2301 Gross-Enzersdorf, Oesterreich, AUSTRIA, EUROPE

Stadtarchiv, A-2812 Gross-Siegharts, Oesterreich, AUSTRIA, EUROPE

Stadtarchiv, A-3701 Grossweikersdorf, Oesterreich, AUSTRIA, EUROPE

Stadtarchiv, A-2352 Gumpoldskirchen, Oesterreich, AUSTRIA, EUROPE

Stadtarchiv, A-2770 Gutenstein, Niederoesterreich, Oesterreich, AUSTRIA, EUROPE

Stadtarchiv, A-3350 Haag, Niederoesterreich, Oesterreich, AUSTRIA, EUROPE

Stadtarchiv, A-4680 Haag am Hausruck, Oesterreich, AUSTRIA, EUROPE

Stadtarchiv, A-2410 Hainburg, Oesterreich, AUSTRIA, EUROPE

Stadtarchiv, A-4540 Bad Hall, Oesterreich, AUSTRIA, EUROPE

Stadtarchiv, A-6060 Solbad Hall (Tirol), Oesterreich, AUSTRIA, EUROPE

Stadtarchiv, Keltenmuseum, A-5400 Hallein, Oesterreich, AUSTRIA, EUROPE

Stadtarchiv, A-3130 Herzogenberg, Oesterreich, AUSTRIA, EUROPE

Stadtarchiv, A-2325 Himberg, Oesterreich, AUSTRIA, EUROPE

Stadtarchiv, A-5639 Bad Hofgastein, Oesterreich, AUSTRIA, EUROPE

Stadtarchiv, A-2273 Hohenau (March), Oesterreich, AUSTRIA, EUROPE

Stadtarchiv, A-3180 Hohenberg, Oesterreich, AUSTRIA, EUROPE

Stadtarchiv, A-2223 Hohenruppersdorf, Oesterreich, AUSTRIA, EUROPE

Stadtarchiv, A-2020 Hollabrunn, Oesterreich, AUSTRIA, EUROPE

Stadtarchiv, A-3343 Hollenstein, Oesterreich, AUSTRIA, EUROPE

Stadtarchiv, A-3580 Horn, Oesterreich, AUSTRIA, EUROPE

Stadtarchiv, A-8262 Ilz, Oesterreich, AUSTRIA, EUROPE

Stadtarchiv, Badgasse 2, A-6020 Innsbruck, Oesterreich, AUSTRIA, EUROPE

Stadtarchiv, A-4820 Bad Ischl, Oesterreich, AUSTRIA, EUROPE

Stadtarchiv, A-8750 Judenburg, Oesterreich, AUSTRIA, EUROPE

Stadtarchiv, A-8262 Kalsdorf bei Ilz, Oesterreich, AUSTRIA, EUROPE

Stadtarchiv, A-4292 Kefermarkt, Oesterreich, AUSTRIA, EUROPE

Stadtarchiv, A-4531 Kematen, Oesterreich, AUSTRIA, EUROPE

Stadtarchiv, A-4560 Kirchdorf (Krems), Oesterreich, AUSTRIA, EUROPE

Stadtarchiv, A-2860 Kirchschlag, Oesterreich, AUSTRIA, EUROPE

Stadtarchiv, A-6370 Kitzbuehel, Oesterreich, AUSTRIA, EUROPE

Kitzbühel. See Kitzbuehel.

Stadtarchiv, A-3400 Klosterneuburg, Oesterreich, AUSTRIA, EUROPE

Stadtarchiv, A-3433 Koenigstetten, Oesterreich, AUSTRIA, EUROPE

Königstetten. See Koenigstetten.

Stadtarchiv, A-2100 Korneuburg, Oesterreich, AUSTRIA, EUROPE

Stadtarchiv, Koernermarkt 13, A-3500 Krems (Donau), Oesterreich, AUSTRIA, EUROPE

Stadtarchiv, A-2851 Krumbach, Oesterreich, AUSTRIA, EUROPE

Stadtarchiv, A-5431 Kuchl, Oesterreich, AUSTRIA, EUROPE

Stadtarchiv, A-6330 Kufstein, Oesterreich, AUSTRIA, EUROPE

Stadtarchiv, A-2136 Laa (Thaya), Oesterreich, AUSTRIA, EUROPE

Stadtarchiv, A-3550 Langenlois, Oesterreich, AUSTRIA, EUROPE

Stadtarchiv, A-3921 Langschlag, Oesterreich, AUSTRIA, EUROPE

Stadtarchiv, A-2361 Laxenburg, Oesterreich, AUSTRIA, EUROPE

Stadtarchiv, A-3552 Lengenfeld, Oesterreich, AUSTRIA, EUROPE

Stadtarchiv, Kirchgasse 6, A-8700 Leoben, Oesterreich, AUSTRIA, EUROPE

Stadtarchiv, Rathaus, Hauptstrasse 1-5, Postfach 1000, A-4041 Linz, Oesterreich, AUSTRIA, EUROPE *(Street address A-4020)*

Stadtarchiv, A-3874 Litschau, Oesterreich, AUSTRIA, EUROPE

Stadtarchiv, A-7442 Lockenhaus, Oesterreich, AUSTRIA, EUROPE

Stadtarchiv, A-7361 Lutzmannsburg, Oesterreich, AUSTRIA, EUROPE

Stadtarchiv, A-2344 Mariz-Enzersdorf, Oesterreich, AUSTRIA, EUROPE

Stadtarchiv, A-7210 Mattersburg, Oesterreich, AUSTRIA, EUROPE

Stadtarchiv, A-5230 Mattighofen, Oesterreich, AUSTRIA, EUROPE

Stadtarchiv, A-3512 Mautern (Donau), Oesterreich, AUSTRIA, EUROPE

Stadtarchiv, A-2130 Mistelbach, Oesterreich, AUSTRIA, EUROPE

Mödling. See Moedling.

Stadtarchiv, A-2340 Moedling, Oesterreich, AUSTRIA, EUROPE

Stadtarchiv, A-8850 Murau, Oesterreich, AUSTRIA, EUROPE

Stadtarchiv, A-8480 Mureck, Oesterreich, AUSTRIA, EUROPE

Stadtarchiv, A-4120 Neufelden, Oesterreich, AUSTRIA, EUROPE

Stadtarchiv, A-4720 Neumarkt (Hausruck), Oesterreich, AUSTRIA, EUROPE

Stadtarchiv, A-5202 Neumarkt (Wallersee), Oesterreich, AUSTRIA, EUROPE

Stadtarchiv, A-3371 Neumarkt (Ybbs), Oesterreich, AUSTRIA, EUROPE

Stadtarchiv, A-2620 Neunkirchen, Oesterreich, AUSTRIA, EUROPE

Stadtarchiv, A-7100 Neusiedl am See, Oesterreich, AUSTRIA, EUROPE

Stadtarchiv, A-2004 Nieder-Fellabrunn, Oesterreich, AUSTRIA, EUROPE

Stadtarchiv, A-4100 Ottensheim, Oesterreich, AUSTRIA, EUROPE

Stadtarchiv, A-2380 Perchtoldsdorf, Oesterreich, AUSTRIA, EUROPE

Stadtarchiv, A-4320 Perg, Oesterreich, AUSTRIA, EUROPE

Stadtarchiv, A-3680 Persenbeug, Oesterreich, AUSTRIA, EUROPE

Pöchlarn. See Poechlarn.

Stadtarchiv, A-3380 Poechlarn, Oesterreich, AUSTRIA, EUROPE

Stadtarchiv, A-8225 Poellau, Oesterreich, AUSTRIA, EUROPE

Pöllau. See Poellau.

Stadtarchiv, A-2170 Poysdorf, Oesterreich, AUSTRIA, EUROPE

Stadtarchiv, A-3251 Purgstall (Erlauf), Oesterreich, AUSTRIA, EUROPE

Stadtarchiv, A-8490 Radkersburg, Oesterreich, AUSTRIA, EUROPE

Stadtarchiv, A-6240 Rattenberg, Oesterreich, AUSTRIA, EUROPE

Stadtarchiv, A-2651 Reichenau (Rax), Oesterreich, AUSTRIA, EUROPE

Stadtarchiv, A-2070 Retz, Oesterreich, AUSTRIA, EUROPE

Stadtarchiv, A-6600 Reutte, Oesterreich, AUSTRIA, EUROPE

Stadtarchiv, A-4910 Ried im Innkreis, Oesterreich, AUSTRIA, EUROPE

Stadtarchiv, A-4150 Rohrbach, Oberoesterreich, Oesterreich, AUSTRIA, EUROPE

Stadtarchiv, A-3602 Rossatz, Oesterreich, AUSTRIA, EUROPE

Stadtarchiv, Conradplatz 1, A-7071 Rust, Oesterreich, AUSTRIA, EUROPE

Stadtarchiv, A-5760 Saalfelden, Oesterreich, AUSTRIA, EUROPE

Stadtarchiv, Schloss, Museumsplatz 6, A-5020 Salzburg, Oesterreich, AUSTRIA, EUROPE

Stadtarchiv, A-5600 Sankt (=St.) Johann im Pongau, Oesterreich, AUSTRIA, EUROPE

Stadtarchiv, A-9462 Bad Sankt (=St.) Leonhard, Oesterreich, AUSTRIA, EUROPE

Stadtarchiv, A-3352 Sankt (=St.) Peter in der Au, Oesterreich, AUSTRIA, EUROPE

Stadtarchiv, Rathaus, A-3100 Sankt (=St.) Poelten, Oesterreich, AUSTRIA, EUROPE

Sankt (=St.) Pölten. See Sankt Poelten.

Stadtarchiv, A-4780 Schaerding, Oesterreich, AUSTRIA, EUROPE

Schärding. See Schaerding.

Stadtarchiv, A-4861 Schoerfling, Oesterreich, AUSTRIA, EUROPE

Schörfling. See Schoerfling.

Stadtarchiv, A-2641 Schottwien, Oesterreich, AUSTRIA, EUROPE

Stadtarchiv, A-8541 Schwanberg, Oesterreich, AUSTRIA, EUROPE

Stadtarchiv, A-2320 Schwechat, Oesterreich, AUSTRIA, EUROPE

Stadtarchiv, A-5201 Seekirchen, Oesterreich, AUSTRIA, EUROPE

Stadtarchiv, A-3541 Senftenberg, Oesterreich, AUSTRIA, EUROPE

Stadtarchiv, A-8510 Stainz, Oesterreich, AUSTRIA, EUROPE

Stadtarchiv, Stadtplatz 27, A-4400 Steyr, Oberoesterreich, Oesterreich, AUSTRIA, EUROPE

Stadtarchiv, A-4221 Steyregg, Oesterreich, AUSTRIA, EUROPE

Stadtarchiv, A-2000 Stockerau, Oesterreich, AUSTRIA, EUROPE

Stadtarchiv, A-5204 Strasswalchen, Oesterreich, AUSTRIA, EUROPE

Stadtarchiv, A-2153 Stronsdorf, Oesterreich, AUSTRIA, EUROPE

Stadtarchiv, A-5580 Tamsweg, Oesterreich, AUSTRIA, EUROPE

Stadtarchiv, A-5660 Taxenbach, Oesterreich, AUSTRIA, EUROPE

Stadtarchiv, A-4850 Timelkam, Oesterreich, AUSTRIA, EUROPE

Stadtarchiv, A-2514 Traiskirchen, Oesterreich, AUSTRIA, EUROPE

Stadtarchiv, A-3133 Traismauer, Oesterreich, AUSTRIA, EUROPE

Stadtarchiv, A-3430 Tulln, Oesterreich, AUSTRIA, EUROPE

Stadtarchiv, A-3363 Ulmerfeld, Oesterreich, AUSTRIA, EUROPE

Stadtarchiv, A-2242 Unterwaltersdorf, Oesterreich, AUSTRIA, EUROPE

Stadtarchiv, A-5261 Uttendorf, Oberoesterreich, Oesterreich, AUSTRIA, EUROPE

Vienna. See Wien.

Stadtarchiv, Widmannsgasse 38, A-9500 Villach, Oesterreich, AUSTRIA, EUROPE

Vöcklabruck. See Voecklabruck.

Stadtarchiv, A-4840 Voecklabruck, Oesterreich, AUSTRIA, EUROPE

Stadtarchiv, A-2540 Bad Voeslau, Oesterreich, AUSTRIA, EUROPE

Stadtarchiv, A-8250 Vorau, Oesterreich, AUSTRIA, EUROPE

Vöslau. See Bad Voeslau.

Stadtarchiv, Rathaus, A-3830 Waidhofen (Thaya), Oesterreich, AUSTRIA, EUROPE

Stadtarchiv, Oberer Stadtplatz 32, A-3340 Waidhofen (Ybbs), Oesterreich, AUSTRIA, EUROPE

Stadtarchiv, A-3610 Weissenkirchen, Oesterreich, AUSTRIA, EUROPE

Stadtarchiv, Rathaus, A-4601 Wels, Oesterreich, AUSTRIA, EUROPE

Stadtarchiv, A-5450 Werfen, Oesterreich, AUSTRIA, EUROPE

Stadtarchiv, A-3355 Weyer (Enns), Oesterreich, AUSTRIA, EUROPE

Wiener Stadt- und Landesarchiv, Magistratsabteilung 8, Felderstrasse 1, Rathaus, A-1010 Wien/Vienna, Oesterreich, AUSTRIA, EUROPE

Stadtarchiv, Petersgasse 2, A-2700 Wiener Neustadt, Oesterreich, AUSTRIA, EUROPE

Stadtarchiv, A-9400 Wolfsegg (Hausruck), Oesterreich, AUSTRIA, EUROPE

Stadtarchiv, A-2120 Wolkersdorf, Oesterreich, AUSTRIA, EUROPE

Stadtarchiv, A-3370 Ybbs (Donau), Oesterreich, AUSTRIA, EUROPE

Stadtarchiv, A-3341 Ybbsitz, Oesterreich, AUSTRIA, EUROPE

Stadtarchiv, A-5700 Zell am See, Oesterreich, AUSTRIA, EUROPE

Stadtarchiv, A-2225 Zistersdorf, Oesterreich, AUSTRIA, EUROPE

Stadtarchiv, A-3910 Zwettl, Oesterreich, AUSTRIA, EUROPE

MUNICIPAL ARCHIVES Switzerland (alphabetical by city, town, or village)

Stadtarchiv, Rathaus, CH-5000 Aarau, Schweiz,
SWITZERLAND

Stadtarchiv, Rathaus, CH-4663 Aarburg, Schweiz,
SWITZERLAND

Stadtarchiv, Berglischulhaus, CH-9320 Arbon, Schweiz,
SWITZERLAND

Stadtarchiv, Rathaus, CH-5400 Baden (Aargau), Schweiz,
SWITZERLAND

Stadtarchiv Basel-Stadt, Martinsgasse 2, CH-4000
Basel, Schweiz, SWITZERLAND

Stadtarchiv, Erlacherhof, Junkerngasse 47, CH-3003
Bern, Schweiz, SWITZERLAND

Bienne. See Biel.

Stadtarchiv, Marktgasse 17, CH-9220 Bischofszell,
Schweiz, SWITZERLAND

Stadtarchiv, Rathaus, CH-5620 Bremgarten, Schweiz,
SWITZERLAND

Stadtarchiv, Stadthaus, CH-5200 Brugg, Schweiz,
SWITZERLAND

Buergerarchiv, CH-8253 Diessenhofen, Schweiz,
SWITZERLAND

Stadtarchiv, Rathaus, CH-8500 Frauenfeld, Schweiz,
SWITZERLAND

Stadtarchiv, Rathaus, CH-8454 Kaiserstuhl, Schweiz,
SWITZERLAND

Stadtarchiv, Probsteigebaeude, CH-5313 Klingnau,
Schweiz, SWITZERLAND

Stadtarchiv, Rathaus, CH-4335 Laufenburg, Schweiz,
SWITZERLAND

Stadtarchiv, Rathaus, CH-5699 Lenzburg, Schweiz,
SWITZERLAND

Lucerne. See Luzern.

Stadtarchiv, Winkelriedstrasse 12a, CH-6000
Luzern/Lucerne, Schweiz, SWITZERLAND

Stadtarchiv, Rathaus, CH-5507 Mellingen, Schweiz,
SWITZERLAND

Stadtarchiv, Rathaus, CH-3280 Murten, Schweiz,
SWITZERLAND

Stadtarchiv, Stadthaus, CH-4600 Olten, Schweiz,
SWITZERLAND

Stadtarchiv der Ortsgemeinde Rapperswil, CH-8640
Rapperswil, Schweiz, SWITZERLAND

Stadtarchiv, Rathaus, CH-4310 Rheinfelden, Schweiz,
SWITZERLAND

Stadtarchiv, Vadiana, Notkerstrasse 22, CH-9000
Sankt (=St.) Gallen, Schweiz, SWITZERLAND

Stadtarchiv, Fronwagplatz 24, CH-8200 Schaffhausen,
Schweiz, SWITZERLAND

Buergerarchiv, CH-8266 Steckborn, Schweiz,
SWITZERLAND

Stadtarchiv, Rathaus, CH-8260 Stein am Rhein, Schweiz,
SWITZERLAND

Stadtarchiv, Stadthaus, Muehlestrasse 5, CH-8400
Winterthur, Schweiz, SWITZERLAND

Stadtarchiv, Rathaus, CH-4800 Zofingen, Schweiz,
SWITZERLAND

Stadtarchiv, Stadthausquai, CH-8001 Zuerich, Schweiz,
SWITZERLAND

Stadtarchiv, Rathaus, CH-6300 Zug, Schweiz,
SWITZERLAND

Zürich. See Zuerich.

CATHOLIC AND ORTHODOX

ARCHDIOCESES   Subordinate Dioceses
BAMBERG   Eichstaett, Speyer, Wuerzburg
COLOGNE   Aachen, Muenster, Osnabrueck, Limburg,Trier, Essen
FREIBURG   Mainz, Rottenburg-Stuttgart
MUNICH-FREISING   Augsburg, Passau, Regensburg
PADERBORN   Hildesheim, Fulda, Berlin

GERMANY.

Roemisch-katholische Kirche in Deutschland
Sekretariat der Deutschen Bischofskonferenz
Kaiserstrasse 163
D-53113 Bonn
GERMANY
(headquarters of Roman Catholic church hierarchy in
former West Germany)

Roemisch-katholische Kirchenprovinz
Franzoesische Strasse 34
D-10117 Berlin
GERMANY
(headquarters of Roman Catholic church in former German
Democratic Republic (East Germany); district includes
bishoprics of Berlin and Dresden-Meissen)

Katholisches Bistum der Alt-Katholiken in Deutschland
Gregor-Mendel-Strasse 28
D-53115 Bonn
GERMANY
(headquarters of the small "Old Catholic" conservative
church in Federal Republic of Germany (West Germany),
founded 1870 protesting papal infallibility)

Altkatholische Kirche
Georgstrasse 7
D-13129 Blankenburg
GERMANY
(headquarters of the small "Old Catholic" conservative
church in the former German Democratic Republic (East
Germany) founded 1870 protesting doctrine of papal
infallibility)

Katholisches Kirchenbuchamt des Verbands der Dioezesen
    Deutschlands Muenchen
Dachauer Strasse 50/II Rgb.
D-80335 Muenchen
GERMANY
(general headquarters of Catholic church book offices in
Germany; Munich)

Militaerkirchenbuchamt
Adenauerallee 115
Postfach 3099
D-53113 Bonn
GERMANY
(Catholic chaplaincy books of German military personnel
and their families)

Kirchliches Archiv des Katholischen Militaerbischofs
Kaiserstrasse 14
D-53113 Bonn
GERMANY
(church archive of the Catholic military bishop)

Griechisch-Orthodoxe Metropolie von Deutschland
Niebuhrstrasse 61
D-53113 Bonn
GERMANY
(headquarters of Greek Orthodox church in Germany)

Archiv des Deutschen Caritasverbands (DCV)
Karlstrasse 40
D-79104 Freiburg im Breisgau
GERMANY
(documents on Cahenslyism, German Catholic emigration
to the United States in general, and the *St. Raphaelsverein*
group which assisted immigrants upon their arrival)

Raphaels-Werk e.V.
Adenauerallee 41
D-20097 Hamburg
GERMANY
(St. Raphael's Society headquarters; all its records were
destroyed in the bombing of Hamburg in World War II)

Arbeitsgemeinschaft ostdeutscher Familienforscher e.V.
Kirchenbuchauskunftstelle
Am Muehlenhof
D-26180 Rastede
GERMANY
(information clearing house on location of German-
language church books of communities in eastern areas,
such as present-day Poland, Czech Republic, and Russia)

ALSACE.

Archives de l'Évêché de Strasbourg
16, rue Brûlée
F-67081 Strasbourg
FRANCE
(diocesan archive for diocese of Strasbourg/Strassburg; but
all non-current parish baptismal, marriage, and death
records are at the pertinent *state* archive)

ALSACE-LORRAINE. See ALSACE and LORRAINE.

EUROPEAN RELIGIOUS ARCHIVES: CATHOLIC

AUSTRIA.

Stiftsarchiv
A-8911 Admont
Oesterreich/AUSTRIA
EUROPE
(abbey archive for Admont)

Stiftsarchiv
A-3591 Altenburg (Bezirk Horn)
Oesterreich/AUSTRIA
EUROPE
(abbey archive for Altenburg)

Dioezesanarchiv
St. Rochusstrasse 21
Fach 165
A-7001 Eisenstadt
Oesterreich/AUSTRIA
EUROPE
(diocesan archive for Eisenstadt and the Burgenland)

Bistum Feldkirch
Archiv der Dioezese
Bahnhofstrasse 13
A-6800 Feldkirch
Oesterreich/AUSTRIA
EUROPE
(diocesan archive for diocese of Feldkirch; parish vital registers of diocese from 1839)

Stiftsarchiv
A-6414 Fiecht bei Obermieming
Oesterreich/AUSTRIA
EUROPE
(abbey archive for Fiecht; parish vital registers of Tirol from 1921)

Stiftsarchiv
A-3511 Goettweig Post Furth
Oesterreich/AUSTRIA
EUROPE
(abbey archive for Goettweig/Göttweig)

Bistum Graz-Seckau
Dioezesanarchiv
Bischofsplatz 4
A-8010 Graz
Oesterreich/AUSTRIA
EUROPE
(diocesan archive for diocese of Graz)

Gurk. See Klagenfurt.

Stiftsarchiv
A-2532 Heiligenkreuz bei Baden
Oesterreich/AUSTRIA
EUROPE
(abbey archive for Heiligenkreuz in Lower Austria (Niederösterreich))

Bistum Innsbruck
Dioezesanarchiv
Domplatz 6
Postfach 582
A-6021 Innsbruck
Oesterreich/AUSTRIA
EUROPE
(diocesan archive for diocese of Innsbruck)

Provinzialarchiv der Nordtiroler Kapuziner
Kaiserjaegerstrasse 6
A-6020 Innsbruck
Oesterreich/AUSTRIA
EUROPE
(archive of the North Tyrolean Capuchins in Innsbruck)

Bistum Gurk, Archiv der Dioezese
Gurker Fuerstbischoefliches Palais
Mariannengasse 6
A-9020 Klagenfurt
Oesterreich/AUSTRIA
EUROPE
(diocesan archive for diocese of Klagenfurt; parish vital registers of Carinthia (Kärnten) from 1840)

Stiftsarchiv
A-3400 Klosterneuburg
Oesterreich/AUSTRIA
EUROPE
(abbey archive for Klosterneuburg in Lower Austria (Niederösterreich))

Stiftsarchiv
A-4550 Kremsmuenster
Oesterreich/AUSTRIA
EUROPE
(abbey archive for Kremsmuenster/Kremsmünster in Upper Austria (Oberösterreich))

Stiftsarchiv
A-4650 Lambach
Oesterreich/AUSTRIA
EUROPE
(abbey archive for Lambach in Upper Austria (Oberösterreich))

Stiftsarchiv
A-3180 Lilienfeld
Oesterreich/AUSTRIA
EUROPE
(abbey archive for Lilienfeld in Lower Austria (Niederösterreich))

Bistum Linz, Ordinariatsarchiv
Harrachstrasse 7
A-4020 Linz an der Donau
Oesterreich/AUSTRIA
EUROPE
(diocesan archive for diocese of Linz; parish vital registers of diocese from 1819)

Stiftsarchiv
A-3390 Melk
Oesterreich/AUSTRIA
EUROPE
(abbey archive for Melk in Lower Austria
(Niederösterreich))

Stiftsarchiv
A-4490 St. Florian bei Linz
Oesterreich/AUSTRIA
EUROPE
(abbey archive for St. Florian in Upper Austria
(Oberösterreich))

Stiftsarchiv
A-8813 St. Lambrecht
Oesterreich/AUSTRIA
EUROPE
(abbey archive for St. Lambrecht in Styria (Steiermark))

Dioezesanarchiv
Domplatz 1
A-3100 St. Poelten
Oesterreich/AUSTRIA
EUROPE
(diocesan archive for diocese of St. Poelten/Sankt Pölten;
parish vital registers for diocese from 1785)

Erzbistum Salzburg, Konsistorialarchiv
Kapitelplatz 2
A-5010 Salzburg
Oesterreich/AUSTRIA
EUROPE
(archdiocesan archive for archdiocese of Salzburg; parish
vital registers for diocese from 1816 including Badgastein,
Fusch, Goldegg, Kleinarl, Maria Alm, Pfarrwenden, St.
Georgen im Pinzgau, St. Johann im Pongau, St. Martin am
Tennengebirge, St. Veit im Pongau, Taxenbach,
Viehhofen, Wagrain, Weissbach, and Werfen)

Erzabtei St. Peter
Archiv St. Peter
Postfach 113
A-5010 Salzburg
Oesterreich/AUSTRIA
EUROPE
(archive of the archabbey of St. Peter)

Stiftsarchiv
A-4553 Schlierbach bei Kirchdorf
Oesterreich/AUSTRIA
EUROPE
(abbey archive for Kirchdorf in Upper Austria
(Oberösterreich))

Stiftsarchiv
A-8732 Seckau
Oesterreich/AUSTRIA
EUROPE
(abbey archive for Seckau near Graz; parish vital registers
from 1835)

Stiftsarchiv
A-3353 Seitenstetten bei St. Peter in der Au
Oesterreich/AUSTRIA
EUROPE
(abbey archive for Seitenstetten)

Stiftsarchiv
A-6422 Stams
Oesterreich/AUSTRIA
EUROPE
(abbey archive for Stams in Tirol)

*Vienna. See *Wien.

Stiftsarchiv
A-8250 Vorau
Oesterreich/AUSTRIA
EUROPE
(abbey archive for Vorau in Styria (Steyer))

Erzbistum Wien, Dioezesanarchiv
Wollzeile 2
A-1010 Wien/Vienna
Oesterreich/AUSTRIA
EUROPE
(archdiocesan archive for archdiocese of Vienna (Wien);
parish vital registers from 1797 for Lower Austria
(Niederösterreich) and Districts XX through XXVI of
Vienna (Wien); from 1812 for Districts I through IXX of
Vienna (Wien); deaths from 1648)

Alt-Katholische Kirche Oesterreichs
Schottenring 17
A-1010 Wien/Vienna
Oesterreich/AUSTRIA
EUROPE
(headquarters of "Old Catholic" conservative minority
Catholic church body in Austria)

Alt-Katholische Kirchengemeinde Wien-Innen
Riemergasse 1
A-1010 Wien/Vienna
Oesterreich/AUSTRIA
EUROPE
("Old Catholic" church parish of Vienna)

Stiftsarchiv
A-4073 Wilhering
Oesterreich/AUSTRIA
EUROPE
(abbey archive for Wilhering in
Upper Austria (Oberösterreich))

Stift Wilten, Archiv
Klostergasse 7
A-6020 Wilten (Tirol)
Oesterreich/AUSTRIA
EUROPE
(abbey archive for Wilten near Innsbruck in Tirol)

EUROPEAN RELIGIOUS ARCHIVES: CATHOLIC

BADEN.

Badisches Generallandesarchiv
Noerdliche Hilda-Promenade 2
D-77133 Karlsruhe
GERMANY
(has church book duplicates for communities in Baden
1810-1869)

Erzbistumsarchiv
Herrenstrasse 35, Eingang Schoferstrasse
D-79098 Freiburg im Breisgau
GERMANY
(archdiocesan archive for archdiocese of Freiburg)

BAVARIA.

Bischoefliches Ordinariat
Archiv des Bistums Augsburg
Hafnerberg 2/II
D-86152 Augsburg
GERMANY
(diocesan archive for diocese of Augsburg; has ca. 500
parish vital registers and family books, for over half of the
parishes in the diocese)

Erzbistumsarchiv
Domplatz 5
D-96049 Bamberg
GERMANY
(archdiocesan archive for archdiocese of Bamberg; has
many parish vital registers for diocese of Bamberg)

Bischoefliches Ordinariatsarchiv
Luitpoldstrasse 2
Postfach 1362
D-85067 Eichstaett
GERMANY
(diocesan archive for diocese of Eichstaett/Eichstätt)

Erzbischoefliches Ordinariatsarchiv Muenchen und
    Freising
Matrikelamt
Karmeliterstrasse 1 (Eingang Pacellistrasse)
D-80333 Muenchen/Munich
GERMANY
(archdiocesan archive and parish vital register office for
archdiocese of Munich and Freising)

Erzbischoefliches Matrikelamt
Rochusstrasse 5
D-80333 Muenchen/Munich
GERMANY
(parish vital register branch of the archdiocesan archive of
Munich and Freising; covers Munich area up to 1876)

Archiv des Bistums Passau
Luragogasse 4
D-94032 Passau
GERMANY
(diocesan archive for diocese of Passau; many parish vital
registers)

Bischoefliches Zentralarchiv
St. Petersweg 11-13
Postfach 110228
D-93015 Regensburg *(Street address D-93047)*
GERMANY
(diocesan archive for diocese of Regensburg; parish vital
registers for all of diocese to 1876; also Catholic church
books of former eastern areas)

Bischoefliches Ordinariatsarchiv
Domerschule 2
D-97070 Wuerzburg *(located Am Bruderhof 1)*
GERMANY
(diocesan archive for diocese of Wuerzburg/Würzburg)

BERLIN.

Dioezesanarchiv
Goetzstrasse 65
D-12099 Berlin
GERMANY
(diocesan archive for diocese of Berlin)

Katholisches Dompfarramt St. Hedwig
Hinter der Katholischen Kirche 3
D-10117 Berlin
GERMANY
(Catholic cathedral parish, in East Berlin)

BOEHMEN. (BOHEMIA.) See CZECH REPUBLIC.

BOHEMIA. See CZECH REPUBLIC.

BÖHMEN. (BOHEMIA.) See CZECH REPUBLIC.

BRAUNSCHWEIG. See LOWER SAXONY.

BRUNSWICK. See LOWER SAXONY.

CZECH REPUBLIC.
(Note: Most pre-1870 Czech parish vital registers are now
deposited at regional state archives rather than diocesan
archives)

Bischoefliches Zentralarchiv
St. Petersweg 11-13
Postfach 110228
D-93015 Regensburg
GERMANY *(Street address D-93047)*
(diocesan archive for diocese of Regensburg, including
duplicates of parish vital registers for western Bohemia for
1780-1820)

Katedrála římsko-katolické
97600 Banská Bystrica
CZECH REPUBLIC
(diocesan archive for diocese of Neusohl, now Banská
Bystrica)

Katedrála římsko-katolické
Brno
CZECH REPUBLIC
(diocesan archive for diocese of Bruenn/Brünn, now Brno)

Katedrála římsko-katolické
České Budějovice
CZECH REPUBLIC
(diocesan archive for diocese of Budweis, now České
Budějovice)

Katedrála římsko-katolické
Hradec Králové
CZECH REPUBLIC
(diocesan archive for diocese ofKoeniggraetz/Königgrätz,
now Hradec Králové)

Katedrála římsko-katolické
Košicė
CZECH REPUBLIC
(diocesan archive for diocese of Kaschau, now Košicė)

Katedrála římsko-katolické
Litoměřice
CZECH REPUBLIC
(diocesan archive for diocese of Leitmeritz, now
Litoměřice)

Katedrála římsko-katolické
94900 Nitra
CZECH REPUBLIC
(diocesan archive for diocese of Neutra, now Nitra)

Katedrála římsko-katolické
Olomouc
CZECH REPUBLIC
(diocesan archive for diocese of Olmuetz/Olmütz, now
Olomouc)

Katedrála římsko-katolické
Praha
CZECH REPUBLIC
(diocesan archive for diocese of Prag (English: Prague),
now Praha)

Katedrála římsko-katolické
08000 Prešov
CZECH REPUBLIC
(diocesan archive for diocese of Preschau (Hungarian:
Eperjes), now Prešov)

Katedrála římsko-katolické
Rožnavá
CZECH REPUBLIC
(diocesan archive for diocese of Rosenau, now Rožnavá)

Katedrála římsko-katolické
Spišská
CZECH REPUBLIC
(diocesan archive for diocese of Szepes, now Spišská)

EAST PRUSSIA. See also PRUSSIA.

Geheimes Staatsarchiv
Archivstrasse 12-14
D-14195 Berlin
GERMANY
(state archive holding some Catholic parish vital registers
from East Prussia)

Bischoefliches Zentralarchiv
St. Petersweg 11-13
Postfach 110228
D-93015 Regensburg *(Street address D-93047)*
GERMANY
(repository for some Catholic parish vital registers from
eastern areas, including Berent, Briesen, Danziger
Hoehe/Höhe, Dirschau, Graudenz, Karthaus, Konitz,
Löbau/Loebau, Marienburg, Marienwerder, Neustadt,
Preussisch Stargard, Putzig, Rosenberg, Schlochau,
Strasburg, Stuhm, Thorn, and Tuchel, possibly also other
places in West Prussia, until 1 January 1978 formerly held
in Muenchen/Munich)

EASTERN GERMANY. (Areas no longer German)

Bischoefliches Zentralarchiv
St. Petersweg 11-13
Postfach 110228
D-93015 Regensburg *(Street address D-93047)*
GERMANY
(some Catholic parish vital registers from Posen, West
Prussia, and East Prussia)

Saechsisches Staatsarchiv Leipzig
Abteilung Deutsche Zentralstelle fuer Genealogie
Schongauerstrasse 1
D-04109 Leipzig-Paunsdorf
GERMANY
(some parish vital registers for eastern Germany, mostly
pre-1820; held here since 24 July 1995)

ESTONIA. See also RUSSIA.

Eesti Riigi Keskariiv
ulica Manezi 4
Tallinn
ESTONIA
(parish registers to 1834; later registers are now at local
district office (ZAGS))

FRANCE. See ALSACE and LORRAINE.

HAMBURG.
South of Elbe River, diocese of Hildesheim
(see LOWER SAXONY).
North of Elbe River, diocese of Osnabrück/Osnabrueck
(see LOWER SAXONY).

HANNOVER.
See LOWER SAXONY, OLDENBURG, WESTPHALIA.

EUROPEAN RELIGIOUS ARCHIVES: CATHOLIC

HESSEN.

Staatsarchiv fuer Hessen-Darmstadt
Karolinenplatz 3
D-64289 Darmstadt
GERMANY
(state archive for Hessen-Darmstadt; has church book
duplicates from 1818)

Bischoefliches Generalvikariat
Paulustor 5
Postfach 147
D-36001 Fulda
GERMANY
(diocesan headquarters for diocese of Fulda)

Bistumsarchiv
Rossmarkt 4
D-65549 Limburg/Lahn
GERMANY
(diocesan archive for diocese of Limburg; parish vital
registers and some civil registers which were kept by
priests; has records of Frankfurt cathedral, Höchst/Hoechst,
and Oberursel, among others)

Erzbistumsarchiv
Kirchenbuchabteilung
Domplatz 3
Postfach 1480
D-33044 Paderborn
GERMANY
(archdiocesan archive for the archdiocese of Paderborn; has
almost all parish vital registers of archdiocese before 1874)

Katholische Kirchenbuchstelle
Buergistrasse 28
D-34125 Kassel
GERMANY
(Catholic parish vital register office for city of Kassel)

HOLLAND.

Allgemeen Rijksarchief
7 Bleijenburg
NL-2500 's Gravenhage
Nederland/NETHERLANDS
(national archive of Holland; most Netherlands records
after 1811, including some Catholic parish vital registers)

Rijksarchief in Gelderland
Markt Straat 1
NL- Arnhem
Nederland/NETHERLANDS
(state archive of Netherlands for Gelderland; has parish
registers of Duiven, Groessen, Huissen, Hulhuizen, Leuth,
Lobith, Oud Sevenaer, and Zevenaar)

HUNGARY.

Magyar Országos Levéltár
Bécsikapu-tér 4
H-1014 Budapest 1
HUNGARY
(Hungarian national archive; has microfilms of all parish
vital registers to 1895, but only books to 1867 are open,
with church permission)

Ferences Levéltár
II Martirok ut 23
H-1024 Budapest
HUNGARY
(Hungarian Catholic church headquarters)

LATVIA.

Latvijas PSR
Centràlais Valsta vèstures arhívs
ulica Skjunju 11
Riga
LATVIA
(parish registers to 1834; later registers are now at local
district office (ZAGS))

LIPPE. See WESTPHALIA.

LITHUANIA.

Lietuvos TSR Centrinis Valsybinis Istorijos Archyvas
ulica Vrublevskogo 6
Vilna
LITHUANIA
(parish registers to 1834 except for Vilnius city; later
registers are now at local district office (ZAGS))

Zapisi Aktev Grazhdanskogo Sostoninia
Vilna
LITHUANIA
(parish registers for Vilnius city)

LORRAINE.

Archives de l'Évêché de Metz
F-57000 Metz
FRANCE
(diocesan archive for the diocese of Metz)

LOWER SAXONY.
See also OLDENBURG and WESTPHALIA.

Bistumsarchiv
Pfaffenstieg 2
D-31134 Hildesheim
GERMANY
(diocesan archive for the diocese of Hildesheim)

Kirchenbucharchiv der Dioezese Hildesheim
Postfach 100263
D-31102 Hildesheim
GERMANY
(has Catholic church books of the Duchy of
Braunschweig/Brunswick from the beginnings ca.
1750-1800 to ca. 1850)

Dioezesanarchiv des Bistums Osnabrueck
Bischoefliches Generalvikariat
Grosse Domfreiheit 10
D-49074 Osnabrueck
GERMANY
(diocesan archive for the diocese of
Osnabrück/Osnabrueck)

LUXEMBOURG.

Bistumsarchiv
4, rue Genistre
L- Luxembourg
Luxembourg
(diocesan archive for the diocese of Luxembourg)

MAEHREN. (MORAVIA.) See CZECH REPUBLIC.

MÄHREN. (MORAVIA.) See CZECH REPUBLIC.

MECKLENBURG.

Bischoefliches Amt Schwerin
Lankower Strasse 14/16
D-19057 Schwerin
GERMANY

MORAVIA. See CZECH REPUBLIC.

NETHERLANDS. See HOLLAND.

NORDRHEIN-WESTFALEN. See NORTH RHINE-
WESTPHALIA.

NORTH RHINE-WESTPHALIA. See RHINELAND,
WESTPHALIA.

OLDENBURG.

Bischoefliches Offizialat
Archivstrasse
Bahnhofstrasse
D-49377 Vechta
GERMANY
(branch of diocesan archive of Muenster/Münster covering
the region of Oldenburg; has a number of parish vital
registers from about 1832)

PALATINATE.

Archiv des Bistums Speyer
Kleine Pfaffengasse 16-18
Postfach 1160
D-67321 Speyer/Rhein *(Street address D-67346)*
GERMANY
(diocesan archive for the diocese of Speyer; has microfilms
of Catholic parish vital registers for the diocese)

Bistumsarchiv
Jesuitenstrasse 13 b
Postfach 1340
D-54203 Trier
GERMANY
(diocesan archive for the diocese of Trier; has some
Catholic parish vital registers)

POLAND. See also POSEN, SILESIA, etc.

Sekretariat Prymasa Polski
ulica Miodowa 17
PL-00246 Warszawa/Warsaw
Polska/POLAND
(Catholic church headquarters for Poland)

Archiwum Diecezji Chelmno
Plac Katedralny
PL-83130 Pelplin pow. Tczew
Polska/POLAND
(diocesan archive for the diocese of Kulm, now Chelmno)

Archiwum Diecezji
PL-Gdańsk
Polska/POLAND
(diocesan archive for the diocese of Danzig, now Gdańsk)

Archiwum Archidiecezalne
PL-62200 Gniezno-Katedra
Polska/POLAND
(diocesan archive for the diocese of Gnesen, now Gniezno)

Archiwum Diecezji
PL- Gorzów
Polska/POLAND
(diocesan archive for the diocese of Landsberg, now
Gorzów)

Archiwum Diecezji
PL- Olsztyn
Polska/POLAND
(diocesan archive for the diocese of Allenstein, now
Olsztyn)

Archiwum Diecezji
PL- Opole
Polska/POLAND
(diocesan archive for the diocese of Oppeln, now Opole)

Archiwum Diecezjalne
pl. Katedralny 4A
PL-27700 Przemyśl
Polska/POLAND
(diocesan archive for the diocese of Przemyśl, Galicia)

Archiwum Diecezji
PL- Piła
Polska/POLAND
(diocesan archive for the diocese of
Schneidemuehl/Schneidemühl, now Piła)

Archiwum Diecezji
PL- Poznań
Polska/POLAND
(diocesan archive for the diocese of Posen, now Poznań)

Archiwum Diecezji
PL- Warszawa
Polska/POLAND
(diocesan archive for the diocese of Warsaw (German:
Warschau), now Warszawa)

Archiwum Diecezji
PL- Włocławek
Polska/POLAND
(diocesan archive for the diocese of Leslau, now
Włocławek)

Archiwum Diecezji
ulica Kanonia 12
PL-50328 Włocław
Polska/POLAND
(diocesan archive for the diocese of Breslau, now
Wrocław)

Katolicki Universytet Lubelski
Zakład Duszpasterstwa i Migracji Polonijnej
Alejc Racławickie 14
PL-20950 Lublin
Polska/POLAND
(institute at the Catholic university of Lublin compiling a
historical and geographical directory of Polish parishes in
the United States and Canada)

POMERANIA. See under POLAND.

POMMERN. (POMERANIA.) See under POLAND.

POSEN. See also POLAND.
(Note: There is some overlap of Posen with West Prussia
owing to border changes. Most places now have Polish
names; German is listed here.)

Bischoefliches Zentralarchiv
St. Petersweg 11-13
Postfach 110228
D-93015 Regensburg *(Street address D-93047)*
GERMANY
(repository of Catholic parish vital registers for eastern
areas, including Posen; has registers for Bromberg,
Culm/Kulm, Leipe, Rippin, Stargard, Thorn, and Wirsitz)

PREUSSEN. See PRUSSIA.

PRUSSIA.
Here, EAST PRUSSIA and WEST PRUSSIA only!

*Note: Prussia in the 19th century encompassed most of
northern Germany and even Hohenzollern in southern
Germany. There is some overlap between West Prussia and
Posen. Most places now have Polish names; German is
listed here.*

Bischoefliches Zentralarchiv
St. Petersweg 11-13
Postfach 110228
D-93015 Regensburg *(Street address D-93047)*
GERMANY
(repository of Catholic parish vital registers for eastern
areas, including East Prussia and West Prussia)

RHINELAND.
See also PALATINATE and WESTPHALIA.

Bischoefliches Dioezesanarchiv Aachen
Klosterplatz 7
Postfach 210
D-52003 Aachen
GERMANY
(diocesan archive for diocese of Aachen/Aix-la-Chappelle)

Domarchiv
Domhof 6
D-52062 Aachen
GERMANY
(cathedral archive for Aachen/Aix-la-Chapelle)

Bistumsarchiv und Muensterarchiv
Zwoelfling 16
D-45127 Essen
GERMANY
(diocesan archive for diocese of Essen)

Historisches Archiv des Erzbistums Koeln
Gereonstrasse 2-4
D-50670 Koeln/Cologne
GERMANY
(archdiocesan archive for the archdiocese of Cologne)

Bistumsarchiv
Grebenstrasse 8-12
Postfach 1160
D-67321 Mainz
GERMANY
(diocesan archive for diocese of Mainz; note that church
books for Frankfurt/Main and vicinity are in the diocesan
archive in Limburg; see under HESSEN)

RUSSIA.

Central State Historical Archives
Naberežnaya Krasnogo Flota 4
St. Petersburg
RUSSIA
(national historical archive for the former Soviet Union;
has copies of records of all churches in Russia, probably
since 1722)

Archiwum Główne Akt Dawnych
ulica Długa 7
PL-00263 Warszawa/Warsaw
Polska/POLAND
(Polish historical archive for older records; has some
Catholic parish vital registers prior to 1850 for formerly
Polish areas now in Russia)

Archiwum Zabuzańskie
Nowy Šwiat 18/20
PL- Warszawa/Warsaw
Polska/POLAND
(Polish historical archive; has some Catholic parish vital
registers after 1850 for formerly Polish areas now in
Russia)

Regional Government Archivist
Kutyakova St. Building 15
410710 Saratov
RUSSIA
(many Catholic parish register transcripts for German
colonies in former Soviet Union)

SAARLAND.

Archiv des Bistums Speyer
Kleine Pfaffengasse 16
Postfach 1160
D-67321 Speyer
GERMANY
(diocesan archive for the diocese of Speyer, including part
of the Saarland)

Bistumsarchiv
Jesuitenstrasse 13 b
Postfach 1340
D-54203 Trier
GERMANY
(diocesan archive for the diocese of Trier, including part of
the Saarland)

SAXONY.

Bistumsarchiv
Domplatz 7
D-01662 Meissen/Sachsen
GERMANY
(diocesan archive for diocese of Meissen)

Archivverwaltung des Domstiftes und des Bischoeflichen
    Ordinariats Meissen
Bei der Peterskirche 6
D-02826 Goerlitz/Neisse
GERMANY
(archive administration for diocese of Meissen and former
bishopric of Meissen)

Erzbistumsarchiv
Domplatz 3
Postfach 1480
D-33044 Paderborn
GERMANY
(archdiocesan archive for the archdiocese of Paderborn; has
Catholic parish vital registers prior to 1874 for the northern
parts of Saxony not in the diocese of Meissen)

Archiv des Domstifts St. Petri
An der Petrikirche 6
D-02625 Bautzen
GERMANY
(cathedral abbey archive in Bautzen)

SCHLESIEN. See SILESIA.

SCHLESWIG-HOLSTEIN.

Bistumsarchiv des Bistums Osnabrueck
Bischoefliches Generalvikariat
Grosse Domfreiheit 10
D-49074 Osnabrueck
GERMANY
(diocesan archive for the diocese of
Osnabrück/Osnabrueck, including all of
Schleswig-Holstein)

SCHWEIZ. See SWITZERLAND.

SILESIA.
See also EASTERN GERMANY and POLAND.

Bistumsarchiv
Biesnitzer Strasse 94
D-02826 Goerlitz/Neisse
GERMANY
(regional branch of Breslau diocesan archive)

former SOVIET UNION. See RUSSIA, ESTONIA, etc.

SUDETENLAND. See CZECH REPUBLIC.

SWITZERLAND.

Stiftsarchiv Beromuenster
CH-6215 Beromuenster
Schweiz/SWITZERLAND
(abbey archive of Beromuenster/Beromünster)

Bischoefliches Archiv Chur
Bischoefliches Schloss
Hof 19
CH-7000 Chur
Schweiz/SWITZERLAND
(diocesan archive for the diocese of Chur)

Stiftsarchiv Disentis
Kloster
CH-7980 Disentis
Schweiz/SWITZERLAND
(abbey archive of Disentis)

Stiftsarchiv Einsiedeln
Kloster
CH-8840 Einsiedeln
Schweiz/SWITZERLAND
(abbey archive of Einsiedeln)

Stiftsarchiv Engelberg
CH-6390 Engelberg
Schweiz/SWITZERLAND
(abbey archive of Engelberg)

Archives de l'Évêché de Lausanne, Genève et Fribourg
86 rue de Lausanne
CH-1003 Lausanne
Schweiz/SWITZERLAND
(diocesan archive for the diocese of Lausanne, Geneva, and
Fribourg)

Archives de Chapitre Saint-Nicolas de Fribourg
4 chemin des Archives
CH-1700 Fribourg
Schweiz/SWITZERLAND
(archive of the chapter of St. Nicholas at Fribourg)

Archiv des Bischoeflichen Ordinariats Sankt Gallen
Klosterhof 6 b
CH-9000 Sankt Gallen
Schweiz/SWITZERLAND
(diocesan archive for the diocese of St. Gallen)

Stiftsarchiv St. Gallen
Regierungsgebaeude
CH-9001 St. Gallen
Schweiz/SWITZERLAND
(abbey archive of St. Gallen)

Archiv des Bistums Basel
Baselstrasse 61
CH-4500 Solothurn
Schweiz/SWITZERLAND
(diocesan archive for the present diocese of Basel)

Archives de l'Ancien Évêché de Bâle
Hôtel de Gleresse
10 rue de Annonciades
CH-2900 Porrentruy/Pruntrut
Schweiz/SWITZERLAND
(archive of the former diocese of Basel)

UKRAINE.

Kuria Arcybiskupa w Lubaczowie
ulica Mickiewicza 85
PL-37600 Lubaczów
Polska./POLAND
(archive of the archdiocese of Lubaczów)

WESTPHALIA.

Bistumsarchiv Muenster (BAM)
Kardinal-von-Galen-Stift
Georgskommende 19
D-48143 Muenster
GERMANY
(diocesan archive for the diocese of Muenster/Münster; has
many parish vital registers of diocese; does not do research)

Erzbistumsarchiv
Kirchenbuchabteilung
Domplatz 3
Postfach 1480
D-33044 Paderborn *(Street address D-33098)*
GERMANY
(archdiocesan archive for the archdiocese of Paderborn; has
almost all parish vital registers of archdiocese prior to
1874)

WEST PRUSSIA. See also PRUSSIA.

Bischoefliches Zentralarchiv
St. Petersweg 11-13
Postfach 110228
D-93015 Regensburg *(Street address D-93047)*
GERMANY
(repository for Catholic parish vital registers for eastern
areas, including Allenstein, Bartenstein, Braunsberg,
Heilsberg, Heydekrug, Koenigsberg/Königsberg,
Rastenburg, Ruessel/Rüssel, Sensburg, and Tilsit, possibly
also other places in West Prussia)

WUERTTEMBERG.

Dioezesanarchiv
Eugen-Bolz-Platz 5
Postfach 9
D-72101 Rottenburg am Neckar *(Street address D-92108)*
GERMANY
(diocesan archive for diocese of Rottenburg am Neckar)

WÜRTTEMBERG. See WUERTTEMBERG.

(Includes Jewish museums, societies, congregations, cemeteries, institutes, publications, etc. Look across national borders and even continents in this section for other sources.)

GERMANY.

Gesamtarchiv der deutschen Juden
Joachimstaler Strasse 13
D-10719 Berlin
GERMANY
(central archive in Berlin for German Jewry)

Zentralrat der Juden in Deutschland
Oranienburger Strasse 31
D-10117 Berlin
GERMANY
(central council for German Jewry)

Leo Baeck Institute
15 W. 16th St.
NEW YORK NY 10011
USA
(private archive in New York City for Jewry, especially German Jews; the collection's strong points include Worms, Baden, the Palatinate, Berlin, and northern Germany; has offices also in London and in Jerusalem)

International Tracing Service
Grosse Allee 5
D-34454 Arolsen
GERMANY
(central archive in Germany with master index of over 46,000,000 entries covering 13,000,000 people from 3,735,000 documents of 20th century concentration camp name lists, deportation lists, lists of towns with Jews, etc.; Buchenwald and Dachau records nearly complete; Flossenburg, Mauthausen, Mittelbau, Natzweiler, Niederhagen-Wewelsburg, and Stutthof fairly complete; Auschwitz, Gross-Rosen, Krakow-Plaszow, Lublin, Neuengamme, Ravensbruck, and Sachsenhausen few; can be accessed through American Red Cross, Family Assistance Department)

Bundesarchiv
Am Woellershof 12
D-56068 Koblenz
GERMANY
(national archive of Federal Republic of Germany; has vital registers of Jewish congregations in East Prussia, Pomerania, Silesia, West Prussia, possibly other formerly German eastern areas; has listing of Jews in the governing district of Breslau/Wrocław in 1812 with their newly adopted family names)

Archiv des Institutum Judaicum Delitzschianum
Wilmergasse 1-4
D-48143 Muenster
GERMANY
(archive for the history of Jews in Germany; has photocopies of some Jewish parish vital registers for all areas east of the Elbe River, North Rhine-Westphalia, East Frisia, and other parts of Germany, formerly kept in the central archive for German Jewry and in the archive of the synagogue of Breslau/Wrocław)

Verband juedischer Heimatvertriebener und Fluechtlinge in der Bundesrepublik e.V.
Gaussstrasse 18
D-60316 Frankfurt/Main
GERMANY
(association of Jewish expellees and refugees (mostly from eastern areas now Poland, Czech Republic, etc.) in the Federal Republic of Germany)

Zentralrat der Juden in Deutschland
Ruengsdorfer Strasse 6
D-53173 Bonn
GERMANY
(central council of Jews in Germany)

Verband der Juedischen Gemeinden in der DDR
Bautzner Strasse 20
D-01099 Dresden
GERMANY
(association of Jewish congregations in the former German Democratic Republic (East Germany))

Juedische Gemeinde zu Berlin
Fasanenstrasse 79
D-10623 Berlin
GERMANY
(Jewish congregation in West Berlin)

Juedische Gemeinde Berlin
Oranienburger Strasse 28
D-10117 Berlin
GERMANY
(Jewish congregation in East Berlin)

Friedhofsverwaltung Weissensee
Herbert-Baum-Strasse 45
D-13088 Berlin
GERMANY
(Jewish cemetery in East Berlin with over 100,000 graves; records of practically all burials since 1881)

Israelitische Religionsgemeinschaft Wuerttembergs
Hospitalstrasse 36
D-70174 Stuttgart
GERMANY
(Jewish headquarters of Wuerttemberg; has most vital registers of synagogues in Wuerttemberg)

AUSTRIA. See also HUNGARY.
(Note: Austrian Jewish vital records prior to 1781 were
kept in the Catholic parish vital registers.)

Israelitische Gemeide
Schottenring 25
A-1010 Wien/Vienna
Oesterreich/AUSTRIA
EUROPE
(Jewish archive in Wien/Vienna; files on locations of
Austrian Jewish records)

Juedisches Museum der Stadt Wien
Dorotheergasse 11
A-1010 Wien/Vienna
Oesterreich/AUSTRIA
EUROPE
(Jewish museum in Wien/Vienna with special focus on the
Austro-Hungarian monarchy and on Wien/Vienna)

Institut fuer Judaistik der Universitaet Wien
Ferstellgasse 6/12
A-1090 Wien/Vienna
Oesterreich/AUSTRIA
EUROPE
(institute for Jewish studies of the University of
Wien/Vienna)

Friedhofsamt der I.K.G.
Zentralfriedhof 4. Tor
Simmeringer Hauptstrasse
A-1110 Wien/Vienna
Oesterreich/AUSTRIA
EUROPE
(Jewish central cemetery in Wien/Vienna; has card file and
burial register)

Landsarchiv
Landhaus
Freiheitsplatz 1
A-7001 Eisenstadt
Oesterreich/AUSTRIA
EUROPE
(state archive for the Burgenland, including microfilms of
Jewish records)

Institut fuer Geschichte der Juden in Oesterreich
Dr. Albert Lichtblau
Rudolfskai 42
A-5020 Salzburg
Oesterreich/AUSTRIA
EUROPE
(Austrian Jewish historical institute)

Juedisches Museum Hohenems
Villa Hermann Rosenthal
Schweizer Strasse 5
A-6845 Hohenems (Vorarlberg)
Oesterreich/AUSTRIA
EUROPE
(Austrian Jewish historical museum)

AUSTRALIA.

Australian Jewish Genealogical Society
P.O. Box 189
Glenhunty 3163
VICTORIA
AUSTRALIA

CANADA.

The Canadian Jewish Congress
1590 McGregor Ave.
Montréal, Quebec
CANADA H3G 1C5
(records on Jewish immigrants to Canada)

Jewish Genealogical Society of Montreal
4605 St. Kevin, Apt. 2
Montréal, Quebec
CANADA H3W 1N8
(genealogical society for Jewish people in Montreal area)

CZECH REPUBLIC.

Obvodní Narodní Vibor
Vodickova 18
Praha
CZECH REPUBLIC
(archive in Prague containing records on Jews)

Society for the History of Czechoslovakian Jews
25 Mayhew Ave.
LARCHMONT NY 10538
USA
(American society for history of Czechoslovakian Jews)

EASTERN EUROPE.

YIVO Institute for Jewish Research
15 W. 16th St.
NEW YORK NY 10028
USA
(institute for Jewish research in New York City with
archive; major repository on eastern European Jews)

Hebrew Union College
Klau Library
1 W. 4th St.
NEW YORK NY 10012
USA
(collection of cemetery records and memory books from
eastern Europe)

ENGLAND.

Jewish Historical Society of England
25 Westbourne Rd.
GB- Edgbaston, Birmingham
ENGLAND BI5 3TX
(historical society for Jews in England)

Jewish Genealogical Society of England
c/o Graham Jaffe
36 Woodstock Road
Golders Green
GB- London NW
ENGLAND 11 8ER
(genealogical society for Jews in England)

Mocatta Library
University College
Attn.: Mr. Munk
Gower St.
GB- London W 1
ENGLAND
(researcher on Jews in England)

FRANCE.

Cercle de Généalogie Juivre
Boîte postale 707
F-75163 PARIS Cedex
FRANCE
(society for French Jewish genealogical research)

Association Temple Reformée
Boîte postale 74
F-67260 Sarre-Union
FRANCE
(Jews in Alsace-Bossue region)

Beate Klarsfeld Foundation
515 Madison Avenue
NEW YORK NY 10022
USA
(foundation in New York City devoted to French Jewry)

GALICIA.

Gesher Galicia
3128 Brooklawn Terrace
CHEVY CHASE MD 20815-3942
USA
(society for Jewish genealogical research in Galicia)

HUNGARY.

Magyar Országos Levéltár
Bécsikapu-tér. 4
H-1014 Budapest 1
HUNGARY
(Hungarian national archives; contains 314 synagogue registers for areas including the Burgenland areas that became Austrian in 1919)

World Federation of Hungarian Jews
136 E. 39th St.
NEW YORK NY 10016
USA
(foundation of Hungarian Jewry)

Magyar Zsidó Levéltár
József körut 27
H-1085 Budapest
HUNGARY
(Hungarian Jewish archives)

Hungarian Jewish Special Interest Group
P.O. Box 34152
CLEVELAND OH 44134
(Hungarian Jewish genealogical group)

ISRAEL.

Search Bureau for Missing Relatives
The Jewish Agency for Israel
P.O. Box 92
IL-97706 Jerusalem
ISRAEL
(name researched, last residence, date of birth, place of birth (town of origin), who are relatives, deceased Israelis; relatives seeking relatives especially since the Holocaust)

Central Archive for the History of the Jewish People
Sprimzak Building, Givat Ram Campus
Hebrew University
P.O. Box 1149
IL- Jerusalem
ISRAEL
(worldwide Jewish historical archive in Jerusalem; cannot undertake research, but will sell microfilms of town records on German Jews, variously in Hebrew, Yiddish, and German languages, from ca. 1800 to 1876; contains the Diamant collection)

The Jewish National and University Library
Givat Ram Campus
Hebrew University
IL- Jerusalem
ISRAEL
(collection of *pinchassim* (vital registers) from Austria, France, Germany, Hungary, Poland, and Russia)

Moresket Beit Saba
c/o Yehuda Ben-David
17 Kaplan Street
IL- Jerusalem
ISRAEL
(society for the Jewish family heritage)

Yad Vashem
Har HaZikaron
P.O. Box 3477
IL- 91034 Jerusalem
ISRAEL
(Israeli institution dedicated to the memory of victims of the Holocaust 1933-1945. *Yizcor* or "Pages of Memory" department documents the lives of victims, also lists name and address of living person who made the testimony; has 3 parts: Hall of Names, Library, and Central Archives of the Holocaust & Jewish Resistance)

Israel Genealogical Society
c/o Esther Ramon
50 Harav Uziel Street
IL-96424 Jerusalem
ISRAEL
(Jewish genealogical society in Israel)

Dorot - Douglas Goldman Jewish Genealogy Centre
The Dorot Project
Beth Hatefutsoth
Nahum Goldmann Museum of the Diaspora
Tel Aviv University Campus
P.O. Box 39359
IL-61390 Tel Aviv
ISRAEL
(computerized depository for Jewish family trees)

LITHUANIA.

Jesish State Museum
Pamenkalnio 12
Vilnius 2001
LITHUANIA
(Lithuuanian Jewish museum)

Hebrew Union College
Klau Library
1 W. 4th St.
NEW YORK NY 10012
USA
(cemetery records from Lithuania, memory books from Lemberg/Lvov)

MACEDONIA. See former YUGOSLAVIA.

NETHERLANDS.

Nederlands Joods Familienarchief
Amstelkijk 67
NL- Amsterdam
Nederland/NETHERLANDS
(Jewish family archive in the Netherlands)

Nederlanse Kring voor Joodse Genealogie
Rudi Curtissos
da Costalaan 21
NL-3743 HT Baarn
Nederland/NETHERLANDS
(society for Jewish genealogy)

POLAND.

Panstwowe Muzeum
PL-32603 Oswiecim
Polska/POLAND
(ca. 1,500,000 index cards on Auschwitz/Birkenau concentration camp victims)

Żydowaki Instytucji Histoyczny
ulica Gen. Świerczewskiego 79
PL-00090 Warszawa
Polska/POLAND
(Polish Jewish Historical Institute)

Krystyna Maddowa
Panstwowega Muzeum
Droga Meczennikow Majdenska 67
PL-20325 Lublin
Polska/POLAND
(ca. 100,000 index cards of ca. 350,000 victims of Majdanek concentration camp)

ROMANIA.

Romanian Circle of Jewish Genealogy
Bd. Mihail Kogalniceanu 5, Et 7 Sektor 5
70601 Bucharest
ROMANIA
(Jewish genealogical society in Romania)

ROM-SIG
P.O. Box 520583
LONGWOOD FL 32752-0583
USA
(Jewish genealogical society for Romania)

RUMANIA. See ROMANIA.

RUSSIA.

Central State Historical Archives
Nabarežnaya Krasnogo Flota 4
St. Petersburg
RUSSIA
(national historical archive for Russia; has copies of records of all churches in Russia, probably since 1722; it is unknown whether synagogue records are included)

Jewish Genealogical Society in Moscow
Dr. Alexander Kronick
c/o VAAD
72 Varshavskoye sb.
113556 Moskva/Moscoa
RUSSIA
(Jewish genealogical society for Russia)

SOVIET UNION. See RUSSIA.

SWITZERLAND.

Schweizerische Vereinigung fuer juedische Genealogie
Postfach 876
CH-8021 Zuerich
Schweiz
SWITZERLAND
(Swiss Jewish genealogical society; publishes "Maajan die Quelle")

UNITED STATES OF AMERICA.
See also under GERMAN-AMERICAN RELIGIOUS
ORGANIZATIONS: JEWISH.

Leo Baeck Institute
15 W. 16th St.
NEW YORK NY 10011
USA
(collection of records on German-speaking Jews (Austria,
Czech Republic, Germany, Romania, etc.); congregational
histories, vital records; strong points Berlin, northern
Germany; Baden, the Palatinate)

American Jewish Historical Society
2 Thornton Road
WALTHAM MA 02154
USA
(historical society for American Jews; synagogue and
educational records)

American Jewish Archives
Hebrew Union College
Jewish Institute of Religion
3101 Clifton Ave.
CINCINNATI OH 45220
USA
(center for North American Jewish history and genealogy)

American Jewish Periodical Center
3101 Clifton Ave.
CINCINNATI OH 45220
USA
(center for 836 microfilmed Jewish periodicals,
newspapers, and bulletins in various languages)

Hebrew Union College
Klau Library
1 W. 4th St.
NEW YORK NY 10012
USA
(collection of cemetery records and memory books from
eastern Europe)

Jewish Theological Seminary Library
3080 Broadway
NEW YORK NY 10027
USA
(records of European Jewish communities; Hebrew
subscription lists for 8,767 communities in Europe and N.
Africa with names of over 350,000 Jews who paid for book
publication)

Yeshiva University Library
Amsterdam Ave. & 158th St.
NEW YORK NY 10033
USA
(university library with Jewish holdings)

AVOTAYNU
International Review of Jewish Genealogy
155 N. Washington Ave.
P.O. Box 900
BERGENFIELD NJ 07666
USA
(periodical for Jewish genealogy)

USSR. See RUSSIA.

former YUGOSLAVIA.

Arhiv Jugoslavije Makedonike
Kej Dimitar Vlahov
YU-91001 Skopje
YUGOSLAVIA
(Yugoslavian state archive for Macedonia; has some Jewish
registers for 1750-1832)

EUROPEAN RELIGIOUS ARCHIVES: PROTESTANT

(Note: Other than the first two listings for Evangelical churches (the EKD & VELKD) and their constituent bodies, most non-Catholic Christian churches (Methodist, Baptist, etc.) are quite small in Germany and not likely to have much genealogical material available, if any.)

GERMANY.

Evangelische Kirche in Deutschland, Kirchenamt
Herrenhaeuserstrasse 12
Postfach 210220
D-30402 Hannover *(Street address D-30419)*
GERMANY
(main headquarters of Evangelical ("Lutheran") Church in Germany, a union in 1823 of Lutheran and Reformed church bodies; together with Catholics, one of the two major church bodies in Germany; has no parish vital registers or extracts at headquarters; they are held regionally or locally)

Vereinigte Evangelisch-Lutherische Kirche Deutschlands
Richard-Wagner-Strasse 26
D-30177 Hannover *(Street address D-30177)*
GERMANY
(headquarters of an association of Evangelical ("Lutheran") churches in Germany; has no parish vital registers or extracts)

Bund der Evangelischen Kirchen
Auguststrasse 80
D-10117 Berlin
GERMANY
(federation of Evangelical ("Lutheran") churches in former German Democratic Republic (East Germany))

Kirchliches Aussenamt der Evangelischen Kirche in Deutschland
Friedrichstrasse 2-6
D-60323 Frankfurt/Main
GERMANY
(office which supports ecumenism, pastoral care for vacationers and foreigners, and connections with German-speaking Lutheran congregations in other countries)

Umsiedler- und Vertriebenenbeauftragter
Horst Schubring, Propst i.R.
Nelkenweg 38
D-35396 Giessen
GERMANY
(advisor for refugee and expellee problems)

Suchamt der Evangelischen Kirche
D-17268 Rosenow Post Harsenbach ueber Templin
GERMANY
(search office of the Evangelical (Lutheran) church in the former GDR (East Germany) presumably for missing living persons)

Evangelisches Zentralarchiv
Jebensstrasse 3
D-10623 Berlin
GERMANY
(central regional archive for several thousand parish vital registers of Lutheran churches of the old Prussian Union in eastern areas, some now Polish)

Archiv des Diakonischen Werks der Evangelischen Kirche in Deutschland e.V.
Altensteinstrasse 51
D-14195 Berlin
GERMANY
(archive of the deacon work of the EKD)

Deutsches Evangelisches Pfarrhaus-Archiv
Lutherhaus
Lutherplatz 8
D-99817 Eisenach
GERMANY
(German Protestant parsonage archive)

Kirche Jesu Christi der Heiligen der Letzten Tage (HLT)
Abteilung Genealogie
Max-Planck-Strasse 23a
D-61381 Friedrichsdorf
GERMANY
(Church of Jesus Christ of Latter-day Saints "Mormon" administrative headquarters in Germany for genealogy, Family History Centers, etc.; not a place to send queries)

Vereinigung der Deutschen Mennonitengemeinden
Koenigstrasse 132
D-47798 Krefeld
GERMANY
(association of German Mennonite churches)

Archiv des Mennonitischen Geschichtsvereins
D-67297 Weierhof bei Marnheim/Pfalz
GERMANY
(archive of the Mennonite Historical Society located in the Palatinate; no recordkeeping by Mennonite churches, but rather by families)

Religioese Gesellschaft der Freunde in Deutschland (Quäker)
Brombergstrasse 9 a
D-79102 Freiburg im Breisgau
GERMANY
(association of the Society of Friends (Quakers) in Germany; closely related in belief to the more "German" Mennonites)

Europaeisch-Festlaendische Brueder-Unitaet
Herrnhuter Bruedergemeinde
Unitaetshaus
Badwasen 6
D-73087 Bad Boll
GERMANY
(Moravian Church ("Herrnhuter" or "Unitas Fratrum")
headquarters for Europe, founded 1457(!), has 23
congregations in Europe)

Evangelische Brueder-Unitaet
Archiv der Brueder-Unitaet
Zittauer Strasse 24
D-02747 Herrnhut (Oberlausitz)
GERMANY
(archive of the Moravian Church, also known as Unitas
Fratrum or Herrnhuter; has about 25,000 biographies of
members, especially Bohemian, Moravian, Swiss, and
Dutch)

Saechsisches Staatsarchiv Leipzig
Abteilung Deutsche Zentralstelle fuer Genealogie
Schongauer Strasse 1
D-04329 Leipzig
GERMANY
(genealogical center in Leipzig, holds some parish vital
registers for eastern Germany, mostly pre-1920)

Bund Evangelisch-Freikirchlicher Gemeinden in
Deutschland (Baptisten)
Friedberger Strasse 101
D-61350 Bad Homburg vor der Hoehe
GERMANY
(headquarters of the federation of Evangelical Free
Churches ("Baptists") in Germany, founded 1849)

Evangelisch-methodistische Kirche
Wilhelm-Leuschner-Strasse 8
D-60329 Frankfurt/Main
GERMANY
(headquarters of the Methodist Church of Germany)

Bund evangelisch-reformierter Kirchen Deutschlands
Raboisen 18-20
D-20095 Hamburg
GERMANY
(association of Evangelical Reformed churches of
Germany)

Reformierter Bund
Generalsekretariat
Klapperstiege 13
D-48455 Bad Bentheim
GERMANY
(association of Reformed churches of Germany, founded
1884)

Christlicher Gemeinschaftsverband Muehleim/Ruhr
Mollerstrasse 40
D-64289 Darmstadt
GERMANY
(society for Christian fellowship, presumably an
ecumenical organization)

Die Heilsarmee in Deutschland
Nationales Hauptquartier
Salierring 23/27
D-50677 Koeln/Cologne
GERMANY
(national headquarters of Salvation Army in Germany; a
worldwide project of the Salvation Army is to find living
missing living persons (relatives) worldwide, by no means
only derelicts or the homeless; for details contact your local
Salvation Army branch)

Altreformierte Kirchen in Deutschland
Bramerskamp 7
D-49828 Neuenhaus
GERMANY
(association of "Old Reformed" churches in Germany
(those which did not participate in the 1823 union with
Lutherans))

Bund freier evangelischer Gemeinden in Deutschland
Goltenkamp 2
D-58452 Witten-Bommern
GERMANY
(federation of independent Evangelical (Lutheran)
congregations in Germany (which did not participate in the
1823 union with Reformed churches), founded 1854)

Alt-Lutherische Kirche in der DDR
Annenstrasse 53
D-10179 Berlin
GERMANY
(headquarters of "Old Lutheran" church, founded 1830, has
ca. 9,000 members)

Selbstaendige Evangelisch-Lutherische Kirche
Schopenhauerstrasse 7
D-30625 Hannover
GERMANY
(headquarters of "independent" Evangelical ("Lutheran")
church)

Seminar der Evangelischen Gemeinschaft
Evangelisch-methodistische Kirche
Peter-Cornelius-Strasse 26
D-72766 Reutlingen
GERMANY
(seminary of the former Evangelical Association in
Germany, now a part of the Methodist Church)

ALSACE. See FRANCE.

EUROPEAN RELIGIOUS ARCHIVES: PROTESTANT

ANHALT.

Evangelische Landeskirche Anhalts
D-06842 Dessau
GERMANY
(Lutheran church in Saxony-Anhalt)

AUSTRIA.

Evangelischer Oberkirchenrat in Wien
Schellinggasse 12
A-1010 Wien/Vienna
Oesterreich/AUSTRIA
EUROPE
(main headquarters of Evangelical (Lutheran) Church in
Austria)

Archiv des evangelischen Oberkirchenrates
Severin-Schreiber-Gasse 3A
A-1180 Wien/Vienna
Oesterreich/AUSTRIA
EUROPE
(archive of Evangelical (Lutheran) Church in Austria;
parish vital registers for all Protestant parishes of
Austro-Hungarian Empire from 1878 to 1917; Lutheran
vital records will be in local Catholic (!) parish vital
registers prior to 1781)

Evangelisches Dioezesanmuseun
A-9712 Fresach
Oesterreich/AUSTRIA
EUROPE
(museum of Reformation history in Austria)

Standesamt
Waehringerstrasse 39
A-1100 Wien-Alsergrund (Vienna-Als...)
Oesterreich/AUSTRIA
EUROPE
(Austrian special civil registry with duplicate records since
1870 of free-thinkers, Arminian-Orientals, Lipponauers,
Mennonites, Moravian Brethren, Mohammedans, and
members of no recognized denomination, also marriage
records for all marriages that required dispensations)

BADEN.

Evangelischer Oberkirchenrat
Landeskirchliches Archiv
Blumenstrasse 1
Postfach 2269
D-76010 Karlsruhe
GERMANY
(central archive for Evangelical (Lutheran) churches in
Baden; many parish vital registers, especially pre-1810)

Generallandesarchiv
Noerdliche Hilda-Promenade 2
D-76133 Karlsruhe
GERMANY
(has church book duplicates for communities in Baden
1810-1869)

Schoonmaker Library
18 Brodhead Ave.
P.O. Box 339
NEW PALTZ NY 12561
USA
(has French Reformed parish vital records from large
congregation at Mannheim)

BAVARIA. See also PALATINATE.

Evangelisch-Lutherischer Landeskirchenrat
Meiserstrasse 13
D-80333 Muenchen/Munich
GERMANY
(archive for Evangelical (Lutheran) churches in Bavaria
excluding Franconia and the city of Augsburg)

Evangelisch-Lutherische Kirche in Bayern
Landeskirchliches Archiv
Veilhofstrasse 28
D-90489 Nuernberg/Nuremberg
GERMANY
(church historical archive for Evangelical (Lutheran)
churches in Middle Franconia, Lower Franconia, and
Upper Franconia, except Regensburg city; see below)

Evangelisch-Lutherische Kirche in Bayern
Landeskirchliches Archiv
Aussenstelle Kirchenbucharchiv
Am Oelberg 2
D-93047 Regensburg
GERMANY
(new central church book archive for Evangelical
(Lutheran) churches in Middle Franconia, Lower
Franconia, and Upper Franconia, except Regensburg city;
has registers of Ansbach, Feuchtwangen, etc.)

Evangelisch-Lutherisches Pfarrarchiv
Pfarrergasse 5
D-93047 Regensburg
GERMANY
(archive for parish vital registers of the city of Regensburg)

Kirchenarchiv
Herbert Becher
Dollingerstrasse 11
D-93049 Regensburg
GERMANY
(private individual who handles genealogical research for
Regensburg *city* Lutheran church archive)

Evangelisches Kirchenbuchamt
Im Annahof 4
D-86150 Augsburg
GERMANY
(archive for Evangelical (Lutheran) parish vital registers of *city* of Augsburg)

BERLIN.

Archiv des Evangelischen Konsistoriums
    Berlin-Brandenburg
Bachstrasse 1-2
D-10555 Berlin
GERMANY
(archive for Evangelical (Lutheran) church district of Berlin and Brandenburg)

Evangelische Kirche Berlin-Brandenburg
Neue Gruenstrasse 19
D-10179 Berlin
GERMANY
(headquarters for Evangelical (Lutheran) church district of Berlin and Brandenburg in former German Democratic Republic (East Germany))

Evangelisches Zentralarchiv in Berlin
Kirchenbuchstelle
Jebensstrasse 3
D-10623 Berlin
GERMANY
(archive for parish vital registers of Evangelical (Lutheran) churches of the old Prussian Union, eastern Germany, and old Berlin to 1874; has index of baptisms and rough marriage indexes for ca. 40 congregations)

BESSARABIA.

Hilfskomittee der evangelisch-lutherischen Kirche aus Bessarabien
Haus des deutschen Ostens
Koenigsworther Strasse 2
D-30167 Hannover
GERMANY
(aid society for Lutheran churches in Bessarabia)

BOHEMIA. See CZECH REPUBLIC, SUDETENLAND.

BRANDENBURG.

Archiv des Evangelischen Konsistoriums
Berlin-Brandenburg
Bachstrasse 1-2
D-10555 Berlin
GERMANY
(archive for Evangelical (Lutheran) church district of Berlin and Brandenburg)

Evangelische Kirche Berlin-Brandenburg
Neue Gruenstrasse 19
D-10179 Berlin
GERMANY
(headquarters for Evangelical (Lutheran) church district of Berlin and Brandenburg in former German Democratic Republic (East Germany))

Evangelisches Zentralarchiv in Berlin
Kirchenbuchstelle
Jebensstrasse 3
D-10623 Berlin
GERMANY
(archive for parish vital registers of Evangelical (Lutheran) churches of the old Prussian Union, eastern Germany, and old Berlin; several thousand registers)

Domstiftsarchiv Brandenburg
Burghof 11
D-14776 Brandenburg
GERMANY
(archive for the cathedral of Brandenburg)

BRAUNSCHWEIG. See BRUNSWICK.

BREMEN.

Bremische Evangelische Kirche
Archiv der Kirchenkanzlei
Franziuseck 2-4
D-28199 Bremen
GERMANY
(headquarters of Evangelical (Lutheran) church of Bremen; has no parish vital registers)

Staatsarchiv
Praesident-Kennedy-Platz 2
D-28203 Bremen
GERMANY
(52 volumes of Evangelical (Lutheran) parish vital registers from 1581 to 1855 for the city-state of Bremen)

BRUNSWICK. See also LOWER SAXONY.

Braunschweigische Evangelisch-lutherische Landeskirche
Landeskirchliches Archiv
Alter Zeughof 1
Postfach 420
D-38100 Braunschweig
GERMANY
(archive for Evangelical (Lutheran) church district of Braunschweig/Brunswick; has Evangelical (Lutheran) parish vital registers of the district of Braunschweig/Brunswick except for the cities of Braunschweig/Brunswick and Wolfenbuettel/Wolfenbüttel after 1815)

EUROPEAN RELIGIOUS ARCHIVES: PROTESTANT

Stadtkirchenamt
Schuetzenstrasse 23
D-38100 Braunschweig/Brunswick
GERMANY
(archive for Evangelical (Lutheran) parish vital records of
churches in Braunschweig/Brunswick *city* after 1815)

Evangelisch-Lutherisches Kirchenverband Wolfenbuettel
Kirchenverbandsamt
Neuer Weg 1
D-38302 Wolfenbuettel
GERMANY
(archive for Evangelical (Lutheran) parish vital records of 8
churches in Wolfenbuettel/Wolfenbüttel *city* after 1815)

CZECH REPUBLIC. See SUDETENLAND.

DANZIG. See WEST PRUSSIA; for Dutch Reformed: see
NETHERLANDS.

EAST PRUSSIA.

Evangelisches Zentralarchiv in Berlin
Kirchenbuchstelle
Jebensstrasse 3
D-10623 Berlin
GERMANY
(archive for parish vital registers of the Evangelical
(Lutheran) churches of the old Prussian Union to 1874; ca.
7,000 registers)

EASTERN GERMANY.
See also specific areas, such as POSEN, SILESIA,
WEST PRUSSIA, etc.

Evangelisches Zentralarchiv in Berlin
Kirchenbuchstelle
Jebensstrasse 3
D-10623 Berlin
GERMANY
(archive for parish vital registers of the Evangelical
(Lutheran) churches of the old Prussian Union to 1874; ca.
7,000 registers)

Arbeitsgemeinschaft ostdeutscher Familienforscher e.V.
Kirchenbuchauskunftstelle
Am Muehlenhof 5
D-26180 Rastede
GERMANY
(computerized information center in Federal Republic of
Germany set up by genealogical society for eastern areas on
the present location of parish vital registers)

Saechsisches Staatsarchiv Leipzig
Abteilung Deutsche Zentralstelle fuer Genealogie
Schongauer Strasse 1
D-04329 Leipzig
GERMANY
(genealogical center in Leipzig, holds some parish vital
registers for eastern Germany, mostly pre-1920)

ENGLAND.

Len M. Metzner
10, Kingsley Court
25, The Avenue
Worcester Park, Surrey KT4 7EX
UNITED KINGDOM
(index of registers of Hamburg Lutheran Church, Trinity
Lane, London)

Public Record Office
Kew
UK- Richmond, Surrey
ENGLAND TW9 4DU
(records of German Lutheran Royal Chapel, Hamburg
Lutheran Chapel, Germany Lutheran Chapel in Savoy, and
St. George's Lutheran, as well as Fetter Lane Moravian
Church)

ERMLAND.

Historischer Verein fuer das Ermland
Ermlandweg 22
D-48159 Muenster
GERMANY
(church books of the Ermland area)

ESTONIA. See also EASTERN GERMANY, RUSSIA.

Eesti Riigi Keskariiv
ulica Manezi 4
Tallinn
ESTONIA
(parish registers to 1834; later registers are now at local
district office (ZAGS))

FRANCE. (Includes "HUGUENOTS").

Centre de documentation d'histoire protestante
Archives départementales du Gard
20, rue des Chassaintes
F-30000 Nîmes
FRANCE
(center for the documentation of history of French
Protestantism in the state archive at Nîmes)

Bibliothèque de la Société d'histoire du Protestantisme
Français
54, rue des Saint-Pères
F-75007 Paris
FRANCE
(library of the French Protestant Historical Society)

La Bibliothèque de l'Institut de France
23, quai de Couti
F-75005 Paris
FRANCE
(library of the French Institute; has some Protestant parish
vital registers)

La Bibliothèque de l'Arsenal
1, rue de Sully
F-75004 Paris
FRANCE
(library; has some Protestant parish vital registers)

Walloon Library
Central Genealogical Office
Nassau-laen 18
NL-2500 's-Gravenhage/The Hague
Nederland/NETHERLANDS
(has card index of Walloons)

Schoonmaker Library
18 Brodhead Ave.
P.O. Box 339
NEW PALTZ NY 12561
USA
(has French Reformed parish vital registers of Mannheim, Germany)

The Huguenot Library
University College
Gower St.
London WC1E 6BT
UNITED KINGDOM
(Huguenot library)

Arbeitskreis fuer die Geschichte der Hugenotten und Waldenser
Brachterstrasse 15
D-35282 Rauschenberg-Schwabendorf
GERMANY
(working group for the history of Huguenots and Waldensians)

Archives départementales du Bas-Rhin
5-9, rue Fischart
F-67000 Strasbourg
FRANCE
(French state archive for Lower Rhine/northern Alsace area except city of Strasbourg; has most Reformed and Lutheran parish vital registers for Lower Rhine/northern Alsace area prior to ca. 1875)

Archives départementales du Haut-Rhin
Cité administrative
Rue Fleischauer
F-68000 Colmar
FRANCE
(French state archive for Upper Rhine/southern Alsace area; has most Reformed and Lutheran parish vital registers for Upper Rhine/southern Alsace area prior to ca. 1875)

Archives de la ville Strasbourg
8, place de l'Hospital
Boîte Postale No 1049-1050 F
F-67070 Strasbourg
FRANCE
(municipal archive for city of Strasbourg; has most Reformed and Lutheran parish vital registers for *city* of Strasbourg prior to ca. 1875; insufficient staff for research by mail; you must hire a GENEALOGIST, q.v.)

Stadtarchiv
Stadtverwaltung (Amt 41 A)
Karmeliterkloster
Karmelitergasse 5
D-60311 Frankfurt am Main
GERMANY
(archive of the French Reformed congregation at Frankfurt am Main; has records of material and other assistance given to Huguenots, including places of origin and intended destinations)

FRANCONIA. See BAVARIA.

HAMBURG. (Dutch Reformed see NETHERLANDS.)

Evangelisch-lutherische Kirche im Hamburgischen Staat
Archiv
Neue Burg 1
D-20354 Hamburg
GERMANY
(archive for Evangelical (Lutheran) churches of Hamburg proper; has 886 volumes of original parish vital registers from 1816 to 1866; also films and indexes to parish vital registers from 1603 to 1815, originals of which are in the state archive in Hamburg)

Staatsarchiv Hamburg
ABC-Strasse 19, Eingang A
D-20354 Hamburg
GERMANY
(state archive for the city-state of Hamburg; has originals of Evangelical (Lutheran) parish vital registers of old Hamburg from 1603 to ca. 1865)

Nordelbisches Kirchenarchiv Hamburg
Grindelallee 7
D-20146 Hamburg
GERMANY
(Evangelical (Lutheran) church administrative archive for parishes in the region near Hamburg north of the Elbe River; has only a few parish vital registers; information about location of registers; most registers since ca. 1866 kept locally)

Kirchenbuchstelle Altona im Kirchenkreisverband
    Blankenese, Niendorf und Pinneberg
Iserbarg 1
D-22559 Hamburg
GERMANY
(Evangelical (Lutheran) church archive with parish vital
registers for joint church district of Hamburg-Altona,
Blankenese, Niendorf, and Pinneberg)

Kirchenkreisamt Harburg
Kirchenbuch- und Meldewesen
Hoelertwiete 5
D-21073 Hamburg
GERMANY
(Evangelical (Lutheran) district church archive for Harburg
with parish vital registers for Hamburg-Harburg)

HANNOVER. (HANOVER.)

HANOVER. See also LOWER SAXONY.

Kirchenbuchamt der Evangelisch-lutherischen
    Landeskirche Hannovers
Ubbenstrasse 15
D-30159 Hannover
GERMANY
(Evangelical (Lutheran) church book office for the *district*
of Hannover; has some Evangelical (Lutheran) parish vital
registers for the *district* of Hannover)

Evangelisch-lutherische Landeskirche Hannovers
Landeskirchliches Archiv
Am Steinbruch 14 *(Eingang Badenstedter Strasse 41)*
Postfach 3726
D-30037 Hannover *(Street address D-30449)*
GERMANY
(archive for Evangelical (Lutheran) church district of
Hannover; 20,000 church books before 1875; microfilms of
church books to 1852; microfiches of some church books
1853-1875, including Hannover, Goettingen, Hildesheim,
and Hameln-Pyrmont, also available at 14 other places,
including Aurich, Goettingen, and Stade for those regions;
not available for sale or lease or interlibrary loan)

Evangelisch-lutherische Stadtkirchenverband Hannover
Stadtkirchenkanzlei
Kirchenbuchamt
Hildesheimer Strasse 165-167
Postfach 5740
D-30057 Hannover *(Street address D-30173)*
GERMANY
(Evangelical (Lutheran) church book office for the city of
Hannover; has Evangelical (Lutheran) parish vital registers
for the 70 parishes of Hannover *city* only)

HESSE.
See MUNICIPAL ARCHIVES for Frankfurt city; see
NETHERLANDS for Dutch Reformed records of
Frankfurt.

Landeskirchenamt der Evangelischen Kirche von
    Kurhessen-Waldeck
Landeskirchenarchiv
Wilhelmshoeher Allee 330
Postfach 410260
D-34064 Kassel-Wilhelmshoehe *(Street address D-34131)*
GERMANY
(headquarters of the Evangelical (Lutheran) church district
of Hessen-Waldeck; not a repository for parish vital
registers)

Evangelische Kirche von Kurhessen-Waldeck
Archiv des Landeskirchenamts
Heinrich-Wimmer-Strasse 4
D-34131 Kassel-Wilhelmshoehe
GERMANY
(archive of the Evangelical (Lutheran) church district of
Hessen-Waldeck)

Evangelische Kirche in Hessen und Nassau
Paulusplatz 1
D-64285 Darmstadt
GERMANY
(headquarters of the Evangelical (Lutheran) church district
of Hessen and Nassau; not a repository for parish vital
registers)

Evangelische Kirche in Hessen und Nassau
Jakob-Steffan-Strasse 3
D-55122 Mainz
GERMANY
(branch office of Evangelical (Lutheran and Reformed)
church district of Hessen and Nassau)

Evangelische Kirche in Hessen und Nassau
Zentralarchiv
Ahastrasse 5a
D-64285 Darmstadt
GERMANY
(archive of Evangelical (Lutheran and Reformed) church
district of Hessen and Nassau)

Staatsarchiv fuer Hessen-Darmstadt
Karolinenplatz 3
D-64289 Darmstadt
GERMANY
(state archive for Hessen-Darmstadt; has duplicates of
Evangelical (Lutheran and Reformed) parish vital registers
for Hessen-Darmstadt from ca. 1808 to 1875)

Hessische Familiengeschichtliche Vereinigung e.V.
Karolinenplatz 3
D-64289 Darmstadt
GERMANY
(genealogical society for Hessen-Darmstadt; has some
card-files of Evangelical (Lutheran) church books prior to
1808 for Bessungen, Bickenbach, Darmstadt, Eschau,
Gross-Bieberau, Nidda, Nieder-Beerbach, Nieder-Modau,
Seeheim, Stumpertenrod, etc.)

Staatsarchiv fuer Hessen-Kassel
Friedrichsplatz 15
Postfach 540
D-35017 Marburg/Lahn
GERMANY
(state archive for Hessen-Kassel or Kurhessen (Electoral
Hesse); has some duplicates of Evangelical (Lutheran and
Reformed) parish vital registers for Hessen-Kassel from ca.
1808 to 1875)

Evangelischer Gemeinde- und Dekanatsverband Darmstadt
Kirchengemeindeamt
Kiesstrasse 14
D-64283 Darmstadt
GERMANY
(Evangelical (Lutheran and Reformed) parish office for the
city of Darmstadt; has Evangelical (Lutheran and
Reformed) parish vital registers for the *city* of Darmstadt;
Schloss (castle) registers were destroyed in World War II)

HESSEN. (HESSE.)

HOLLAND. See NETHERLANDS.

HOLSTEIN. See SCHLESWIG-HOLSTEIN.

HUGUENOTS. See FRANCE.

HUNGARY.

Magyar Országos Levéltár
Bécsikapu-tér 4
H-1014 Budapest 1
HUNGARY
(has 1,033 Reformed and 297 Lutheran microfilms of
parish vital registers to 1895, but only books to 1867 are
open, with church permission)

Evangélikus Országos Levéltár
Üllöi út 24
H-1085 Budapest
HUNGARY
(Hungarian Lutheran church headquarters)

A Magyarországi Református Egyház Zsinati Léveltára
Reformatus Levéltár
Kálvin tér 8
H-1091 Budapest
HUNGARY
(Hungarian Reformed church headquarters; synodal
archives)

A Magyarországi Baptista Egyház Zsinati Léveltára
Aradi u. 48
H-1062 Budapest
HUNGARY
(Hungarian Baptist Church archive)

LATVIA. See also EASTERN GERMANY, RUSSIA.

Latvijas PSR
Centràlais Valsta vèstures arhìvs
ulica Skjunju 11
Riga
LATVIA
(parish registers to 1834; later registers are now at local
district office (ZAGS))

LIPPE.
See also LOWER SAXONY and WESTPHALIA.

Evangelisch-lutherische Landeskirche von
     Schaumburg-Lippe
Herderstrasse 27
Postfach 1307
D-31665 Bueckeburg
GERMANY
(headquarters of Evangelical (Lutheran) church district of
Schaumburg-Lippe; not a repository of parish vital records)

Lippisches Landeskirchenamt
Archiv der Lippischen Landeskirche
Leopoldstrasse 12
D-32756 Detmold
GERMANY
(headquarters of Evangelical (Reformed and Lutheran)
church district of Lippe-Detmold; has some Evangelical
(Reformed and Lutheran) parish vital registers for
Lippe-Detmold)

Personenstandsarchiv
Staatsarchiv
Willi-Hofmann-Strasse 2
D-32756 Detmold
GERMANY
(Lower Saxony state archive and vital records archive for
Lippe and part of Westphalia; has duplicates of Evangelical
(Reformed and Lutheran) parish vital registers mostly ca.
1815-1874)

LITHUANIA. See also EASTERN GERMANY, RUSSIA.

Lietuvos TSR Centrinis Valsybinis Istorijos Archivas
ulica Vrublevskogo 6
Vilna
LITHUANIA
(Lutheran parish registers to 1834 for Coadjuthen,
Crottingen, Dawillan, Heydekrug, Kairinn, Karkelbeck,
Kinten, Laugszargen, Nattkischken, Nidden, Paleiten,
Paszieszen, Piktopen, Plaschken, Plicken, Prokuls,
Ramutten, Rucken, Russ, Saugen, Schwarzort, Szugken,
Wannagen, Wieszen, and Wischwill; later registers are now
at local district office (ZAGS))

Lietuvos TSR Mokslu Akadam Ijos Centrine Biblioteks
Vilna
LITHUANIA
(Academy of Sciences library; has Reformed parish vital
registers to 1834 except for Vilnius city; later registers are
now at local district office (ZAGS))

Zapisi Aktev Grazhdanskogo Sostoninia
Vilna
LITHUANIA
(parish registers for Vilnius city)

LORRAINE. See FRANCE.

LOWER SAXONY. See also BRUNSWICK, HANOVER,
LIPPE, OLDENBURG, OSTFRIESLAND,
WESTPHALIA, etc.

Evangelisch-lutherische Landeskirche Hannovers
Landeskirchliches Archiv
Am Steinbruch 14
Eingang Badenstedter Strasse 41
Postfach 3726
D-30037 Hannover *(Street address D-30449)*
GERMANY
(archive for Evangelical (Lutheran) church district of
Hannover)

Gesellschaft fuer niedersaechsische Kirchengeschichte
Rote Reihe 6
D-30169 Hannover
GERMANY
(society for Lower Saxony church history)

Archiv der evangelisch-lutherischen Kirche in Oldenburg
Philosophenweg 1
Postfach 1709
D-26007 Oldenburg *(Street address D-26121)*
GERMANY
(archive for Evangelical (Lutheran) church in district of
Oldenburg; most holdings now in Oldenburg state archive;
see also Eutin church archive in Schleswig-Holstein, as that
area formerly was part of Oldenburg)

Evangelisch-reformierte Kirche in Nordwestdeutschland
Archiv des Landeskirchenrats
Saarstrasse 6
Postfach 1380
D-26763 Leer
GERMANY
(archive for Evangelical (Reformed) church district of
Ostfriesland/northwest Germany)

Evangelisch-lutherische Landeskirche Hannovers
D-31543 Loccum
GERMANY
(archive of the Evangelical (Lutheran) abbey and
theological seminary at Loccum)

Evangelisch-lutherische Landeskirche von
    Schaumburg-Lippe
Herderstrasse 27
Postfach 1307
D-31665 Bueckeburg
GERMANY
(headquarters for Evangelical (Lutheran) church district of
Schaumburg-Lippe); not a repository of parish vital
registers)

Staatsarchiv fuer Oldenburg
Damm 43
D-26135 Oldenburg
GERMANY
(Lower Saxony state archive for Oldenburg; has
Evangelical (Lutheran) parish vital registers from 1801 to
(partially) 1955)

Kirchenbuchamt der Evangelisch-lutherischen
    Landeskirche Hannovers
Ubbenstrasse 15
D-30159 Hannover
GERMANY
(Evangelical (Lutheran) church book office for the district
of Hannover; has some Evangelical (Lutheran) parish vital
registers)

Lippisches Landeskirchenamt
Leopoldstrasse 27
D-32756 Detmold
GERMANY
(headquarters of Evangelical (Reformed and Lutheran)
church of Lippe-Detmold; has some Evangelical (Reformed
and Lutheran) parish vital registers for Lippe-Detmold)

Staatsarchiv fuer Osnabrueck
Schlossstrasse 29
D-49074 Osnabrueck
GERMANY
(Lower Saxony state archive for Osnabrück/
Osnabrueck area; has duplicates of some Evangelical
(Lutheran and Reformed) parish vital registers for
Osnabrück/Osnabrueck area prior to 1875)

Niedersaechsisches Staatsarchiv
Am Sande 4 C
D-21682 Stade
GERMANY
(Lower Saxony state archive for Stade area; has duplicates
of some Evangelical (Lutheran) parish vital registers for
former church territories of Bremen and Verden)

Evangelisch-lutherische Stadtkirchenverband Hannover
Stadtkirchenkanzlei, Kirchenbuchamt
Arnswaldtstrasse 28
Postfach 5740
D-30057 Hannover
GERMANY *(Street address D-30159)*
(Evangelical (Lutheran) church book office for the city of
Hannover; has Evangelical (Lutheran) parish vital registers
for Hannover *city* only)

Evangelisch-lutherischer Gesamtverband Osnabrueck
Gemeindeamt
Heger-Tor-Wall 9
Postfach 1824
D-49008 Osnabrueck
GERMANY
(Evangelical (Lutheran) church office for city of
Osnabrück/Osnabrueck; has Evangelical (Lutheran and
Reformed) parish vital registers for *city* of
Osnabrück/Osnabrueck)

LÜBECK. See SCHLESWIG-HOLSTEIN.

LUEBECK. See SCHLESWIG-HOLSTEIN.

MAEHREN. (MORAVIA.) See SUDETENLAND,
CZECH REPUBLIC.

MÄHREN. (MORAVIA.) See SUDETENLAND,
CZECH REPUBLIC.

MECKLENBURG.

Archiv der Landessuperintendentur der
Evangelischen-Lutherischen Landeskirche
Mecklenburgs
Strasse des Friedens 50
D-19370 Parchim
GERMANY
(archive of the administration of the Evangelical (Lutheran)
church of Mecklenburg)

Domarchiv
Domplatz
Domhof 35
Postfach 1266
D-23909 Ratzeburg
GERMANY
(Evangelical (Lutheran) cathedral archive for Ratzeburg
and Evangelical (Lutheran) parish vital registers from all of
Mecklenburg-Schwerin and Mecklenburg-Strelitz except
Wismar area and Rostock, where the church books are in
the municipal archive; these registers were brought to
Ratzeburg near the end of World War II)

Mecklenburgisches Kirchenbuchamt
Muenzstrasse 8
Postfach 001003
D-19010 Schwerin
GERMANY
(archive of Evangelical (Lutheran) church of Mecklenburg;
has church visitation rolls from the 16th through 18th
centuries; has microfilms of parish vital registers)

MORAVIA.
See SUDETENLAND, CZECH REPUBLIC.

"MORAVIANS".

Brueder-Unitaet
Archiv der Brueder-Unitaet
Zittauer Strasse 24
D-02747 Herrnhut (Oberlausitz)
GERMANY
(archive of the Moravian church, also known as Unitas
Fratrum or Herrnhuter, in Europe, including some Volga
River settlements; 25,000 biographies of members)

Baseler Mission
Evangelische Missionsgesellschaft
Missionsstrasse 21
CH-4000 Basel
Schweiz/SWITZERLAND
(archive of the Moravian church in Europe, including some
Volga River settlements)

Archiv der Herrnhuter Brudergemeine
Volandstrasse 18
D-78125 Koenigsfeld
GERMANY
(archive of the Moravian congregation of Koenigsfeld)

NETHERLANDS.

Nederlandse Hervormde Kerk
Postbus 202
NL- Leusden
Nederland/NETHERLANDS
(national headquarters in Holland of Dutch Reformed
Church; church book records of Emden since 1544, Wesel
1544, Cologne 1544, Aachen 1544, Goch 1544, Duisburg
1553, Frankfurt am Main 1554, Emmerich 1560,
Frankenthal 1562, Hamburg, Staken, Danzig)

Rijksarchief in Gelderland
Markt Straat 1
NL- Arnhem
Nederland/NETHERLANDS
(Netherlands state archive for Gelderland; has Dutch
Reformed parish vital registers for Huissen, Lobith, and
Zevenaar)

Gemeentenarchief Amsterdam
Amsteldijk 67
NL-1074 HZ Amsterdam
Nederland/NETHERLANDS
(archive of the community of Amsterdam; has some parish
vital registers)

Vereenigde Doopsgizinde Gemeente Archief
Bureau D.S.
Singel 154
NL- Amsterdam
Nederland/NETHERLANDS
(archive of the Mennonite congregation of Amsterdam)

OLDENBURG. See also LOWER SAXONY.

Staatsarchiv fuer Oldenburg
Damm 43
D-26135 Oldenburg
GERMANY
(Lower Saxony state archive for Oldenburg; has
Evangelical (Lutheran) parish vital registers from 1801 to
(partially) 1955)

Evangelisch-Lutherische Kirche Oldenburgs
Philosophenweg 1
D-26121 Oldenburg
GERMANY
(headquarters of Evangelical ("Lutheran") church of the
former Duchy of Oldenburg)

Evangelisch-Lutherische Kirche in Oldenburg
Archiv
Huntestrasse 14
Postfach 1709
D-26007 Oldenburg *(Street address D-26135)*
GERMANY
(archive for Evangelical (Lutheran) church in district of
Oldenburg; most holdings now in Oldenburg state archive;
see also Eutin church archive in Schleswig-Holstein, as that
area formerly was a part of Oldenburg)

Professor Tony Holtmann
Institut fuer Politikwissenschaft II
Ammerlaender Heerstrasse 114-118
Postfach 2503
D-26111 Oldenburg *(Street address D-26129)*
GERMANY
(professor with major project comparing church books of
Oldenburg with records of emigrants to America)

PALATINATE.

Evangelische Kirche der Pfalz
Landeskirchenrat (Protestantische Landeskirche)
Domplatz 5
Postfach 1720
D-67327 Speyer *(Street address D-67346)*
GERMANY
(archive for Protestant (Reformed and Lutheran) church
district of the Palatinate; has approximately 1,700 volumes
of Protestant (Reformed and Lutheran) parish vital registers
from 1556 to 1940 for the Palatinate except the northern
portion)

Zentralarchiv der Evangelischen Kirche der Pfalz
Kirchenbuchstelle Koblenz
Karmeliterstrasse 1-3
D-56068 Koblenz
GERMANY
(archive of Evangelical (Lutheran and Reformed) parish
vital registers from the Rhineland, the northern portion of
the Palatinate, and the Saarland)

POLAND. See under EAST PRUSSIA, POMERANIA,
POSEN, SILESIA, WEST PRUSSIA, etc.

POMERANIA. See also EASTERN GERMANY.

Pommersche Evangelische Kirche
Evangelisches Konsistorium
Landeskirchliches Archiv
Bahnhofstrasse 35/36
D-17489 Greifswald
GERMANY
(consistory of Evangelical (Lutheran) church of Pomerania)

Evangelisches Zentralarchiv in Berlin
Kirchenbuchstelle
Jebensstrasse 3
D-10623 Berlin
GERMANY
(archive for parish vital registers of the Evangelical
(Lutheran) churches of the old Prussian Union to 1874
including Stettin and 19 other parishes of the Stettin district
of Pomerania)

Evangelisch-lutherische Kirche im Hamburgischen Staat
Archiv
Neue Burg 1
D-20457 Hamburg
GERMANY
(archive of Evangelical (Lutheran) church in Hamburg; has
Evangelical (Lutheran) parish vital registers for Stettin,
Hagen, Falkenwalde, Frauendorf, Kreckow, and
Stolzenhagen in Pomerania from 1613 to 1945, transferred
after World War II)

POMMERN. See POMERANIA.

POSEN. See also EASTERN GERMANY.

Evangelisches Zentralarchiv in Berlin
Kirchenbuchstelle
Jebensstrasse 3
D-10623 Berlin
GERMANY
(archive for parish vital registers of the Evangelical
(Lutheran) churches of the old Prussian Union to 1874
including 31 parishes of Posen)

PREUSSEN. See PRUSSIA.

PRUSSIA.
See EAST PRUSSIA and WEST PRUSSIA.
Note: Prussia in the 19th century encompassed most of
northern Germany and even Hohenzollern in southern
Germany.

RHINELAND.
See also PALATINATE and WESTPHALIA.
(for Dutch Reformed records; NETHERLANDS)

Archiv der Evangelischen Kirche im Rheinland
Evangelische Archivstelle Koblenz
Karmeliterstrasse 1-3
D-56068 Koblenz
GERMANY
(archive of Evangelical (Lutheran and Reformed) church in
the southern portion of the Rhineland; has many
Evangelical (Lutheran) and Reformed parish vital registers)

Archiv der Evangelischen Kirche im Rheinland
Hans-Boeckler-Strasse 7
Postfach 320340
D-40418 Duesseldorf *(Street address D-40476)*
GERMANY
(archive of Evangelical (Lutheran and Reformed) church in
the northern portion of the Rhineland; has some
Evangelical (Lutheran) parish vital registers; publishes
*Monatshefte fuer Evangelische Kirchengeschichte des
Rheinlands*)

Personenstandsarchiv Bruehl
Schlossstrasse 12
D-50321 Bruehl
GERMANY
(vital records archive for the Rhineland; has some
Evangelical (Lutheran and Reformed) parish vital registers
and duplicates for most of the Rhineland from ca. 1798 to
1874)

ROMANIA.

Archiv des Landeskirchenamts der Evangelischen Kirche
    von Westfalen
Landeskirchenamt
Altstaedter Kirchplatz 4
D-33602 Bielefeld
GERMANY
(Evangelical (Reformed and Lutheran) church archive in
Bielefeld, Federal Republic of Germany (West Germany);
believed to hold some Evangelical (Lutheran) parish vital
registers from Siebenbuergen/Transylvania in present-day
Romania)

RUSSIA. See also EASTERN GERMANY.

Central State Historical Archives
Naberežnaya Krasnogo Flota 4
St. Petersburg
RUSSIA
(national historical archive for Russia; has parts of the
archives of the Consistorium General of the Lutheran
church in Russia and copies of records of all churches in
Russia, probably since 1722)

Kirchliche Gemeinschaft der evangelisch-lutherischen
    Deutschen aus Russland
Postfach 410308
D-34065 Kassel
GERMANY
(church association of Lutheran Germans from Russia in
Federal Republic of Germany)

SAARLAND.

Protestantisches Landeskirchenarchiv
Grosse Himmelsgasse 6
D-67346 Speyer
GERMANY
(archive of Protestant (Reformed and Lutheran) churches in
the Palatinate; has many Protestant (Reformed and
Lutheran) parish vital registers, including some from the
Saarland)

Archiv der Evangelischen Kirche im Rheinland
Archivstelle Koblenz
Karmeliterstrasse 1-3
D-56068 Koblenz
GERMANY
(archive of the Evangelical (Lutheran and Reformed)
church in the Rhineland; has many Evangelical (Lutheran
and Reformed) parish vital registers, including some from
the Saarland)

SACHSEN. (SAXONY).

SAXONY. See also THURINGIA.

Evangelisch-Lutherische Landeskirche Sachsens
Landeskirchenarchiv
Lukasstrasse 6
D-01069 Dresden
GERMANY
(Evangelical (Lutheran) state church archive for the former
Kingdom of Saxony)

Evangelische Landeskirche Anhalts
D-06842 Dessau
GERMANY
(headquarters of Evangelical (Reformed and Lutheran)
church district of Saxony-Anhalt)

Evangelisches Konsistorium des Goerlitzer
    Kirchengebietes
Archiv der Evangelischen Kirchen von Schlesien
Berliner Strasse 62
D-02826 Goerlitz
GERMANY
(headquarters of Evangelical (Lutheran) church district of
Goerlitz/Görlitz; 70 volumes of parish registers)

Archiv der Evangelischen Kirche der Kirchenprovinz
 Sachsen
Am Dom 2
D-39104 Magdeburg
GERMANY
(general archive of Evangelical (Lutheran and Reformed)
church district of the former Prussian province of Saxony)

Kirchenbuchstelle Magdeburg
Halberstaedter Strasse 132
D-39112 Magdeburg
GERMANY
(church book archive of the Evangelical (Lutheran and
Reformed) church district of the former Prussian province
of Saxony)

Archiv und Bibliothek des Evangelischen Ministeriums
Comthurgasse 8
D-99084 Erfurt
GERMANY
(archive of documents pertaining to the church authorities
in Erfurt from the 16th century; has some parish vital
registers)

Kirchenbuchamt des Evangelisch-Lutherischen
Kirchengemeindeverbands Leipzig
Burgstrasse 1-5-Hof-3. Stock
D-04109 Leipzig
GERMANY
(church book office of Evangelical (Lutheran) association
of Leipzig; has parish vital registers of Evangelical
(Lutheran) churches in Leipzig *city*)

SCHAUMBURG-LIPPE. See under LIPPE.

SCHLESIEN. See SILESIA.

SCHLESWIG-HOLSTEIN.

Evangelisch-lutherische Landeskirche Schleswig-Holsteins
Daenische Strasse 27-35
Postfach 3449
D-24033 Kiel *(Street address D-24103)*
GERMANY
(administrative headquarters for Evangelical (Lutheran)
church of Schleswig-Holstein)

Kirchenbuchstelle Altona im Kirchenkreisverband
 Blankenese, Niendorf und Pinneberg
Iserbarg 1
D-22559 Hamburg
GERMANY
(church book office for church districts of Altona,
Blankenese, Niendorf, and Pinneberg)

Kirchenbuchamt Angeln
Rentamt des Kirchenkreises Angeln
Wassermuehlenstrasse 12
D-24376 Kappeln/Schlei
GERMANY
(church book office for church district of Angeln; has
Evangelical (Lutheran) parish vital registers for church
district of Angeln)

Kirchenbuchamt Eckernfoerde
Schleswiger Strasse 33
D-24340 Eckernfoerde
GERMANY
(church book office for church district of
Eckernfoerde/Eckernförde; has Evangelical (Lutheran)
parish vital registers for church district of
Eckernfoerde/Eckernförde)

Kirchenbuchamt fuer Eiderstedt
Marienstrasse 16
D-25836 Garding
GERMANY
(church book office for church district of Eiderstedt; has
Evangelical (Lutheran) parish vital registers for church
district of Eiderstedt)

Kirchenbuchamt Elmshorn
Kirchenstrasse 3
D-25337 Elmshorn
GERMANY
(church book office for Rantzau region; has Evangelical
(Lutheran) parish vital registers for town of Elmshorn only)

Kirchenbuchamt Eutin
Schlossstrasse 2
D-23701 Eutin
GERMANY
(church book archive for the Eutin city district of the
former Evangelical (Lutheran) district of Lübeck/Luebeck
in the Free State of Oldenburg; has Evangelical (Lutheran)
parish vital registers for the *city* of Eutin)

Nordelbisches Kirchenarchiv Gleschendorf
Am Kirchberg 4
D-23684 Scharbeutz
GERMANY
(church book archive for the Eutin rural district of the
former Evangelical (Lutheran) district of Lübeck/ Luebeck
in the Free State of Oldenburg; has Evangelical (Lutheran)
parish vital registers for the rural area of Eutin)

Kirchenbuchamt des Kirchenkreises Flensburg
Muehlenstrasse 19
D-24937 Flensburg
GERMANY
(church book office for the church district of Flensburg;
has Evangelical (Lutheran) parish vital registers for the
church district of Flensburg)

Kirchenkreisamt Harburg
Kirchenbuch- und Meldewesen
Hoelertwiete 5
D-21073 Hamburg
GERMANY
(church district office for the Hamburg-Harburg church
district; has Evangelical (Lutheran) parish vital registers for
the church district of Hamburg-Harburg)

Kirchenbuchamt Husum-Bredstedt
Schobueller Strasse 36
D-25813 Husum
GERMANY
(church book office for the church district of Husum and
Bredstedt; has Evangelical (Lutheran) parish vital registers
for Husum and Nordfriesland/North Frisia (Bredstedt))

Kirchenbuchamt Kiel
Falckstrasse 9
D-24103 Kiel
GERMANY
(church book office for city of Kiel; has Evangelical
(Lutheran) parish vital registers for *city* of Kiel only; rural
parish vital registers for church district of Kiel are kept in
local parishes or in Nordelbisches KIrchenarchiv Kiel)

Nordelbisches Kirchenarchiv
Anna-Paulsen-Haus
Winterbeker Weg 51
D-24114 Kiel
GERMANY
(Evangelical (Lutheran) parish vital registers for the Kiel
region)

Zentrale Vermittlungsstelle des Kirchenkreises Herzogtum
    Lauenburg
Schrangenstrasse 2
D-23909 Ratzeburg
GERMANY
(Evangelical (Lutheran) central search bureau for region of
the former Duchy of Lauenburg)

Kirchenbuchamt Luebeck
Baeckerstrasse 3-5
D-23564 Luebeck
GERMANY
(church book office for church district of Lübeck/Luebeck;
has Evangelical (Lutheran) parish vital registers for church
district of Lübeck/Luebeck beginning ca. 1870; earlier
parish vital registers are at Luebeck municipal archive)

Archiv der Hansestadt Luebeck
Muehlendamm 1-3
D-23552 Luebeck
GERMANY
(municipal/state archive for the city/state of
Luebeck/Lübeck; has Evangelical (Lutheran) parish vital
registers for Luebeck/Lübeck up to ca. 1870)

Kirchenbuchamt fuer Muensterdorf
Heinrichstrasse 1
D-25524 Itzehoe
GERMANY
(church book office for church district of
Muensterdorf/Münsterdorf (the Itzehoe area); has
Evangelical (Lutheran) parish vital registers for church
district of Muensterdorf/Münsterdorf)

Kirchenbuchamt Neumuenster
Am alten Kirchhof 5
D-24534 Neumuenster
GERMANY
(church book office for church district of Neumuenster/
Neumünster; has Evangelical (Lutheran) parish vital
registers, information about registers of rural parishes)

Kirchenbuchamt fuer Niendorf
Waidmannstrasse 35
D-22769 Hamburg
GERMANY
(church book office for Niendorf region; has Evangelical
(Lutheran) parish vital registers for Niendorf region)

Kirchenkreis Norderdithmarschen
Markt 27
D-25746 Heide
GERMANY
(church district administration for northern Dithmarschen;
no centralized church book repository)

Kirchenbuchamt fuer Oldenburg/Holstein
Kirchenstrasse 7
D-23730 Neustadt in Holstein
GERMANY
(church book office for Oldenburg/Holstein region; has
Evangelical (Lutheran) parish vital registers for
Oldenburg/Holstein region)

Kirchenbuchamt des Kirchenkreises Ploen
Kirchenstrasse 33
Postfach 229
D-24206 Preetz
GERMANY
(church book office for church district of Ploen/Plön,
including the Probstei; has Evangelical (Lutheran) parish
vital registers for church district of Ploen/Plön)

Kirchenbuchamt Rendsburg
An der Marienkirche 7-9
D-24768 Rendsburg
GERMANY
(church book office for church district of Rendsburg; has
Evangelical (Lutheran) parish vital registers for church
district of Rendsburg and Rendsburg military church books
ca. 1809-1818 and 1889-1945)

Kirchenbuchsammelstelle Schleswig
Norderdomstrasse 6
D-24837 Schleswig
GERMANY
(church book collection for church district of Schleswig;
has Evangelical (Lutheran) parish vital registers for church
district of Schleswig)

Kirchenbuchamt fuer Segeberg
Kirchplatz 1
D-23795 Bad Segeberg
GERMANY
(church book office for church district of (Bad) Segeberg;
has Evangelical (Lutheran) parish vital registers for church
district of (Bad) Segeberg)

Kirchenbuchamt fuer Stormarn
Rockenhof 1
D-22359 Hamburg
GERMANY
(church book office for church district of Stormarn; has
Evangelical (Lutheran) parish vital registers for church
district of Stormarn)

Rentamt des Kirchenkreises Suederdithmarschen
Klosterhof 17
D-25704 Meldorf
GERMANY
(treasurer's office of the church district of
Süderdithmarschen/Suederdithmarschen; no centralized
church book repository; parish vital registers kept locally at
Evangelisches Pfarramt: W-25767 Albersdorf, W-25719
Barlt, W-25541 Brunsbuettel, W-25712
Burg/Dithmarschen, W-27498 Helgoland, W-25770
Hemmingstedt, W-25709 Kronprinzenkoog, W-25746
Lohe-Rickelshof, W-25709 Marne, W-25704 Meldorf,
W-25785 Nordhastedt, W-25693 St. Michaelisdonn,
W-25727 Suederhastedt, W-25729 Windbergen, and
W-25797 Woehrden, respectively)

Rentamt des Kirchenkreises Suedtoendern
Wikinger Strasse 1
D-25917 Leck
GERMANY
(treasurer's office of the church district of
Suedtoendern/Südtöndern; has Evangelical (Lutheran)
parish vital registers for Suedtoendern/Südtöndern)

SIEBENBUERGEN. See ROMANIA.

SIEBENBÜRGEN. See ROMANIA.

SILESIA. See also EASTERN GERMANY.

Evangelisches Konsistorium des Goerlitzer
Kirchengebietes
Archiv der Evangelischen Kirchen von Schlesien
Berliner Strasse 62
D-02826 Goerlitz/Neisse
GERMANY
(archive in former German Democratic Republic (East
Germany) for Evangelical (Lutheran) church of Silesia; has
70 volumes of Evangelical (Lutheran) parish registers)

Evangelisches Zentralarchiv in Berlin
Kirchenbuchstelle
Jebensstrasse 3
D-10623 Berlin
GERMANY
(archive for parish vital registers of the Evangelical
(Lutheran) churches of the old Prussian Union to 1874
including 11 parishes of Silesia from the area between
Goerlitz and Waldenburg)

SOVIET UNION. See RUSSIA.

SUDETENLAND. See also EASTERN GERMANY.

Institut fuer Reformations- und Kirchengeschichte der
      boehmischen Laender
Buchenstrasse 34
D-74906 Bad Rappenau
GERMANY
(institute for Bohemian Reformation and church history)

Archiv des evangelischen Oberkirchenrates
Severin-Schreiber-Gasse 3
A-1180 Wien/Vienna
Oesterreich/AUSTRIA
EUROPE
(archive of the Lutheran chief council in Vienna, with
jurisdiction over Sudetenland)

Gemeinschaft evangelischer Sudetendeutscher
Boltensternstrasse 1
D-40239 Duesseldorf
GERMANY
(association of Lutheran Sudeten Germans in the Federal
Republic of Germany)

SWITZERLAND.
(No unified church book archive system; parish vital
registers sometimes at centralized state archive, sometimes
at local parish, sometimes in custody of civil registrars.)

THUERINGEN. See THURINGIA.

THÜRINGEN. See THURINGIA.

THURINGIA.

Archiv des Landeskirchenrats der
    Evangelisch-Lutherischen Kirche in Thueringen
Dr.-Moritz-Mitzenheim-Strasse 2
D-99817 Eisenach
GERMANY
(Evangelical (Lutheran) church archive for Thuringia,
including Reuss both old and new lines, Saxony-Altenburg,
Saxony-Gotha, Saxony-Meiningen,
Saxony-Weimar-Eisenach, Schwarzburg-Rudolstadt,
Schwarzburg-Sondershausen, and Thuringia; has some
Evangelical (Lutheran) parish vital registers and some
church visitation records)

TRANSYLVANIA. See ROMANIA.

UNITAS FRATRUM. See "MORAVIANS."

USSR. See RUSSIA.

WALDECK. See under HESSE.

WALDENSIANS. See under HUGUENOTS.

WESTPHALIA.
See also RHINELAND, LIPPE, etc.

Evangelische Kirche von Westfalen
Landeskirchenarchiv
Altstaedter Kirchplatz 5
D-33602 Bielefeld
GERMANY
(archive of Evangelical (Reformed and Lutheran) church of
Westphalia; has some Evangelical (Reformed and
Lutheran) parish vital registers)

Lippische Landeskirche
Leopoldstrasse 27
D-32756 Detmold
GERMANY
(headquarters of Evangelical (Reformed and Lutheran)
church in Lippe; has some Evangelical (Reformed and
Lutheran) parish vital registers for Lippe)

Personenstandsarchiv Detmold
Willi-Hofmann-Strasse 2
D-32756 Detmold
GERMANY
(Lower Saxony state archive and vital records archive for
Lippe and part of Westphalia; has duplicates of Evangelical
(Reformed and Lutheran) parish vital registers mostly
1815-1874)

Kreiskirchliches Zentralarchiv
Adolf-Stoecker-Strasse 3
D-44809 Bochum
GERMANY
(church book archive for church district of Bochum)

WEST PRUSSIA. See also EASTERN GERMANY.

Kirchenbuchstelle der Evangelischen Kirche der Union
Jebensstrasse 3
D-10623 Berlin
GERMANY
(archive for parish vital registers of Evangelical (Lutheran)
churches of the old Prussian Union; several thousand
registers)

WUERTTEMBERG.

Evangelischer Oberkirchenrat
Landeskirchliches Archiv fuer Wuerttemberg
Gaensheidestrasse 4
D-70184 Stuttgart
GERMANY
(headquarters of Evangelical (Lutheran) church in
Wuerttemberg/Württemberg; has 3,829 volumes of
duplicates of parish vital registers from 1808 to 1875 (and
two microfilm readers!) but will interlibrary loan films
within Germany)

Evangelische Landeskirche in Wuerttemberg
Lauterbadstrasse 31
D-72250 Freudenstadt
GERMANY
(branch office of Evangelical (Lutheran) church in
Wuerttemberg/Württemberg)

Evangelisches Kirchenregisteramt Stuttgart
Hospitalhof
Gymnasiumstrasse 36
D-70174 Stuttgart
GERMANY
(church registration office for city of Stuttgart; has
Evangelical (Lutheran) parish vital registers for *city* of
Stuttgart)

HEIMATORTSKARTEIEN

These are files registering over 18,000,000 people from former German-speaking territories filed generally by *Kreis* ("county") of residence as of 1 September 1939, with latest known addresses. These may be useful, especially for unusual surnames, if the *Kreis* is known but not the village or town. They were originally set up by German churches and the German Red Cross to help reunite dislocated families, friends, and neighbors after World War II. There have been over 11,000,000 inquiries, of which over 8,000,000 have been successful in establishing contacts. Please note that these files do not cover persons deceased by 1939 and are not primarily genealogical; however, they may be helpful in locating living members of a given family. Many files give birthdates and birthplaces of individuals.

Kirchlicher Suchdienst
Zentralstelle der Heimatortskarteien
Lessingstrasse 1
D-80336 Muenchen
GERMANY
(central headquarters for administration of all of the various homeland card files)

Heimatortskartei fuer Nordosteuropa
Abteilung Ostpreussen und Memelland
Meesenring 13
D-23566 Luebeck
GERMANY
(for East Prussia and northeastern Europe)

Heimatortskartei fuer Nordosteuropa
Abteilung Danzig-Westpreussen
Meesenring 13
D-23566 Luebeck
GERMANY
(for West Prussia and Danzig)

Heimatortskartei fuer Nordosteuropa
Abteilung Pommern
Meesenring 13
D-23566 Luebeck
GERMANY
(for Pomerania)

Heimatortskartei Mark Brandenburg
Auf dem Kreuz 41
Postfach 101420
D-86004 Augsburg
GERMANY
(for the march (border area) of Brandenburg)

Zentralkartei fuer Stadt- und Landkreis Landsberg/Warthe
Irma Krueger
Neuendorfer Strasse 83
D-13385 Berlin
GERMANY
(for the county of Landsberg on the Warthe)

Heimatkreiskartei fuer Stadt- und Landkreis Koenigsberg
(Neumark)
Eiermarkt 6
D-38100 Braunschweig/Brunswick
GERMANY
(for the county of Koenigsberg/Königsberg in the Neumark)

Zentralkartei fuer Stadt- und Landkreis Sorau
Guenther Krause
Osterymweg 3
D-44319 Dortmund
GERMANY
(for the county of Sorau)

Heimatortskartei
Abteilung Niederschlesien
Traenkgasse 9
Postfach 2187
D-96007 Bamberg *(Street address D-96052)*
GERMANY
(for Lower Silesia)

Heimatortskartei
Abteilung Oberschlesien-Breslau
Ostuzzistrasse 4
D-94032 Passau
GERMANY
(for Upper Silesia and Breslau/Wrocław)

Heimatortskartei Deutsche aus dem Wartheland und Polen
Engelbosteler Damm 72
D-30167 Hannover
GERMANY
(for the Wartheland district and Poland)

Heimatortskartei Nordosteuropa
Abteilung Deutsch-Balten
Meesenring 13
D-23566 Luebeck
GERMANY
(for Baltic Germans from Estonia and Latvia)

Heimatortskartei Nordosteuropa
Abteilung Litauen
Waldstrasse 1
D-25712 Burg (Dithmarschen)
GERMANY
(for Lithuania)

Heimatortskartei Suedosteuropa-Umsiedler
Abteilung Deutsche aus Russland, Bessarabien, Bulgarien
und Dobrudscha
Rosenbergstrasse 50
D-70176 Stuttgart
GERMANY
(for Germans from Russia, Bessarabia, Bulgaria, and Dobrogea)

HEIMATORTSKARTEIEN

Heimatortskartei fuer Sudetendeutsche
Von-der-Tann-Strasse 9 I
D-93047 Regensburg
GERMANY
(for Sudeten Germans (Czech Republic))

Heimatortskartei Suedosteuropa-Ostumsiedler
Abteilung Deutsche aus Ungarn, Rumaenien, Jugoslawien,
     Slowakei und Ruthenien
Rosenbergstrasse 50
D-70176 Stuttgart
GERMANY
(for Germans from Germany, Romania, Yugoslavia, Slovak
Republic, and Ruthenia)

EUROPEAN NATIONAL AND REGIONAL GENEALOGICAL AND HISTORICAL SOCIETIES

(Mostly staffed by unpaid volunteers who can't do extensive research, but will try to reply to well-put, specific questions in German, sometimes even English, referring you to somebody who can help, but do your homework - give full names, religion, all dates, occupation, & places; send ancestor charts, photocopies of old writing, 2 or 3 or more International Reply Coupons (available at post office) or $2.00 cash, keeping each family on a separate sheet, each with your name & address; use enough postage; write one letter to the right place, not dozens! These societies receive ca. 20,000 letters per year.)

EUROPE and WORLDWIDE.

Confédération Internationale de Généalogie et d'Héraldique
Secrétariat général
448 New Jersey Ave. SE
WASHINGTON DC 20003
USA
(international "umbrella organization" of major genealogical and heraldry societies; may be able to furnish current addresses of societies not found in this book, outdated, or otherwise not deliverable)

GERMANY. See also ALSACE, AUSTRIA, etc.

Deutsche Arbeitsgemeinschaft genealogischer Verbaende
      e.V., Sitz Stuttgart
NRW Personenstandsarchiv Rheinland
Schlossstrasse 12
D-50321 Bruehl
GERMANY
("umbrella organization" of German genealogical societies; all requests which cannot be directed to a specific society should be addressed here; will forward inquiries to the proper society)

Gesamtverein der deutschen Geschichts- und
      Altertumsvereine
Severinstrasse 222-228
D-51145 Koeln
GERMANY
(association of German historical and antiquity societies)

Bund der Familienverbaende e.V.,
      Bundesgeschaeftstelle Unterpoerlitz
Kirchgasse 18
D-98693 Ilmenau
GERMANY
("umbrella organization" of German family associations, i.e. surname societies)

Akademie fuer Genealogie, Heraldik und verwandte
      Wissenschaften e.V., Sitz Braunschweig
Gutenbergstrasse 12B
D-38118 Braunschweig
GERMANY
(genealogical educational academy; publishes *Basiswissen Genealogie*)

Verband der Lebensversicherungs-Unternehmer e.V.
Eduard-Pflueger-Strasse 55
D-53113 Bonn
GERMANY
(association of life insurance companies; useful in tracing current addresses of insured persons)

Deutscher Soldatenbund Kyffhaeuser e.V.
Taunusstrasse 63
D-65183 Wiesbaden
GERMANY
(German soldier society, much like the American Legion)

Zentralstelle fuer Personen- und Familiengeschichte
Seulberg
Birkenweg 13
D-61381 Friedrichsdorf
GERMANY
(German national genealogy and family history foundation headquarters for collecting, registering, and archiving all sorts of material for research; suggestions for further research; no individual memberships)

Verein zur Foerderung der Zentralstelle fuer
      Personen- und Familiengeschichte e.V.
Archivstrasse 11
D-14195 Berlin
GERMANY
(society for the furtherance of the above German national genealogy and family history foundation)

Der HEROLD, Verein fuer Heraldik, Genealogie und
      verwandte Wissenschaften, Sitz Berlin
Archivstrasse 12-14
D-14195 Berlin
GERMANY
(German national genealogical and heraldic society; official register of German coats of arms (over 150,000); publication: *Der Herold*)

Michael Becker (HG)
Strasse zum Loewen 16a
D-14109 Berlin
GERMANY
(corresponding secretary for HEROLD society)

Helmut Eckardt (HG)
Donnersmarckallee
D-13465 Berlin
GERMANY
(genealogical committee advisor for HEROLD society)

Genealogisch-Heraldische Gesellschaft mit dem Sitz in
      Goettingen e.V.
Evangelisch-reformiertes Gemeindehaus
Untere Karspuele 10
Postfach 2062
D-37010 Goettingen *(Street address D-37073)*
GERMANY
(genealogy and heraldry society)

EUROPEAN NATIONAL AND REGIONAL GENEALOGICAL AND HISTORICAL SOCIETIES

Heraldischer Verein zum Kleeblatt e.V.
Erhardt Haacke
Berliner Strasse 14e
D-30457 Hannover
GERMANY
(society for heraldry and nobility)

Gesellschaft fuer deutsche Sprache
Postfach 2669
D-6200 Wiesbaden
GERMANY
(Society for the German Language, including name
research; scientific German surname search for a fee)

Institut fuer niederdeutsche Sprache
Schnoor 41
D-28195 Bremen
GERMANY
(Institute for Low German language = *Plattdeutsch*)

Gesellschaft fuer deutsche Postgeschichte
Schaumainkai 53
Postfach 700420
D-60554 Frankfurt (Main) *(Street address D-60596)*
GERMANY
(German postal history society)

Ahnenlistenumlauf (ALU)
Rainer und Jutta Bien
Hauptstrasse 70
D-31699 Beckedorf bei Stadthagen
GERMANY
(central file of individual German pedigrees sent in by
participants; at least 14 volumes published)

Friedrich-Wilhelm-Euler-Institut fure
personengeschichtliche Forschung e.V., Sitz   Bensheim
Ernst-Ludwig-Strasse 21
D-64625 Bensheim
GERMANY
(institute for research on historical upper class; does not
answer private requests, only scientific or official inquiries)

Saechsisches Staatsarchiv Leipzig
Abteilung Deutsche Zentralstelle fuer Genealogie
Schongauer Strasse 1
Postfach 274
D-04002 Leipzig *(Street address D-04329)*
GERMANY
(source for genealogical records in the German Democratic
Republic; also has old ancestor file of a former all-German
national genealogical society, the ASTAKA or
Ahnenstammkartei, with hundreds of thousands of
ancestors listed)

Verein fuer das Deutschtum im Ausland
Landsberger Strasse 509
D-81241 Muenchen
GERMANY
(society for all German natives and German citizens living
outside Germany)

Arbeitsgemeinschaft historischer Kommissionen und
        landesgeschichtlicher Institute
Hauptstaatsarchiv
Mainzer Strasse 80
D-65189 Wiesbaden
GERMANY
(association of German regional historical commissions and
institutes; may be able to refer you to one for your area of
interest)

Hansischer Geschichtsverein
Archiv der Hansestadt Luebeck
Muehlendamm 1/3
D-23552 Luebeck
GERMANY
(historical society for the Hanseatic League)

Deutsche Burgenvereinigung e.V.
Marksburg
D-56338 Braubach am Rhein
GERMANY
(histories, pictures, and plans of castles in Europe;
publishes a magazine)

Amerika-Gesellschaft
Auswandererarchiv
Luebecker Strasse 10a
D-23795 Bad Segeberg
GERMANY
(archive of emigration to America)

Staedte-Bruecke e.V.
Postfach 76 04 44
D-22054 Hamburg
GERMANY
(international German-American town affiliation program
in which American families are linked with German
namesakes)

Deutsches Adelsarchiv
Schwanallee 21
D-35037 Marburg/Lahn
GERMANY
(archive of nobility of German lands)

Volksbund deutsche Kriegsgraeberfuersorge
Werner-Hilpert-Strasse 2
D-34117 Kassel
GERMANY
(society for upkeep of German military graves and
cemeteries)

Verein zur Foerderung EDV-gestuetzter familienkundlicher
        Forschungen e.V., Sitz Luenen
Schorlemmers Kamp 20
D-44536 Luenen
GERMANY
(computer genealogy society in Germany; publishes
Computergenealogie)

EUROPEAN NATIONAL AND REGIONAL GENEALOGICAL AND HISTORICAL SOCIETIES

Genealogischer Kreis in der Kameradschaft Siemens
    Erlangen e.V.
Theo Lonicer
Postfach 3240
D-91020 Erlangen
GERMANY
(genealogical society for employees of Siemens Co., a large
German corporation)

Genealogischer Kreis im Kulturkreis Siemens e.V.,
    Sitz Berlin
Siemensdamm 50
D-13629 Berlin
GERMANY
(genealogyical society for employees in the Berlin factory
of Siemens Co., a large German corporation)

Gruppe Familien- und Wappenkunde im
    Bundesbahn-Sozialwerk, Sitz Frankfurt
Gueter Strasse 9
D-60327 Frankfurt (Main)
GERMANY
(national network of local groups of German Federal
Railway employees and retirees working on genealogy and
heraldry; see local groups listed under particular regions:
Essen, Frankfurt, Hamburg, Hannover, Karlsruhe, Koeln,
Muenchen, Nuernberg, Saarbruecken, Stuttgart)

Genealogische Gesellschaft von Utah
Filiale Europa
Mr. G. Grasser
Lohweg 7
D-92367 Pilsach
GERMANY
(European branch of the Genealogical Society of Utah, the
microfilming arm of the Church of Jesus Christ of Latter-
day Saints)

Karin Beie (GK)
Eythstrasse 5
D-91058 Erlangen
GERMANY
(corresponding secretary for Siemens genealogical society)

Bund der Vertriebenen
Kreisverband Braunschweig e.V.
Arbeitskreis Genealogie, Auskunftsstelle
Gutenbergstrasse 12 b
D-38118 Braunschweig
GERMANY
(genealogy working group of the society of refugees and
expellees, concerned with research in middle and eastern
Germany now Polish, Czech, USSR, etc.)

Genealogyical Association of English-Speaking Researchres
    in Europe, Sitz Heidelberg
Zengerstrasse 1 (Mark-Twain-Village)
D-69126 Heidelberg
GERMANY
(mostly U.S. military personnel researching in Europe)

Verband Deutscher Heimat- und Volkstrachtenvereine
Dorotheenstrasse 21
D-81825 Muenchen
GERMANY
(society of German folk costume and local history societies;
publishes *Deutsche Trachtenzeitung*)

Forschungsstelle fuer Nationalitaeten und Sprachfragen
Rotenberg 21
D-35037 Marburg/Lahn
GERMANY
(research center for questions of nationality & language)

ALSACE.
See also FRANCE and HUGUENOTS and under
LORRAINE.

Cercle généalogique d'Alsace
Archives départementales
5, rue Fischart
F-67000 Strasbourg
FRANCE
(genealogical society for Alsace)

AUSTRIA.
See also SALZBURGERS, SUDETENLAND.

Institut fuer historische Familienforschung
Doeblinger Hauptstrasse 56/4
A-1190 Wien/Vienna
Oesterreich/AUSTRIA
EUROPE
(contact point for any genealogical research in Austria)

Heraldisch-Genealogische Gesellschaft "Adler"
Haarhof 4a
Postfach 25
A-1014 Wien/Vienna *(Street address A-1040)*
Oesterreich/AUSTRIA
EUROPE
(Austrian genealogy and heraldry society)

Arbeitsbund fuer Oesterreichische Familienkunde
Buergergasse 2A/1
A-8010 Graz
Oesterreich/AUSTRIA
EUROPE
(Austrian genealogical society)

Landesleitung Kaernten des Arbeitsbundes fuer
Oesterreichische Familienkunde
Dr. Frhr. von Krafft-Ebbing
Villacherring
A-9010 Klagenfurt
Oesterreich/AUSTRIA
EUROPE
(Carinthian branch of Austrian genealogical society)

Tiroler-Matrikel-Stiftung (Peestiftung)
Anichstrasse 18
A-6020 Innsbruck
Oesterreich/AUSTRIA
EUROPE
(Tirolean genealogical society)

Oberoesterreichische Landesstelle fuer Familienkunde
Bundesrealschule
A-4010 Linz
Oesterreich/AUSTRIA
EUROPE
(Upper Austrian genealogical society)

Deutschordens-Zentralarchiv
Singerstrasse 7
A-1010 Wien/Vienna
Oesterreich/AUSTRIA
EUROPE
(archive of the Teutonic Knights)

BADEN-WUERTTEMBERG.
See BADEN and WUERTTEMBERG.

BADEN.

Verein fuer Familien- und Wappenkunde in Wuerttemberg
    und Baden e.V.
Konrad-Adenauer-Strasse 8
(Wuerttembergische Landesbibliothek, Zimmer 103)
Postfach 105441
D-70047 Stuttgart *(Street address D-70173)*
GERMANY
(genealogy and heraldry society for both Baden and
Wuerttemberg)

Landesverein Badische Heimat e.V., Sitz Bretten
Ausschuss fuer Familienforschung
Heilbronnerstrasse 3
D-75015 Bretten
GERMANY
(regional genealogical group within the historical society
for northern Baden)

Freiburger Genealogischer Arbeitskreis
Dr. Hans Bartsch
Vogesenstrasse 4
D-79189 Bad Krozingen
GERMANY
(genealogical working group for southwestern Baden)

Interessentenkreis fuer Familienforschung
Karl Friedrich Kirner
Beyerlestrasse 12
D-78464 Konstanz
GERMANY
(genealogy group for southeastern Baden)

Verein fuer Geschichte des Bodensees und Umgebung
Stadtarchiv Konstanz
Benediktinerplatz 5
D-78467 Konstanz
GERMANY
(society for history of Lake Constance and vicinity)

Verein fuer Geschichte des Hegau e.V.
August-Ruf-Strasse 7 (Stadtarchiv)
D-78224 Singen
GERMANY
(society for history of the Hegau region, near Singen)

Verein fuer Geschichte und Naturgeschichte des Baars
Fuerstlich Fuerstenbergisches Archiv
Haldenstrasse 3
D-78166 Donaueschingen
GERMANY
(society for history and natural history of the Baar region)

Geschichtsverein Bachgau
Stettiner Strasse 6
D-63762 Grossostheim
GERMANY
(historical society for the Grossostheim area)

Breisgau-Geschichtsverein Schauinsland
Gruenwalder Strasse 15
D-79098 Freiburg (Breisgau)
GERMANY
(historical society for the Breisgau region)

Historischer Verein fuer Mittelbaden
Postfach 1569
D-77605 Offenburg
GERMANY
(historical society for the central Baden region)

Geschichtsverein Hochrhein e.V., Waldshut-Tiengen
Rathausstrasse 19
D-79761 Waldshut-Tienge
GERMANY
(historical society for the upper (southern) Rhine)

Gruppe Familien- und Wappenkunde im
        Bundesbahn-Sozialwerk, Ortsgruppe Karlsruhe
Winfried Bucker
Bahndirektion, Buero M
D-76139 Karlsruhe
GERMANY
(railway employee genealogy group for Karlsruhe area)

Historischer Verein Wertheim
Muehlenstrasse 26
D-97877 Wertheim
GERMANY
(historical society for Wertheim)

Centralarkiv for Invanderer fra Hessen/Pfalz 1759-64
Jan Hyllested
Markedsgade 34
DK-8900 Randers
Danmark/DENMARK
(central registry for emigrants from Baden-Durlach and the
Kraichgau to Denmark from 1759 to 1764)

BALTIC GERMANS.

Deutsch-Baltische Genealogische Gesellschaft
Reinhard-Zinkann-Haus (Haus der Deutsch-Balten)
Herdweg 79
D-64285 Darmstadt
GERMANY
(genealogical society for Germans from Baltic areas)

Forschungsstelle Baltikum der AGoFF
Winno von Loewenstein
Parkstrasse 45
D-51427 Bergisch-Gladbach
GERMANY
(Baltic subgroup of genealogical society for eastern areas)

Baltische Ahnen- und Stammtafeln
Isabella von Pantzer
Wahner Strasse 2
D-51143 Koeln
GERMANY
(publisher of Baltic ancestor charts and family lines)

Deutsch-Baltische Landsmannschaft im Bundesgebiet e.V.
Widmannstrasse 20
D-30519 Hannover
GERMANY
(homeland association for Baltic Germans in Germany)

Historischer Verein fuer Ermland
Ermlandweg 22 (Ermlandhaus)
D-45159 Muenster
GERMANY
(historical society for the Baltic region)

Heimatauskunftstelle Baltikum
Landesausgleichsamt Hessen
Luisenstrasse 13
D-65195 Wiesbaden
GERMANY
(German government Baltic information center)

Archiv der Estlaendischen Ritterschaft
c/o Georg von Krusenstjern
Weitlstrasse 81
D-81477 Muenchen
GERMANY
(archive of the Estonian knighthood)

Baltische Briefe
Deefkamp 13
D-29227 Grosshansdorf
GERMANY
(publishes Baltic genealogical material)

BANAT.

Landsmannschaft der Banater Schwaben und Rumaenien
    in Deutschland e.V.
Sendlinger Strasse 55
D-80331 Muenchen
GERMANY
(homeland association for Banat and Romanian Germans in
Germany)

BATSCHKA

Arbeitsgemeinschaft ostdeutscher Familienforscher
Dr. Helmut Flacker
Steingasse 4
D-79189 Bad Krozingen
GERMANY
(genealogical society for the Batschka region)

BAVARIA.
See also FRANCONIA, PALATINATE.

Bayerischer Landesverein fuer Familienkunde
Hauptstaatsarchiv
Ludwigstrasse 14, I
D-80539 Muenchen/Munich
GERMANY
(all-Bavarian genealogical society; publishes list of
researchers by region)

Hans-Peter Kaiserswerth (BL)
Lessingstrasse 7b
D-93049 Regensburg
GERMANY
(corresponding secretary for Bavarian genealogical society)

Helmut Schmidt
Bautzener Strasse 24
D-86167 Augsburg
GERMANY
(Augsburg local group of Bavarian genealogical society)

Lolo Anwander
Trivastrasse 15c
D-80637 Muenchen
GERMANY
(Munich local group of Bavarian genealogical society)

Gerhart Nebinger
Taxisstrasse 6
Postfach 1832
D-86623 Neuburg
GERMANY
(Neuburg local group of Bavarian genealogical society)

Lore Schretzenmayr
Erikaweg 58
D-93053 Regensburg
GERMANY
(Regensburg local group of Bavarian genealogical society)

Michael Fischl
Wilhelm-Niedermayer-Strasse 15
D-94104 Tittling
GERMANY
(Tittling local branch of Bavarian genealogical society)

Vereinigung des Adels in Bayern
Holbeinstrasse 5/II
D-81679 Muenchen *(Munich)*
GERMANY
(Bavarian nobility association)

Institut fuer bayrische Geschichte an der Uni Muenchen
Ludwigstrasse 14
D-80539 Muenchen *(Munich)*
GERMANY
(Munich University institut for Bavarian history)

Kommission fueer bayerische Landesgeschichte bei der
    Bayerischen Akademie der Wissenschaften
Marstallplatz 8
D-80539 Muenchen *(Munich)*
GERMANY
(Bavarian academy of sciences commission for Bavarian
history)

Verband fuer Orts- und Flurnamenforschung in Bayern
Leonrodstrasse 57
D-80626 Muenchen *(Munich)*
GERMANY
(society for Bavarian place-name and field-name research)

Verband bayerischer Geschichtsvereine
Marstallplatz 8
D-80539 Muenchen *(Munich)*
GERMANY
(association of Bavarian historical societies)

Historischer Verein fuer Bad Aibling und Umgebung
Heimatmuseum Bad Aibling
Wilhelm-Leibl-Platz 2
D-83043 Bad Aibling
GERMANY
(Bad Aibling regional historical society)

Gesellschaft fuer altbayrische Geschichte und Kultur der
    Weltenburger Akademie
Osterriedergasse 6
D-93326 Abensberg
GERMANY
(society for history and culture of old Bavaria, including
Upper Bavaria, Lower Bavaria, and the Upper Palatinate;
conducts workshops on genealogical research)

Historischer Verein fuer Mittelfranken e.V.
Staatliche Bibliothek (Schlossbibliothek)
D-91522 Ansbach
GERMANY
(historical society for Middle Franconia)

Geschichts- und Kunstverein Aschaffenburg
Schoenborner Hof
Wermbachstrasse 15
D-63739 Aschaffenburg
GERMANY
(Aschaffenburg historical and art society)

Heimatverein fuer den Landkreis Augsburg e.V.
Landratsamt
Prinzregentenplatz 4
D-86150 Augsburg
GERMANY
(Augsburg local history society)

Historischer Verein fuer Schwaben
Stadtarchiv
Fugger Strasse 12
D-86150 Augsburg
GERMANY
(historical society for the Swabia region)

Historischer Verein fuer Oberfranken
Ludwigstrasse 2 (Neues Schloss)
D-95444 Bayreuth
GERMANY
(historical society for Upper Franconia)

Verein fuer Heimatkunde des Berchtesgadener Landes e.V.
Salzburger Strasse 18
D-83471 Berchtesbaden
GERMANY
(historical society for the Berchtesgaden area)

Heimatverein Burghausen am Salzach
Burg 17
D-84489 Burghausen
GERMANY
(local history society for Burghausen)

Historische Gesellschaft Coburg e.V.
Eupenstrasse 108
D-96450 Coburg
GERMANY
(historical society for Coburg)

Historischer Verein Dillingen an der Donau
Ostendstrasse 7
D-89407 Dillingen (Donau)
GERMANY
(historical society for Dillingen)

Fuerstlich und Graeflich Fuggersches Familien- und
    Stiftungsarchiv
Ziegelstrasse 29
D-89047 Dillingen (Donau)
GERMANY
(Fugger family (financiers, philanthropists) and foundation
archive)

Historischer Verein Eichstaett
Universitaetsbibliiothek
Am Hofgarten 1
D-85072 Eichstaett
GERMANY
(historical society for Eichstaett)

Heimatverein Erlangen und Umgebung
Verein fuer Heimatschutz e.V.
Marktplatz 1
D-91054 Erlangen
GERMANY
(local history society for Erlangen and vicinity)

Zentralinstitut fuer fraenkische Landeskunde und
    allgcmcinc Rcgionalforschung dcr Uni Erlangcn-
    Nuernberg
Kochstrasse 4
D-91054 Erlangen
GERMANY
(University of Erlangen institute for Franconian local and
regional history)

Historischer Verein Freising e.V.
Stadtarchiv Freising
Rathaus
Obere Hauptstrasse 2
D-85354 Freising
GERMANY
(historical society for Freising)

Alt-Fuerth
Verein fuer Geschichte und Heimatforschung e.V.
Schlosshof 12
D-90768 Fuerth
GERMANY
(historical and local history society for Fuerth)

Arbeitsgemeinschaft fuer Heimatkunde Grafing e.V.
Dobelweg 16
D-90768 Fuerth
GERMANY
(local history society for Grafing)

Historischer Verein Guenzburg e.V.
Sophienstrasse 3
D-89312 Guenzburg
GERMANY
(historical society for Günzburg/Guenzburg)

Verein fuer Heimatkunde Gunzenhausen e.V.
Theodor-Heuss-Strasse 8
D-91710 Gunzenhausen
GERMANY
(local history society for Gunzenhausen)

Nordoberfraenkischer Verein fuer Natur-, Geschichts- und
    Landeskunde e.V.
Stadtarchiv
Unteres Tor 9
D-95028 Hof (Saale)
GERMANY
(natural history, history, and local history society for
northern Upper Franconia)

Historischer Verein Ingolstadt
Stadtarchiv
Auf der Schanz 45
D-85049 Ingolstadt (Donau)
GERMANY
(historical society for Ingolstadt)

Heimatverein Kempten e.V.
Grasmueckenweg 1
D-87439 Kempten
GERMANY
(local history society for Kempten)

Historischer Verein fuer Niederbayern
Residenz
Altstadt 79
D-84028 Landshut
GERMANY
(historical society for Lower Bavaria)

Historischer Verein fuer Stadt und Kreis Landsberg
    am Lech
Schanzwiese 34
D-86899 Landsberg (Lech)
GERMANY
(historical society for Landsberg and vicinity)

Museumsverband Lindau
Altes Rathaus
Reichsplatz
Postfach 2145
D-88111 Lindau *(Street address D-88131)*
GERMANY
(museum society for Lindau)

Muenchener Arbeitskreis fuer Familienforschung und
    Heimatgeschichte, Sitz Muenchen
Kleiststrasse 10
D-85521 Ottobrunn bei Muenchen
GERMANY
(genealogical and local history branch for Upper Bavaria,
near Munich)

Historischer Verein von Oberbayern
Winzererstrasse 68
D-80797 Muenchen *(Munich)*
GERMANY
(historical society of Upper Bavaria)

Historischer Verein Neu-Ulm
Illerholzweg 18
D-89231 Neu-Ulm
GERMANY
(historical society for Neu-Ulm)

Historischer Verein fuer Noerdlingen und das Ries
Stadtarchiv Noerdlingen
Rathaus
Marktplatz 1
D-86720 Noerdlingen
GERMANY
(historical society for Noerdlingen and vicinity)

Verein fuer Geschichte der Stadt Nuernberg
Stadtarchiv
Egidienplatz 23
D-90403 Nuernberg *(Nuremberg)*
GERMANY
(society for the history of Nuremberg)

Heimatverein Pottenstein
Hauptstrasse 19
D-91278 Pottenstein
GERMANY
(local history society for Pottenstein)

Historischer Verein fuer Oberpfalz und Regensburg
Dachauplatz 4
D-93047 Regensburg
GERMANY
(historical society for the Upper Palatinte and Regensburg)

Colloquium Historicum Wirsbergense
Heimat- und Geschichtsfreunde am Obermain e.V.
Neubaustrasse 2
D-92657 Redwitz
GERMANY
(historical society for the Würzburg/Wuerzburg area)

Historischer Verein Rosenheim
Kulturamt
Max-Bram-Platz 2a
D-83022 Rosenheim
GERMANY
(historical society for Rosenheim)

Heimatverein fuer Wasserburg am Inn und Umgebung e.V.
Arnikaweg 10
D-83543 Rott (Inn)
GERMANY
(local history society for Wasserburg am Inn and vicinity)

Historischer Verein Schrobenhausen
Paarstrasse 5
D-86529 Schrobenhausen
GERMANY
(historical society for Schrobenhausen)

Historischer Verein Schweinfurt e.V.
Friedrich-Rueckert-Bau
Martin-Luther-Platz
D-97421 Schweinfurt
GERMANY
(historical society for Schweinfurt)

Heimatverein Spalter Land e.V.
Hauptstrasse 43
D-91174 Spalt
GERMANY
(local history society for the Spalt area)

Historischer Verein fuer Straubing und Umgebung e.V.
Fraunhoferstrasse 9
D-94315 Straubing
GERMANY
(local history society for Straubing and vicinity)

Historischer Verein Tittmoning e.V.
Stadtplatz 12
D-84529 Tittmoning
GERMANY
(historical society for Tittmoning)

Historischer Verein fuer den Chiemgau zu Traunstein e.V.
Herzog-Otto-Strasse 7
D-83278 Traunstein
GERMANY
(historical society for Traunstein and the Chiemgau region)

Verein fuer Kunst und Altertum in Ulm und Oberschwaben
Stadtarchiv
Weinhof 12 (Schwoerhaus)
Postfach 3940
D-89029 Ulm (Donau) *(Street address D-89073)*
GERMANY
(society for art and antiquity in Ulm and Upper Swabia)

Heimatkundlicher Arbeitskreis im Oberpfaelzer Waldverein
Staatsarchiv
Kulturzentrum Hans Bauer
Pfarrplatz 4
D-92637 Weiden (Oberpfalz)
GERMANY
(local history group of the Upper Palatine Forest society)

Heimat- und Museumsverein Weissenhorn und Umgebung
Schulstrasse 5
Postfach 1206
D-89259 Weissenhorn *(Street address D-89264)*
GERMANY
(local history and museum society for Weissenhorn and vicinity)

Gruppe Familien- und Wappenkunde im
     Bundesbahn-Sozialwerk, Ortsgruppe Muenchen
Helmut Drobnitsch
Bahndirektion Buero B
D-80335 Muenchen *(Munich)*
GERMANY
(railway employee genealogy branch for Munich area)

Gruppe Familien- und Wappenkund im
    Bundesbahn-Sozialwerk, Ortsgruppe Muenchen
Erhard Nadler
Am Bergsteig 9
D-81541 Muenchen *(Munich)*
GERMANY
(railway employee genealogy branch for Munich area)

Gruppe Familien- und Wappenkunde im
    Bundesbahn-Sozialwerk, Ortsgruppe Nuernberg
Adolf Fischer
Juttastrasse 20
D-90480 Nuernberg *(Nuremberg)*
GERMANY
(railway employee genealogy branch for Nuremberg area)

Gruppe Familien- und Wappenkunde im
    Bundesbahn-Sozialwerk, Ortsgruppe Neuburg/Donau
Gerhart Nebinger
Postfach 1832 (VBW)
D-86623 Neuburg/Donau
GERMANY
(railway employee genealogy branch for area of Neuburg
on the Danube)

Gruppe Familien- und Wappenkunde im
    Bundesbahn-Sozialwerk, Ortsgruppe Augsburg
Dr. Friedrich Blendinger
Thanellerstrasse 3
D-86163 Augsburg
GERMANY
(railway employee genealogy branch for Augsburg area)

Dr. Wolfgang Knabe
Schwaebische Forschungsgemeinschaft
Universitaet Augsburg
Universitaetsstrasse 10
D-86159 Augsburg
GERMANY
(project to find descendants of the ca. 20,000 emigrants
between 1800 and 1914 from Bavaria Swabia (the
Augsburg area) from the 4,532 towns and villages of the
area)

Gesellschaft fuer Familienforschung in Franken e.V.
Archivstrasse 17
D-90408 Nuernberg *(Nuremberg)*
GERMANY
(society for genealogy in Franconia)

Gesellschaft fuer Familienforschung in der Oberpfalz e.V.,
Sitz Regensburg
Pustetstrasse 13
D-93155 Hemau
GERMANY
(society for genealogy in the Upper Palatinate)

Hans-Peter Kaiserswerth (GO)
Lessingstrassc 7b
D-93049 Regensburg
GERMANY
(contact person for Upper Palatinate genealogical society)

BELARUS.

E-mail: pkp2@pkp2.belpsk.minsk.by
(Minsk genealogical society)

BELGIUM.

Service de Centralisation des Études Généalogiques et
Démographiques de Belgique
Maison des Arts
Chaussée de Haecht Schaerbeck147
B-1030 Bruxelles/Brussels
Belgique/BELGIUM
(centralized referral service for inquiries on genealogical
research in Belgium)

Genealogicum Belgique
36 boulevard Lambermont
B- Bruxelles/Brussels
Belgique/BELGIUM
(Belgian genealogical society)

L'Office Généalogique et Héraldique de Belgique
Musées Royaux d'Art et d'Histoire
10 avenue des Nerviens
B-1040 Bruxelles/Brussels
Belgique/BELGIUM
(Walloon genealogical society in Belgium)

Vlaamse Vereniging voor Familiekunde
Centrum voor Familiegeschiedenis
E.A. v. Haverbckc
Van Heybeeckstraat 3
B-2060 Antwerpen-Merksem
Belgique/BELGIUM
(Flemish genealogical society with Center for Family
History, publishes *Vlaamse Stam*)

Genealogie ohne Grenzen
Postbus 10
NL-6343 ZG Klimmen
Nederland/NETHERLANDS
(publication covering the area of Liège, Aachen, and
Maastricht)

Fédération Généalogique et Héraldique de Belgique
rue de la Procession 39
B-1460 Ittre
Belgique/BELGIUM
(Belgian genealogy and heraldry society)

BERLIN.

Der HEROLD, Verein fuer Heraldik, Genealogie und
    verwandte Wissenschaften, Sitz Berlin
Archivstrasse 12-14
D-14195 Berlin
GERMANY
(national genealogical and heraldry society for all of
Germany, but located in Berlin)

Verein zur Foerderung der Zentralstelle fuer Personen- und
    Familiengeschichte, Sitz Berlin
Archivstrasse 12-14
D-14195 Berlin
GERMANY
(society for the advancement of the Center for German
Genealogy)

Helmut Eckardt
Dommersmarckallee 27
D-13465 Berlin
GERMANY
(contact person for society for advancement of the CGG
above)

Interessengemeinschaft Genealogie im Kulturverband
    Berlin e.V., Sitz Berlin
Heinrich-Heine-Strasse 11
D-10179 Berlin
GERMANY
(genealogy interest group in Berlin cultural association)

Verein fuer die Geschichte Berlins
Frau L. Gruendahl
Damaschkestrasse 33
D-10711 Berlin
GERMANY
(Berlin historical society)

Arbeitsgemeinschaft fuer Familienkunde im Kulturkreis
    Siemens e.V., Sitz Berlin
Goebelstrasse 143-145
D-13629 Berlin-Siemensstadt
GERMANY
(genealogical society for Siemens company employees;
Berlin, also all of Germany)

Historische Gesellschaft zu Berlin
Habelschwerdter Allee 45
D-14195 Berlin
GERMANY
(historical society for Berlin)

Historische Kommission zu Berlin
Kirchweg 33
D-14129 Berlin
GERMANY
(historical commission for Berlin)

BESSARABIA. See also RUSSIA.

Landsmannschaft der Bessarabiendeutschen
Florianstrasse 17
D-70188 Stuttgart
GERMANY
(homeland association for Bessarabian Germans)

Heimatmuseum der Deutschen aus Bessarabien
Lindach Strasse 37
D-75417 Muehlacker
GERMANY
(local history museum of the Germans from Bessarabia)

Arbeitsgemeinschaft ostdeutscher Familienforscher
Dr. Paul Edel
Ziegelstrasse 11
Postfach 1232
D-73402 Aalen
GERMANY
(genealogical society for genealogists for Bessarabia)

BOHEMIA. See CZECH REPUBLIC, SUDETENLAND.

BRANDENBURG.
See also MIDDLE GERMANY.

Forschungsstelle Ostbrandenburg-Neumark der AGoFF
Dipl.-Ing. Alfred Bley
Luetzelsachsen
Im Langewann 65
D-69469 Weinheim
GERMANY
(genealogical research center for eastern Brandenburg and
the Neumark)

Historische Kommission fuer Berlin und die
    Mark Brandenburg
Kirchweg 33
D-14129 Berlin
GERMANY
(historical commission for Berlin and the Brandenburg
border area)

Heike Brachwitz
Am Muehlenhof 5
D-26180 Rastede
GERMANY
(contact person for above eastern Brandenburg and
Neumark group)

Heimatkreis Koenigsberg (Neumark)
Kreuzstrasse 97
D-38118 Braunschweig *(Brunswick)*
GERMANY
(local history group for Koenigsberg in the Neumark)

Armin Weist
Sallgaster Strasse 31
D-13439 Berlin
GERMANY
(contact person for Brandenburg genealogical
association)

W. Heiduck
fruehere Leninallee 153
D-10360 Berlin
GERMANY
(contact for Brandenburg genealogical association)

Landesgeschichtliche Vereinigung fuer die Mark
Brandenburg e.V.
Eisenpfuhlstrasse 46
D-13437 Berlin
GERMANY
(historical society for Brandenburg, publishes
*Mitteilungsblatt und Jahrbuch fuer Brandenburgische
Landesgeschichte*)

BRAUNSCHWEIG. See BRUNSWICK.

BREMEN.

"Die Maus"
Gesellschaft fuer Familienforschung e.V., Sitz Bremen
Praesident-Kennedy-Platz 2
D-28203 Bremen
GERMANY
(genealogical society for Bremen and vicinity)

Uta Bothe (MS)
Platjenwerbe
Am Lohhof 17
D-27721 Ritterhude
GERMANY
(genealogical society for Bremen and vicinity)

Historische Gesellschaft Bremen e.V.
Am Staatsarchiv 1/Fedelhoeren
D-28203 Bremen
GERMANY
(historical society for Bremen)

Familienkundliche Kommission fuer Niedersachsen und
    Bremen sowie angrenzende ostfaelische Gebiete e.V.,
    Sitz Hannover
Georg W. Jahn
Schloss Ricklingen
Steinfeldstrasse 34
D-30826 Garbsen
GERMANY
(elite private genealogical society for Lower Saxony and
Bremen; membership by invitation only)

BRUNSWICK.

Braunschweigischer Geschichtsverein e.V.
Loewenwall 18B
D-38100 Braunschweig *(Brunswick)*
GERMANY
(historical society for Braunschweig/Brunswick)

Harzverein fuer Geschichte und Altertumskunde
Burgplatz 1
D-38100 Braunschweig *(Brunswick)*
GERMANY
(historical and antiquity society for the Harz region)

BUCHENLAND. See BUKOVINA.

BUKOVINA.

Forschungsstelle Galizien und Bukowina der AGoFF
Ernst Hexel (deceased)
Buchenauer Strasse 28
D-82256 Fuerstenfeldbrueck
GERMANY
(genealogical research center for Galicia, including
Bukovina, in Germany)

Arbeitsgemeinschaft ostdeutscher Familienforscher,
    Abteilung Bukowina
Dipl.-Ing. Kurt Neumann
Platanenstrasse 13
D-58644 Iserlohn
GERMANY
(Buchenwald genealogical society)

Raimund-Friedrich-Kaindl-Gesellschaft
Prof. Dr. Herbert Mayer
Raingarten 19
D-73650 Winterbach
GERMANY
(research group in Federal Republic of Germany for
Bukovina Germans)

Landsmannschaft der Buchenlanddeutschen e.V.
Artilleriestrasse 20
D-80636 Muenchen *(Munich)*
GERMANY
(homeland association for Bukovina Germans in Germany)
BURGENLAND.

Forschungsstelle Burgenland der AGoFF
Heinz Somargyvár
Bei der Rolandsmuehle 9
D-22763 Hamburg
GERMANY
(research group in Federal Republic of Germany for
Germans from western Hungary or Burgenland)

CARPATHIAN GERMANS.

Gymnasial Professor a.D. Erich Sirchich
Dammerstockstrasse 11
D-76199 Karlsruhe
GERMANY
(research group in Germany for Carpathian Germans)

Karpathendeutsche Landsmannschaft Slowakei
Breslauer Strasse 32
D-70806 Kornwerstheim
GERMANY
(homeland association for Slovakian Carpathian Germans
in Germany)

CENTRAL GERMANY. See MIDDLE GERMANY.

EUROPEAN NATIONAL AND REGIONAL GENEALOGICAL AND HISTORICAL SOCIETIES

CZECH REPUBLIC. See also SUDETENLAND.

Vereinigung sudetendeutscher Familienforscher, Sitz
    Regensburg
Adolf Fischer
Juttastrasse 20
D-90480 Nuernberg *(Nuremberg)*
GERMANY
(researchers working on German families in present-day
Czech Republic)

Collegium Carolinum e.V.
Forschungsstelle fuer die boehmischen Laender
Hochstrasse 8/II
D-80538 Muenchn *(Munich)*
GERMANY
(research center for Bohemia)

DANUBE SWABIANS.

Forschungsstelle Donauschwaben der AGoFF
Winfried Kniesel
Pommernstrasse 24
D-27749 Darmstadt-Eberstadt
GERMANY
(genealogical research center for Danube Swabians)

Forschungsstelle Donauschwaben der AGoFF
Dr. Helmut Flacker
Steingasse 4
D-79189 Bad Krozingen
GERMANY
(genealogical research center for Danube Swabians)

Arbeitskreis donauschwaebischer Familienforscher, Sitz
Schriesheim
Goldmuehlestrasse 30
D-71069 Sindelfingen
GERMANY
(genealogical working group for Danube Swabians)

Werner Weissmueller (AD)
Im Rossgarten 17
D-88348 Saulgau
GERMANY
(contact person for Danub Swabian genealogical group)

Landsmannschaft der Donauschwaben aus Jugoslawien-
    Burgenland e.V.
Charlottenplatz 17 II
D-70123 Stuttgart
GERMANY
(homeland association for Danube Swabians from former
Yugoslavia and the Burgenland area of Austria)

DANZIG. See also WEST PRUSSIA.

Bund der Danziger
Muehlenbruecke 1
D-23552 Luebeck
GERMANY
(federation of Danzigers)

Arbeitsgemeinschaft ostdeutscher Familienforscher,
    Gruppe Danzig
Dieter God
Schorlemmers Kamp 20
D-44536 Luenen
GERMANY
(Danzig genealogy group)

DENMARK. See also SCHLESWIG-HOLSTEIN.

Centralarkiv for Invandrere 1759-1764
Jan Hyllested
Markedsgade 34
DK-8900 Randers
Danmark/DENMARK
(private research center for immigrants from the
Bergstrasse, the Durlach area, the Kraichgau, and the
Palatinate to the Alheide region of Denmark in 1759-1764)

Sammenslutningen of Slaegtshistoriske Foreninger
DK-8210 Aarhus V
Danmark/DENMARK
(federation of Danish genealogy societies)

Samfundet for Dansk Genealogi og Personalhistorie
Finn Andersen
Grysgårdsvej 22
DK-2400 København NV *(Copenhagen)*
Danmark/DENMARK
(Danish society for genealogy and personal history)

Det Danske Udvandrerarkiv
Arkivstrade 1
P.O. Box 731
DK-9100 Aalborg
Danmark/DENMARK
(Danish emigration library and archive affiliated with
Aalborg University; has emigrant file)

Dansk Genealogisk Institut
Nørre Volgade 80
DK-1358 København *(Copenhagen)*
Danmark/DENMARK
(private Danish genealogical institute)

Slaegtshistorisk Forening for Sto København
Snerlevej 33
DK-2820 Gentofte
Danmark/DENMARK
(genealogical society for Copenhagen area)

Heimatkundliche Arbeitsgemeinschaft fuer Nordschleswig
Vestergade 30
DK-60200 Aabenraa
Danmark/DENMARK
(genealogical society for North Schleswig)

EUROPEAN NATIONAL AND REGIONAL GENEALOGICAL AND HISTORICAL SOCIETIES

DOBRUDSCHA/DOBRUDJA

Landsmannschaft der Dobrudscha- und Bulgariendeutschen
Hasenbergstrasse 35
D-70839 Gerlingen
GERMANY
(homeland association for Dubrudja and Bulgarian
Germans in Germany)

EAST PRUSSIA. See PRUSSIA.

EASTERN GERMANY. See also POLAND, GERMANY,
BANAT, BATSCHKA, BESSARABIA, BUKOVINA,
CARPATHIAN GERMANS, GALICIA, MIDDLE
GERMANY, POMERANIA, PRUSSIA (EAST AND
WEST), SILESIA, SLOVAKIA, TRANSYLVANIA,
VOLHYNIA.

Arbeitsgemeinschaft ostdeutscher Familienforscher e.V.,
    Sitz Herne
z.H. Martin Opitz
Bibliothek, Kulturzentrum
Berliner Platz 11
D-44623 Herne
GERMANY
("umbrella organization" of all pre-World War II
genealogical groups for eastern Germany (east of the
former German Democratic Republic), publishes
Ostdeutsche Familienkunde and *Archiv ostdeutscher
Familienforscher*)

Johann-Gottfried-Herder-Institut
Gisonenweg 5-7
D-35037 Marburg
GERMANY
(institute for history and culture of eastern Germany (east
of the former German Democratic Republic))

Gesellschaft fuer ostmitteleuropaeische Landeskunde und
    Kultur
Zum Nordhaag 5
D-58313 Herdecke
GERMANY
(society for east central European geography and culture;
membership by invitation only)

Studienstelle ostdeutsche Genealogie der Forschungsstelle
    Ostmitteleuropa
Universitaet Dortmund
Emil-Fisse-Strasse 50
D-44227 Dortmund
GERMANY
(study center for eastern German genealogy; has a large
West Prussian index)

Herbert Sylvester
Nachtigallenweg 14
D-50997 Koeln
GERMANY
(corresponding secretary for eastern German genealogical
"umbrella organization"; has regional list of researchers)

Lore Schretzenmayr
Erikaweg 58
D-93053 Regensburg
GERMANY
(keeper of ancestral card-file for eastern German
genealogical organization)

Arbeitsgemeinschaft fuer mitteldeutsche Familienforschung
    e.V. (AMF)
Prof. Dr. Hans-Joachim Anderson
Cappel
Goldbergstrasse 23
D-35043 Marburg/Lahn
GERMANY
(working group of genealogists for central Germany (the
former DDR), publishes *Mitteldeutsche Familienkunde*)

Bund der Vertriebenen
Kreisverband Braunschweig e.V.
Arbeitskreis Genealogie, Auskunftsstelle
Gutenbergstrasse 12 b
D-38118 Braunschweig
GERMANY
(genealogy working group of the society of refugees and
expellees from eastern areas)

EASTPHALIA. See OSTFALEN.

EAST PRUSSIA. See PRUSSIA.

EGERLAND. See SUDETENLAND.

ENGLAND.

Anglo-German Family History Society
Peter Towey
14 River Reach
Teddington, Middlesex TW11 9QL
UNITED KINGDOM
e-mail: 100535.2632@compuserve.com
(German genealogical society for German-British persons)

ESTONIA. See BALTIC GERMANS.

FRANCE. See also ALSACE, BELFORT, HUGUENOTS,
LORRAINE.

Federation des Sociétés françaises de Généalogie,
    d'Héraldique et de Sigillographie
11, boulevard Pershing
F-78000 Versailles
FRANCE
(federation of French genealogy, heraldry, and seal
societies)

Federation française de Genealogie
2, Rue de Turbigo
F-75001 Paris
FRANCE
(French genealogical federation)

Les Cieux Noms de France
12, rue Caumartin
F-75009 Paris
FRANCE
(genealogical society for all of France)

Centre d'entr'aide généalogique
Boîte postale 101
F-75862 Paris Cedex 18
FRANCE
(genealogists' mutual aid group)

Le Société du Grand Armorial de France
179, Boulevard Haussmann
F-75000 Paris
FRANCE
(heraldry society for France)

Féderation Française des généalogistes
64, rue Richelieu
F-75002 Paris
FRANCE
(French society of genealogists)

Chambre Syndicale des généalogistes
18, rue du Cherche-Midi
F-75006 Paris
FRANCE
(French association of genealogists)

Centre International Huguenot
47, rue de Clichy
F-75009 Paris
FRANCE
(world Huguenot information center)

Cercle Généalogique et Héraldique de Normandie
17, rue Louis Malliot
F-76000 Rouen
FRANCE
(genealogical society with card index of ca. 40,000 passengers through LeHavre)

Groupement gênêalogique du Havre & Seine-Maritime
Boîte postale 80
F-76050 LeHavre Cedex
FRANCE
(LeHavre genealogical society; has card index of some emigrants via LeHavre 1784-1844)

France Génealogique
Jacques dell' Acquo
Les Frènes 52
55 Boulevard de Charonne
F-75011 Paris
FRANCE
(genealogy publication for France)

FRANCONIA (in northern BAVARIA).

Gesellschaft fuer Familienforschung in Franken
Archivstrasse 17 (Staatsarchiv)
D-90408 Nuernberg *(Nuremberg)*
GERMANY
(genealogical society for Franconia, publishes *Blaetter fuer Fraenkische Familienkunde* and a diskette with regional list of researchers)

Edgar Hubrich (GF)
Steinbuehlstrasse 7
D-91301 Forchheim
GERMANY
(research contact for Franconian genealogical society)

Gesellschaft fuer fraenkische Geschichte
Robert-Koch-Strasse 4
D-99096 Erlangen
GERMANY
(historical society for Franconia)

Historischer Verein fuer Mittelfranken
Regierungsbibliothek
Schloss
D-91522 Ansbach
GERMANY
(historical society for Middle Franconia)

Historischer Verein fuer Oberfranken
Luitpoldplatz 7
D-95444 Bayreuth
GERMANY
(historical society for Upper Franconia)

FULDA. See HESSEN-KASSEL.

GALICIA.

Forschungsstelle Galizien und Bukowina der AGoFF
Ernst Hexel *(now deceased)*
Buchenaustrasse 28
D-82256 Fuerstenfeldbrueck
GERMANY
(genealogical center for Galicia)

GERMANY. See first listings in this section, before ALSACE.

HAMBURG.

Genealogische Gesellschaft, Sitz Hamburg, e.V.
Alsterchaussee 11
Postfach 302042
D-20307 Hamburg
GERMANY
(genealogical society for Hamburg, Schleswig-Holstein, northern Lower Saxony, and Mecklenburg, co-publishes *Niederdeutsche Familienkunde*)

Verein fuer Hamburgische Geschichte
ABC-Strasse 19
D-20354 Hamburg
GERMANY
(historical society for Hamburg)

Sigrun Ulbrich (GH)
Schulstrasse 22
D-22880 Wedel
GERMANY
(she is contact person for the Hamburg society)

Arbeitskreis Bergedorf der Genealogischen Gesellschaft
    Hamburg
(located Torturm Schloss Bergedorf, Erdgeschoss)
Harald Richart
Wentorfer Strasse 84a
D-21029 Hamburg
GERMANY
(local branch of Hamburg society)

Vereinigung fuer Heimatkunde und Heimatpflege im
    Alsterraum
Herrn Dr. E. Reusch
Basaltweg 72
D-22395 Hamburg
GERMANY
(society for local history and preservation in the Alster
area)

HESSE.

Arbeitsgemeinschaft der Familienkundlichen
    Gesellschaften in Hessen
Ernst-Otto Braasch
Graefestrasse 35
Postfach 410338
D-34065 Kassel-Wilhelmshoehe *(Street address D-34121)*
GERMANY
(umbrella organization of genealogical societies in Hesse,
publishes *Hessische Familienkunde* and *Hessische
Ahnenlisten*)

Centralarkiv for Invanderer fra Hessen/Pfalz 1759-64
Jan Hyllested
Markedsgade 34
DK-8900 Randers
Danmark/DENMARK
(central registry for emigrants from Hessen
to Denmark from 1759 to 1764)

Hessische Familiengeschichtliche Vereinigung e.V., Sitz
    Darmstadt
Karolinenplatz 3 (Staatsarchiv)
D-64289 Darmstadt
GERMANY
(genealogical society for Hesse-Darmstadt; computer
diskette with regional list of researchers)

Geschichts- und Museumsverein
Rittergasse 3-5
D-36304 Alsfeld
GERMANY
(historical and museum society for Alsfeld)

Verein fuer Geschichte und Landeskunde e.V.
Ernst-Moritz-Arndt-Strasse 2B
D-61348 Bad Homburg vor der Hoehe
GERMANY
(historical and local history society for Bad Homburg)

Heimat- und Geschichtsverein Bischofsheim
Schillerstrasse 25
D-65474 Bischofsheim
GERMANY
(local history and historical society for Bischofsheim)

Buedinger Geschichtsverein
In der Langgewann 58
D-65654 Buedingen
GERMANY
(historical society for Buedingen)

Geschichtsverein fuer Butzbach und Umgebung
Marktplatz 3
D-35510 Butzbach
GERMANY
(historical society for Butzbach and vicinity)

Frankfurt Historische Kommission
Karmelitergasse 5 (Stadtarchiv)
D-60311 Frankfurt (Main)
GERMANY
(historical commission for Frankfurt am Main)

Frankfurter Verein fuer Geschichte und Altertumskunde
    e.V.
Karmelitergasse 5 (Stadtarchiv)
D-60311 Frankfurt (Main)
GERMANY
(Frankfurt society ofr history and antiquity)

Friedberger Geschichtsverein e.V.
Haagstrasse 16 (Stadtarchiv)
D-61169 Friedberg
GERMANY
(historical society for Friedberg)

Fuldaer Geschichtsverein e.V.
Stadtschloss
D-36037 Fulda
GERMANY
(historical society for Fulda)

Geschichtsverein Herborn e.V.
Schlossstrasse 3
D-35745 Herborn
GERMANY
(historical society for Herborn)

Huenfelder Kultur- und Museumsgesellschaft e.V.
Am Kirchplatz
D-36088 Huenfeld
GERMANY
(culture and museum society for Huenfeld)

Verein fuer Heimatkunde Koenigstein im Taunus
Hauptstrasse 3
D-61462 Koenigstein (Taunus)
GERMANY
(society for local history of Koenigstein)

Verein fuer Geschichte und Heimatkunde der Stadt
    Kronberg im Taunus e.V.
Koenigsteiner Strasse 6d
D-61476 Kronberg (Taunus)
GERMANY
(society for history and local history of Kronberg)

Historische Kommission fuer Hessen
Friedrichsplatz 15
D-35037 Marburg
GERMANY
(historical commision for Hesse)

Verein fuer Geschichte- und Heimatkunde Oberursel e.V.
Postfach 1146
D-61401 Oberursel
GERMANY
(society for history and local history of Oberursel)

Hanauer Geschichtsverein
Schlossplatz 2
D-63450 Hanau
GERMANY
(historical society for Hanau)

Heimatmuseum Walldorf
Waldstein 100 (Stadthalle)
D-64546 Moerfelden-Walldorf
GERMANY
(local history museum for Walldorf)

Waldeckischer Geschichtsverein e.V.
Schlossstrasse 24
D-34454 Arolsen
GERMANY
(historical society for Waldeck region)

Dieter Zwinger (HV)
Osannstrasse 24
D-64285 Darmstadt
GERMANY
(contact person for Hessian genealogical society)

Rainer Koetting
Am Karlshof 12
D-64287 Darmstadt
GERMANY
(keeps ancestral file of Hessian genealogical society)

Historischer Verein fuer Hessen
Schloss
D-64283 Darmstadt
GERMANY
(historical society for Hesse-Darmstadt)

Oberhessischer Geschichtsverein Giessen e.V.
Stadtarchiv
Berliner Platz 1
D-35390 Giessen
GERMANY
(historical society for Upper Hesse (Lahn-Giessen area))

Gruppe Familien- und Wappenkunde im
    Bundesbahn-Sozialwerk
Ortsgruppe Frankfurt/Main
Gueterstrasse 9
D-60327 Frankfurt am Main
GERMANY
(railroad employee local genealogy branch for Frankfurt
area)

Gesellschaft fuer Familienkunde in Kurhessen und
    Waldeck e.V.
Postfach 101346
D-34065 Kassel-Wilhelmshoehe
GERMANY
(genealogical society for Hesse-Kassel (Electoral Hesse)
and Waldeck)

Friedrich Hamm
Geibelstrasse 2
D-34117 Kassel
GERMANY
(corresponding secretary for Hesse-Kassel genealogical
society)

Genealogisch-Heraldische Gesellschaft mit dem Sitz in
    Goettingen e.V.
Ev.-ref. Gemeindehaus
Untere Karspuele 11
D-37073 Goettingen
GERMANY
(genealogical society for Goettingen and vicinity)

Vereinigung fuer Familien- und Wappenkunde Fulda e.V.,
    Sitz Fulda
Taunusstrasse 4
D-36043 Fulda
GERMANY
(genealogy and heraldry society for Fulda and vicinity; co-
publishes *Hessische Familienkunde* and *Hessische
Ahnenlisten*)

Familienkundliche Gesellschaft fuer Nassau und Frankfurt
    e.V., Sitz Wiesbaden
Hessisches Hauptstaatsarchiv
Mosbacher Strasse 55
D-65187 Wiesbaden
GERMANY
(genealogical society for Hesse-Nassau and Frankfurt)

Norbert Michel (FG)
Milanstrasse 4
D-65201 Wiesbaden
GERMANY
(corresponding secretary for Hesse-Nassau genealogical
society above)

Arbeitsgemeinschaft fuer Walldorfer Geschichte und
  Genealogie, Sitz Walldorf
Klagenfurter Ring 23
D-65187 Wiesbaden-Biebrich
GERMANY
(historical and genealogical working group for local area of
Walldorf near Frankfurt)

Verein fuer hessische Geschichte und Landeskunde e.V.
  Kassel
Moenchebergstrasse 19
Postfach 101380
D-34013 Kassel *(Street address D-34125)*
GERMANY
(local history society for Hesse)

HESSEN. See HESSE.

HOLLAND.

Nederlanse genealogische Vereniging
Postbus 976
NL-1000 AZ Amsterdam
Nederland/NETHERLANDS
(Dutch genealogical society; publishes *Gens Nostra*)

Centraal Bureau voor Genealogie
Prins-Willem-Alexander-Hof 22
Postbus 11755
NL-2595 AT 's Gravenhage/The Hague
Nederland/NETHERLANDS
(Dutch genealogy office; publishes *Mededelingen*; index of
4,000,000 deaths between 1940 and 1970; millions of
newspaper clippings 1795-present; 55,000 genealogical
manuscripts)
Internet:
http://ourworld.compuserve.com/homepages/paulvanV/

Koninklijk Nederlandsch Genootschap voor Geschlacht- en
Wappenkunde
Prins-Willem-Alexander-Hof 24
NL-2529 AB 's Gravenhage
Nederland/NETHERLANDS
(Dutch genealogy and heraldry society; publishes *De
Nederlandsche Leeuw*)

Werkgroep genealogisch Onderzoek Duitsland
P. C. Hooftlaan 9
NL-3018 HG Amersfoort
Nederland/NETHERLANDS
(Dutch genealogical working group for families with
German connections)

Brabantse Leeuw
Drukkerij-Juten
Parade 17
NL- s'Hertogenbosch
Nederland/NETHERLANDS
(genealogical society for Brabantine people)

Zuidhollandse Vereniging voor Genealogie
Postbus 404
NL- Rotterdam
Nederland/NETHERLANDS
(genealogical society for Zuidholland
province, publishes *Ons Voorgeslacht*)

Fryske Akademy
Coulonhus
Doelestrjitte 8
NL-8911 DX Ljouwert/Leeuwarden
Nederland/NETHERLANDS
(Frisian academy for Frisian culture)

Hoge Raad van Adel
71 Zeestraat
NL- s'Gravenhage
Nederland/NETHERLANDS
(arbiters of armorial bearings in Holland)

Niederlaendische Ahnengemeinschaft
Mittelburgwall 46
D-25840 Friedrichstadt/Eider
GERMANY
(German genealogical society for those with Dutch
ancestry)

Genealogie ohne Grenzen
Postbus 10
NL-6343 ZG Klimmen
Nederland/NETHERLANDS
(publication covering the area of Liège, Aachen, and
Maastricht)

HOLSTEIN. See also SCHLESWIG-HOLSTEIN.

Vereinigung fuer Familienkunde, Sitz Elmshorn
Besenbeker Strasse 121
D-25535 Elmshorn
GERMANY
(genealogical society for Elmshorn-Pinneberg area)

Luebecker Arbeitskreis fuer Familienforschung
Erich Gercken
Moltkestrasse 20
D-23564 Luebeck
GERMANY
(genealogy working group for Luebeck and vicinity)

Heimatbund Eiderstedt
Friedrich Johannsen
D-25881 Tating
GERMANY
(local history society for the Eiderstedt region)

HUGUENOTS. See also FRANCE.

Deutscher Hugenotten-Verein e.V.
Deutsches Hugenotten-Zentrum
Hafenplatz 9a
D-34385 Bad Karlshafen
GERMANY
(genealogical research center for society of Huguenots in
Germany)

Ute Bilshausen-Lasalle (DH)
An der Schule 14
D-30938 Burgwedel
GERMANY
(contact person for Huguenot branch of society above)

Dr. Theo Kiefner (DH)
Lehengasse 5
D-75365 Calw
GERMANY
(contact person for Waldensian branch of Huguenot
society)

Centre International Huguenot
47, rue de Clichy
F-75009 Paris
FRANCE
(genealogical and historical society for Huguenots in all
countries)

HUNGARY. See DANUBE SWABIANS.

Magyar Országos Levéltár Konyvtara
Bécsikapu-tér 4
H-1250 Budapest 1
HUNGARY
(Hungarian genealogical society)

Koezep-Europa Intezet
Teleki Laszlo Alapstvany
Szilagyi Erzebetfasor 22c
H-1125 Budapest
HUNGARY
(Hungarian emigration research center)

Landsmannschaft der Deutschen aus Ungarn
Bundesverband
D-80538 Muenchen *(Munich)*
GERMANY
(homeland association of Germans from Hungary in
Germany)

Arbeitsgemeinschaft ostdeutscher Familienforscher
Dr. Helmut Flacker
Steingasse 4
D-79189 Bad Krozingen
GERMANY
(German genealogical society for Germans in the Batschka)

Arbeitsgemeinschaft ostdeutscher Familienforscher
Antal von Könczöl
Schwarzwaldstrasse 34a
D-79296 Reute
GERMANY
(genealogical society for Germans from Hungary)

Bács-Kiskun Megyei Levéltár
Kossuth tér 1
Pf. 7
H-6001 Kecskemét
HUNGARY
(center for the Batschka region)

Baranja Begyei Levéltár
Kossuth Lajos u. 11
Pf. 392
H-7601 Pécs
GERMANY
(center for the Fünfkirchen area)

IRELAND.

The Palatine Society of Ireland
30-31 Wicklow Street
Dublin 2
IRELAND

Irish Palatine Heritage Center
N21
Rathkeale, Co. Limerick
IRELAND

LATVIA. See BALTIC GERMANS.

LIPPE. See also LOWER SAXONY.

Naturwissenschaftlicher und Historischer Verein fuer das
Land Lippe e.V.
Willi-Hofmann-Strasse 2
D-32756 Detmold
GERMANY
(historical and natural history society for Lippe)

Lipper Heimatbund
Bismarckstrasse 8
D-32756 Detmold
GERMANY
(local history society for Lippe)

Arbeitsgemeinschaft fuer schaumburgische Familienkunde
Gut Nienfeld
D-31867 Pohle ueber Hameln
GERMANY
(genealogical society for Schaumburg-Lippe)

Schaumburg-Lippischer Heimatverein
Dr. Roswitha Somer
Luebingstrasse 4
D-31675 Bueckeburg
GERMANY
(local history society for Schaumburg-Lippe)

LITHUANIA. See BALTIC GERMANS.

LORRAINE. See also FRANCE.

Union des cercles généalogiques d'Alsace, Lorraine,
    Meurthe et Moselle, Meuse et Vosges
Archives départementales de Meurthe et Moselle
1, rue de la Monnaie
F-54000 Nancy
FRANCE
(umbrella organization of genealogical societies for the
Lorraine region)

Cercle généalogique de Lorraine
Archives départementales de Meurthe et Moselle
1, rue de la Monnaie
F-54000 Nancy
FRANCE
(genealogical society for Lorraine)

Union des Cercles Généalogiques de la Lorraine
Boîte postale 8
F-54131 Saint Max Cedex
FRANCE
(federation of genealogical societies in Lorraine)

Cercle généalogique de la Moselle
1, allee du Château
F-57050 Saint-Julien-les-Metz
FRANCE
(genealogical society for the Moselle region)

Societe d'Histoire et d'Archeologie de la Lorraine
Hôtel de la Préfecture
F-75000 Metz
FRANCE
(historical and archaeological society for Lorraine)

LOWER SAXONY.

Niedersaechsischer Landesverein fuer Familienkunde e.V.
Am Bokemahle 14-16 (Stadtarchiv)
D-30171 Hannover
GERMANY
(genealogical society for Lower Saxony; co-publishes
Niederdeutsche Familienkunde)

Historischer Verein fuer Niedersachsen
Hauptstaatsarchiv
Am Archiv 1
D-30169 Hannover
GERMANY
(historical society for Lower Saxony)

Olaf Meyer (NL)
Waldstrasse 25
D-31712 Niedernwoehren
GERMANY
(contact person for Lower Saxony genealogical society
above)

Familienkundliche Kommission fuer Niedersachsen und
    Bremen sowie angrenzende ostfaelische Gebiete e.V.,
    Sitz Hannover
Georg W. Jahn
Schloss Ricklingen
Steinfeldstrasse 34
D-3008 Garbsen 5
GERMANY
(elite private genealogical society for Lower Saxony and
Bremen; membership by invitation only)

Maenner vom Morgenstern, Heimatbund an Elb- und
    Wesermuendung
Mueggenburgweg 2
D-27607 Langen
GERMANY
(private society for local history of the lower Elbe and
Weser River area)

Gruppe Familien- und Wappenkund im
    Bundesbahn-Sozialwerk
Ortsgruppe Hannover
Klaus-Peter Wulf
Bahndirektion, Buero SF
D-30159 Hannover
GERMANY
(German railway employee genealogy study group for
Hannover area)

Ostfriesische Landschaft
Arbeitsgruppe Familienkunde, Genealogie und Heraldik,
    Sitz Aurich
Landschaftshaus
Buergermeister-Mueller-Platz 2
Postfach 1580
D-26585 Aurich
GERMANY
(genealogy and heraldry working group for area of
Ostfriesland/East Frisia, publishes *Quellen und
Forschungen zur Ostfriesischen Familien- und
Wappenkunde* and *Ostfriesische Familienkunde*)

Gisela Haltrich (OS)
Roentgenstrasse 23
D-26789 Leer/Ostfriesland
GERMANY
(contact person for Ostfriesland society above)

Arbeitskreis Bergedorf der Genealogisch-Heraldischen
    Gesellschaft mit dem Sitz in Goettingen e.V.
    Bergedorfer Schloss
D-21029 Hamburg-Bergedorf
GERMANY
(genealogical society for the Bergedorf area)

Arbeitskreis fuer Familienforschung
Sackstrasse 4
Postfach 1268
D-31666 Bueckeburg
GERMANY
(genealogical society for the Schaumburg area and
neighboring Westphalia)

Arbeitsgruppe Familienforschung Dinklage
Walter Wendeln
Riedenweg 11
D-49413 Dinklage
GERMANY
(genealogical society for Dinklage)

Genealogisch-Heraldische Gesellschaft mit dem Sitz in
    Goettingen e.V.
Ev.-ref. Gemeindehaus
Untere Karspuele 11
Postfach 2062
D-37010 Goettingen
GERMANY
(genealogy and heraldry society for Goettingen and
vicinity)

Geschichtsverein fuer Goettingen und Umgebung e.V.
Neues Rathaus
Geismarlandstrasse 4
D-37083 Goettingen
GERMANY
(historical society for Goettingen and vicinity)

Geschichts- und Heimatschutzverein Goslar
Stadtarchiv
Zehntstrasse 24
Postfach 2569
D-38615 Goslar *(Street address D-38640)*
GERMANY
(historical and local preservation society for Goslar)

Deutscher Familienverband
Kreisverband Harz e.V.
Petersilienstrasse 14
D-38640 Goslar
GERMANY
(association of family societies in Goslar and the Harz area)

Familienkundlicher Verein Hildesheim
Feldbergen Nr. 66
D-31185 Soehlde
GERMANY
(genealogical society for the Hildesheim area)

Arbeitsgemeinschaft fuer Familienforschung
Leinstrasse 4 (Museum)
D-31582 Nienburg
GERMANY
(genealogical society for the Nienburg area)

Heimat- und Museumsverein fuer Northeim und Umgegend
Postfach 1323
D-37143 Northeim
GERMANY
(local history and museum society for Northeim and
vicinity)

Oldenburgische Gesellschaft fuer Familienkunde
Wolfgang Buesing
Lerigauweg 14
D-2900 Oldenburg
GERMANY
(genealogical society for the former Duchy of Oldenburg
area; publishes *Oldenburgische Familienkunde*)

Arbeitskreis Familienforschung Osnabrueck
Michael G. Ahrenhoevel
Kiwittstrasse 1A
D-49080 Osnabrueck
GERMANY
(genealogical society for the Osnabrueck area)

Stader Geschichts- und Heimatverein
Inselstrasse 12 (Museum)
D-21335 Lueneburg
GERMANY
(historical and local history society for Lueneburg)

Dierk Feye (OL)
Fichtenstrasse 10
D-26316 Varel
GERMANY
(contact person for Oldenburg genealogical society above)

Verein fuer Geschichte und Landeskunde von Osnabrueck
Staatsarchiv
Schlossstrasse 29
D-49074 Osnabrueck
GERMANY
(historical and local history society for Osnabrueck)

Heimat- und Geschichtsverein Osterode am Harz und
    Umgebung e.V.
Am Suedbahnhof 10
D-37520 Osterode (Harz)
GERMANY
(local history and historical society for Osterode and
vicinity)

Arbeitsgemeinschaft fuer schaumburgische Familienkunde
Hafenstrasse 1
D-31737 Rinteln
GERMANY
(genealogy working group for Schaumburg-Lippe)

Heimat- und Familienkundliche Arbeitsgemeinschaft
An den Zehn Eichen 14
D-29525 Uelzen
GERMANY
(local history and genealogy working group for Uelzen
area)

Familienkundlicher Arbeitskreis im Geschichtsausschuss
    des Heimatbundes fuer das Oldenburger Muensterland
Friedrich Bunge
Grosse Strasse 101
D-49377 Vechta
GERMANY
(genealogical working group for Oldenburg Muensterland)

EUROPEAN NATIONAL AND REGIONAL GENEALOGICAL AND HISTORICAL SOCIETIES

Upstalsboom - Gesellschaft fuer historische
Personenforschung und Bevoelkerungsgeschichte in
Ostfriesland e.V.
z.H. Herrn Prof. Dr. Harro Buss
Flotowweg 4
D-26386 Wilhelmshaven
GERMANY
(genealogical and historical society for East Frisia)

Prof. Tony Holtmann
Institut fuer Politikwissenschaft II
Carl-von-Ossietzky-Universitaet Oldenburg
Ammerlaender Heerstrasse 114-118
Postfach 2503
D-26011 Oldenburg
(Street address D-26129; post office box D-26015)
GERMANY
(research on emigration from northern Germany to
America)

Wolfgang Riechmann
Schillingskamp 4
D-32469 Petershagen
GERMANY
(researching cause of emigration of ca. 17,000 emigrants
from the county of Minden)

Schaumburg-Lippischer Heimatverein
Lange Strasse 32
D-31675 Bueckeburg
GERMANY
(local history association for Schaumburg-Lippe region)

LUXEMBOURG.

Association Luxembourgeoise de Généalogie et
d'Héraldique
Jean-Claude Muller
Postfach 13
L-8501 Redange/Attert
LUXEMBOURG
(Luxembourg genealogy and heraldry society; publishes *De
Familljefuerscher*)

Association Luxembourgeoise de Généalogie et
d'Héraldique
Georges Kiessel
Kuebenek 1
L-5404 Bech-Kleinmacher
LUXEMBOURG
(Luxembourg genealogy and heraldry society; publishes *De
Familljefuerscher*)

Centre de Documentaion des Migrations Humaines
54 Bd de la Petrusse
L-2320 Luxembourg
LUXEMBOURG
(Luxembourg emigration center)

Conseil Héraldique du Luxembourg
3 rue Bellevue
L-1000 Luxembourg
LUXEMBOURG
(heraldry council for Luxembourg)

MASOVIA. See PRUSSIA.

MASUREN. See PRUSSIA.

MECKLENBURG.

P. Goetze
Eggerstrasse 4
D-18059 Rostock
GERMANY
(contact person for Mecklenburg genealogical association)

Genealogische Gesellschaft, Sitz Hamburg, e.V.
Alsterchaussee 11
Postfach 302042
D-20307 Hamburg
GERMANY
(genealogical society for Hamburg, also covering
Mecklenburg due to long-standing historical ties)

Heraldische Fachgruppe "Zum Greifen" beim Kulturbund
e.V., Sitz Wismar
Eggerstrasse 4
D-18059 Rostock
GERMANY
(Mecklenburg heraldry society)

Arbeitsgemeinschaft Genealogie und Heraldik
Roland Bornschein
Zum Netzboden 14
D-23966 Wismar
GERMANY
(genealogy and heraldry society for Mecklenburg)

Institute for Migration and Ancestral Research
Richard-Wagner-Strasse 31
D-18119 Warnemuende
GERMANY
(possibly a commercial genealogical research firm?)

MEURTHE ET MOSELLE. See under LORRAINE.

MEUSE. See under LORRAINE.

MIDDLE GERMANY. See also BRANDENBURG,
MECKLENBURG, SAXONY, THURINGIA.

Arbeitsgemeinschaft fuer mitteldeutsche Familienforschung
e.V., Sitz Marburg
E. Joachim Mueller
Waldweg 5
D-04416 Leipzig-Markkleeberg
GERMANY
or

Arbeitsgemeinschaft fuer mitteldeutsche Familienforschung
e.V., Sitz Marburg
Strasse der Freundschaft 2
D-99706 Sondershausen
GERMANY
(genealogical society for all of central Germany, roughly
the former DDR/GDR, publishes *Mitteldeutsche
Familienkunde*; has regional list of researchers)

Walter Beie (AM)
Eythstrasse 5
D-91058 Erlangen
GERMANY
(contact person for central German society above)

MOEMPELGARD. See MONTBÉLIARD.

MÖMPELGARD. See MONTBÉLIARD.

MONTBÉLIARD.

Centre d'entr'aide généalogique de Franche Comté
12 rue Oehmichen
F-25200 Montbéliard
FRANCE
(genealogical society for Montbéliard area)

MORAVIA. See CZECH REPUBLIC, SUDETENLAND.

"MORAVIANS." See under RELIGIOUS ARCHIVES.

MOSELLE.

Cercle généalogique de la Moselle
1, allee du Château
F-57050 Saint-Julian-les-Metz
FRANCE
(genealogical society for Moselle area)

NASSAU. See HESSE.

NETHERLANDS. See HOLLAND.

DIE NEUMARK. See BRANDENBURG.

NIEDERSACHSEN. See LOWER SAXONY.

NORDRHEIN-WESTFALEN. See RHINELAND and
WESTPHALIA.

NORTH RHINE-WESTPHALIA. See RHINELAND and
WESTPHALIA.

OLDENBURG. See LOWER SAXONY.

OSTFALEN.

Familienkundliche Kommission fuer Niedersachsen und
Bremen, sowie angrenzende ostfaelische Gebiete,
e.V., Sitz Hannover
Mueggenburgweg 2
D-27607 Langen
GERMANY
(genealogical society for Lower Saxony, Bremen, and
Ostfalen, membership by invitation only)

OSTFRIESLAND. See LOWER SAXONY.

OSTPREUSSEN. See PRUSSIA.

PALATINATE.

Arbeitsgemeinschaft fuer Pfaelzisch-Rheinische
Familienkunde e.V., Sitz Ludwigshafen
Rottstrasse 17 (Stadtarchiv)
D-67061 Ludwigshafen/Rhein
GERMANY
(genealogical society for the Palatinate with local branches
in Ludwigshafen, Kaiserslautern, Neustadt/Weinstrasse,
Alzey, Konken, Mutterstadt, Pirmasens, and Worms,
publishes *Pfaelzisch-Rheinische Familienkunde*)

Klaus Dufner (AP)
Baltersbacherweg13
D-66564 Ottweiler
GERMANY
(contact person for Palatinate genealogical society above)

Arbeitsgemeinschaft fuer Pfaelzisch-Rheinische
Familienkunde e.V.
Ortsgruppe Kaiserslautern
Institut fuer pfaelzische Geschichte und Volkskunde
Benzinoring 6
D-67657 Kaiserslautern
GERMANY
(Kaiserslautern branch)

Arbeitsgemeinschaft fuer Pfaelzisch-Rheinische
Familienkunde e.V.
Ortsgruppe Neustadt
Heinz R. Anheuser
Goethestrasse 15
D-67435 Neustadt (Haardt)
GERMANY
(branch in Neustadt an der Haardt = Neustadt an der
Weinstrasse)

Arbeitsgemeinschaft fuer Pfaelzisch-Rheinische
Familienkunde e.V.
Ortsgruppe Speyer
Studienrat Hermann Hauber
Rosenweg 16
D-67354 Roemerberg
GERMANY
(Speyer branch)

Arbeitsgemeinschaft fuer Pfaelzisch-Rheinische
    Familienkunde e.V.
Ortsgruppe Zweibruecken
Walter Bohrer
Stadtarchiv Zweibruecken
Herzogstrasse 13
D-66482 Zweibruecken
GERMANY
(Zweibruecken branch)

Historischer Verein der Pfalz
Historisches Museum der Pfalz
Grosse Pfaffengasse 7
D-67346 Speyer
GERMANY
(historical society for the Palatinate)

Verein fuer Heimatkunde fuer Stadt und Kreis Bad
    Kreuznach e.V.
Fronwingert 20
D-55566 Sobernheim
GERMANY
(local history society for the county of Bad Kreuznach)

Zweibruecker Arbeitsgemeinschaft fuer Familienkunde
Fritz Leonhardt
Wallstrasse 43
D-66482 Zweibruecken
GERMANY
(genealogy working group for Zweibruecken area)

Centralarkiv for Invanderer fra Pfalz 1759-64
Jan Hyllested
Markedsgade 34
DK-8900 Randers
Danmark/DENMARK
(central registry for emigrants from the Palatinate to
Denmark from 1759 to 1764)

PFALZ. See PALATINATE.

POLAND. See also BRANDENBURG, EASTERN
GERMANY, GALICIA, POMERANIA, PRUSSIA (EAST
and WEST), POSEN, SILESIA, VOLHYNIA, and
EASTERN GERMANY.

Towaryzstwo Genealogiczno-Heraldyczne
Societas Genealogica AC Heraldica
ulica Wodna 27
Pałac Górków
PL-61781 Poznań
Polska/POLAND
(genealogical society for Poland; publishes quarterly,
GENS)

Osrodek Badan Genealogicznych Piast
Krakowskie Przedmiescie 64
PL-00322 Warszawa
POLAND
(genealogical society for Poland)

Heimatauskunftstelle Polen I, Bereich Łodz
Bankstrasse 4
D-40476 Duesseldorf
GERMANY
(information center for persons from the Łodz region)

Heimatauskunftstelle Polen II
Schoonworth 7
D-30167 Hannover
GERMANY
(information center for persons from a certain region of
Poland)

Instytut Historyczny Universytetu Wroclawskięgo
ulica Szewska 49
PL-50139 Wroclaw
POLAND
(publishes *Genealogia* in Polish with some German and
English)

Forschungsstelle Polen der AgoFF
Dieter God
Schorlemmers Kamp 20
D-44536 Luenen
GERMANY
(genealogical research center in Germany for Poland)

Forschungsstelle Mittelpolen, Wolhynien der AGoFF
Heinz Ulbrich
Sperberweg 6
Postfach 1039
D-92661 Altenstadt an der Waldnaab
GERMANY
(genealogical research center in Germany for central
Poland and Volhynia)

Heimatkreisgemeinschaft Kolmar
Erwin Krause
Max-Planck-Strasse
D-40607 Meerbusch
GERMANY
(local history society for Kolmar area)

POMERANIA. See also SWEDEN.

Forschungsstelle Pommern der AGoFF
Elmar Bruhn
Lohkamp 13
D-22117 Hamburg
GERMANY
(Pomeranian genealogical research center)

Pommersches Familien-Archiv
Martin Hermann
Lorenz-von-Stein-Ring 20
D-24340 Eckernfoerde
GERMANY
(Pomeranian family research center)

Gesellschaft fuer pommersche Geschichte, Altertumskunde
    und Kunst
Dr. Berger
Farinastrasse 42
D-29525 Uelzen
GERMANY
(history, antiquity and art society for Pomerania)

Pommerscher Zentralvorstand e.V. und Pommersche
    Landsmannschaft
Europaweg 4
D-23570 Luebeck-Travemuende
GERMANY
(homeland association for Pomeranians; publishes *Die
Pommersche Zeitung* and *Pommern*)

Pommersche Landsmannschaft
Johnsallee 18
D-20148 Hamburg
GERMANY
(homeland association for Pomeranians in Germany)

Historische Kommission fuer Pommern
Rotenberg 16
D-35057 Marburg (Lahn)
GERMANY
(historical commission for Pomerania)

Stiftung Pommern
Schloss Rantzaubau
Daenische Strasse 44
D-24103 Kiel
GERMANY
(foundation for Pomerania)

Landesheimatverband Mecklenburg-Vorpommern e.V.
Aussenstelle
Woldegker Strase 35
D-17036 Neubrandenburg
GERMANY
(local history association for the Nearer Pomerania area)

Vorpommersche Forschungsstelle fuer Geschichte e.V.
Ernst-Moritz-Arndt-Museum
An den Anlagen 1
D-18574 Garz
GERMANY
(historical society for Nearer Pomerania and Ruegen)

Hans-Juergen Schmitz
Kungsmarksvagen 79
S-37144 Karlskrone
Sverige/SWEDEN
(contact person for Swedish research group on Swedish
emigration to Pomerania)

POSEN. See also EASTERN GERMANY.

Forschungsstelle Posen der AgoFF
Hilde Moller
Oppenheimer Strasse 50
D-60594 Frankfurt (Main)
GERMANY
(genealogical research group for Posen)

Otto Firchau
Nachtigallenweg 6
D-32105 Bad Salzuflen
GERMANY
(genealogical research center for Netze district near
Bromberg)

Historisch-Landeskundliche Kommission fuer Posen und
    Deutschtum in Polen
Saarstrasse 21
D-55122 Mainz
GERMANY
(historical and local history commission for Posen and
Germans in Poland)

Posener Archiv
D.-Paul-Blau-Haus
D-21335 Lueneburg
GERMANY
(Posen research center)

POZNAN. See POSEN.

PRUSSIA. See also EASTERN GERMANY. Here, only
EAST and WEST PRUSSIA. Note, though, that "Prussia"
after 1866 had grown to include nearly all of northern
Germany.

Verein fuer Familienforschung in Ost- und Westpreussen
    e.V., Sitz Hamburg
Reinhard Wenzel
An der Leegde 23
D-29223 Celle
GERMANY
(genealogical society for East and West Prussia and Danzig
only, publishes *Altpreussische Geschlechterkunde*)

Forschungsstelle Ostpreussen der AGoFF
Dr. Wolf Konietzko
Eichstrasse 6
D-25336 Elmshorn
GERMANY
(East Prussia genealogical research center, especially for
eastern Masuren (Masovia))

Kurt-Walter Friedrich (VFOW)
Weissenburger Strasse 16
D-22049 Hamburg
GERMANY
(contact person for society on emigrants from East and
West Prussia)

Historische Kommission fuer ost- und westpreussische
    Landesforschung
Houverath
Auf dem Muehlberg 11
D-53902 Bad Muenstereifel
GERMANY
(commission for research on East and West Prussia,
publishes *Preussenland*)

Studienstelle ostdeutscher Genealogie der Forschungsstelle
    Ostmitteleuropas
Universitaet Dortmund
Emil-Figge-Strasse 50
D-44227 Dortmund
GERMANY
(has large genealogical index for West Prussia)

Landsmannschaft Preussen e.V.
Parkallee 86
D-20144 Hamburg
GERMANY
(homeland association for East Prussians; publishes *Das
Ostpreussenblatt*)

RAD Traditionsgemeinschaft Ostpreussen
Siegfried Kloss
Sudetenstrasse 8
D-21698 Harsefeld
GERMANY
(East Prussian (military) society)

Forschungsstelle Westpreussen-Danzig der AGoFF
Dr. Wolf Konietzko
Eichstrasse 6
D-25336 Elmshorn
GERMANY
(genealogical center for West Prussia and Danzig with card
file of over 285,000)

Copernicus-Vereinigung zur Pflege der Heimatkunde und
    Geschichte Westpreussens e.V.
von-Kluck-Strasse 23
D-48151 Muenster
GERMANY
(society for local history and history of West Prussia)

Landsmannschaft Westpreussen
von-Kluck-Strasse 23
D-48151 Muenster
GERMANY
(homeland association for West Prussians)

RHINELAND. See also PALATINATE and
WESTPHALIA.

Genealogie ohne Grenzen
Postbus 10
NL-6343 ZG Klimmen
Nederland/NETHERLANDS
(publication covering the area of Liège, Aachen, and
Maastricht)

Westdeutsche Gesellschaft fuer Familienkunde, Sitz Koeln
Am Draitschbusch 18
D-53177 Bonn-Bad Godesberg
GERMANY
(genealogical society headquarters for the area along the
Rhine with branches in Aachen, Bonn, Cologne,
Duesseldorf, Duisberg, Essen, Gummersbach, Kleve,
Krefeld, Koblenz, Moenchengladbach, Trier, and
Wuppertal, publishes *Mitteilungen der Westdeutschen
Gesellschaft fuer Familienkunde*)

Westdeutsche Gesellschaft fuer Familienkunde e.V.
Bezirksgruppe Aachen
Hans Strack
Gruener Weg 9
D-52146 Wuerselen-Broichweiden
GERMANY
(Aachen local branch of above genealogical society)

Aachener Geschichtsverein e.V.
Stadtarchiv
Fischmarkt 3
D-52062 Aachen
GERMANY
(historical society for Aachen)

Bergischer Verein fuer Familienkunde e.V., Sitz Wuppertal
Dr. Wolfram Lang
Zanellastrasse 52
D-42287 Wuppertal
GERMANY
(Bergisch Land local genealogical society; publishes
regional list of researchers)

Historischer Verein fuer die Grafschaft Ravensberg e.V.
Rohrteichstrasse 19
D-33602 Bielefeld
GERMANY
(historical society for Bielefeld and the Ravensberg area)

Vereinigung der Heimatfreunde am Mittelrhein e.V.,
    Sitz Bingen
Staedtisches Verkehrsamt
Rheinkai 21
D-55411 Bingen
GERMANY
(society for local history of the Middle Rhine region)

Westdeutsche Gesellschaft fuer Familienkunde e.V.
Bezirksgruppe Bonn
Adolf Paul Quilling (WG)
Grossenbuschstrasse 30
D-53229 Bonn
GERMANY
(Bonn local branch of above genealogical society,
publishes *Die Laterne*)

EUROPEAN NATIONAL AND REGIONAL GENEALOGICAL AND HISTORICAL SOCIETIES

Bonner Heimat- und Geschichtsverein
Stadtarchiv
Stadthaus
Berliner Platz 2
D-53111 Bonn
GERMANY
(Bonn local history and historical society)

Historischer Verein fuer den Niederrhein (das alte
    Erzbistum Koeln)
Am Hof 28
Postfach 2227
D-53012 Bonn *(Street address D-53113)*
GERMANY
(historical society for the Lower Rhine, the area of the old
Archbishopric of Cologne)

Historischer Verein fuer Dortmund und die Grafschaft
    Mark e.V.
Stadtarchiv Dortmund
Stadthaus
Olpe 1
D-44135 Dortmund
GERMANY
(historical society for Dortmund and the County of Mark)

Duerner Geschichtsverein
Stadt- und Kreisarchiv Dueren
Rathaus
Kaiserplatz 2-4
D-52349 Dueren
GERMANY
(Dueren historical society)

Westdeutsche Gesellschaft fuer Familienkunde e.V.
Bezirksgruppe Duesseldorf
Dr. Franz Josef Bender
Angermunder Weg 17
D-40880 Ratingen
GERMANY
(Duesseldorf local branch of above genealogical society)

Duesseldorfer Verein fuer Familienkunde e.V., Sitz
    Duesseldorf
Monika Degenhard
Krummenweger Strasse 26
D-40885 Ratingen
(genealogical society for Duesseldorf area, publishes
Duesseldorfer Familienkunde)

Duesseldorfer Geschichtsverein e.V.
Hauptstaatsarchiv
Mauerstrasse 55
D-40476 Duesseldorf
GERMANY
(Duesseldorf historical society)

Westdeutsche Gesellschaft fuer Familienkunde e.V.
Bezirksgruppe Duisburg
Dr. med. Ursula Budde-Ihmer
Sonnenwall 19
D-47051 Duisburg
GERMANY
(Duisburg local branch of above genealogical society)

Mercator-Gesellschaft
Stadtarchiv
Alter Markt 21
D-47051 Duisburg
GERMANY
(local history society for Duisburg)

Westdeutsche Gesellschaft fuer Familienkunde e.V.
Bezirksgruppe Essen
Dr. med. Wilfried Vogeler
Hendrik-Witte-Strasse 4
D-45128 Essen/Ruhr
GERMANY
(Essen local branch of above genealogical society)

Historischer Verein fuer Stadt und Stift Essen
Stadtarchiv
Steeler Strasse 29
D-45127 Essen
GERMANY
(historical society for Essen)

Gruppe Familien- und Wappenkunde im
    Bundesbahn-Sozialwerk
Ortsgruppe Essen
Ernst Huels
Bahndirektion, Buero B
D-45257 Essen
GERMANY
(German railway employee genealogy and heraldry study
group for Essen area)

Verein der Geschichts- und Heimatfreunde des Kreises
    Euskirchen e.V.
Kreisverwaltungsarchiv
Juelicher Ring 32
Postfach 1145
D-53861 Euskirchen *(Street address D-53879)*
GERMANY
(historical and local history society for the county of
Euskirchen)

Historischer Verein fuer Geldern und Umgegend e.V.
Kreisarchiv
Kapuzinerstrasse 34
D-47608 Geldern
GERMANY
(historical society for Geldern and vicinity)

Verein fuer Orts- und Heimatkunde Gelsenkirchen-Buer
Postfach 200417
D-45839 Gelsenkirchen
GERMANY
(society for local history of Gelsenkirchen-Buer)

Westdeutsche Gesellschaft fuer Familienkunde e.V.
Bezirksgruppe Gummersbach
Henning Schroeder
Im Sohl 60
D-51643 Gummersbach
GERMANY
(Gummersbach (Oberberg) local branch of above
genealogical society)

Arbeitskreis Familienforscher im Hagener Heimatbund
    e.V., Sitz Hagen
Hochstrasse 74
Postfach 1368
D-58013 Hagen *(Street address D-58095)*
GERMANY
(genealogical society for Hagen area)

Geschichtsverein Heiligenhaus e.V.
Rathaus
D-42579 Heiligenhaus
GERMANY
(historical society for Heiligenhaus)

Historischer Verein Ingelheim
Rathaus
D-55218 Ingelheim
GERMANY
(historical society for Ingelheim)

Westdeutsche Gesellschaft fuer Familienkunde e.V.
Bezirksgruppe Kleve
Hermann Th. Dellmann
Heldstrasse 41
D-47533 Kleve/Niederrhein
GERMANY
(Kleve local branch of above genealogical society)

Mosaik-Familienkundliche Vereinigung fuer das Klever
    Land e.V., Sitz Kleve
Mosaik-Archiv
Christus-Koenigschule
Lindenallee 54
D-47533 Kleve
GERMANY
(Kleve local genealogical society)

Westdeutsche Gesellschaft fuer Familienkunde e.V.
Bezirksgruppe Koblenz
Markenbildchenweg 13
D-56068 Koblenz
GERMANY
(Koblenz local branch of above genealogical society)

Verein fuer Geschichte und Kunst des Mittelrheins
Landeshauptarchiv
Karmeliterstrasse 1/3
D-56065 Koblenz
GERMANY
(society for history and art of the Middle Rhine)

Westdeutsche Gesellschaft fuer Familienkunde e.V.
Bezirksgruppe Koeln
Dr. Guenter Junkers
Bergische Landstrasse 210
D-51375 Leverkusen
GERMANY
(Cologne local branch of above genealogical society)

Koelnischer Geschichtsverein
Birburger Strasse 4
D-50935 Koeln
GERMANY
(historical society for Cologne)

Gruppe Familien- und Wappenkunde im
    Bundesbahn-Sozialwerk
Ortsgruppe Koeln
Werner Derrix
Bruehlscher Weg
D-47608 Geldern
GERMANY
(German railway employee genealogy and heraldry study
group for Koeln/Cologne area)

Westdeutsche Gesellschaft fuer Familienkunde e.V.
Bezirksgruppe Krefeld
Dr. Guenter Jacobs
Horstdyk 75a
D-47803 Krefeld
GERMANY
(Krefeld local branch of above genealogical society)

Westdeutsche Gesellschaft fuer Familienkunde e.V.
Bezirksgruppe Mittelrhein
Hans Finzel
Muehlweg 13-15
D-56321 Brey
GERMANY
(Middle Rhine local branch of above genealogical society)

Westdeutsche Gesellschaft fuer Familienkunde e.V.
Bezirksgruppe Moenchengladbach
Margret Schopen
Duesseldorfer Strasse 25
D-41238 Moenchengladbach
GERMANY
(Moenchengladbach local branch of above genealogical
society)

Geschichtsverein des Monschauer Landes
Trierer Strasse 66
D-52156 Monschau
GERMANY
(historical society for the Monschau region)

Verein fuer Orts- und Heimatkunde Recklinghausen
Haltener Strasse 4
D-45657 Recklinghausen
GERMANY
(society for local history of Recklinghausen)

Geschichts- und Altertumsverein fuer Siegburg und den
    Rhein-Sieg-Kreis e.V.
Rathaus
D-53721 Siegburg
GERMANY
(society for history and antiquity of the Siegburg area)

Westdeutsche Gesellschaft fuer Familienkunde e.V.
Bezirksgruppe Trier
Heinz Grundhoefer
Gestade 5
D-55470 Bernkastel-Kues
GERMANY
(Trier local branch of above genealogical society)

Arbeitsgemeinschaft fuer Landesgeschichte und
    Volkskunde des Trierer Raumes
Stadtarchiv
Weberbach 25
D-54290 Trier
GERMANY
(society for history and local history of the Trier region)

Werler Arbeitsgemeinschaft fuer Familienforschung
Stadtarchiv Werl
Rathaus
Hedwig-Dransfeld-Strasse 23
Postfach 6040
D-59445 Werl *(Street address D-59457)*
GERMANY
(Werl local genealogical society)

Gesellschaft fuer Rheinische Geschichtskunde
Severinstrasse 222-228
D-51145 Koeln
GERMANY
(society for Rhine history)

Roland zu Dortmund e.V.
Hansastrasse 61
Postfach 103326
D-44033 Dortmund
GERMANY
(genealogical society for Dortmund area)

Erich-W. Riekenbrauck (RD)
Hollmannstrasse 2b
D-44229 Dortmund
GERMANY
(contact person for Dortmund area genealogical society
above)

Verein fuer geschichtliche Landeskunde der Rheinlande
Am Hofgarten 22
D-55113 Bonn
GERMANY
(local history society for the Rhineland)

Historischer Verein fuer den Niederrhein
Charlottenstrasse 80-86
D-40210 Duesseldorf
GERMANY
(historical society for the Lower (northern) Rhine area)

ROMANIA. See also DANUBE SWABIANS.

Dr. Helmut Flacker
Steingasse 4
D-79189 Bad Krozingen
GERMANY
(genealogical research center for Romanian Germans)

Forschungsstelle Rumaenien der AgoFF
Manfred Huber
Bussardweg 20
D-79110 Freiburg (Breisgau)
GERMANY
(genealogical research center for Romanian Germans)

RUSSIA (GERMANS FROM RUSSIA). See also
POLAND, GALICIA, BALTIC GERMANS, etc.

Forschungsstelle Russlanddeutsche der AGoFF
Dr. Paul Edel
Ziegelstrasse 11
Postfach 1232
D-73402 Aalen *(Street address D-73431)*
GERMANY
(genealogical center for Germans from Russia)

Landsmannschaft der Deutschen aus Russland
Raitelsbergstrasse 49
D-70188 Stuttgart
GERMANY
(homeland association of Germans from Russia, publishes
magazine, *Volk auf dem Weg*)

Genealogy and Family History Society
P.O. Box 459
127349 Moscow
RUSSIA
(RAGAS/Moscow reorganized as a non-profit organization
registered with Moscow Ministry of Justice)

SAARLAND.

Arbeitsgemeinschaft fuer Saarlaendische Familienkunde im
    Historischen Verein fuer die Saargegend e.V., Sitz
    Saarbruecken
Norbert Emanuel
Hebbelstrasse 3
D-66346 Puettlingen
GERMANY
(genealogical working group of Saarland historical society,
publishes *Saarlaendische Familienkunde,
Informationsdienst*, and *Saarlaendische Ahnen- und
Stammreihen*)

Gruppe Familien- und Wappenkunde im
    Bundesbahn-Sozialwerk
Ortsgruppe Saarbruecken
Josef Friedrich
Bahndirektion, Buero T
D-66111 Saarbruecken
GERMANY
(German railway employee genealogy and heraldry study
group for Saarbruecken area)

Historischer Verein fuer die Saargegend
Landesarchiv
Scheidter Strasse 114
D-66130 Saarbruecken
GERMANY
(historical society for the Saar region)

Historische Kommission fuer saarlaendische
    Landesgeschichte und Volksforschung
Landesarchiv
Scheidter Strasse 114
D-66130 Saarbruecken
GERMANY
(historical commission for history and demography of the
Saarland)

Institut fuer Landeskunde im Saarland
Universitaet
Bau 35
D-66123 Saarbruecken
GERMANY

Vereinigung fuer die Heimatkunde im Landkreis Saarlouis
    e.V.
Arbeitsgruppe Familienforschung
Landratsamt
Postfach 360
D-66740 Saarlouis
GERMANY
(genealogy working group of historical society for the
Saarlouis area of the Saarland)

SACHSEN. See SAXONY.

SALZBURGERS.

Salzburger Verein e.V.
Wohnstift Salzburg
Memeler Strasse 35
D-33605 Bielefeld
GERMANY
(historical and genealogical society for Protestants expelled
from Salzburg in 1730's; many settled in East Prussia, some
in Georgia)

Salzburger Verein e.V.
Harro Janetzke
Knatenserweg 8
D-31675 Bueckeburg
GERMANY
(genealogical researcher for Salzburger society in
Germany)

Salzburger Verein e.V.
Herbert Nolde
Am Brachfelde 2
D-37077 Goettingen
GERMANY
(genealogical researcher for Salzburger society in
Germany)

SAXONY. See also MIDDLE GERMANY and
THURINGIA. (Includes SAXONY-ANHALT).

Prof. Dr. W. Lorenz
Burgauenstrasse 3
D-04177 Leipzig
GERMANY
(contact person for Saxony genealogical association)

Studiengruppe fuer Saechsische Geschichte und Kultur
Wallensteinstrasse 10
D-80807 Muenchen/Munich
GERMANY
(study group for Saxon history and culture)

Bernd Hofestaedt
Block 109/1
D-06124 Halle-Neustadt
GERMANY
(contact person for Saxony-Anhalt genealogical
association)

Arbeitsgemeinschaft Genealogie Annaberg-Buchholz
Hauptstrasse 118
D-09477 Arnsfeld
GERMANY
(local genealogical society for Annaberg-Buchholz and
vicinity)

Adam-Ries-Bund e.V., Sitz Annaberg-Buchholz
Adam-Ries-Haus
Johannesgasse 23
D-09456 Annaberg-Buchholz
GERMANY
(local historical society for Annaberg-Buchholz)

Interessengemeinschaft Genealogie Dresden, Sitz Dresden
Krenkelstrasse 9
D-01309 Dresden
GERMANY
(local genealogical society for Dresden and vicinity)

Arbeitsgemeinschaft Genealogie
Armin Lippmann
Strasse Usti nad Labem 23
D-09119 Chemnitz
GERMANY
(genealogical association for Erzgebirge and some central
Germany)

Genealogischer Abend "Ekkehard" Halle, Sitz Halle
Eilenburger Strasse 17
D-06116 Halle/Saale
GERMANY
(genealogical society for Halle and vicinity)

Neuer Hallescher Genealogischer Abend, Sitz Halle
R. Maerz
Brotuffstrasse 9
D-06127 Merseburg
GERMANY
(genealogical society for Halle and vicinity)

Leipziger Genealogische Gesellschaft, Sitz Leipzig
Deutsche Zentralstelle fuer Genealogie
Schongauer Strasse 1
Postfach 274
D-04002 Leipzig *(Street address D-04329)*
GERMANY
(genealogical society for Leipzig and vicinity, publishes
Genealogische Blaetter)

Arbeitsgemeinschaft Genealogie Magdeburg, Sitz
 Magdeburg
Siegfried Reincke
Thiemstrasse 7
D-39104 Magdeburg
GERMANY
(genealogical association for Magdeburg area)

Arbeitskreis vogtlaendischer Familienforscher im Verein
 fuer vogtlaendische Geschichte, Volks- und
 Landeskunde e.V., Sitz Plauen
Juergen Uhlmann
Auguststrasse 18
D-08523 Plauen
GERMANY
(Vogtland genealogical society)

Arbeitsgemeinschaft Genealogie
Heinz Mocker
Weststrasse 73
D-08523 Plauen
GERMANY
(Vogtland genealogical society)

Arbeitsgemeinschaft vogtlaendischer Familienforscher
Genealogische Gruppe Reichenbach
Dr. Werner Mahlberg
Zwickauer Strasse 95
D-08468 Reichenbach Vogtland
GERMANY
(Reichenbach local group of Vogtland society)

Arbeitsgemeinschaft vogtlaendischer Familienforscher
Genealogische Gruppe Treuen-Auerbach
Reinhard Huettner
Poststrasse 4
D-08233 Treuen Vogtland
GERMANY
(Treuen and Auerbach local group of Vogtland society)

SCHAUMBURG-LIPPE. See LOWER SAXONY.

SCHLESIEN. See SILESIA.

SCHLESWIG-HOLSTEIN. See also DENMARK,
HOLSTEIN.

Schleswig-Holsteinische Gesellschaft fuer
 Familienforschung und Wappenkunde e.V., Sitz Kiel
Postfach 3809
D-24037 Kiel
GERMANY
(genealogical society for Schleswig-Holstein, library at
Harmsstrasse 13, Kiel; publishes genealogical yearbook,
ancestor and descendant charts, and newsletters;
co-publishes *Niederdeutsche Familienkunde*)

Gesellschaft fuer Schleswig-Holsteinische Geschichte
Schloss Gottorf
D-24837 Schleswig
GERMANY
(historical society for Schleswig-Holstein)

Schleswig-Holsteinischer Heimatbund
Rathausstrasse 2
D-24103 Kiel
GERMANY
(local history society for Schleswig-Holstein)

Genealogische Gesellschaft, Sitz Hamburg, e.V.
Alsterchaussee 11
Postfach 302042
D-20307 Hamburg *(Street address D-20149)*
GERMANY
(genealogical society for Hamburg and area including
Schleswig-Holstein)

Arbeitskreis Bergedorf der Genealogischen Gesellschaft
 Hamburg
(Torturm Schloss Bergedorf, Erdgeschoss)
Wentorfer Strasse 84a
D-21029 Hamburg
GERMANY
(local working group of genealogical society for Hamburg
and area including Schleswig- Holstein)

Vereinigung fuer Familienkunde Elmshorn
Besenbeker Strasse 121
D-25335 Elmshorn
GERMANY
(genealogical society for the Elmshorn-Pinneberg area)

Arbeitsgemeinschaft Fehmarner Familienforscher
Postfach 33
D-23770 Petersdorf (Westfehmarn)
GERMANY
(genealogical society for Fehmarn)

EUROPEAN NATIONAL AND REGIONAL GENEALOGICAL AND HISTORICAL SOCIETIES

Gesellschaft fuer Flensburger Stadtgeschichte e.V.
Stadtarchiv
Rathaus
D-24937 Flensburg
GERMANY
(historical society for Flensburg)

Heimatbund fuer den Kreis Steinburg e.V.
Dieter Pape
Viktoriastrasse 16-18 (Kreishaus)
D-25524 Itzehoe
GERMANY
(local history society for Itzehoe and Steinburg County)

Gesellschaft fuer Kieler Stadtgeschichte
Stadtarchiv
Rathaus, Zimmer 442
Fleethoern 9-17
D-24103 Kiel
GERMANY
(historical society for Kiel)

Verein fuer luebeckische Geschichte und Heimatkunde
Archiv der Hansestadt Luebeck
Muehlendamm 1/3
D-23552 Luebeck
GERMANY
(society for history and local history of Luebeck)

Arbeitskreis fuer Familienforschung e.V., Sitz Luebeck
Muehlentorplatz 2 (Muehlentorturm)
D-23552 Luebeck
GERMANY
(genealogical society for Luebeck area, publishes
Luebecker Beitraege zur Familien- und Wappenkunde)

Heimatbund und Geschichtsverein Herzogtum Lauenburg
    e.V.
Domhof 13 (Kreisarchiv)
Postfach 1140
D-23901 Ratzeburg *(Street address D-23909)*
GERMANY
(local history and historical society for the Ratzeburg and
Duchy of Lauenburg region)

Rolt Heitmann
Hauptstrasse 15
D-23611 Bad Schwartau
GERMANY
(contact person for Luebeck genealogical society above)

Institut fuer Regionale Forschung und Information im
    Deutschen Grenzverein e.V.
Waitzstrasse 5
D-24937 Flensburg
GERMANY
(study group for northern portion of Schleswig-Holstein;
cultural exchanges in Wisconsin and Iowa)

Heimatkundliche Arbeitsgemeinschaft fuer Nordschleswig
Vestergade 30
DK-6200 Aabenraa
Danmark/DENMARK
(local history society for North Schleswig)

Auswanderer Archiv Schleswig-Holstein der Amerika-
    Gesellschaft
Luebecker Strasse 10a
D-23795 Bad Segeberg
GERMANY
(emigrant archive; collects books, brochures, letters,
drawings of Schleswig-Holstein and pertaining to
Schleswig-Holsteiners in America)

Nordfriisk Instituut
Paul-H. Pauseback
Sueder Strasse 300
D-25821 Bredstedt
GERMANY
(central institute for recording, promoting, and preserving
Frisian language and culture; file of ca. 4,000 Frisian
emigrants)

SIEBENBUERGEN. See TRANSYLVANIA.

SILESIA. See also EASTERN GERMANY,
SUDETENLAND.

Forschungsstelle Schlesien der AGoFF
Neithard von Stein
Talstrasse 3
D-31707 Bad Eilsen
GERMANY
(genealogical center for Silesia)

Ślaskie Towarzstwo Genealogiczne
Ulanowskięgo 24A
P.O. Box 312
PL-50950 Wroclaw 2
POLAND
(Silesian genealogical society; publishes *Chronicle*,
newsletter in 4 languages, including English and German)

Landsmannschaft Schlesien, Nieder- und Oberschlesien
    e.V.
Haus Schlesien
Heisterbacherrott
D-53639 Koenigswinter
GERMANY
(homeland association for Silesia, including Lower and
Upper Silesia)

Landsmannschaft der Oberschlesien
Bahnhofstrasse 67-69
D-40883 Ratingen (Hoesel)
GERMANY
(homeland association for Upper Silesia)

Forschungsstelle Grafschaft Glatz
Dr. Dieter Pohl
Forststrasse 3
D-64397 Modautal
GERMANY
(research center for the County of Glatz (Klodzko, Nowa
Ruda) in Lower Silesia)

Forschungsgruppe Kreis Lauban
Kurt Michael Beckert
Kiefelhorn 13
D-38154 Koenigslutter
GERMANY
(research group for the County of Lauban (Luban), Lower
Silesia)

SLAVONIA.

Forschungsstelle Slawonien der AgoFF
Dr. Helmut Flacker
Steingasse 4
D-79189 Bad Krozingen
GERMANY
(research group for Slavonia)

SLOVAK REPUBLIC.

Forschungsstelle Slowakien der AgoFF
Antal von Könczöl
Schwarzwaldstrasse 34a
D-79276 Reute
GERMANY
(genealogical center for Slovakia)

SLOVENIA.

Slovenian Genealogical Society (SGS)
Peter Hawlina
Lipica 7
64220 Skofia Loka
SLOVENIA
(Slovenian genealogical society)

Slovenska Genealogicko-Heraldicka Spolocnost prî Matîcî
     Slovenskej
Novomeskeho 32
03252 Martin
SLOVENIA
(Slovenian genealogy and heraldry society)

Karpatendeutsche Landsmannschaft Slowakei
Brreslauer Strasse 32
D-70806 Kornwestheim
GERMANY
(homeland association for Slovakia)

SOUTH AFRICA.

Genealogical Society of South Africa
Postbus 3057
Coetzenburg
Stellenbosch 7602
SOUTH AFRICA
(has a researcher, Rolf Schaible, for German families)

SOUTHEASTERN EUROPE.
See also specific areas.

Forschungsstelle Suedosteuropa der AGoFF
Dr. Martin Armgart
Graitengraben 41
D-45326 Essen/Ruhr
GERMANY
(genealogical center for western Hungary, Romania,
Slovakia, Slovenia in Yugoslavia, and the Ukraine)

SOVIET UNION. See RUSSIA.

SREM.

Forschungsstelle Srem der AGoFF
Dr. Helmut Flacker
Steingasse 4
D-79189 Bad Krozingen
GERMANY
(genealogical center for Srem)

SUDETENLAND.

Forschungsstelle Sudetenland der AGoFF
Prof. Richard W. Eichler
Steinkirchner Strasse 16
D-81475 Muenchen *(Munich)*
GERMANY
(genealogical center for Sudeten Germans)

Vereinigung sudetendeutscher Familienforscher (VSFF)
Wittelsbacher Strasse 33
D-93155 Hemau
GERMANY
(genealogical society for Sudeten German researchers,
including Bohemia, Moravia, and Austrian Silesia)

Reinhold Wurdack (VS)
Von-Brunn-Strasse 2
D-96110 Schesslitz
GERMANY
(contact person for Sudetenland genealogical society
above)

Arbeitsstelle Oesterreich (VS)
Dr. Heinz Schoeny
Boschstrasse 24/7
A-1190 Wien/Vienna
Oesterreich/AUSTRIA
EUROPE
(Austrian contact person for Sudetenland genealogical
center above)

Sudetendeutsches Genealogisches Archiv
Lore Schrezenmayr
Erikaweg 58
D-93053 Regensburg
GERMANY
(genealogical archive for Sudeten Germans)

Historische Kommission fuer die Sudetenlaender
Guellstrasse 7
D-80538 Muenchen *(Munich)*
GERMANY
(historical commission for the Sudetenland)

Historische Kommission der Sudetenlaender e.V.
Hochstrasse 8
D-81669 Muenchen *(Munich)*
GERMANY
(historical commission for the Sudetenland)

Arbeitsgemeinschaft fuer kulturelle Heimatsammlungen bei
    dem Sudetendeutschen Archiv e.V.
Thierschstrasse 11-17
D-80538 Muenchen/Munich
GERMANY
(working group for cultural collections pertaining to
Sudetenland Germans)

Arbeitskreis Egerlaender Familienforscher
Guenther Schoen
Schwabstrasse 6
D-73479 Ellwangen
GERMANY
(working group of genealogists for the Egerland)

SWABIA. See BAVARIA, WUERTTEMBERG.

SWEDEN.

Hans-Juergen Schmitz
Kungsmarksvagen 79
S-37144 Karlskroe
Sverige/SWEDEN
(contact person for Swedish research group on Swedish
emigration to northern Germany)

Centrala Soldatregistret
Regementsmuseet P4/Fo35
Box 604
S-54129 Skövde
Sverige/SWEDEN
(Swedish military archive)

SWITZERLAND.

Schweizerische Gesellschaft fuer Familienforschung
(SGFF)
Zentralstelle fuer genealogische Auskuenfte
Manuel Aicher
Vogelaustrasse 34
CH-8953 Dietikon
Schweiz/SWITZERLAND
(Swiss genealogical society information center with 80,000
files; send all data, documents, & information previously
obtained + $20)

Schweizerische Gesellschaft fuer Familienforschung
(SGFF)
Schweizerische Landesbibliothek
Hallwylstrasse 15
CH-3003 Bern
Schweiz/SWITZERLAND
(headquarters of above Swiss genealogical society)

Schweizerische Gesellschaft fuer Familienforschung
(SGFF)
Dr. phil. Hans Boecklin
Steinbuehlallee 189
CH-4054 Basel
Schweiz/SWITZERLAND
(library of above Swiss genealogical society)

Schweizerische Gesellschaft fuer Familienforschung
(SGFF)
Werner Hug
Unterwartenweg 23/8
CH-4132 Muttenz
Schweiz/SWITZERLAND
(documentation for above Swiss genealogical society)

SGFF
Kreuzackerweg 12
CH-4148 Pfefflingen
Schweiz/SWITZERLAND
(branch of Swiss genealogical society for Basel area)

Cercle généalogique de l'Ancien Êvéché de Bâle
Jean-Philippe Gobat
50, rue de Condémine
CH-2740 Moutier
SGFF
(genealogical society for the old Bishopric of Basel)

Peter Werner Imhof
Burgisteinstrasse
CH-3135 Wattwil
Schweiz/SWITZERLAND
(branch of Swiss genealogical society for Bern area)

SGFF
Dreilindenstrasse 26
CH-6006 Luzern/Lucerne
Schweiz/SWITZERLAND
(branch of Swiss genealogical society for Lucerne area)

SGFF
rue des Beaux-Arts 3
CH-2000 Neuenburg/Neuchâtel
Schweiz/SWITZERLAND
(branch of Swiss genealogical society for Neuchâtel area)

SGFF
Landvogt-Waser-Strasse 70
CH-8405 Winterthur
Schweiz/SWITZERLAND
(branch of Swiss genealogical society for St. Gallen area)

SGFF
Anton Rechsteiner
Buebenloostrasse 20
CH-9500 Wil
Schweiz/SWITZERLAND
(branch of Swiss genealogical society for St. Gallen area)

Vereinigung fuer Familienkunde
Notkerstrasse 22 (Stadtarchiv)
CH-9000 St. Gallen
Schweiz/SWITZERLAND
(genealogical society for St. Gallen and Appenzell area)

Walliser Vereinigung fuer Familienforschung
Jean-B. Buetzberger
49, avenue Maurice Troillet
Case Postale 58
CH-1951 Sion
Schweiz/SWITZERLAND
(genealogical society for Valais/Wallis canton)

Genealogische Gesellschaft Zuerich
H. Peyer
Eichholzstrasse 19
CH-8706 Feldmeilen
Schweiz/SWITZERLAND
(genealogical society for Zuerich area)

Genealogisch-Heraldische Gesellschaft Zuerich
Eggwiesenstrasse
CH-8332 Russikon
Schweiz/SWITZERLAND
(genealogical and heraldic society for Zuerich area)

Schweizerische Heraldische Gesellschaft
Joseph M. Galliker
Luetzelmattstrasse 4
CH-6006 Luzern
Schweiz/SWITZERLAND
(Swiss heraldry society for German-speaking areas)

Société suisse d'Héraldique
16 rue St. Michel
CH-1700 Fribourg
Schweiz/SWITZERLAND
(Swiss heraldry society for French-speaking areas)

Heraldik & Grafik
Atelier Galloway
Museggstrasse 35
CH-6004 Luzern
Schweiz/SWITZERLAND
(private studio with information on Swiss coats of arms)

Verband schweizerischer Berufsfamilienforscher
Rietstrasse 25
CH-8703 Erlenbach-Zuerich
Schweiz/SWITZERLAND
(association of Swiss professional genealogists)

THURINGIA. See also MIDDLE GERMANY, SAXONY, and GERMANY.

Arbeitsgemeinschaft Genealogie Thueringen e.V., Sitz
     Weimar
Helmut Wlokka
Martin-Andersen-Nexoe-Strasse 62
D-99096 Erfurt
GERMANY
(Thuringian genealogical society; publishes *Genealogie in Deutschland*)

Arbeitsgemeinschaft Genealogie Thueringen e.V.
Peter-Juergen Klippstein
Herderstrasse 35
D-99096 Erfurt
GERMANY
(president ofThuringian genealogy society with branches in Erfurt, Gera, and Weimar)

Dr. Siegfried Mildner (THe)
Franz-Liszt-Strasse 8
D-99706 Sondershausen
GERMANY
(branch of Thuringian genealogical society for Erfurt and vicinity)

Dr. Harald Bergner (THg)
Heinrich-Heine-Strasse 16
D-07749 Jena
GERMANY
(branch of Thuringian genealogical society for Gera and vicinity)

Dr. Egbert Seidel (THw)
Otto-Schwarz-Strasse 58
D-07768 Jenz-Winzerla
GERMANY
(branch of Thuringian genealogical society for Weimar and vicinity)

TRANSYLVANIA.

Genealogische Sektion des Arbeitskreises fuer
Siebenbuergische Landeskunde
Siebenbuergische Buecherei
Schloss Horneck
D-74831 Gundelsheim/Wuerttemberg
GERMANY
(genealogical subbranch of the working group on
Transylvanian studies)

Arbeitskreis fuer Siebenbuergische Landeskunde
Abteilung Genealogie
Michael Fleischer
Holderbaumstrasse 9
D-67549 Worms
GERMANY
(genealogy group for Transylvania)

Landsmannschaft der Siebenbuerger Sachsen in
Deutschland e.V.
Sendlinger Strasse 48
D-80331 Muenchen *(Munich)*
GERMANY
(homeland association for Transylvanian Saxons in
Germany)

TURKEY.

Forschungsstelle Tuerkei der AgoFF
Dr. Helmut Flacker
Steingasse 4
D-79189 Bad Krozingen
GERMANY
(genealogy center for Germans from Turkey)

UKRAINE.

Forschungsstelle Ukraine der AgoFF
Antal von Könczöl
Schwarzwaldstrasse 34a
D-79276 Reute
GERMANY
(genealogy center for the Ukraine)

VOGTLAND. See SAXONY.

VOLHYNIA.

Forschungsstelle Mittelpolen-Volhynia der AGoFF
Heinz Ulbrich
Sperberweg 6
Postfach 1039
D-92661 Altenstadt an der Waldnaab
GERMANY
(genealogy center for central Poland/Volhynia)

Historischer Verein fuer Wolhynien
Hugo Schmidt, Pastor i.R.
Breslauer Strasse 10
D-91126 Schwabach
GERMANY
(historical society for Volhynia)

The Wandering Volhynians
Joerg Werner
Markusweg 82
D-32257 Buende
GERMANY
(German representative for Volhynian newsletter; for
America see section on American societies)

WALDECK. See HESSEN.

WALDENSER. See HUGUENOTS.

WALDENSIANS. See HUGUENOTS.

WEST PRUSSIA. See PRUSSIA.

WESTFALEN. See WESTPHALIA.

WESTPHALIA. See also LIPPE and RHINELAND.

Westfaelische Gesellschaft fuer Genealogie und
Familienforschung
Warendorfer Strasse 24
D-48145 Muenster
GERMANY
(genealogical society for Westphalia)

Historische Kommission fuer Westfalen
Racume 405-497
Warendorfer Strasse 24
D-48145 Muenster
GERMANY
(historical commission for Westphalia)

Provinzialinstitut fuer westfaelische Landes- und
Volksforschung des Landesverbandes
Westfalen-Lippe
Schorlemer Strasse 16
D-48183 Muenster
GERMANY
(institute for Westphalian studies)

Verein fuer Geschichte und Altertumskunde Westfalens
Abteilung Muenster
Schorlemer Strasse 16
D-48183 Muenster
GERMANY
(historical and antiquity society for Muenster area)

Familiengeschichtliche Vereinigung fuer die Kreise
Iserlohn und Altena
Letmathe
D-58642 Iserlohn
GERMANY
(genealogical society for Iserlohn and Altena areas)

Mindener Geschichtsverein
Kommunalarchiv Minden
Tonhallenstrasse 7
D-32423 Minden
GERMANY
(historical society for Minden)

Gruppe Familien- und Wappenkunde im
    Bundesbahn-Sozialwerk
Ortsgruppe Minden/Westfalen
Gerhard Heese-Golm
BOAR, BZA, Bahnhof
D-32427 Minden/Westfalen
GERMANY
(German railroad employee genealogy group for Minden
area)

Verein fuer Geschichte und Alteretumskunde Westfalens
Abteilung Paderborn
Leostrasse 21
D-33098 Paderborn
GERMANY
(history and antiquity society for Paderborn area)

Verein fuer Geschichte und Heimatpflege Soest e.V.
Stadtarchiv
Haus "Zum Spiegel"
Jakobistrasse 13
D-59494 Soest
GERMANY
(history and local history society for Soest)

Werler Arbeitsgemeinschaft fuer Familienforschung
Heinrich Josef Deisting
Lerchenweg 2
D-58730 Froendenberg/Ruhr
GERMANY
(genealogical working group for Werl and vicinity)

Familienkundlicher Abend DAGV im Hagener Heimatbund
    e.V.
Hochstrasse 74
Postfach 1368
D-58013 Hagen
GERMANY
(genealogical working group for Hagen (Westphalia) and
vicinity)

WESTPREUSSEN. See PRUSSIA.

WUERTTEMBERG.

Verein fuer Familien- und Wappenkunde in Wuerttemberg
    und Baden e.V.
Konrad-Adenauer Strasse 8
Wuerttembergische Landesbibliothek
Zimmer 103
Postfach 105441
D-70047 Stuttgart *(Street address D-70173)*
GERMANY
(genealogical society for Wuerttemberg and Baden,
publishes *Suedwestdeutsche Blaetter fuer Familien- und
Wappenkunde*)

Kurt Bihlmaier
Baachstrasse 27
D-71364 Winnenden
GERMANY
(contact person for genealogical society for Wuerttemberg
and Baden above)

Gruppe Familien- und Wappenkunde im
    Bundesbahn-Sozialwerk
Ortsgruppe Stuttgart
Alfons Hoffmann
Hammerstrasse 2
D-71638 Ludwigsburg
GERMANY
(Stuttgart area branch of German railroad employee
genealogy branch)

Wuerttembergischer Geschichts- und Altertumsverein
Konrad-Adenauer-Strasse 4
D-70173 Stuttgart
GERMANY
(history and antiquity society for Wuerttemberg)

Wuerttembergische Geschichts- und Altertumsverein
    e.V.
Konrad-Adenauer-Strasse 4
Hauptstaatsarchiv
D-70173 Stuttgart
GERMANY
(historical and antiquity society for Wuerttemberg)

Institut fuer geschichtliche Landeskunde an der
    Universitaet Tuebingen
Wilhelmstrasse 36
D-72074Tuebingen
GERMANY
(historical geography institute for Wuerttemberg at
University of Tuebingen)

Gesellschaft fuer Heimatpflege, Kunst- und
    Altertumsverein Biberach
Kreiskultur- und Archivamt
Rollinstrasse 9
D-88400 Biberach
GERMANY
(preservation, art, and antiquity society for Biberach)

Heimatgeschichtsverein fuer Schoenbuch und Gaeue e.V.
Galgenberg 48
D-71032 Boeblingen
GERMANY
(local history society for Boeblingen and the Schoenbuch area)

Geschichts- und Altertumsverein Esslingen am Neckar e.V.
Foehrenweg 1
D-73732 Esslingen
GERMANY
(historical and antiquity society for Esslingen)

Geschichts- und Altertumsverein Goeppingen
Kreisarchiv
Lorcher Strasse 6
Postfach 809
D-73008 Goeppingen *(Street address D-73033)*
GERMANY
(historical and antiquity society for Goeppingen)

Historischer Verein Heilbronn e.V.
Deutschhof
Eichgasse 1 (Stadtarchiv)
Postfach 2030
D-74010 Heilbronn *(Street address D-74072)*
GERMANY
(historical society for Heilbronn)

Historischer Verein Ludwigsburg fuer Stadt und Kre3is
    e.V.
Wilhelmstrasse 3
D-71638 Ludwigsburg
GERMANY
(historical society for the county of Ludwigsburg)

Verein fuer Heimatgeschichte Nagold e.V.
Hauffstrasse 13
D-72202 Nagold
GERMANY
(local history society for Nagold)

Suelchgauer Altertumsverein
Bischof-von-Keppler-Strasse 32
D-72108 Rottenburg
GERMANY
(antiquity society for the Rottenburg area)

Historischer Verein fuer Wuerttembergisch Franken
Muenzstrasse 1
D-74523 Schwaebisch Hall
GERMANY
(historical society for Schwaebisch Hall and vicinity)

Hohenzollerischer Geschichtsverein
Karlstrasse 3
Postrfach 526
D-72482 Sigmaringen *(Street address D-72488)*
GERMANY
(historical society for Sigmaringen and Hohenzollern)

Landeskundliche Forschungsstelle Hohenzollern in der
    Kommission fuer geschichtliche Landeskunde in
    Baden-Wuerttemberg
Karlstrasse 3
Postrfach 526
D-72482 Sigmaringen *(Street address D-72488)*
GERMANY
(historical research center for Hohenzollern)

YUGOSLAVIA. See DANUBE SWABIANS,
SOUTHEASTERN EUROPE.

ABC-Buecherdienst
Burgweinting
Junkersstrasse 11
D-93055 Regensburg
(international bookseller)

Address D Plus
Multi-Media Vertriebs GmbH
Am Neckartor 2
D-70190 Stuttgart
GERMANY
(sells German phone book CD-ROMs, outdated but
searchable by address)

Aschendorffsche Verlagsbuchhandlung
Soester Strasse 13
Postfach 1124
D-48001 Muenster
GERMANY
(publisher/distributors for books on Westphalian local
history and emigration)

Buch- und Kunstantiquariat Reinhold Berg
Wahlenstrasse 6
D-93047 Regensburg
GERMANY
(antiquarian book and art store)

Buchhandlung Bouvier
Am Hof 28
D-53113 Bonn
GERMANY
(books about the Rhineland)

Braunsche Universitaetsbuchhandlung
Antiquariatsabteilung
Kaiserstrasse 120
D-76133 Karlsruhe
GERMANY
(bookseller with antiquarian section for rare and
out-of-print publications)

Bund fuer deutsche Schrift und Sprache
Ahlhorn
Postfach 1110
D-26189 Grossenkneten
GERMANY
(association for German script and language; has teaching
and learning materials for old script)

Verlag Degener & Co.
Inhaber Manfred Dreiss
Nuernberger Strasse 27
Postfach 1340
D-91403 Neustadt (Aisch)   *(Street address D-91413)*
GERMANY
(major publishing house for books on German genealogy,
also the bimonthly "Familienkundliche Nachrichten,"
which is distributed with newsletters of nearly all German
genealogical societies)

Deutsche Post AG
Direktion Erfurt
Zentrallager Post
Privatkundenbertrieb
D-99081 Erfurt
GERMANY
(German post office distribution center for postal code
books and postal code maps)

Zeitschrift "Deutschland"
Postfach 100801
D-60008 Frankfurt (Main)
GERMANY
(magazine on politics, culture, business, and science)

Buchversand und Antiquariat Matthias Flury
Eduard-Buchner-Strasse 17
D-97204 Wuerzburg
GERMANY
(antiquarian bookstore; has old city directories)

Verlag Walter de Gruyter & Co.
Genthiner Weg 13
D-10785 Berlin
GERMANY
(publishing house for *MINERVA* reference books,
including handbooks on German archives)

N.G. Elwert Verlag
Postfach 1128
D-35001 Marburg/Lahn
GERMANY
(publishing house for books on local history, folklore,
geography, and dialectology)

Otto Harrassowitz
Taunusstrasse 5
D-65183 Wiesbaden
GERMANY
(international book dealer)

Herold GmbH
Guntramsdorfer Strasse 105
A-2340 Moedling
Oesterreich/AUSTRIA
EUROPE
(sells Austrian phone book CD-ROMs)

Hoelty-Stube
Johannisstrasse 28
D-37073 Goettingen
GERMANY
(books on Lower Saxony, Eichsfeld region, genealogy)

Galerie Huelchrath
Reichsgraf Finck v. Finkenstein
Huelchrather Strasse 6
D-50670 Koeln
GERMANY
(books on genealogy, the Gotha series on nobility)

Institut fuer pfaelzische Geschichte und Volkskunde
Benzinoring 6
Postfach 2860
D-67616 Kaiserslautern
GERMANY
(quasi-official institute for Palatine history and folk culture
which publishes books on the Palatinate/Pfalz, emigration,
Palatines abroad, and Pennsylvania Germans/
"Pennsylvania Dutch")

Antiquariat Karpinski
Am Schiessendahl 12
D-50374 Erftstadt
GERMANY
(antiquarian bookstore for Judaica, Silesia, Pomerania, East
and West Prussia, Poland, Russia)

Antiquariat Klittich-Pfannkuch
Kleine Burg 12
Postfach 1133
D-38001 Braunschweig *(Street address D-38100)*
GERMANY
(books on Braunschweig, the Harz region, genealogy, and
dialect)

Uni-Buchladen Peter Koehler
Emil-Warburg-Weg 28
D-95447 Bayreuth
GERMANY
(university bookstore; local history of Franconia and Upper
Palatinate, Reformation history, genealogy)

Antiquariat Marsilius
Kutschergasse 22
D-67346 Speyer
GERMANY
(antiquarian bookstore for the Palatinate)

Heinz Moos Verlag
Rottenbucherstrasse 30
D-82166 Graefelfing vor Muenchen
GERMANY
(publishing house for books, buttons, bumper stickers, wall
charts, etc., on emigration, the 1983 German-American
Tricentennial, German-Americans)

Antiquariat Karlhein Mueller
Lahnstrasse 14
D-65606 Villmar
GERMANY
(antiquarian bookstore for genealogy, history, military
science)

Versandantiquariat Robert A. Mueller Nachfolger
Bothfelder Strasse 11
D-30916 Isernhagen
GERMANY
(mail order antiquarian bookseller)

PAN Service Center
Postfach 102
A-1103 Wien *(Vienna)*
Oesterreich/AUSTRIA
EUROPE
(Austrian telnet service, including online phone directory)

Polygraphischer Verlag AG
Helenastrasse 3
CH-8034 Zuerich 8
Schweiz/Switzerland
(publishing house for *Familiennamenbuch der Schweiz*,
volumes listing all surnames in Switzerland and
home-towns where rights of citizenship are granted)

Ingenierbucro Pracfckc
Holzvogtkamp 55
D-24220 Flintbek
GERMANY
www.services@iway.de
(German mail order CD-ROM distributor)

Radio Deutsche Welle
Postfach 100444
D-50444 Koeln/Cologne
GERMANY
(official German overseas radio and satellite/cable TV
program service; publishes monthly program schedules)

Heinz Reise-Verlag
Kurmainzer Weg 22
Postfach 3141
D-37021 Goettingen
GERMANY
(publishing house for books on local history, also *Der
Schluessel*, an index to genealogical articles in Germany)

Verlag Hans Rohn
Oberdorfstrasse 5
Raemipostfach
CH-8024 Zuerich
Schweiz/Switzerland
(publishing house for books on genealogy and antiquarian
bookstore)

Wilhelm Rost Verlag
Vor dem Oberntore 27
D-31848 Bad Muender/Deister
GERMANY
(publishing house for reprints, books on local history,
genealogical books, and *Glenzdorfs Internationales
Genealogen-Lexikon*, an ongoing series of directories of
genealogists with surnames, places, time periods, and
special research interests listed and indexed)

Versandantiquariat Henning Schroeder
Kaiserstrasse 12
Postfach 100822
D-51608 Gummersbach *(Street address D-51643)*
GERMANY
(mail order genealogical and antiquarian bookseller)

Schropp Buchhandlung
Lauterstrasse 14/15
D-12159 Berlin
GERMANY
(bookseller)

Klaus Siefert
Beim Weissen Stein 29
D-77933 Lahr-Dinglingen
GERMANY
(*Ortssippenbücher*, local books of families for Baden)

Antiquariat J. Stargardt
Radestrasse 10
D-35037 Marburg
GERMANY
(antiquarian bookstore with books on genealogy, heraldry,
local history)

C.A. Starke Verlag
Frankfurter Strasse 51/53
D-65549 Limburg/Lahn
GERMANY
(major publishing house for books on German genealogy,
also the journal *Archiv fuer Sippenforschung* with its query
section entitled "Praktische Forschungshilfe")

Antiquariat und Aktionshaus J. A. Stargard
Clausewitzstrasse 4
Postfach 126826
D-10595 Berlin *(Street address D-10629)*
GERMANY
(antiquarian bookstore for documents, genealogy, heraldry)

Antiquariat Stauderhoff
Alter Fischmarkt 21
Postfach 7620
D-48041 Muenster
GERMANY
(antiquarian bookstore)

Franz Steiner Verlag GmbH Wiesbaden
Birkenwaldstrasse 44
Postrach 101526
D-70014 Stuttgart
GERMANY
(publishing house for books on German genealogy and
local history)

Tele-Info Verlag GmbH
Carl-Zeiss-Strasse 27
D-30827 Garbsen
GERMANY
(publisher of CD-ROMs of German telephone books)

Konrad Theiss Verlag
Villastrasse 11
D-70190 Stuttgart
GERMANY
(publishing house with many books on emigration by
Werner Hacker)

TopWare
Quadrat O 3,2
D-68161 Mannheim
GERMANY
(publisher of CD-ROMs of German telephone books)

Verlag fuer Standesamtswesen
Hanauer Landstrasse 197
D-60314 Frankfurt (Main)
GERMANY
(official publishing house for books on names, civil
registration and the law, and gazetteers (place-name
books), including the periodically updated *Ortsbuch der
Bundesrepublik Deutschland*, which lists civil registration
jurisdictions in the Federal Republic of Germany)

WEKA-Verlag GmbH & Co. KG
J.-Wassermann-Strasse 12
Postfach 1561
D-86305 Friedberg
GERMANY
(publishing house for travel brochures of cities and
communities)

Friedrich R. Wollmershaeuser
Herrengasse 8-10
D-89610 Oberdischingen
GERMANY
(publisher and distributor of German genealogical books)

Zielke Verlag
Stadtlohnweg 13C 407
D-48161 Muenster
GERMANY
(books in German on research in former Soviet Union and
Baltic areas)

J.P. Zwicky Verlag
Fraumuensterstrasse 13
CH-8001 Zuerich
Schweiz/SWITZERLAND
(publishing house for books on Swiss genealogy)

Dieter Zwinger
Osannstrasse 24
D-64285 Darmstadt
GERMANY
(computer diskettes with regional lists of researchers)

NATIONAL AND REGIONAL LIBRARIES

Nationalbibliothek = national library
Staatsbibliothek = national library
Landesbibliothek = state library
Universitaetsbibliothek = university library
Most libraries would be willing to photocopy their card catalogs on a limited subject or specific pages from an identified book. Some have Interlibrary Loan, even worldwide. But libraries cannot be expected to do even brief searches; you must hire a researcher for that.

GERMANY.

Deutsche Bibliothek
Zeppelinallee 8
D-60325 Frankfurt (Main)
GERMANY

Deutsche Staatsbibliothek
Unter den Linden 8
D-10117 Berlin
GERMANY

Deutsche Buecherei
Haus der Deutschen Buecherei
Deutscher Platz
D-04103 Leipzig
GERMANY

Bibliothek des Germanischen Nationalmuseums
Kartaeusergasse 1
D-90402 Nuernberg/Nuremberg
GERMANY

Universitaet Bremen
Deutsche Presseforschung
Postfach 330160
D-28331 Bremen
GERMANY
(German newspaper research)

Wehrbereichsbibliothek II
Hans-Boeckler-Allee 18
D-30173 Hannover
GERMANY
(military history library)

USAREUR Library and Resource Center
Zengerstrasse 1 (Mark Twain Village)
D-69126 Heidelberg
GERMANY
(library at U.S. military base in Heidelberg)

AUSTRIA.

Oesterreichische Nationalbibliothek
Josefplatz 1
A-1014 Wien/Vienna
Oesterreich/AUSTRIA
EUROPE

Universitaetsbibliothek Wien
Dr.-Karl-Lueger-Ring
A-1010 Wien/Vienna
Oesterreich/AUSTRIA
EUROPE

BADEN.

Badische Landesbibliothek
Karlstrasse 1
Nymphengarten
D-76133 Karlsruhe
GERMANY

Universitaetsbibliothek Heidelberg
Ploeck 107-109
D-67119 Heidelberg
GERMANY

Universitaetsbibliothek Freiburg
Rempartstrasse 15
Postfach 1629
D-79016 Freiburg im Breisgau
GERMANY

Wuerttembergische Landesbibliothek
Konrad-Adenauer-Strasse 8
D-70173 Stuttgart
GERMANY

BAVARIA.

Bayerische Staatsbibliothek
Ludwigstrasse 16
D-80539 Muenchen *(Munich)*
GERMANY
(the largest newspaper collection in Germany)

Universitaetsbibliothek
Geschwister-Scholl-Platz 1
D-80539 Muenchen *(Munich)*
GERMANY

Universitaetsbibliothek
Universitaetsstrasse 4
Postfach 3509
D-91023 Erlangen *(Street address D-91054)*
GERMANY

BAYERN. See BAVARIA.

NATIONAL AND REGIONAL LIBRARIES

BELGIUM.

Bibliothèque Royale de Belgique
4 Boulevard de l'Empereur
B- Bruxelles/Brussels
Belgique/BELGIUM

BERLIN.

Universitaetsbibliothek
Garystrasse 39
D-14195 Berlin
GERMANY

Universitaetsbibliothek der Humboldt-Universitaet zu
    Berlin
Clara-Zetkin-Strasse 27
D-10117 Berlin
GERMANY

BRANDENBURG.

Universitaetsbibliothek
Garystrasse 39
D-14195 Berlin
GERMANY

BRAUNSCHWEIG. See also LOWER SAXONY.

Herzog August Bibliothek
Lessingplatz 1
D-38304 Wolfenbuettel
GERMANY

BREMEN.

Universitaetsbibliothek Bremen
Breitenweg 27
D-28195 Bremen
GERMANY

Staats- und Universitaetsbibliothek
Moorweidenstrasse 40
D-20146 Hamburg
GERMANY

BRUNSWICK. See BRAUNSCHWEIG.

CZECH REPUBLIC.

Czech National Library
Klementinum 190
CS-11001 Praha/Prague 1
CZECH REPUBLIC

DENMARK.

Det Kongelige Bibliothek
Christians Brygge 8
Postbox 2149
DK-1016 København/Copenhagen
Danmark/DENMARK

Schleswig-Holsteinische Landesbibliothek
Warnemuender Strasse 16-18
D-24106 Kiel
GERMANY

EASTERN EUROPE.

Buecherei des deutschen Ostens
Hauptbuecherei
Berliner Platz 11
D-44623 Herne
GERMANY

Bibliothek der Stiftung Haus des deutschen Ostens
Bismarckstrasse 90
D-40210 Duesseldorf
GERMANY

Niedersaechsische Landesbibliothek
Waterloostrasse 8
D-30169 Hannover
GERMANY

Universitaetsbibliothek
Postfach 1521
D-48004 Muenster
GERMANY

Johann-Gottfried-Herder-Institut
Gisonenweg 5-7
D-35037 Marburg/Lahn
GERMANY

EMIGRATION.

Bibliothek des Instituts fuer Auslandsbeziehungen
Charlottenplatz 17
D-70173 Stuttgart
GERMANY
(large library on German emigration)

FRANCE.

Bibliothèque Nationale
58, rue de Richelieu
F-75084 Paris
FRANCE
(contains genealogies of French noble families prior to
1789 in *Carrés d'Hozier* and coats of arms of notable
French families in 1696 in *d'Hozier Armorial Géneral
Officiel*)

HAMBURG.

Staats- und Universitaetsbibliothek Hamburg "Carl von
    Ossietzky"
Von-Melle-Park 5
D-20146 Hamburg
GERMANY

HANNOVER. See LOWER SAXONY.

NATIONAL AND REGIONAL LIBRARIES

HESSE.

Hessische Landesbibliothek
Heinrich-von-Bibra-Platz
Postfach 665
D-36006 Fulda
GERMANY

Murhardsche Bibliothek der Stadt Kassel und
Landesbibliothek
Brueder-Grimm-Platz 4 A
D-34117 Kassel
GERMANY

Hessische Landesbibliothek Wiesbaden
Rheinstrasse 55
D-65185 Wiesbaden
GERMANY

Stadt- und Universitaetsbibliothek
Bockenheimer Landstrasse 134-138
D-60325 Frankfurt/Main
GERMANY

HOLLAND. See NETHERLANDS.

HUNGARY.

Bibliotheque Nationale Széchényi
Múzeum Körút 14-16
H-1013 Budapest VIII
HUNGARY

LIPPE.

Lippische Landesbibliothek
Hornsche Strasse 41
D-32756 Detmold
GERMANY

LOWER SAXONY.

Niedersaechsische Landesbibliothek
Waterloostrasse 8
D-30169 Hannover
GERMANY

Staats- und Universitaetsbibliothek
Prinzenstrasse 1
D-37073 Goettingen
GERMANY

LUXEMBOURG.

Bibliothèque Nationale
37 Boulevard F.D. Roosevelt
L- Luxembourg
LUXEMBOURG

MECKLENBURG.

Mecklenburgische Landesbibliothek
Domkreuzgang
D-19055 Schwerin
GERMANY

NETHERLANDS.

Koninklijke Bibliotheek
Lange Voorhout 34
NL- s'Gravenhage/The Hague
Nederland/NETHERLANDS

NIEDERSACHSEN. See LOWER SAXONY.

NORTH RHINE-WESTPHALIA. See RHINELAND,
LIPPE, and WESTPHALIA.

OLDENBURG.

Landesbibliothek
Ofener Strasse 15
D-26121 Oldenburg
GERMANY

PALATINATE.

Pfaelzische Landesbibliothek
Otto-Mayer-Strasse 9
Postfach 1709
D-67327 Speyer   *(Street address D-67346)*
GERMANY

Wuerttembergische Landesbibliothek
Konrad-Adenauer-Strasse 8
D-70173 Stuttgart
GERMANY

PFALZ. See PALATINATE.

POLAND. See also EASTERN EUROPE.

Biblioteka Narodowa
ulica Hankiewicza 1
PL- Warszawa/Warsaw
Polska/POLAND

Niedersaechsische Landesbibliothek
Waterloostrasse 8
D-30169 Hannover
GERMANY

POMERANIA.

Bibliothek der Pommernstiftung
Schloss Rantzaubau
Daenische Strasse 44
D-24103 Kiel
GERMANY

POMMERN. See POMERANIA.

NATIONAL AND REGIONAL LIBRARIES

PRUSSIA (EAST AND WEST).

Staatsbibliothek Preussischer Kulturbesitz
Potsdamer Strasse 33
D-10785 Berlin
GERMANY

Nordostdeutsches Kultuswerk
Conventstrasse 1
D-21335 Lueneburg
GERMANY

RHINELAND.

Universitaetsbibliothek Koeln
Universitaetsstrasse 33
D-50931 Koeln-Lindenthal *(Cologne)*
GERMANY

Badische Landesbibliothek
Nymphengarten
Karlstrasse 1
D-76133 Karlsruhe
GERMANY

Universitaetsbibliothek Duesseldorf
Universitaetsstrasse 1
D-40225 Duesseldorf
GERMANY

ROMANIA.

Suedostdeutsches Kulturwerk
Bibliothek
Guellstrasse 7
D-80336 Muenchen/Munich
GERMANY

Siebenbuergische Buecherei
Schloss Horneck
D-74831 Gundelsheim
GERMANY
(library on Transylvania)

RUMANIA. See ROMANIA.

SAARLAND.

Universitaetsbibliothek
Am Stadtwald
D-66123 Saarbruecken
GERMANY

Wuerttembergische Landesbibliothek
Konrad-Adenauer-Strasse 8
D-70173 Stuttgart
GERMANY

SCHLESWIG-HOLSTEIN.

Schleswig-Holsteinische Landesbibliothek
Warnemuender Strasse 16-18
D-24106 Kiel
GERMANY

Universitaetsbibliothek
Ohlshausenstrasse 29
D-24118 Kiel
GERMANY

Staats- und Universitaetsbibliothek
Moorweidenstrasse 40
D-20146 Hamburg
GERMANY

SWITZERLAND.

Schweizerische Landesbibliothek
Hallwylstrasse 15
CH-3003 Bern
Schweiz/SWITZERLAND

TRANSYLVANIA. See ROMANIA.

WESTPHALIA.

Stadt- und Landesbibliothek
Hansaplatz
D-44137 Dortmund
GERMANY

WUERTTEMBERG.

Wuerttembergische Landesbibliothek
Konrad-Adenauer-Strasse 8
D-70173 Stuttgart
GERMANY

Badische Landesbibliothek
Nymphengarten
Karlstrasse 1
D-76133 Karlsruhe
GERMANY

WÜRTTEMBERG. See WUERTTEMBERG.

EUROPEAN MUSEUMS

(a representative selection covering many occupations and representations of the way of life of our ancestors, transportation, or local history; for almost any occupation there will be a museum)

Deutscher Museumsbund
Senckenberganlage 25
D-60325 Frankfurt am Main
GERMANY
(association of German museums; can refer you to museums in your geographic area or field of interest)

Deutsches Museum
Museumsinsel
D-80538 Muenchen/Munich
GERMANY
(German museum of science and technology, somewhat like the Smithsonian Institution)

Deutsches Apotheken-Museum
Schloss
D-69117 Heidelberg
GERMANY
(German apothecary/pharmacy museum)

Bayerisches Nationalmuseum
Prinzregentenstrasse 3
D-80538 Muenchen *(Munich)*
GERMANY
(Bavarian national museum)

Deutsches Brotmuseum
Fuerstenecker Strasse 17
D-89077 Ulm
GERMANY
(German bread museum)

Deutsches Brauerei-Museum
St. Jakobs-Platz 1
D-80331 Muenchen/Munich
GERMANY
(German brewery museum)

Deutsches Uhrenmuseum
Gerwig Strasse 1
D-78120 Furtwangen
GERMANY
(German clock museum; includes mechanical and cuckoo clocks)

Wappen- und Siegelsammlung
Staatsarchiv Hamburg
Rathaus
ABC-Strasse 19, Eingang A
D-20354 Hamburg
GERMANY
(German coat of arms and seal collection)

Foerderverein German Emigrant Museum
Insclstrassc 6
D-27568 Bremerhaven
GERMANY
(foundation for German emigrant museum on history of emigration; archives, library, photograph collection)

Dirk Schroeder
Messe Bremen Expo 2000
Faulenstrasse 23/29
D-28195 Bremen
GERMANY
(emigration exposition in Bremen planned for the year 2000)

Museum fuer baeuerliche Arbeitsgeraete
Adolf-Waechter-Strasse 17
D-95447 Bayreuth
GERMANY
(German farm tool museum)

Mainfraenkisches Museum
Festung Marienberg
D-97082 Wuerzburg
GERMANY
(museum for the Franconia area)

Germanisches Nationalmuseum
Kornmarkt 1
D-90402 Nuernberg *(Nuremberg)*
GERMANY
(German national historic museum)

Hutmuseum
Tannenwaldweg 102
D-61350 Bad Homburg
GERMANY
(German hat museum)

Musikantenmuseum
Burg Lichtenberg
D-66871 Thallichtenberg
GERMANY
(German itinerant musician museum)

Schmuckmuseum
Reuchlinhaus
Stadtgarten
D-75172 Pforzheim
GERMANY
(German jewelry museum)

Deutsches Leder- und Schuhmuseum
Frankfurter Strasse 86
D-63067 Offenbach
GERMANY
(German leather and shoe museum)

Lippisches Landesmuseum
Ameide 4
D-32756 Detmold
GERMANY
(Lippe regional museum)

Landesmuseum Mainz
Grosse Bleiche 49
D-55116 Mainz
GERMANY
(Mainz regional museum)

Wehrgeschichtliches Museum
Karlstrasse 1
Postfach 1633
D-76406 Rastatt *(Street address D-76437)*
GERMANY
(German military history museum)

Deutsches Bergbaumuseum
Am Bergbaumuseum
D-44791 Bochum
GERMANY
(German mining museum and archive)

Siegfried's Mechanisches Musikkabinett
Oberstrasse 29
D-65385 Ruedesheim am Rhein
GERMANY
(automated music instrument museum)

Historisches Museum der Pfalz
Grosse Pfaffengasse 7
D-67346 Speyer
GERMANY
(historical museum of the Palatinate)

Gutenbergmuseum
Liebfrauenplatz 5
D-55116 Mainz
GERMANY
(German printing museum)

Rheinisches Landesmuseum
Colmantstrasse 14
D-53115 Bonn
GERMANY
(Rhine museum)

Rheinisches Landesmuseum
Ostallee 4
D-54290 Trier
GERMANY
(Rhineland museum)

Roemisch-Germanisches Museum
Roncalliplatz 4
D-50667 Koeln *(Cologne)*
GERMANY
(museum of the Roman and Germanic peoples)

Roemisch-Germanisches Museum
Ernst-Ludwig-Platz 2
D-55116 Mainz
GERMANY
(museum of the Roman and Germanic peoples)

Salzmuseum
Bergwerkstrasse
D-83471 Berchtesgaden
GERMANY
(German salt museum)

Antikes Schiffahrtsmuseum
Neutorstrasse
D-55116 Mainz
GERMANY
(museum of ancient ships)

Museum Steinarbeiterhaus
Hohburg
Martin-Luther-Strasse 5
D-04808 Hohburg
GERMANY
(German stoneworking museum)

Stiftung Schweizerisches Freilichtmuseum Ballenberg
CH-3855 Brienz (Berner Oberland)
Schweiz/SWITZERLAND
(Swiss open-air museum between Brienzwiler and
Hofstetten with 55 reconstructed rural houses from 17
cantons of Switzerland, demonstrations of customs and
traditions of 17th and 18th centuries)

Klingenmuseum
Wuppertaler Strasse 161
D-42653 Solingen
GERMANY
(German sword and blade museum; cutlery, surgical
instruments, scissors, razors, etc.)

Deutsches Tabak- und Zigarrenmuseum
Finfhausenstrasse 8-12
D-32257 Buende
GERMANY
(German tobacco and cigar museum)

Spielzeugmuseum
Karl Strasse 13
D-90403 Nuernberg *(Nuremberg)*
GERMANY
(toy museum)

Verkehrsmuseum
D-90403 Nuernberg *(Nuremberg)*
GERMANY
(German transportation museum; first German railway car
(1835))

Museumsdorf
D-449661 Cloppenburg
GERMANY
(German village museum with north German farmhouses of
16th to 19th centuries, craftsmen's studios, windmills)

EUROPEAN MUSEUMS

Freilichtmuseum
D-77793 Gutach
GERMANY
(German village museum; reconstructed Black Forest farm
houses; water-operated machines)

Geigenbaumuseum
Ballenhausgasse 3
D-82481 Mittenwald
GERMANY
(German violin museum)

Windmuehlen- und Landwirtschaftsmuseum
Petersdorf-Lemkenhafen
D-23769 Westfehmarn
GERMANY
(German windmill and agriculture museum)

Rheingau- und Wein-Museum Broemserburg
Rheinstrasse 2
D-65385 Ruedesheim
GERMANY
(German wine museum)

Museum fuer Weinkultur
Weinstrasse
D-67146 Deidesheim
GERMANY
(museum for wine culture)

Wald- und Holzmuseum
Burgstrasse
D-56154 Boppard
Federal Republic of Germany
(German wood museum)

GENEALOGISTS

No guarantees are expressed or implied by the inclusion of the following in this listing. Some are not full-time genealogists. Make clear arrangements in advance whenever requesting professional help. Send a self- addressed, stamped envelope within your own country or else 2 or 3 International Reply Coupons (available from post office) for foreign countries or $2 or $3 cash.

Verband deutschsprachiger Berufsgenealogen e.V.
Friedrichstrasse 25
Postfach 1720
D-49347 Diepholz
GERMANY
(association of German-speaking professional genealogists
in Europe)

Bruno Alder-Neveling
Im Grund 14c
CH-9012 St. Gallen
Schweiz/SWITZERLAND
(Cantons Appenzell-Ausserrhoden and St. Gallen)

Christine Bachelet
Residence Bel Horizon
191 Rue du Carmel
F-76230 Baisguillaune
FRANCE
(Rouen archive research, including Le Havre passenger
lists)

Waldtraud Beckmann
Celler Heerstrasse 301
D-38112 Braunschweig *(Brunswick)*
GERMANY
(Braunschweig area)

Wladimir von Berens
Pjarnuskoe Schosse 191 mut. 191
200016 Tallin
ESTONIA
(Estonia and Latvia; knows English)

Karl-Heinz Bernardy
Deutschherrenstrasse 42
D-56070 Koblenz
GERMANY
(Koblenz archives)

Udo Blankenhahn
Jaerkenweg 9
D-59494 Soest
GERMANY
(Westphalia and the Rhineland)

Pierre-Arnold Borel
Belle-Combe 8
CH-2300 La Chaux-de-Fonds
Schweiz/SWITZERLAND
(Canton Neuchâtel)

Inge Bork
5700 S. China Clay Dr.
SALT LAKE CITY UT 84118
USA
(research in LDS Family History Library)

Klaus Brand
Niflandring 5
D-22559 Hamburg
GERMANY
(Hamburg)

Edward R. Brandt
13 - 27th Ave. SE
MINNEAPOLIS MN 55414-3101
USA
(eastern European Germans)

Madame J.M. Brower
8, rue de la Closerie
F-78240 Chambourcy
FRANCE
(Huguenot/French research done in Paris)

Lois Byrem
P.O. Box 280
STRASBURG PA 17579
USA
(German Baptist Brethren)

Gastone Cambin
Via Camara 58
CH-6932 Bregenzano-Lugano
Schweiz/SWITZERLAND
(Tessin, Graubuenden/Grisons cantons of Switzerland)

Jane Adams Clarke
634 Naomi St.
PHILADELPHIA PA 19144
USA
(Pennsylvania Germans)

James A. Derheim
700 Meadowbrook Lane
SIOUX FALLS SD 57103
USA
(photographs of ancestral villages, landmarks, homes in
Europe)

Dr. Richard W. Dougherty
476 E. South Temple #189
SALT LAKE CITY UT 84111
USA
(German & German-American research)

Carolyn B. Dryfoos
Pennsylvania German Research
RD 1
SUGARLOAF PA 18249
USA
(research, genealogy tours)

GENEALOGISTS

Frau Dr. Irmtraut Eder-Stein
Archivoberraetin a.D.
Magdeburger Strasse 35
D-56075 Koblenz
GERMANY
(Koblenz archives)

Jean Ensch
33, rue Lankheck
L-7542 Mersch
LUXEMBOURG
(Luxembourg)

Jason Epstein
Av. Epitacio Pessoa 2330
1550 Lagoa
22471 Rio de Janeiro
BRAZIL
(Germans in Brazil)

Kurt Ewald
Johann-Schmidt-Strasse 33
D-85716 Unterschleissheim
GERMANY
(Germany, Austria, Switzerland)

Family Tree
Zöldlomb u. 16-18/B
H-1025 Budapest
HUNGARY
(Hungary)

Frl. Kathrin Fiechter
Alpenstrasse 27 d
CH-3400 Burgdorf BE
Schweiz/SWITZERLAND
(Switzerland)

Pfarrer i.R. Rolf Finkentey
Holte-Lastrup
Ziegelei 78
D-49774 Laehden
GERMANY
(Koblenz archives)

Eva Fintelmann
Korfiz-Holm-Strasse 21
D-81245 Muenchen/Munich
GERMANY
(Bavaria)

Hans Finzel, Oberstaatsrat a.D.
Salinenstrasse 19
D-55543 Bad Kreuznach
GERMANY
(Koblenz archives)

Boy Friedrich
Estedeich 82
D-21129 Hamburg
GERMANY
(Hamburg passenger lists)

Kermit Frye
152 Spring Valley Center
BLOOMINGTON MN 55420-5535
USA
(German translations)

G.-Alexander Fuelling
Ernst-Ludwig-Strasse 21
D-64625 Bensheim
GERMANY
(Hesse, Palatinate/Pfalz, southern Rhineland)

Duncan B. Gardiner
12961 Lake Ave.
LAKEWOOD OH 44107
USA
(Czech Republic and surrounding areas)

German Research Specialists
P.O. Box 582155
MINNEAPOLIS MN 55458-2155
USA
(lists of villages in Pomerania, East Prussia, West Prussia, Brandenburg, Posen, and Silesia)

Frau Ella Gieg
Rimhorn
Goldbachstrasse 3
D-6129 Luetzelbach 5
GERMANY
(emigration from the Odenwald)

Manfred Gillissen
Taubhausstrasse 47
D-56112 Lahnstein
GERMANY
(Koblenz archives)

Bernd Goelzer
7, rue des Vergers
F-57350 Stiring-Wendel
FRANCE
(the Palatinate/Pfalz & Saarland; knows English)

Delbert Gratz
RR 2, Box 89
8990 Augsburger Rd.
BLUFFTON OH 45817
USA
(Mennonites, Anabaptists, Switzerland, Alsace-Lorraine, southern Germany)

Jacques Julien de Guise
Cabinet d'Etudes Généalogiques
Boîte postale 227
CH-1211 Genève 25
Suisse/SWITZERLAND
(Switzerland, Alsace, southwestern Germany)

Yvonne Gygli
Ringstrasse 3
CH-3052 Zollikofen BE
Schweiz/SWITZERLAND
(Aargau, Basel, Bern, Solothurn cantons of Switzerland)

Gordon Hartig
71 Sleigh Rd.
WESTFORD MA 01886
USA
(German translations)

Harold M. Hegyessy, Jr.
1030 E. Grove Dr.
PLEASANT GROVE UT 84062
USA
(Germany, Switzerland)

John W. Heisey
728 S. George St.
YORK PA 17403
USA
(Pennsylvania Germans)

Eckhard Hensel
111 Fisherman's Lane
WRIGHTSVILLE PA 17368
USA
(Germany, Switzerland, etc.; translations)

Hans-Joachim Hinners
Wurster Strasse 390 b
D-2850 Bremerhaven-Weddewarden
GERMANY
(northwestern Germany near Bremerhaven)

Adolph Hirsch
P.O. Box 4368
N HOLLYWOOD CA 91607
USA
(translations)

Sonja R. Hoeke-Nishimoto
5663 W 11200 N
HIGHLAND UT 84003-9413
USA
(German translations)

Ursula Huelsbergen
1908 Alabama St.
LAWRENCE KS 66046
USA
(German research; translations)

John Hueppi
Sustenstrasse 24
CH-3604 Thun
Schweiz/SWITZERLAND
(Bern and Solothurn cantons, Switzerland)

Werner Hug
Unterwartweg 23/8
CH-4132 Muttenz BL
Schweiz/SWITZERLAND
(Aargau, Basel, Solothurn cantons, Switzerland)

Friedrich Ernst Hunsche
Am Ortfelde 28
D-30916 Isernhagen
GERMANY
(Duchy of Tecklenburg; emigration; northwestern Germany)

Jim Ivey
Czech-Mates
1135 20th Ave.
DEER PARK WI 54007
USA
(data base of German-Bohemian names)

Dr. Lutz Jacob & Katharina Kahlert
Gohliser Strasse 1
D-04105 Leipzig
GERMANY
(origins and meanings of German names)

Christian Jaehne
Muelbergstrasse 9
D-73728 Esslingen
GERMANY
(Wuerttemberg, Baden, southwestern Germany; knows English)

Hank Jones (= Henry Z Jones, Jr.)
P.O. Box 261388
SAN DIEGO CA 92196-1388
USA
("Palatines" of 1708-1710 to New York state; other immigrants prior to 1750; has traced over 550 of 849 of "1709ers" back to European origins)

Peggy Shomo Joyner
5088 Dogwood Trail
PORTSMOUTH VA 23703
USA
(Germans and Swiss in Pennsylvania, western Maryland, and the valley of Virginia prior to 1800)

Walter Kamphoefner
1208 Airline
COLLEGE STATION TX 77860
USA
(emigration from Westphalia)

Michail Jurewitsch Katin-Jarzew
uliza Gerzen 49, #33
121069 Moskva/Moscow
RUSSIA
(Russian and Baltic Germans; knows English)

GENEALOGISTS

Frau Mathilde Kielholz-Mueller
Isenringstrasse 12
CH-9202 Gossau
Schweiz/SWITZERLAND
(eastern Switzerland)

J. William Klapper
1900 Richmond Dr.
LOUISVILLE KY 40205
USA
(translations of German letters, documents)

Robert M. Knebel
184 Crescent Dr.
GRANBURY TX 76049-5334
USA
(Germany)

Dr. Conrad Koch
Buerenweg 216
CH-4146 Hochwald
Schweiz/SWITZERLAND
(places of origin of emigrants from Germany and
Switzerland)

Gunnar Kohl
Langlosenweg 13
D-64385 Reichelsheim
GERMANY
(card-file of inhabitants of the Odenwald)

Martin Kreder
Hoelderlinstrasse 11
D-89522 Heidenheim/Brenz
GERMANY
(Wuerttemberg)

Wilhelm Krueggeler
Am Rothoborn 4
D-33098 Paderborn
GERMANY
(Westphalia, Rhineland, Hesse)

Franz Walter Kummer-Beck
Herrengrabenweg 3
CH-4053 Basel
Schweiz/SWITZERLAND
(Switzerland)

Franz Kurt Laube
Stoecklimattstrasse 38
CH-4513 Langendorf SO
Schweiz/SWITZERLAND
(Canton Solothurn, Switzerland)

Alfred Laun
Aspenwaldstrasse 2
D-70195 Stuttgart
GERMANY
(card file of 42,000 emigrants from Wuerttemberg
1818-1819, 1830-1852, 1856-1857)

Hugh T. Law
1216 Lillie Circle
SALT LAKE CITY UT 84121
USA
(France, including Alsace and Lorraine)

Angelica Eva Lemmer
Liessem
Drachenburgweg 5
D-53343 Wachtberg
GERMANY
(American-born translator)

Falk Liebezeit
Friedrichstrasse 25
D-19356 Diepholz
GERMANY
(Braunschweig, Bremen, Hannover, Hildesheim,
Niederstift Muenster, Oldenburg, Osnabrueck)

Inger Ludlow
558 K St.
SALT LAKE CITY UT 84103
USA
(Denmark, northern Germany)

Markus Lischer
Felsbergstrasse 6
CH-6006 Luzern LU
Schweiz/SWITZERLAND
(Canton Lucerne, Switzerland)

Johann Hinrich Lueschen
Schulstrasse 6
D-26340 Zetel
GERMANY
(northwest Germany)

Karl Marbacher
Gebeneggweg 8
CH-6005 Luzern
Schweiz/SWITZERLAND
(central Switzerland, including Luzern and Zuerich)

Sieglinde Martin
5410 Burlingame Ave.
BUENA PARK CA 90621-1524
USA
(German translation)

John H. Marvin
2039 Irwin Place
MADISON WI 53713
USA
(Bohemian, Moravian, Slovakian genealogy)

I.M. Maslenikov
Marzikevitschst. 10-57
220092 Minsk
BELARUS
(Minsk area of Belarus; knows English)

GENEALOGISTS

Reinhard Mayer
Jaegerstrasse 42/44
D-83308 Trostberg
GERMANY
(southern Germany; over 140,000 emigrants from Bavaria indexed; knows English)

Gisela Stuehrk Mead
P.O. Box 18258
RENO NV 89511
USA
(translations)

Joachim Memmert
Kopenhagener Allee 18
D-24109 Kiel
GERMANY
(file of "Hollanders" from Schleswig-Holstein and Mecklenburg)

Ernst Michel
Hohruetistrasse 39
CH-6020 Emmenbruecke LU
Schweiz/SWITZERLAND
(interior Switzerland, Graubuenden/Grisons)

Roger Minert
1001 S 1020 W
WOODS CROSS UT 84087
USA
(German translations; research in LDS Family History Library)

Dr. Sylvia Moehle
Calsowstrasse 11
D-37085 Goettingen
GERMANY
(Hannover and Hildesheim area)

Mogens Mogensen-Gallati
Berglistrasse 27
CH-9320 Arbon
Schweiz/SWITZERLAND
(Switzerland)

Merriam Moore
12175 Royal Lutham Row
Rancho Bernardo
SAN DIEGO CA 92128-4472
USA
(Saxony, Thuringia; German translations)

Mario von Moos
Neugrundstrasse 5
CH-8320 Fehraltdorf
Schweiz/SWITZERLAND
(Cantons Zuerich and Schaffhausen, Switzerland)

Lothar Mueller-Westphal
Binsfelder Strasse 45
D-52351 Dueren
GERMANY
(heraldry; illustrations; research at Bruehl vital records archive)

Helg Munko
Koenitgseerstrasse 14
D-98708 Gehren
GERMANY
(Thuringia, Saxony)

Ing. George Musat
Bucarest 1
St. B-dul 1 Mai Nr. 111, Bloc 12A Sc. 1, Ap. 1
ROMANIA
(Romania)

Paul Anthon Nielson
Stygli
Blochstrasse 7
CH-3653 Oberhofen am Thuner See BE
Schweiz/SWITZERLAND
(Switzerland)

Bernhart Nothdurft
Robert-Koch-Strasse 32
D-30853 Langenhagen
GERMANY
(Lower Saxony, Hannover area)

Rolf Nowak
Muehlenstrasse 12
D-37170 Uslar
GERMANY
(Uslar and Solling region)

Bruno J. Nussbaumer
Felsenstrasse 84
CH-9000 St. Gallen
Schweiz/SWITZERLAND
(eastern Switzerland)

Joachim Nuthack
11418 70th St.
Edmonton, Alberta
CANADA T5B 1T4
(Pomerania, Mecklenburg, West Prussia)

Historisch-Demographische Dokumentationsstelle fuer
  Suedwestdeutschland
Prof. Dr. Burkhart Oertel
Brunhildenstrasse 4 B
D-85579 Neubiburg
GERMANY
(card file with over 390,000 surnames and 2,800,000 persons, especially from Baden, Wuerttemberg, and Franconia; also some from Hesse and Schleswig-Holstein; send 2 IRC's or $3.00; several requests $5.00)

GENEALOGISTS

Michael P. Palmer
P.O. Box 765
CLAREMONT CA 91711-0765
USA
(Germany)

Marie-Odile Pérès
24, quai Rouget de Lisle
F-67000 Strasbourg
FRANCE
(Alsace-Lorraine)

MITEK
Julia Petrakis
812 Vista Dr.
CAMANO ISLAND WA 98292
USA
(has research agreements with historic and diplomatic
archives, state libraries, and databases of Russia, Ukraine,
Belarus, and the Baltic states)

Irene Petrauskiene
Vilniaus 26-15
5610 Telsiai
LITHUANIA
(Lithuanian; knows German)

Klaus Pfitzner
Zeisspfad 78a
D-12305 Berlin
GERMANY
(Brandenburg and Berlin)

PIAST Genealogy Research Center
Osradan Badan Genealogicznych
P.O. Box 9
PL-00957 Warszawa 36
POLAND
(Poland)

Dr. Igor Plehre
Radisheva st. 41
410601 Saratov
RUSSIA
(Volga Germans)

Prof. Terence M. Punch
P.O. Box 895
Armdale, Nova Scotia
CANADA B3L 4K5
(German emigrants to Nova Scotia 1749-1753; pre-1850
Germans to Nova Scotia)

Ronald J. Putz
201 Salzburg Ave.
BAY CITY MI 48706-5317
USA
(translations)

Heinz v. Quennaudon
Brandenburgischer Ring 42
D-03172 Guben
GERMANY
(extensive files; send 2 single dollar bills; does not read or
write English; send names, dates, places)

RAGAS (Russian-American Genealogical Archival Source)
P.O. Box 236
GLEN ECHO MD 20812
USA
(official source for genealogical contact with archives in
most parts of former Soviet Union)

Gerhard Reiche, Ing.
Salzbrunnen 4
D-38835 Osterwieck
GERMANY
(Osterode area)

Richard Reinert
Suederquerring 489
D-21037 Hamburg
GERMANY
(Hamburg)

Horst Reschke
P.O. Box 27161
SALT LAKE CITY UT 84127-0161
USA
(Germany)

Mrs. Donald V. Rhoads
9508 Wheel Pump Lane
PHILADELPHIA PA 19118
USA
(descendants of German immigrants of 1683 to
Germantown, PA)

Albert J. Robichaux, Jr.
780 Terry Parkway
TARRYTOWN LA 70056-4752
USA
(Louisiana Germans)

Reinhard Rosenbusch
Kuefsteingasse 29/6
A-1140 Wien/Vienna
Oesterreich/AUSTRIA
(eastern Austria, southern Bohemia, Moravia)

Walter H. Ruf
Helvetiastrasse 43
CH-3800 Unterseen
Schweiz/SWITZERLAND
(Switzerland)

GENEALOGISTS

Karl-Michael Sala
P.O. Box 11584
Pioneer Station
SALT LAKE CITY UT 84147-0584
USA
(Germany; research trips)

Auguste Schaaf
6 quai Anselmann
F-67100 Wissembourg
FRANCE
(Alsace)

Jaroslav Schabanov
Uliza 2 - Nowoostankinskaja 13-23
129075 Moskva/Moscow
RUSSIA
(Saratov area and Volga Germans; knows English)

Horst Scharffs
1046 E. Milbert Ave.
SALT LAKE CITY UT 84106
USA
(Germany)

Trudy Schenk
1230 Kensington Ave.
SALT LAKE CITY UT 84105
USA
(Germany and France)

Henning Schillig
Gneisenaustrasse 6
D-38102 Braunschweig
GERMANY
(church books of the city and Duchy of Braunschweig)

Helmut Schmahl
Burgunderstrasse 3
D-55232 Ober-Floersheim
GERMANY
(Rhineland, Palatinate/Pfalz, Rhine Hesse, Hesse-Darmstadt, Huguenot families; knows English)

Georg Schmidbauer
Dachauer Strasse 267
D-80637 Muenchen/Munich
GERMANY
(video histories of ancestral homes, villages, documents)

Brian H. Schneden
1355 W. Kimberley
DAVENPORT IA 52806
USA
(Schleswig-Holstein; Hamburg passenger lists)

Lore Schretzenmayr
Erikaweg 58
D-93053 Regensburg
GERMANY
(eastern Germany, now Poland, etc.)

Henning Schroeder
Postfach 100822
D-51608 Gummersbach
GERMANY
76702-2411@compuserve.com
(Rhineland, Hesse, Westphalia, Thuringia, Saxony, Silesia, emigration research, Jewish research, Germans from Russia; German Emigrant Register of army deserters 1871-1918, missing men of draft age 1871-1918, missing heirs 1871-1918, and persons absent from home towns in the entire German Empire)

Franz Schubert
Konrad-Adenauer-Strasse 19
D-37075 Goettingen
GERMANY
(Mecklenburg, nearer Pomerania, Schleswig-Holsteins southern Lower Saxony)

Hans Schulthess
Postfach 161
CG-8304 Wallisellen ZH
Schweiz/SWITZERLAND
(Aargau, Schaffhausen, St. Gallen (Protestant part), and Zuerich cantons, Switzerland)

Ann C. Sherwin
1918 Medfield Rd.
RALEIGH NC 27607
USA
(translations; American Translators Association certified German-English)

Elizabeth S. Simons
P.O. Box 608322
CHICAGO IL 60626
USA
(translations)

Ernst Singer
Roemergasse 40/9
A-1160 Wien/Vienna
Oesterreich/AUSTRIA
(Austria, Czech Republic, Slovak Republic, Hungary)

Henryk Skrzupinski
ulica Grunwaldzka 10a/68
PL-85236 Bydgoszcz
POLAND
(the Bromberg area, now Poland)

Karl-Heinz Steinbruch
Wittenberger Strasse 6
D-19063 Schwerin
GERMANY
(Mecklenburg)

GENEALOGISTS

Max Studer
Swiss Roots
17 Chemin des Frenes
CH-1295 Tannay VD
Schweiz/SWITZERLAND
(Switzerland; trips to ancestral villages)

Jared H. Suess
736 Cana Circle
SANDY UT 84070
USA
(Germany, Switzerland)

Rolf Sutter
Julius-Hoelder-Strasse 48
D-70597 Stuttgart
GERMANY
(southwestern Germany)

Dr. Ludovit Szabo
Schlierseestrasse 23
D-81541 Muenchen/Munich
GERMANY
(Czech Republic)

Dorothy R. Tharp
12147 Harvard Ave.
CHICAGO IL 60628
USA
(Saxony, Hesse)

Roland Thommen
Sonnenbergstrasse 7
CH-9400 Rorschacherberg TG
Schweiz/SWITZERLAND
(Canton Thurgau, Switzerland)

Hargen Thomssen
Am Boedjebarg 6 B
D-25767 Bunsoh
GERMANY
(Dithmarschen and neighboring areas; has photocopies of
all Dithmarschen church books and 2,600 charts)

Eva Uhlmann
Lueginslandstrasse 497
CH-8051 Zuerich ZH
Schweiz/SWITZERLAND
(Canton Zuerich, Switzerland)

Urbana Technologies. See under Julia Petrakis.

Albert Voegtlin
Blaeserstrasse 65
D-79576 Weil am Rhein
GERMANY
(Baden and southern Germany)

Heinrich Waber
Hoeheweg 10
CH-3515 Oberdiessbach
Schweiz/SWITZERLAND
(Canton Bern, Switzerland)

Miriam Weiner
136 Sandpiper Key
SECAUCUS NJ 07094
USA
(Jewish research)

Frau Weiss
Seitenstettenstrasse 4
A-1010 Wien *(Vienna)*
Oesterreich/AUSTRIA
EUROPE
(Jewish research in Vienna 1840-1938)

Armin Weist
Moellendorffstrasse 64
D-10567 Berlin
GERMANY

Karen B. Whitmer
The Luxembourg Connection
7627 Blaisdell Ave.
RICHFIELD MN 55423
USA
(Luxembourg surname index)

Marion Wolfert
2541 Campus Dr.
SALT LAKE CITY UT 84121
USA
(German research)

Friedrich R. Wollmershaeuser
Herrengasse 8-10
D-89610 Oberdischingen
GERMANY
(Germany, especially southwestern Germany; many indexes
available; German-American emigration; knows English)

Dr. Christian Wolff
Cercle généalogique d'Alsace
5, rue Fischart
F-67000 Strasbourg
FRANCE
(Alsace)

Walter Wyss-Sunier
Krummackerweg 31
CH-4600 Olten SO
Schweiz/SWITZERLAND
(Cantons Aargau, Solothurn, and Jura, Switzerland)

Josef Wyss-Zehnder
Aberenrain 30
CH-6340 Baar ZG
Schweiz/SWITZERLAND
(Canton Zug, Switzerland)

FORMLETTER FOR CHURCH PARISHES

Mr. John Q. SMITH
12345 South Main Street
ANYTOWN YOURSTATE 67890-9876
United States of America

AIR MAIL
POSTAGE

VIA AIR MAIL / PAR AVION / LUFTPOST

(**Evangelisches Pfarramt** or **Katholisches Pfarramt**)
D-##### Xxxxxx
GERMANY

12345 South Main Street
ANYTOWN YOURSTATE 67890-9876
United States of America
den 31.01.1997   (day.month.year in this order)

Evangelisches Pfarramt or **Katholisches Pfarramt** (see below; use just one or the other)
D-##### Xxxxxx (D- plus 5-digit postal code, followed by name of town (Xxxxxx))
GERMANY (the U.S. Postal Service prefers that all country names be typed in ALL CAPITAL LETTERS)

Sehr geehrter Herr Pfarrer!
    Laut der von mir gesammelten Ahnenforschungsquellen sollen meine Vorfahren aus (name of town: Xxxxxx) stammen. Daher bitte ich hoeflich um einige Angaben aus den dortigen Kirchenbuechern.
    Ich lege eine Ahnentafel bei, damit Sie genau ersehen koennen, um wen es sich handelt.
    Deshalb bitte ich Sie hoeflich um einen vollstaendigen Auszug bzw. um Ablichtungen aus den betreffenden Tauf-, Trau- und Begraebnisregistern fuer meine Vorfahren aus Ihrem Ort und deren Eltern.
    Ich lege zwei Coupons bei, die auf Ihrem Postamt gegen Briefmarken umgetauscht werden koennen. Bitte geben Sie die Gebuehren an.
    Fuer Ihre Bemuehungen und Ihre Mithilfe im voraus dankend, verbleibe ich
                hochachtungsvollst
                John Q. Smith
Beilagen: Ahnentafel
          2 Internationale Antwortscheine

To (Protestant, Lutheran or Reformed)/(Catholic) parish, in Xxxxxx (town), Germany, 31 January 1997

Esteemed pastor (here presumed to be male, although some Protestant parishes have female pastors):

According to the genealogical sources I have collected, my ancestors supposedly come from (name of town: Xxxxxx). I am enclosing an ancestor chart so that you can see exactly whom this concerns. Therefore I most courteously request a complete transcript or photocopies from the pertinent baptismal, marriage, and burial records for my ancestors from your town and their parents. I am enclosing two coupons which can be exchanged for stamps (of your country) at your post office. Please indicate the charges. Thanking you in advance for your efforts and your cooperation, I remain
                Most respectfully
                John Q. Smith
Enclosures: Ancestor chart and 2 International Reply Coupons.

(At this writing, International Reply Coupons cost $1.05 each and are exchangeable for 2 DM worth of postage in Germany; the simplest air mail letter from Germany to America costs 3 DM postage.)

NOTE: This letter is for writing to Lutheran/Reformed (**Evangelisches**) or Catholic (**Katholisches**) parishes.
The D-#### is a new German postal code. Use CH-#### and **Schweiz/SWITZERLAND** for Switzerland, A-#### and **Oesterreich/AUSTRIA, EUROPE** for Austria, if you know the ZIP codes. Otherwise omit the ZIP code, giving name of province or region.

Type everything. Make a copy for yourself of everything. Send a photocopy of your documentation showing the origin. See list of additional phrases; if this is insufficient for your purposes, then good, simple, clear English is better than poor German. See also instructions under other formletters. If your place is in Wuerttemberg, then ask for Family Registers: "Ich bitte um Familienregister." These exist since 1807 at local church parishes in Wuerttemberg.

FORMLETTER FOR CIVIL REGISTRATION OFFICES

Mrs. Mary A. JONES
Rural Route 2, Box 123
ANYTOWN YOURSTATE 11111-1111
United States of America

AIR MAIL
POSTAGE

VIA AIR MAIL / PAR AVION / LUFTPOST

Standesamt
D-##### Xxxxxx
GERMANY

Rural Route 2, Box 123
ANYTOWN YOURSTATE 11111-1111
United States of America
den 31.01.1997   (day.month.year in this order)

Standesamt
D-##### Xxxxxx
GERMANY

Sehr geehrte Damen und Herren!

Laut der von mir gesammelten Ahnenforschungsquellen sollen meine Vorfahren aus (name of town: Xxxxxx) stammen. Daher bitte ich hoeflich um einige Angaben aus den dortigen Standesregistern.

Ich lege eine Ahnentafel bei, damit Sie genau ersehen koennen, um wen es sich handelt.

Deshalb bitte ich Sie hoeflich um einen vollstaendigen Auszug bzw. Ablichtungen aus den betreffenden Geburts-, Heirats- und Sterberegistern fuer meine Vorfahren aus Ihrem Ort sowie Eltern, falls moeglich.

Ich lege zwei Coupons bei, die auf Ihrem Postamt gegen Briefmarken umgetauscht werden koennen. Bitte geben Sie die Gebuehren an.

Fuer Ihre Bemuehungen und Ihre Mithilfe im voraus dankend, verbleibe ich

           hochachtungsvoll

           Mary A. Jones

Beilagen: Ahnentafel
           2 Internationale Antwortscheine

To Civil Registration Offfice in Xxxxxx (town), Germany, 31 January 1997

Ladies and Gentlemen: According to the genealogical sources I have collected, my ancestors supposedly come from (name of town: Xxxxxx). I am enclosing an ancestor chart so that you can see exactly whom this concerns. Therefore I most courteously request a complete transcript or photocopies from the pertinent birth, marriage, and death records for my ancestors from your town, as well as their parents, ir possible. I am enclosing two coupons which can be exchanged for stamps (of your country) at your post office. Please indicate the charges. Thanking you in advance for your efforts and your cooperation, I remain

           Respectfully

           John Q. Smith

Enclosures: Ancestor chart and 2 International Reply Coupons.

Use **Standesamt** in Germany with the prefix D- and Austria with prefix A-; substitute **Zivilstandsamt** in Switzerland with prefix CH-. See also instructions under other formletters.

Many civil vital records are available on LDS "Mormon" microfilm or from centralized archives such as Bruehl or Detmold. German privacy laws sometimes cause difficulties in obtaining records; state that you are a descendant or you may have to show that you are a descendant.

Civil registration begins in Germany and Switzerland on 1 January 1876, in Austria 1938, some areas earlier: former Prussia 1 October 1874, Rhineland and Palatinate west of the Rhine 1 May 1798, Basel-Land 1827, Glarus & Schaffhausen 1849, Solothurn 1836, St. Gallen 1867, Wiener Neustadt 1872. For Bremen, Frankfurt/Main, Hamburg, Luebeck see **Municipal Archives**. For Baden, Hesse, Westphalia see **State Archives**.

"ALL-PURPOSE" FORMLETTER

Miss Nancy A. BROWN
Post Office Box 4321
ANYTOWN YOURSTATE 98765-4321
United States of America

AIR MAIL
POSTAGE

VIA AIR MAIL / PAR AVION / LUFTPOST

(Society, Genealogist, etc., from this Address Book)
D-##### Xxxxxx
GERMANY

Post Office Box 4321
ANYTOWN YOURSTATE 98765-4321
United States of America
den 31.01.1997 (day.month.year in this order)

(Society, Genealogist, etc.)
D-##### Xxxxxx
GERMANY

Sehr geehrte Damen und Herren!/Sehr geehrter Herr MEYER!/Sehr geehrte Frau BRAUN!
   Laut der von mir gesammelten Ahnenforschungsquellen sollen meine Vorfahren aus (name of town: Xxxxxx) stammen. Ich lege eine Ahnentafel bei, damit Sie genau ersehen koennen, um wen es sich handelt.
   Koennten Sie mir gegen Honorar Sucharbeiten durchfuehren? Falls nicht, so bitte ich hoeflich um genaue Anschriften von Ahnenforschen, Archiven, Bibliotheken, genealogischen Vereinen, Kirchenaemtern usw., die mir bei dieser Suche behilflich sein koennen.
   Fuer Ihre Bemuehungen und Ihre Mithilfe im voraus dankend, verbleibe ich
                  mit freundlichem Gruss
                  Nancy A. BROWN
Beilagen: Ahnentafel
                  2 Internationale Antwortscheine

To Society, genealogist, etc., in Xxxxxx (town), GERMANY, 31 January 1997

Ladies and Gentlemen:/Dear Mr. MEYER:/Dear Ms. BRAUN: (It is correct to use **Frau** even for single women)

According to the genealogical sources I have collected, my ancestors supposedly come from (name of town: Xxxxxx). I am enclosing an ancestor chart so that you can see exactly whom this concerns. Could you carry out research for me for a fee? If not, I most courteously request exact addresses of family researchers, archives, libraries, genealogical societies, church offices, etc., which could be of assistance to me in this search. Thanking you in advance for your efforts and your cooperation, I remain
                  Respectfully
                  Nancy A. Brown

Note: This formletter is a generic "all-purpose" letter suitable as a first inquiry to genealogists, church offices, genealogical societies, archives, libraries, etc. The D-##### is a postal code for Germany. Archivists, librarians, and somebody at most major societies in Germany know English. Local genealogists, local civil registrars, and local church pastors, especially in the former German Democratic Republic where Russian was the major foreign language taught, do not necessarily know English. See also instructions under other formletters and list of useful phrases.

USEFUL PHRASES FOR INSERTING IN FORMLETTERS

Sehr geehrter Herr! – Dear Sir:
Sehr geehrte Frau! – Dear Madam:
Sehr geehrter Herr Dr. MUELLER! – Dear Dr. MUELLER: (male)
Sehr geehrte Frau Dr. MUELLER! – Dear Dr. MUELLER: (female)
Sehr geehrte Damen und Herren! – Ladies and Gentlemen:
Hochachtungsvoll, – Respectfully,

Sehr geehrter Herr KLEIN! – Dear Mr. KLEIN:
Sehr geehrte Frau MEYER! – Dear Ms. MEYER:

Mit freundlichem Gruss, – Sincerely/Cordially,

Ich habe einen alten Brief aus Deutschland. – I have an old letter from Germany.
Ich habe schon an eine andere Stelle geschrieben. – I already wrote to another place. (Then name it.)
Ich besitze eine Urkunde in deutscher Sprache. – I own a document (written) in German.
Ich lege eine Ablichtung bei. – I am enclosing a photocopy.

Was fuer genealogische Quellen gibt es dort? – What kind of genealogical sources are there?
Haben Sie eine (Zzzzz-)Familiengeschichte? – Do you have a family history (of the Zzzzz family)?
Haben Sie eine Ahnentafel? – Do you have an ancestor chart?
Haben Sie ein Bild vom RAU-Haus? – Do you have a photo of the house of the RAU family? (Insert name.)
Gibt es eine Ansichtskarte von der Kirche in (Altdorf)? – Is there a postcard of the church in (Altdorf)?
    (Substitute the name of the place.)
Gibt es eine Landkarte von dieser Gegend? – Is there a map of this region?
Gibt es ein Heimatbuch ueber diese Gegend? – Is there a (local history) book about this region?
Ich moechte gerne eine Kopie davon haben. – I would like to have a copy (of it).
    ("It" could be anything: a picture, picture postcard, book, map, chart, typewritten family history, etc.)

Ich heisse auch KLINGENHAUSENDORFER. Sind wir vielleicht miteinander verwandt? –
    My name is also KLINGENHAUSENDORFER. Are we possibly related to each other?
Ich habe Ihren Namen von einem Telefonverzeichnis bekommen. – I got your name from a phone book.
Ich habe Ihren Namen aus einem Buch bekommen. – I got your name from a book.
    Examples would be the Glenzdorf series, the *Ahnenlistenkartei* series, or the *Foko* series.
Ich habe Ihren Namen von einem Freund bekommen. – I got your name from a (male) friend.
Ich habe Ihren Namen von einer Freundin bekommen. – I got your name from a (female) friend.
Bitte antworten Sie in englischer Sprache, wenn moeglich. – Please reply in English if possible.
Leider kann ich kein Deutsch. – Unfortunately I don't know any German.
Mein Brief kommt aus einem Buch. – My letter comes out of a book.

Bevor Sie die Sucharbeit durchfuehren, bitte teilen Sie mit, wieviel die Unkosten betragen werden. –
    Before you perform the research, please inform me how much the expenses will amount to.
Bitte ueberschreiten Sie nicht die Summe von $50,oo US. –
    Please do not exceed the sum of $50.00 US. (or whatever sum you choose)
(Charges vary considerably and it is hard to generalize about them. When you get a *Rechnung* (bill), either pay in bank drafts denominated in the foreign currency (Deutsche mark, Swiss franc, etc.) or allow about $3.00 extra to cover typical foreign charges for currency exchange. Or use Ruesch International Monetary Services.)

For more detail see *Writing to Germany: A Guide to Genealogical Correspondence with German Sources* by Kenneth L. Smith; also "When You Write to Germany..." by Friedrich R. Wollmershaeuser in *Genealogical Research Directory* for 1985. To find German postal codes consult *Das Postleitzahlenbuch*, alphabetical and numerical editions, available from Ernest Thode, RR 7, Box 306, AB Kern Road, MARIETTA OH 45750-9437. For Austria, France, and Switzerland, consult separate postal code books or any telephone book of the country. If you don't know the exact village of origin, your letter is likely to be useless, so before writing abroad, literally exhaust all sources at home, such as family papers and traditions, church and cemetery records, marriage and death certificates, obituaries (especially in German-language papers), naturalizations, passenger arrival records, published histories and indexes, known origins of relatives and fellow settlers, and indexes such as the IGI and others found at local LDS (Mormon) Family History Centers. Mention in your letter if you only *suspect* a certain place as an origin, but don't know for sure.

GERMAN GENEALOGY ON THE INTERNET

In the WorldWideWeb, addresses (URLs) change rather frequently. I have tried to choose representative samples, and WWW sites that are likely to have links to other sites even when their URLs change, so that you can update your bookmarks or notes.

WorldWideWeb links

Federation of Eastern European Family History Societies (Salt Lake City, UT; Davis, CA) - http://www.feefhs.org
Forscherkontakte (**Foko**) **researcher list** - http://w3g.med.uni-giessen.de/~geneal/foko.html
German archives, societies, and genealogical sources - http://www.bawue.de/~hanacek/info/dgenepag.htm
German genealogy homepage - http://www.genealogy.com
FAQs (frequently asked questions about German genealogy) - http://www.genealogy.com/gene/www/ghlp/sgg.html
Germanic Genealogy Society - http://www.mtn.org/mgs/branches/german.html
German geography - http://www.chemie.fu-berlin.de/adressen/brd-fact.html#area
German maps (historical) - http://dcn.davis.ca.us/~feefhs/
German news service (English version) - http://www.mathematik.uni-ulm.de/germnews
German people - http://www.chemie.fu-berlin.de/adressen/brd-fact.html#people
German rulers (emperors, kings, heads of state) - http://www.chemie.fu-berlin.de/diverse.bib/de-kks.html
German states (modern) - http://www.chemie.fu-berlin.de/adressen/bl/bundeslaender.html
German translation service (free) - http://www.genealogy.com/gene/www/abt/translation.html
Germany country information: cities, islands, states, indexes, government, maps, news, organizations, reference (geographic server; German postal codes), society and culture (history; genealogy), East German studies, Prussia - http://www.yahoo.com/text/Regional/Countries/Germany/
Palatines to America (Columbus, OH; PA) - http://genealogy.org/~palam/

e-mail addresses
Anglo-German Family History Society (England) - 100535.2632@compuserve.com
German Genealogical Society of America (LaVerne, CA) - JCBH98A@prodigy.com
Germanic Genealogy Society (St. Paul, MN) - kermit.e.frye@cdev.com
Immigrant Genealogical Society (Burbank, CA) - NEPSUND@aol.com
Sacramento German Genealogical Society (Sacramento, CA) - SacGermGS1@aol.com

FAQs (frequently asked questions about German genealogy, received by e-mail)
Send message to: LISTSERV@RZ.UNI-KARLSRUHE.DE
Message body: GET GEN-DE-L.FAQ.02

FTP
ftp ftp.genealogy.com
        Name: anonymous
        Password: your @ Email.Address
        ftp> cd genealogy/gene/faqs
        ftp> get sgg.faq
        ftp> quit